When someone is murdered, the police investigate the spouse first. That should tell you everything you need to know about marriage.
- **Unknown** -

DEAD MEN DO TELL TALES SERIES
"I Want to Come Home Tonight" (2017)
Blood, Guns & Valentines (2023)
Bloody Chicago (2006)
Bloody Hollywood (2008)
Bloody Illinois (2008)
Dead Men Do Tell Tales (2008)
Fallen Angel (2013)
Horribly Mutilated (2021)
Blood, Bullets & Booze (2023)
Murder by Gaslight (2013)
Murdered in Their Beds (2016)
One August Morning (2015)
One Night at the Biograph (2016)
Suffer the Children (2018)
Two Lost Girls (2016)
Until Death Do Us Part (2024)
Victims of the Ax Fiend (2020)
Without a Trace (2020)

DEAD MEN DO TELL TALES

UNTIL DEATH DO US PART

Mayhem, Murder and Malevolent Tales of Love Gone Wrong

AN AMERICAN HAUNTINGS INK BOOK

UNTIL DEATH DO US PART

Murder, Mayhem & Malevolent Tales of Love Gone Wrong

© Copyright 2024 by Troy Taylor

All Rights Reserved.
ISBN: 978-1-958589-16-8
First Edition

Published by American Hauntings Ink
P.O. Box 249 - Jacksonville IL - 62651
www.americanhauntingsink.com

Publisher's Note:
No part of this publication may be reproduced, distributed, or transmitted in any form or by any means, including photocopying, recording, or other electronic or mechanical methods, without the prior written consent of the publisher, except in case of brief quotations embodied in critical reviews or other noncommercial uses permitted by copyright law.

Cover Design by April Slaughter
Interior Design by Troy Taylor

Printed in the United States of America

Table of Contents

INTRODUCTION — PAGE 7

PART ONE: "THE COUPLE THAT SLAYS TOGETHER"

GO DOWN TOGETHER --- PAGE 15
The Ballad of Bonnie and Clyde

"THE GHOST IN THE ATTIC" – PAGE 108
The Story of Dolly and Otto

"THE DUMB-BELL MURDER" --- PAGE 120
Ruth Snyder and Henry Judd Gray

THE "LONELY HEARTS KILLERS" – PAGE 140
Raymond Fernandez and Martha Beck

BADLANDS – PAGE 158
Charles Starkweather and Caril Ann Fugate

THE SHOE FETISH KILLER'S WIFE – PAGE 171
Jerry and Darcie Brudos

THE "SUNSET STRIP KILLERS" – PAGE 182
Doug Clark and Carol Bundy

DOWN ON THE FARM – PAGE 191
Ray and Faye Copeland

THE "TOY BOX" – PAGE 198
David Ray and Cindy Hendy

PART TWO: "LOVE YOU MADLY"

THE CASE OF THE "RAGGED STRANGER" – PAGE 214
Killing Ruth Wanderer

"BLACK WIDOW" – PAGE 235
The Murderous Career of Louise Peete

"THE MURDERING MINISTER" – PAGE 243
Lawrence Hight and Elsie Sweetin

THE DOCTOR, HIS WIFE, AND THE OTHER WOMAN – PAGE 251
Betrayal and Forbidden Love in Roaring 20s Detroit

"FORBIDDEN LOVE" – PAGE 270
Dr. James Howard Snook and Theora Hix

"THE BLUEBEARD OF THE QUIET DELL" – PAGE 295
The Murderous Harry Powers

"MY WIFE HAS BEEN GASSED!" – PAGE 314
Richard and Delores Gladden

"THE CLEAVER WIDOW" – PAGE 327
Betty and Jerry Ferreri

THE PRICE OF OBSESSION – PAGE 338
The Vanishing of Dorothy Jane Scott

"MEET THE CREEPER" – PAGE 347
The Madness of Dennis Depue

"THIS IS NOT ACCIDENTAL" – PAGE 353
The Story of Zack and Addie

"COME PREPARED TO STAY FOREVER" – PAGE 362
The Murder Farm of Belle Gunness

BIBLIOGRAPHY – PAGE 486

INTRODUCTION
Until Death Do Us Part

IF YOU HAVE EVER BEEN A BARTENDER, you know you hear many weird things when you are working. Trust me, though – you have never heard anything this weird.

On Thanksgiving weekend, 1994, a bartender working at a dive called The Last Stop in Fairmont, West Virginia, had just poured a drink for a 28-year-old customer named Forrest Fuller. He picked up his glass and casually mentioned to his bartender that his dead fiancée was in the backseat of his car.

The bartender called the police.

Whispers spread through the bar, but the police were already on the way. They had started searching the highway after a woman had called them saying that she was worried that her daughter, Jodie Lynn Myers, had been murdered.

When the cops arrived, they found out that Forrest was telling the truth – Jody's body was sitting in the front seat of his 1994 Camaro. Her wedding dress was in the trunk. The police were already disturbed before they started questioning Forrest about the death of his fiancée, but they weren't prepared for what they were about to hear.

Forrest and Jodie had been in a volatile, on-again / off-again relationship for years. On the night of November 23, 1994, though, Jodie decided to break things off for good. Enough was enough.

But Forrest wasn't going to accept that – he flew into a rage and started beating Jodie. He tried to choke her, both with his hands and a necktie. When that failed, he stabbed Jodie to death with a kitchen knife.

Jodie couldn't argue with him now. He was going to marry her – dead or alive.

He put her body into the front seat of his car, drove to the convenience store where he worked, stole nearly $700, and then drove off, leaving Jodie and the vehicle in his garage overnight.

On a bright and sunny Thanksgiving Day, Forrest belted Jodie into the Camaro next to him, stuffed a wedding dress into the trunk, and hit the highway. He left his home in Pemberton Township, New Jersey, and headed for California, where he planned to marry his corpse bride.

On the road, Forrest stopped and called Jodie's mother to explain his plans. He admitted that he had murdered her daughter but that he still planned to marry her. Before ending the call, he promised to send her a souvenir of the wedding -- Jodie's ring finger, which would be wearing a wedding ring inscribed with the words, "I do."

Jodie's mom called the police.

Forrest only made it as far as West Virginia before the police stopped their honeymoon trip.

Forrest Fuller was eventually found guilty at trial and sentenced to serve 30 years behind bars with the possibility of parole. He remains behind bars today – but, by the time you read this, not for much longer.

He'll soon be released --- so my advice to the ladies would be that if you meet a man who just *really* wants to get married, you may want to think twice about it.

LOVE IS STRANGE.

And that's not just a lyric from the Mickey and Sylvia song.

I think we can all agree that some of the best – and worst – things that have ever happened were inspired by love.

LEGEND SAYS THAT A TROJAN PRINCE fell so deeply in love with Helen of Sparta that he kidnapped her and took her away to his distant kingdom, provoking a war with the Greek army that left Troy in ruins. This probably mythical woman had a "face that launched 1,000 ships."

AND THEN THERE'S THE STORY OF Antony and Cleopatra, a romance that went so wrong that Shakespeare saw it fit to be one of his tragedies. The lovers met at the height of turmoil in the Roman Republic, and the Egyptian queen seduced the powerful, married general into an alliance between their two countries.

But that alliance turned sour when future emperor Octavian convinced the Roman senate that Antony was power-hungry and bewitched by Cleopatra and declared war on him. In the aftermath of the battle, Antony is falsely informed that Cleopatra is dead, and Antony stabs himself with his sword. After burying Antony, Cleopatra took her own life in despair.

WHILE HISTORY TELLS US THERE WERE MANY reasons why England was transformed into a Protestant nation, Henry VIII's infatuation with a young woman named Anne Boleyn undoubtedly played a large part in it.

By 1525, Henry had tired of his first wife – the devoutly Catholic and very popular Catherine of Aragon, who had failed to give him a male heir. His wandering eye landed on Anne, a devious and beautiful lady-in-waiting whose father was an ambitious knight and diplomat. But Anne ignored the king's overtures and refused to be seduced without the promise of marriage.

This led Henry to ask the Pope for an annulment of his marriage to Catherine but was refused. Encouraged by advisors who hated the Church, Henry rebelled, married Anne, broke with the Catholic Church, and appointed himself head of the Church of England.

He had changed history – seemingly for love. But it wouldn't last. He soon tired of Anne, too, since she also proved incapable of giving him the male heir he wanted. He had Anne arrested and charged with witchcraft, incest, and adultery. She was found guilty and beheaded. Next, he married Jane Seymour, the third of his six wives, 11 days later.

In the decades that followed, questions about the official state religion fractured and weakened the kingdom, and it would not be until the reign of Elizabeth I – Henry's daughter with Anne – that a permanent Protestant church was established.

IN 1954, TWO OF AMERICA'S BIGGEST celebrities – Marilyn Monroe and baseball great Joe DiMaggio – were married. The wedding made headlines worldwide, but the "dream romance" was never meant to last. Joe was the jealous type who thought that Marilyn would drop out of the movie business and become a housewife, something she was never destined to be. Just nine months later, they separated and were later divorced.

But they stayed in each other's lives. After Marilyn's marriage to Arthur Miller ended in 1961, she fell apart and had to be hospitalized. In 1961, her analyst convinced her to enter the psychiatric ward of the Payne Whitney Clinic, where she was confined for seven horrifying days. Subjected to a locked, padded cell, Marilyn, now even more distraught, called Joe and asked him to rescue her. He immediately arranged for a discharge and did all he could to try and convince her to steer clear of the people causing the most problems in her life – you know, like the Kennedys.

After Marilyn's tragic death, Joe came to her rescue again. He flew to Los Angeles to supervise her funeral arrangements and helped put Marilyn to rest at Westwood Memorial Park. For the next several decades, red roses were delivered to her crypt each week, courtesy of Joe DiMaggio.

Joe died at the age of 85 in 1999, and until the day he died, he regretted losing Marilyn and told friends that he had hoped to remarry her after she left the psychiatric hospital.

Reportedly, not long before his death, Joe told his longtime attorney and friend, Morris Engelberg, that he wasn't sorry that the end of his life was near. "I'll finally get to see Marilyn again," he said.

ONE OF THE MOST CONTROVERSIAL OF ALL of America's presidential first ladies was Rachel Donelson, who had married Andrew Jackson in 1791. She had previously been married to Lewis

Robards of Kentucky and believed that he had finalized their divorce before her marriage to Jackson – he hadn't. In fact, he didn't file the papers until two years later. At that time, even a simple divorce was considered scandalous, so this was even worse. Jackson's opponents used Rachel's past against him during his run for the presidency, calling her a woman of loose morals.

This led to Jackson fighting numerous men in "affairs of honor" – as duels were referred to at the time. And Jackson was no slouch. He was a hardened soldier who'd seen action most of his life. Much blood was spilled because people didn't know when to keep their mouths shut. Besides that, Jackson had the support of ordinary people, who helped him win the election.

Tragically, though, Rachel didn't live long enough to see her husband become president. The stress of the horrible things being spoken and written about her aggravated a pre-existing heart condition, and she suffered a fatal heart attack just two months before he took office.

Jackson was so shocked and grief-stricken by her death that he clung to Rachel for hours after she died, hoping that he could bring her back to life.

PRESIDENT WILLIAM MCKINLEY'S WIFE, Ida, was once a high-spirited socialite, but the deaths of her two young daughters and epileptic seizures left her frail and withdrawn. As McKinley's political career led him toward the White House, Ida spent most of her time in a rocking chair, sewing, and waiting for her husband to come home. She was growing old before her time.

But when McKinley took office in 1897, he didn't keep Ida out of sight. Instead, defying the protocol of the day, he insisted that his wife be seated next to him during state dinners so that he could help her if a seizure struck.

He was utterly devoted to her – even in death.

When President McKinley was fatally shot in 1901, his thoughts weren't for himself but for his fragile Ida. Before he died, he whispered to his secretary, "My wife – be careful how you tell her."

LOVE IS STRANGE.
Love can be tragic.

Love can even be murderous, twisted, horrible, and cruel.

Even the most romantic of holidays – St. Valentine's Day – has a terrible and cruel side. We often laugh and say it's a holiday created by greeting card companies and florists, but if so, it was for the best. Someone needed to tone down *both* the pagan tradition of the season and the one the Catholic Church concocted to replace it.

The pagans called it Lupercalia, which means "the feast of the wolf." It was a time of celebration, violence, and fertility, where you literally purified yourself through sex – lots and lots of sex – fornication, bondage, whippings, group sex, just pretty much any kind of hedonistic activity you could think of.

Needless to say, a holiday that celebrated every sort of sex imaginable had the founders of the Church clutching their pearls and looking for something – really anything – to replace it.

So, they decided that Lupercalia would become a feast day for St. Valentine, which turned out to be, well, a rather unusual choice.

In some ways, it's fitting. He was chosen to be the saint of secular love, healed people, and seems to have been a decent guy. He helped a lot of persecuted Christians from the early Church – back when the Romans were feeding them to the lions – and reminded them of love by cutting out heart shapes from paper and giving them to those who were condemned to the arena.

But, like every good Catholic saint from the old days, he also died a horrible martyr's death. He was murdered by being stabbed, beaten with clubs, and beheaded – on February 14. And now we celebrate the day he was slaughtered with cards, chocolates, and flowers.

Sorry, but that's weird.

Or is it? As you'll find when you turn the pages that follow, it might actually be fitting.

I mean, St. Valentine's Day is probably most famous for the event that occurred on the morning of February 14, 1929, and it had nothing to do with candy and flowers.

On that St. Valentine's Day, six mobsters and a wanna-be gangster who was actually an optometrist were murdered in a garage on Chicago's North Side. The seven men, who owed their allegiance to a gang once run by Irish bootlegger Dean

O'Banion and now run by George "Bugs" Moran, were massacred by none other than Al Capone.

The St. Valentine's Day Massacre has since become the most famous crime ever linked to a romantic holiday. It's become a legendary event that has spawned stories of cursed bricks from when the garage was torn down, hauntings at the present-day site on North Clark Street, and several generations of people who want more than anything to be linked by family ties to mobsters.

If I had a dollar for every person I took to the site of that garage over the years who told me their uncle, grandfather, cousin, or whatever had been a driver for Al Capone... you wouldn't be reading this book because I'd be retired.

But this is not a book about the St. Valentine's Day Massacre. However, it is a book about other crimes from American history linked to love and romance.

Love is strange – but it can also be scary.

Ahead of us, we have strange tales of love, murder, and insanity -- wronged lovers, couples who kill, murderous revenge, and a handful of ghosts, too.

So, buckle up. It's going to get weird.

Troy Taylor
Winter 2023-2024

Part One
"THE COUPLE THAT SLAYS TOGETHER"

"I LOVE YOU TO DEATH."

It's a common enough phrase; most of the time, it's not meant how it's said.

But there's no question that intense love is a form of madness that can inspire extreme behavior. In many cases, neither partner may have exhibited the merest inkling of strange behavior before meeting and becoming entangled with their lover.

Or perhaps an underlying mental disorder is unmasked by an intense love affair and spirals completely out of control. This particular kind of madness has led to torture, abuse, and, yes, even murder – by both men and women. And then there are those couples who simply seem to share their madness between them, resulting in dire and horrific events.

Sometimes, lovers can bring out the best in one another; other times, not so much.

GO DOWN TOGETHER
The Ballad of Bonnie and Clyde

DURING THE DARKEST DAYS OF THE GREAT Depression, Bonnie Parker and Clyde Barrow's murderous love story captivated a nation sick of the government and the banks. They were looking for anti-heroes like Dillinger, Baby Face Nelson – and Bonnie and Clyde.

But in May 1934, Bonnie and Clyde were shot to pieces in a police ambush on a country road in Louisiana. Their deaths became as sensational as their lives, and thousands demanded to see the bodies of the notorious outlaws. The people came, they stared, and they went away. Soon after, Bonnie and Clyde were buried separately in Dallas, Texas.

And then, they were largely forgotten. They might have stayed that way if a movie hadn't been made about them in 1967, starring Faye Dunaway and Warren Beatty, reviving their legend, and making them much more glamorous than they ever were in real life.

Bonnie and Clyde weren't bank robbers. They were two-bit crooks who robbed travelers, shopkeepers, farmers, and grocery clerks. John Dillinger called Bonnie and Clyde "snot-nosed punks," who gave outlaws a bad name. Over two years, they murdered 12 people, most of them lawmen.

One lawman who took part in the ambush had no regrets. As he told a reporter, "I hate to bust a cap on a woman, especially when she was sitting down. However, if it hadn't been her, it would have been us."

So, why do we still talk about Bonnie and Clyde today? Why are their books, movies, and more about the bloodthirsty duo who committed several inept robberies and spent most of their time tired and broke?

It's that love story. No matter how twisted, broken, and sad it might have been, it's the one thing we'll never forget about the pair.

HENRY BARROW AND HIS NEW WIFE, CUMIE, had big plans when they married in December 1891. The young couple moved to

Swift, a small farming community in East Texas, and couldn't wait to start a family and farm of their own. Elvin, known as Jack, was their first son, followed by a daughter named Artie. Then came Marvin, whom everyone called Buck, then Nell two years later, followed by Clyde in 1910 and L.C. in 1912. When their last child, Marie, arrived in 1918, Jack and Artie were already grown.

As a child, Clyde was a "good boy, playful, and full of life," his mother recalled. The family nicknamed him "Bud." He got in a bit of trouble, but not much. A local store owner caught him stealing candy, but rather than punish him, he required Clyde to whistle whenever he came into the store. It was easy to keep an eye on him that way.

A young Clyde Barrow

All the children worked on the farm, and when Clyde wasn't picking cotton or some other chore, he loved to play. He shot marbles with his brothers or pretended to be Jesse James or some other western outlaw like the ones the Barrow children walked three miles to the movie theater to watch on the big screen.

Clyde loved to dance and sing, taught himself to play guitar, and hoped to join a music group someday. He also loved to shoot. All the Barrow kids knew how to use guns – they lived on a farm, and it was necessary – but Clyde was a crack shot. He didn't like hunting, though, because he liked animals, so he'd spend hours plinking away at cans and bottles.

Life was tough for the Barrows. They never made much of a living off the land. They lived in a three-room house so crowded that most of the family slept on makeshift pallets on the floor. They rarely had new clothes or much to eat, even when cotton prices tripled during World War I.

To make up for what they didn't produce on their own farm, Henry and Cumie often worked for others, following the harvest from farm to farm as migrant workers. While they were on the road, the children lived with an uncle. Like at home, they did chores and worked in the field, but they also went fishing and played with their cousins. At their uncle's house, there was always plenty of food on the table.

Henry and Cumie Barrow, later in life. They would remain devoted to Clyde for his entire life, no matter what he might be accused of.

Cumie pushed her children to go to church and sent them to school as much as possible. Henry had never learned to read or write, and Cumie wanted more for her family. Some of the children did better than others. Clyde probably attended school the most, but Buck preferred the outdoors and, like his father, never really learned to read or write.

Times got even tougher after the war. Prices for cotton and other crops dropped after the fighting ended in Europe, making it even harder for the family to scrape together enough money to live.

By then, Jack had married and had become an auto mechanic in Dallas, working out of a garage behind his home. Artie had become a hairdresser in the city, and Nell had gotten married and joined her. Buck had gotten restless and followed his siblings into the city.

By now, Henry and Cumie were in their late 40s and saw fewer possibilities in farming. They packed up what little they had and headed to the city with four-year-old Marie, nine-year-old L.C., and Clyde, who was almost a teenager.

It was a move that would change their lives forever.

WHEN THE BARROWS ARRIVED IN DALLAS IN 1922, the city was on the verge of leaving its past behind and stepping into the modern age. It was no longer the Cowtown of yesterday. Its downtown was thriving with theaters, stores, and restaurants, and the following year, it would have its first skyscraper, the 29-story Magnolia Building.

America in the Roaring Twenties saw an explosion in music, movies, and dance. Radio

The slums of West Dallas in the 1920s

could be found in American homes and real estate, and stock prices soared. Prohibition was the law of the land, but liquor was easy to find in nightclubs and speakeasies nationwide. Families bought their first cars, and women finally had the right to vote. America was a shiny, happy place – at least on the surface.

As many Americans grew wealthier, up to four out of every ten Americans were poor, barely making enough to put food on the table and a roof over their heads. Southern farmers were among those hurting the most.

When the Barrows first arrived in Dallas, they camped with other poverty-stricken families under one of the bridges that ran from downtown across the Trinity River. The city wasn't fond of the "idle farm hands" who had come to Dallas desperate for work and urged them to move on to West Dallas, an unincorporated area outside the city limits near the river bottoms.

The conditions were terrible. Raw sewage flowed into the river from two waste dumps, nearby factories spewed smoke into the air, and oil and chemical plants operated ponds not far from the camp where they contained spills. Most of the streets in Dallas were paved, but the roads in West Dallas were dirt or gravel. When it rained, they turned into mud. Most of West Dallas wouldn't get electricity, running water, or toilets until the 1950s.

Living in a squatter's camp near the river, the Barrows slept under their wagon for a time, eventually adding some tents. The prize was a job in one of the factories, but until he could get one, Henry used the family's horse and wagon to collect junk and scrap metal to sell to the neighborhood salvage yards. Clyde and Buck sometimes helped out by stealing metal their father could sell.

Both food and money were scarce. Many days, the families relied on charities that delivered bologna sandwiches – nicknamed "West Dallas round steak" – or stale bread. Christmas brought presents of fruit, nuts, and candy from the Salvation Army.

Diseases like typhoid, cholera, and diphtheria were a constant worry, and at one point, Clyde, Marie, and Henry became so sick that they were all admitted to a local hospital.

Despite the squalid conditions, people in West Dallas looked out for each other. No one locked their doors – they didn't have anything worth stealing – and while there might not be food in your own home, if your neighbor had a pot of beans going, you knew you'd at least get some supper.

Clyde got away from West Dallas as often as he could. He stayed with his uncle part of the time, and when he was home, Cumie tried to keep him in school. She didn't have much luck with that, though, and Clyde only finished up to the sixth grade.

Back then, though, that didn't stop him from finding jobs, though none of them paid well. He started at a candy company, making $1 a day, then moved to the Proctor & Gamble soap factory for $4 a day. He jumped from job to job, searching for higher pay, working briefly as a theater usher, at the NuGrape bottling plant, United Glass Company, and A&K Auto Top and Paint Shop.

Like his siblings, Clyde gave his parents money when he could afford it. Henry and Cumie continued to struggle, although they had saved enough money to build themselves a new shack a few blocks farther away from the river.

Clyde often stayed with his sister, Nell, in Dallas. She'd married in 1925, and her husband worked during the day but was a bandleader at night. He taught Clyde to play the saxophone.

By now, Clyde was a teenager and wasn't the same playful boy that he had been. He now worried about his clothes and appearance and was rarely happy with the money he was making. His mother blamed this on "wayward women in the neighborhood," although she considered "wayward" to be any girl who wore lipstick and rouge, of which she strongly disapproved.

But girls were definitely on Clyde's mind. The pursuit of one of his first loves was also the first time Clyde got into serious trouble. He fell for a girl named Eleanor and liked her enough to have her initials, EBW, tattooed on his left arm.

After a disagreement in late 1926, Eleanor took off for East Texas to see relatives. Clyde decided to rent a car and bring her back. He took Eleanor's mother with him, and they ended up staying in East Texas longer than he was supposed to. The owner reported it stolen, and when the police went to get it, Clyde hid it from them.

In a move that pretty much ended his chance of winning over Eleanor's family, Clyde went home, leaving his girlfriend and her mother behind. Later, he was arrested for theft and thrown in jail. Since the car was recovered, though, the charges were eventually dropped.

Soon after, Clyde and Buck were caught with a truckload of stolen turkeys. Buck took the blame, so Clyde narrowly avoided another arrest.

Clyde continued working his dead-end, low-paying jobs, but by the late 1920s, he'd made some new friends – and picked up some new skills, like stealing cars.

Thanks to Henry Ford's inexpensive Model T and Model A automobiles and General Motors' willingness to allow people to pay off new cars over time, most families owned a car by the end of the decade. Hundreds of thousands of miles of road had been paved, including new cross-country highways like Route 66.

The increased number of cars on the roads led to increased crime. Cars gave criminals an easy way to escape from the law and helped bootleggers transport illegal liquor to speakeasies.

Clyde and his pals tapped into the new stolen car market, but they also committed burglaries, engaged in petty thefts, and became skilled at cracking safes.

It didn't take long for Clyde to become well-known to the cops. Since Dallas officers didn't want to hunt him down in poverty-plagued West Dallas, they often went to his work to pick him up for questioning about local crimes. Whenever a car was stolen or a house was robbed, the police would drag him downtown. He was never charged with anything, but they'd beat him up and try to get him to confess to whatever crime they needed to have solved.

Hoping to avoid the heat, Clyde started leaving Dallas to commit crimes, but that didn't help. The cops continued to come around his work, causing him to lose jobs. He became increasingly angry and distrustful of authority. His mother later wrote, "After he was picked up so many times, he just came to have a hatred of the law, and figured it didn't do much, if any, good to try and do right."

WHILE CLYDE BARROW WAS GROWING UP AND getting acquainted with the wrong side of the law, Bonnie Parker was falling in love.

Born in a little town called Rowena in West Texas on October 1, 1910, Bonnie was the middle child of Charles and Emma Parker. She had an older brother, Buster, and a little sister named Billie Jean. Her father was a bricklayer, and the family regularly attended the local Baptist church – until tragedy struck.

A young Bonnie Parker

Charles suddenly died when Bonnie was only four, and with few other choices, Emma packed up the three children and moved to her parents' home in West Dallas. They lived near an area dubbed Cement City, a company town of a few hundred people next to a cement plant. Emma went to work as a seamstress in a factory while her mother watched the children. On Sundays, they walked to the Baptist church downtown.

Bonnie was a beautiful girl – with "cotton-colored curls and the bluest eyes you ever saw" – but she was a handful. She constantly acted up for attention, and even though her grandmother frequently spanked her with a hairbrush, Bonnie regularly misbehaved. Like Clyde, she was musical. Emma taught all three children how to play piano, but she ended Bonnie's lessons when it became clear that she could play whatever she heard by ear.

In school, she was a clever, quick learner. In 1922, when she was 11, Bonnie competed in the Dallas County literary contest and won the elementary spelling competition.

Bonnie's pretty face, blonde hair, and bright blue eyes attracted many boys, all of whom tried to woo her with candy and chewing gum gifts. But she had a quick temper and regularly fought with both boys and girls. Despite the trouble she got into, she was popular with the drama teacher, who recognized her knack for writing and making speeches and cast her in school plays and musicals.

Bonnie loved performing, and on Saturdays, when she went fishing with her little sister, Billie complained that Bonnie frightened away the fish with her singing. "I'd tell her to be quiet because I couldn't catch any fish for dinner," Billie later recalled. Bonnie waved off her complaints. "She'd tell me that when she was on Broadway and had her name in lights, I'd be sorry I talked to her that way."

Girls from West Dallas may have had big dreams, but they didn't have many options. Most married young, dropped out of school and got a job.

Bonnie Parker was no exception.

When she was 15, she fell head over heels for Roy Thornton, an older classmate. She even had their names tattooed inside hearts on her upper right thigh. Though her mother was reluctant, she eventually consented for them to marry. The ceremony was held on September 25, 1926, just a week before Bonnie's sixteenth birthday.

The marriage was rocky from the start. The couple rented a house about two blocks from her family, but Bonnie missed her mother. She demanded that Roy take her to her mother's house every evening. The visits were so frequent that Emma actually felt sorry for Roy, who couldn't seem to keep his wife at home.

A few weeks after the wedding, Bonnie and Roy moved with Bonnie to a rental home in Dallas. Emma would later claim that the arrangement suited everyone, but Roy's actions don't make that sentiment ring true.

After less than a year of marriage, Roy began disappearing for long stretches of time – 10 days in August 1927, nearly three weeks in October, and then for several weeks starting in December. In a January 1, 1928, diary entry, 17-year-old Bonnie wrote, "I wish to tell you that I have a roaming husband with a roaming mind. I am not going to take him back."

Though she loved and missed him, Bonnie was angry. She went to the movies and on dates with other men, but she missed Roy, noting in her diary things like, "Sure am lonesome" and "Sure am blue tonight."

Roy had become a heavy drinker and had turned to crime. He did show back up in early 1929, but – as she'd promised herself – she didn't

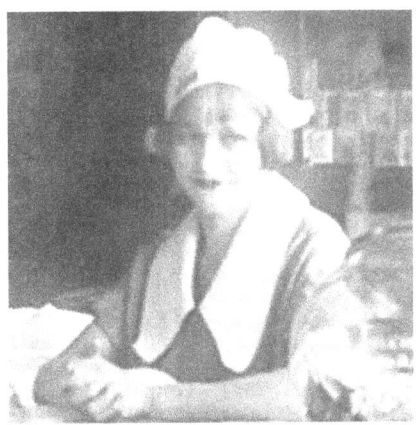

An 18-year-old Bonnie working as a waitress at Hargrave's Cafe

take him back. A few months later, he was arrested, convicted of burglary, and sent to the state penitentiary. Bonnie never saw her husband again, although they never divorced. She told her mother that she didn't think it was fair to do to him while he was in prison.

With Roy gone, Bonnie went to work. She landed a job as a waitress at Hargrave's Café, and the charming, energetic young woman made a lot of extra money in tips. In 1929, she switched jobs and went to work at a café near the courthouse. Judges, lawyers, and lawmen ate there regularly. Ted Hinton, a deputy sheriff who would later spend years trying to catch her, remembered Bonnie well. She was always ready with a joke and would casually flirt with the customers. "Bonnie could turn heads," he later said.

After the stock market crash that October, Bonnie joined the millions of others who lost their jobs. The nation had gone into a financial tailspin as investors lost billions overnight. Businesses closed, and the number of Americans out of work skyrocketed. The café where Bonnie worked closed, and though she looked, she could not find another job.

In January 1930, Bonnie was at her brother and sister-in-law's house in West Dallas when a dark-haired young man named Clyde Barrow came to visit.

Sparks flew.

Bonnie's mother, Emma Parker

The two immediately hit it off and soon became a couple. Bonnie's family liked him, too. Emma Parker found Clyde charming and very handsome with his "dark wavy hair, dancing brown eyes, and a dimple that popped out now and then when he smiled." She thought he looked like a young law student. "He had what they call charm," she said. "He was good company and full of fun, always laughing and joking. I could see why Bonnie liked him."

During one visit to the Parker home, Clyde stayed so late that Emma allowed him to stay the night and loaned him a pair of Bonnie's brother's pajamas.

He was still sleeping on the couch when the police arrived the next day. As usual, they had been looking for him and guessed he would be with his girlfriend. But they didn't count on his girlfriend's reaction. Bonnie wept and screamed and held onto Clyde, begging the cops to leave him alone.

Emma later said she thought her daughter was going crazy.

DESPITE BONNIE'S BEST EFFORTS, the police took Clyde to jail. The Dallas police held him for a few days and then sent him to Denton, about 40 miles away. It turned out that Clyde had been busy before he started romancing Bonnie and was wanted in three towns for burglary and auto theft.

In late 1929 – just a couple of months before he'd met Bonnie – Clyde and his brother, Buck, had stolen a car with a friend. They'd also robbed a home in Denton and lifted a safe from a garage in town. In his rush to get away from a police officer who appeared on the scene, Clyde drove into a curb and broke an axle. All three of them stumbled out of the car and ran. The cop gave chase and opened fire at them. Buck was wounded in both legs and was severely injured. The friend was also caught.

Clyde, however, managed to escape and hide overnight before making his way back to West Dallas.

Buck and their friend had already been convicted of the crime and sent to prison. After Clyde's arrest, he was facing time, too.

And this didn't make Bonnie happy.

While he was locked up in Denton, she wrote him passionate letters that swung between declaring her love for him and worrying about how much time he might serve.

Denton officials didn't have enough evidence to charge him, but Waco, about 100 miles south of Dallas, was waiting. Clyde was transferred there in March and charged with burglary and auto theft.

Bonnie was determined to follow, arguing with her mother until she was allowed to go. She and Cumie Barrow traveled together and stayed with Bonnie's cousin, May, in Waco. Bonnie was thrilled to see Clyde and visited him at least once daily, even after his mother returned to Dallas.

On March 3, Clyde was hauled into court and charged with seven counts. Two days later – without a lawyer – he pled guilty and received a sentence of two years for each count. The judge graciously allowed him to serve them concurrently, which meant he got a two-year sentence instead of 14 years behind bars.

Clyde was supposed to be sent to the state prison to serve his time, but at the same time, state prison officials were closed to newly convicted inmates. The Texas penitentiaries were overflowing, and men were sleeping on the floor between bunks. Overcrowded and filthy, they lacked the space to lock up anyone else. Just weeks before, Texas Governor Dan Moody had declared the main state prison in Huntsville as "unfit for human habitation." He told the state legislature, "I have a dog, and I think a lot of that dog, but I'd kill him before I'd put him down there to stay."

This meant that anyone recently convicted had to stay in a city or county jail for the time being. This delay gave Clyde and two cellmates, William Turner and Emery Abernathy, time to devise an escape plan.

On the evening of March 11, Turner asked one of the guards for a bottle of milk. When the jailer entered their cell, Turner blocked the door, and Abernathy rushed him. They grabbed his keys, and the three inmates pushed their way out of the cell, locking the guard inside.

They ran downstairs, overpowered another guard, and stole his keys. They walked out of the jail and disappeared into the night. By dawn, they had stolen and abandoned four different cars.

With cops all over Texas looking for them, the trio stayed on the run for the next week, finally making an embarrassing mistake several states away in Middletown, Ohio. They'd been busy robbing filling stations, shops, and a railroad ticket office and were on their way out of town with Clyde at the wheel. But he got confused by the dark and winding roads and accidentally drove back into town. They passed by the railroad station again, and the police on the scene recognized the license plate on their stolen car.

The cops opened fire on the car. Turner and Abernathy immediately jumped out and surrendered, but Clyde sped away. He managed to elude the police, who chased him for over an hour but was finally cornered near a river. After exchanging a few shots with his pursuers, Clyde tossed his gun into the river and surrendered.

The newspapers ridiculed "Waco's Dumbbell Bandits" when they were brought back to Texas, but their jailers were not amused. The trio was placed alone in a more secure area on the jail's third floor, and no visitors were allowed.

Back in court, the judge now changed Clyde's sentence to the original 14 years. He claimed he was saving the young man's life by locking him up so that he wouldn't end up in the electric chair someday.

Waco officials were eager to get Clyde and the others out of their jail, but they had nowhere to send them. The state prisons were still not allowing additional inmates. McLennan County Sheriff Leslie Stegall called the head of the state penitentiary commission to plead his case, but he was turned down.

Soon, though, Clyde had other things to worry about. Officials in Houston decided that he might be responsible for a murder in July 1929 and charged him with the crime.

"Horse feathers," Clyde responded. He'd been in Dallas at the time and knew nothing about the murder. His mother insisted that she had receipts that proved he was home when the crime occurred. Even so, plans were made to take him to Houston and put him on trial. Before that happened, though, a more likely suspect was found, and the charges against Clyde were dropped.

That probably felt like a lucky break until April 21, when the "one-way wagon" showed up at the county jail. A few inmates from the state prison had been released - or, more likely, had died - and there was finally room for Clyde.

He was on his way to Eastham Farm, one of the Texas prison system's most brutal sites.

RECORDS FROM CLYDE'S INITIAL PHYSICAL listed him as five feet, five inches tall, weighing a scrawny 127 pounds, with brown hair and brown eyes. He had a few tattoos, including the initials EBW with a heart and dagger on his left forearm, a U.S. Navy tattoo - although he was never in the Navy - and the image of a girl's face - another old girlfriend - on his right forearm.

On the way to the prison camp, he'd met Ralph Fults, an Eastham escapee who'd been caught and was returning to the farm. When Clyde asked him what the camp was like, Fults' words filled him with dread.

Clyde met Ralph Fults at the Eastham prison farm and they soon became fast friends.

The guards would kill you, Fults warned, for two things - escaping and not working fast enough. For a first escape, a convict could expect a severe beating. A second escape? A bullet in the back of the head. The guards would claim you'd tried to escape.

When the two men arrived at Eastham, they were assigned to Camp 2. It wasn't long before Clyde got his first look at the brutality Fults had promised. While the two men were working together on a woodpile, three guards surrounded Fults and beat him with pistol butts until his head was bloody and his eyes were swollen shut.

At some risk to his own safety, Clyde stayed close by, watching and drawing the attention of other guards who gathered around. When the beating ended, he was brave enough to help the man up. Clyde's willingness to be a witness probably saved the other man's life. It also earned him the undying loyalty of Ralph Fults.

For Clyde, though, it lit an angry fire toward authority that would blaze in his heart for the rest of his life. If anyone ever wonders why Clyde was so willing to gun down lawmen, they need look no further than this incident for an answer.

But before Clyde could seek any kind of revenge, he first had to survive being a prisoner at Eastham Farm. The men worked between eight and nine hours each day. Inmates were expected to run in a single-file line at full speed for about two miles to the fields and then run back after a long day of work. Those who couldn't keep up were beaten.

Lunch was a 10-minute break of cornbread and water. Dinner wasn't much better. Food suppliers dumped their spoiled goods at the prison. Everything else came out of a can. The farm lacked a proper sewage system, meaning filth and garbage were everywhere.

Punishments were brutal – beatings, whippings, isolation cells, and one when a handcuffed prisoner was forced to stand on a small barrel for hours on end, even all night. If his legs went numb and he fell, he was hoisted back onto the barrel again and again.

Records from just six months in 1931 showed that 128 prisoners were officially flogged – and many more were beaten that weren't reported. The guards were as hardened as the men they watched over. One Eastham inmate later said that he saw five inmates murdered during the time he was there.

Clyde's sister, Nell, visited her brother when she could and remembered one visit where his eyes were black and blue. Later, he told her he'd been beaten for not keeping up in the fields. Another time, he was beaten for allegedly slipping Nell a letter.

Ralph Fults later recalled that, even in that terrible place, Clyde still joked around and loved to laugh. He talked about his family and his brother, Buck, who'd been sent to prison in January 1920. However, two months after getting locked up, Buck simply walked out, stole a car, and headed to Dallas.

Clyde also told Fults about Bonnie, his "little blue-eyed girl," and how much he loved her. Clyde's absence was hard on Bonnie. She didn't visit, but she wrote him numerous letters.

The friendship between Clyde and Ralph was severed when Clyde was relocated to Eastham's Camp 1. There, he encountered a new kind of abuse.

Prison officials relied on prisoners known as "building tenders" and "trustees" to help keep order among the inmates. These men were often prisoners facing long sentences who were unofficial enforcers, contributing to the violence. They held down prisoners while they were whipped. They often thrashed fellow inmates themselves without facing penalties.

Camp 1 had a vicious trustee named Ed Crowder, a hulking man standing over six feet tall. He was a monster with many enemies serving time for bank robbery. He singled out Clyde for harsh treatment and, according to Ralph Fults, sexually assaulted him.

But then, in October 1931, Crowder mysteriously died.

According to reports, he was killed in a knife fight with an inmate named Aubrey Scalley, who was serving a 50-year sentence for multiple robberies.

But in truth, Clyde was behind the man's death. He hatched a plan with Scalley, who also hated Crowder. Late one evening, Clyde headed to the toilet with a piece of pipe hidden in his pants. Crowder, as he often died, followed him to the bathroom. But when he walked in the door, Clyde struck him in the head with the pipe. The large man fell to the floor, and Clyde hit him again and again with the pipe. Then Scalley stepped in and sliced up Crowder with a homemade knife. Crowder bled to death on the bathroom floor.

Scalley, who already had a lengthy prison sentence ahead of him, took the blame for the murder. He spent some time in solitary confinement, but there was no real investigation.

Clyde Barrow had gotten away with his first murder.

BACK IN WEST DALLAS, CLYDE'S PARENTS were doing a little better financially. One of the children had bought a piece of land on Eagle Ford Road, and Henry and Cumie had loaded their small, hand-built house onto a truck and moved it to the farm. Henry turned the front room into a filling station, selling gas,

The Barrow filling station on Eagle Ford Road -- as well as cash from Clyde -- helped Henry and Cumie survive the Depression.

sodas, and snacks. He had the only fresh well in the area and sold water to locals or traded water for produce and other items.

Rumor has it that he also sold bootleg liquor in those waning days of Prohibition, but if so, no one ever caught him.

The rest of the house was rough. There was no electricity, and they used an outhouse in the back, but the family was doing better than most people were. The Depression was devouring the nation, and more and more people were losing their jobs and homes. The campground where the family had lived when they arrived in West Dallas was now more crowded than ever with people who had lost everything.

But there was another reason the Barrows were doing better besides bootleg booze -- Buck had escaped prison and was busy committing robberies. Most of that money was used to hire lawyers to work on Clyde's behalf.

In November 1931, those lawyers wrote to the state's pardon board that Clyde had been treated unfairly in 1930. The family of one of his Waco accomplices had been able to hire a lawyer to appeal their son's sentence, getting it reduced. At that time, though, Clyde couldn't afford a lawyer, which his new attorneys claimed was an injustice. They also lied a bit for sympathy, claiming that Cumie was a widow and needed Clyde for financial support.

The lawyers managed to drum up more support in the following weeks, even getting a letter from a Waco district attorney who said that Clyde was "a young fellow of nice appearance" and had "plenty of sense to make a good citizen." Letters from a judge and a former McLennan County sheriff also supported his parole, saying that his mother needed help.

On January 7, the state pardon board asked Governor Ross Sterling to consider his release. Things were looking up for Clyde, but he didn't know it. His mother had been telling him for more than a year that she was working to get him released, but as months passed and nothing happened, he became increasingly despondent.

Eastham was wearing him down -- the backbreaking work, the whippings, the punishments, and the long stretches without seeing his family. Over the years, dozens of Eastham prisoners, suffering from exhaustion and mistreatment, had sliced their own Achilles tendons to get out of the fields. Others purposely broke bones or took the drastic step of cutting off fingers and toes. The injuries usually put the inmates in the Huntsville prison hospital, at least for a little while.

Even in pain, that must have seemed like a relief.

In mid-January, Clyde convinced a fellow inmate to cut off two toes on his left foot with a sharp tool. This sent him to the infirmary at Huntsville.

And then, on January 27, Governor Sterling signed Clyde's parole papers.

On February 2, Clyde limped out of the prison gates on crutches, a very different man than the teenager who'd been placed behind bars two years earlier. Ralph Fults later said that prison turned Clyde from "a schoolboy to a rattlesnake." His foot would heal, but his anger wouldn't go away.

Unfortunately, Buck was back behind bars. His wife and mother convinced him to finish his term rather than live as a fugitive.

But now that Clyde was out of prison, he could do what his lawyers had promised: take Buck's place and help support his mother.

But it wouldn't be in the way they expected.

SOON AFTER CLYDE RETURNED TO WEST DALLAS, he cleaned up, put on fresh clothes, and went to see Bonnie Parker. When he arrived, she was visiting with a new boyfriend, but when she saw Clyde, she threw herself into his arms. She hadn't known he was out of prison. The boyfriend got the message and left.

Emma Parker wasn't as thrilled to see Clyde as her daughter was. She tried to talk some sense into him, urging him to get a job and stay out of trouble. But Clyde turned on the charm, gave her his smile and dimple, and told her he'd try, but it was unlikely anyone would want to hire him. If they wouldn't, he promised her, he'd start repairing cars behind his father's gas station.

Clyde didn't make any effort to do that, but he did try and go straight – sort of. He took a construction job that his sister Nell lined up for him in Massachusetts, but that was too far from home, and he left after two weeks. He returned to work at United Glass and Mirror, but the police kept showing up and dragging him downtown, just like in the old days. With so many people out of work because of the Depression, the company didn't need an ex-con who kept missing work, so they let him go.

Clyde's short attempt at a straight life was over.

Clyde Barrow never worked an honest job again. He was fed up, angry, and thirsty for revenge. He swore that he'd never go back to someplace like Eastham again – the cops would have to kill him instead. The more he thought about the prison camp, the angrier he got. While they'd been locked up, Clyde had often talked to Ralph Fults about returning to Eastham for a big prison break when they got out. It would be payback for all the abuse he and the other inmates had suffered.

But a prison break would take money and guns, and the young men didn't have either. So, Clyde and Ralph returned to doing what they did best – committing crimes. Their first robbery was a flop. Tipped off about a big payroll, they tried to rob a local oil company. They tied up the employees and broke into the safe, but it was empty.

The two should have known better. When they'd been locked up, they'd been schooled by veteran bank robbers about the best ways to commit heists. They'd been taught to research their targets, stake them out, and make careful plans. Clyde, Ralph, and a friend, Raymond Hamilton, decided to try out what they'd learned on the way home from a road trip to Minnesota.

There's no record of what bank they hit or where it was located, but Fults later stated they'd stolen "thousands of dollars." Truth or fiction? No one knows, but they hit someplace because the success of the robbery gave them cash and the confidence to do it again. Along the way, they stopped for weapons and ended up with high-powered rifles, a Thompson machine gun, and some bulletproof vests. They hauled them all and their cash back to West Dallas.

And found out they'd been cheated. Gathering with some friends at a remote lake between Dallas and Denton, Clyde and Ralph put the bulletproof vests to the test and watched as they fell apart under fire. The guns quickly jammed, and the Tommy gun was defective.

Hanging on to the money was also difficult. Clyde burned through his share, giving it away to family and friends. He felt good about doing it since they desperately needed it, but generosity also bought him loyalty. When the cops came around asking questions, his neighbors didn't have any answers to give them.

Clyde planned to use the money he had left to stage the raid on Eastham, but he wanted more men and weapons. In April, he and Ralph traveled to the Texas panhandle to look up some old friends who might help them but had no luck tracking them down. They were on their way home when their car broke down in Electra, Texas, a little town near the Oklahoma border.

Strangers strolling toward the town center was a bad sign in Electra, mainly because someone claimed they'd seen Charles "Pretty Boy" Floyd passing through recently. A businessman who spotted Clyde and Ralph alerted the police – even though the two young men were just walking, looking for a garage, and minding their own business.

Police Chief James T. Taylor soon arrived with another city official. Taylor would later claim that Clyde and Ralph pulled guns on him right away. Of course, that wasn't what Ralph recalled. He said that the chief immediately pulled out handcuffs and told them they were under arrest.

It was then when Ralph pulled a pistol and pointed it at the police chief's nose. He took away the cop's gun while Clyde kept his pistol pointed at the other official.

Right at that moment, another man arrived on the scene, who apparently wasn't clear about what was happening. The third man was businessman A.F. McCormick, who'd called the police about Clyde and Ralph in the first place. When he realized what he walked up on, McCormick tried to run, but Clyde grabbed him and pushed him over next to the other two men.

They forced all three of them into McCormick's car at gunpoint, and Clyde took the wheel, speeding off out of town.

About 10 miles later, they dropped the Electra men off near a local ranch, promised to take care of McCormick's car and the police chief's gun, and drove away.

But they only made it a few miles before they ran out of gas. Clyde and Ralph pulled their guns on the first driver they saw, mail carrier W.N. Owens. With the mailman in the backseat, they sped along dirt roads to the Oklahoma border. Unable to pay the bridge toll at the state line, Clyde tore through a chain gate. The toll-takers shot at them but didn't hit anything.

Along the way, the would-be bandits took eight cents from Owens and traded some of his postage stamps for gasoline. By then, they were hungry and convinced a lunch stand owner to give them some food. They shared it with their hostage before dropping him off at the side of the road with his mailbags.

Clyde and Ralph were on their way to Denton to regroup and make plans for the prison break.

ON APRIL 17, CLYDE AND RALPH PICKED UP Bonnie from her mother's house, and the three of them drove to Eastham Farm. Bonnie went in alone, telling the guards she was Aubry Scalley's cousin. When the guards brought him in for a visit, Bonnie told Scalley that Clyde was planning to bust him out soon.

That day was the first time Ralph spent time with Bonnie, and he immediately liked her. The pretty, bright waitress was friendly, chatty, and - to Ralph - didn't seem cut out for a life of crime. But Bonnie quickly dismissed his concerns. "I'm just a loser - like Clyde," she told him. "Folks like us haven't got a chance."

The next night, the trio headed to East Texas to steal cars that would be big enough to transport a bunch of freed prisoners. On the way, they stopped in Kaufman to buy some ammunition and admire the guns on display.

Clyde and Ralph snagged two big cars - a Buick and a Chrysler - but then decided to steal some of the guns from the store they'd visited in Kaufman.

It was a terrible decision, even for them.

A night watchman spotted them hanging around and came their way. Clyde fired a warning shot, and the watchman fired back – and he also set off the town fire bell. In just minutes, locals were rushing toward the store.

Clyde and Bonnie jumped into one car, and Ralph got in the other, but the first road they took was blocked by construction equipment. They circled back through the square – twice – until they found a narrow alley to escape.

And then things got worse. The sky opened up, and it began to pour. The road was soggy at first and then turned into a swamp. Before long, both cars were settled deep in East Texas mud. They weren't going any farther.

Clyde ran to a nearby farmhouse to look for a car. They didn't have one, so he stole two mules. With rain still falling, Clyde and Bonnie got on one mule, and Ralph got on the other. They trudged along most of the night, hoping to find another car and end the disastrous misadventure. Near dawn, they spotted a vehicle at a farmhouse and traded the mules for a better ride. Of course, they didn't get far because they quickly ran out of gas.

For the rest of that day, they hid from pursuers in Kaufman. Eventually, they were spotted, and the posse closed in. The trio ducked into some brush near Cedar Creek to hide as gunshots rang out. By then, Bonnie had lost her shoes and torn her dress. Clyde and Ralph fired back. More shots rang out, and Ralph was winged in the left arm.

Certain they were about to be captured, Clyde decided to make a run for it. He told Bonnie and Ralph that he'd return with help and took off. He managed to slip away while the posse was reloading their guns.

Bonnie and Ralph were soon in custody.

The two were taken to the town of Kemp and locked up in the calaboose, a small brick building with a dirt floor that seemed more like an outhouse than a jail. Bonnie spent the first couple of hours standing at the iron grate door, demanding that the townspeople get Ralph some medical treatment for his arm. But no help was coming. The last car they'd stolen had belonged to the town doctor, who refused to bandage the wound. The pair spent the entire night there on display.

The next day, April 20, they were taken to the large Kaufman County Jail, where Ralph's arm was finally treated. Neither of the prisoners would identify their missing accomplice.

Within a week, Ralph had been linked to the kidnappings in Electra and was transferred to Wichita Falls. He was quickly tried and sentenced to a decade in prison.

Bonnie, meanwhile, was left in the Kaufman County Jail until a grand jury could meet and decide if she should be charged with a crime. The jailer and his wife were kind to her and let her sit outside in the evenings, where she played with their children. Clyde's younger brother, L.C., and his brother Buck's wife, Blanche, checked on Bonnie, and Cumie Barrow sent her a new dress and some shoes.

Emma Parker visited, too, but seeing her daughter behind bars was heart-wrenching to her. She wanted to bail Bonnie out but didn't have the money. There was no money for a lawyer either. The jailer's wife urged Emma to be patient, telling her it was unlikely that Bonnie would be charged with a crime and that a stay in jail might be good for her.

WHILE BONNIE WAS LOCKED UP, CLYDE QUICKLY returned to the business of crime. The same day his friends were moved to the Kaufman jail, Clyde and some pals stole rifles and shotguns from a hardware store.

A few days later, he and two friends checked out a combination filling station and jewelry store in Hillsboro, south of Dallas. After sizing the place up, they made plans to rob the store later that night.

Some believe Clyde went into the store, but his family always insisted he was only the getaway driver. What is known is that someone banged on the door and called for the owner, John Bucher, by name, asking to buy guitar strings. He let them in, and they tried to pay for the strings with a $10 bill. Bucher had to open the safe to make the change and had trouble with the combination.

Or so he pretended.

Bucher sensed the young men were trouble and went for his gun. But one of the robbers fired first. The bullet struck Bucher in the chest. He died later that night.

The bandits left the store with only $40 in cash but about $2,500 worth of diamond rings.

Bonnie and Clyde weren't infamous yet – but they soon would be.

It was another screw-up for Clyde Barrow. They'd failed to get cars, Bonnie was locked up, and now he'd been part of a senseless murder.

And things were getting worse. His photo went out on the wire, and the police chief in Electra identified him from his mugshot. Mailman Owens described tattoos that matched Clyde's. The Texas governor was offering a $250 reward for the capture of the dangerous thieves who'd killed John Bucher.

The Eastham prison break would have to wait.

IN MID-JUNE, THE GRAND JURY IN KAUFMAN finally met to decide Bonnie's fate. Bonnie testified that she didn't know the men she was with, and charges against her were dropped. She was soon on her way home, where her mother constantly lectured her about Clyde and the dangerous path he was on. She told Bonnie she should keep her distance, and to her surprise, Bonnie agreed. She told Emma, "I'm through with him."

Bonnie, of course, was lying through her teeth.

In late June, she told her family she had a job prospect in Wichita Falls and left town. In truth, she was meeting Clyde, who'd rented a little house there to get out of Dallas.

Over the next two years, the couple would regularly take refuge in such hideouts, spending a few days or a few weeks. They were usually unknown wherever they went, but in some cases, they were sheltered by family members, fellow outlaws, or locals who needed the money so badly during the Depression that they didn't mind keeping quiet about some new folks in town.

While lying low, Clyde studied foldout maps of Texas, Oklahoma, Arkansas, Kansas, Missouri, and other states. He didn't have much of an education but had a sharp memory and created routes in his head. He also practiced his driving, coaxing high speeds from various car models. He perfected fast U-turns that would allow him to avoid roadblocks and elude the police.

Clyde drove like a devil, but so far, he hadn't had the luck of one. But that was soon going to change.

Clyde began applying that luck to his skill with weapons. He had some experience shooting guns when he was growing up, but those weapons were nothing like the ones he was dealing with now. His favorite weapon was the Browning Automatic Rifle – the BAR – a gun designed for World War I that weighed about 16 pounds. As an automatic, the BAR could fire off a magazine of 20 bullets in seconds with a single trigger pull. The gun had a stiff recoil, though, and Clyde had to learn to adjust his balance when using it. The first few times he fired one of the heavy rifles, he was knocked to the ground.

Any police officers who came after Clyde Barrow would find themselves out-gunned and unable to keep up with his slick driving skills. He could literally run circles around anyone who tried to catch up to him and leave them in the dust.

A new era in the life and crimes of Clyde and Bonnie was about to begin.

DURING THE SUMMER OF 1932, BONNIE AND CLYDE shared their Wichita Falls place with Raymond Hamilton, a pal who'd been involved in robberies with Clyde. Raymond had just turned 19 and had grown up in West Dallas. One of his sisters was best friends with Clyde's little sister, Marie.

On a steamy Monday in early August, Clyde dropped Bonnie off at his dad's gas station, where she and Clyde stopped by almost every day to say hello. "Listen to the radio, honey," he told her, "and see if we make a getaway."

The two young men drove off, traveling only a few miles to the Neuhoff Brothers Packing Company, where they planned to steal the company's payroll cash. They timed their arrival just right, finding the cash being counted when they walked through the door just before 5:00 P.M.

"Where's that money?" one of them demanded. He held a gun pointed at the office workers as the other slid $440 off the table and into a bag.

They ripped the telephones off the walls when they left. They jumped into their stolen car and roared off, whipping past two vehicles filled with heavily armed police officers who were heading for the river bottoms for some target practice. They tried to give chase, but Clyde and Raymond were long gone.

Clyde (Left) with Raymond Hamilton

Later that week, the boys decided to take a short road trip to Oklahoma and dropped Bonnie off at her mother's house. Emma was overjoyed to see her, and they spent the evening chatting and catching up on the front porch swing. Emma asked Bonnie if she'd seen Clyde.

"I haven't seen him, and I don't want to see him," Bonnie shook her head, keeping up the lie she'd told her earlier in the summer. Her mother would soon learn otherwise, but that night, Emma later said, "I wanted to believe her more than anything in the world."

MEANWHILE, CLYDE, RAYMOND, AND ANOTHER FRIEND named Ross Dyer were speeding along the backroads of southeast Oklahoma. As they cruised into Stringtown, they spotted an outdoor dance that was taking place. A band was playing, the crowd was growing, and Ross wanted to take a turn on the dance floor.

Clyde grudgingly agreed to stop, and while he rarely drank, he likely had a cold beer or two on that hot summer night. Ross joined the dance while his friends stayed close to the car Clyde parked behind the band.

Atoka County Sheriff Charles Maxwell and Undersheriff Eugene Moore were also at the dance. They'd met up because Maxwell wanted to take a spin in Moore's new Chevrolet. At some point, Sheriff Maxwell spotted the two strangers leaning on their car and walked in that direction. He may have seen them drinking or been intolerant of outsiders in his small town, but when he approached them, he said, "Consider yourselves under arrest."

An outlaw like John Dillinger would have just grinned and smooth-talked the sheriff into leaving him alone. He might have even gotten him to share a beer with him.

But Clyde Barrow was no John Dillinger.

The sheriff had barely gotten the words out when Clyde shot him. Raymond pulled his gun, too, and Maxwell went down with six bullets in his chest, arm, leg, and wrist. Though badly injured, Maxwell managed to get his gun out of its holster and get a few shots off, but they went wild. He survived the shootout, but his wounds crippled him, and he never served as a lawman again.

Undersheriff Eugene Moore wasn't even that lucky. He rushed to the scene, his gun drawn, but a stray bullet struck him in the chest, and he died on the spot.

The sound of gunfire put an end to the party. The band crashed to a stop, and dancers screamed and scattered. Flying bullets shattered lights. The crowd ran off in every direction, ducking behind parked cars and under tables.

Clyde and Raymond – leaving Ross behind – jumped into their car and tried to speed away, but one tire caught in a ditch, and the vehicle rolled over. In the chaos, they scooted out of the wreck and stole a car.

Before they got out of Oklahoma, that car lost a wheel, and it slid off to the side of a dusty road. Spotting a farmhouse nearby, Clyde banged on the door, saying they needed a car to get an injured woman to the hospital. The home's owner, Mamie

Redden, later said that Clyde told such a sob story that she sent her son, Haskell Owens, to give them a ride in their family car.

Once Haskell was behind the wheel, Clyde shoved a gun into his side, forcing him to drive in a different direction. They sped off, but after a while, that car broke down, too. When Clyde and Raymond weren't looking, Haskell ran off into the night.

The details of what happened next have been lost, but the two bandits eventually stole another car and made it back to Dallas. Clyde picked up Bonnie, and they hit the road.

By then, lawmen all over Southeast Oklahoma were using bloodhounds and volunteers to search for the two unknown killers, but all they found were abandoned cars until they grabbed Ross Dyer, trying to board a bus for Dallas.

They couldn't pin anything on him, but he tried to warn the cops that the men they were chasing wouldn't be easy to catch. They'd never surrender, he said and would fight to the death.

The police laughed off his warnings, telling reporters they expected to make arrests "before the end of the week."

That was some bragging they'd come to regret.

AFTER RUNNING INTO TROUBLE IN TEXAS AND NOW, Oklahoma, Bonnie suggested they go to New Mexico. In 1932, local police couldn't pursue criminals over city, county, or state lines. That would change in a few years – largely thanks to outlaws like Clyde and Bonnie – but they could cool off outside of Texas for now.

Clyde, Bonnie, and Raymond went to visit an aunt of Bonnie's on her father's side, Nellie Parker Stamps. Nellie was thrilled to see her niece but wasn't sure about the two young men she'd brought with her. Clyde introduced himself as Bonnie's husband, "James White," and Raymond became "Jack Smith." They seemed to have a lot of cash and were driving a shiny new Ford V-8 coupe – a car that no one Nellie knew could afford.

Nellie was so concerned about the situation that she told the local sheriff's office about her visitors.

On a Sunday morning in mid-August, Deputy Sheriff Joe Johns knocked on the door. Bonnie answered, and Johns asked her whose Ford was parked out front. Bonnie said that it belonged to her friends. She said they'd be right down in a moment; they're getting dressed.

The farmhouse outside of Carlsbad, New Mexico, where Bonnie's Aunt Nellie lived – and where they kidnapped Deputy Sheriff Joe Johns.

Inside the house, Clyde and Raymond were instantly on alert – "getting dressed" was a signal they'd made up for trouble outside. But things were worse than just a cop on the porch. Not only were their guns locked inside the Ford, but Nellie and her husband, Melvin, were also in the house, and Clyde didn't want to scare them or for them to get hurt. But Clyde did find an old shotgun in a closet, so he grabbed it, and the pair of outlaws slipped out the back door.

Deputy Johns was peering into the window of the Ford with his back to the men. Clyde and Raymond snuck up behind him, put the shotgun muzzle against the back of his neck, and ordered him to put his hands up. Johns hesitated, his hand hovering near his gun, but Raymond took it away before he was tempted to pull it.

The deputy was shoved into the car, and Clyde, Raymond, and Bonnie followed. Aunt Nellie begged them not to hurt the lawmen, but Raymond told her to shut up. Clyde turned to the Johns, though, and assured him that they wouldn't hurt him.

Without a wave of goodbye to Nellie and Melvin, they roared off down the road.

Word of the kidnapping spread quickly, and a desperate search began for the missing deputy using officers from New Mexico and Texas. Worried that the gangsters might head for Mexico, about 250 volunteers were added along the border.

When a dead man was found later that day about 90 miles northeast of El Paso, newspapers ran frightening headlines about the lawman's murder. The victim turned out to be someone else.

As it turned out, Deputy Johns was on the ride of his life to Central Texas. Clyde flew down muddy, unpaved roads at breakneck speeds, weaving around traffic and knocking off more than one bumper as he swerved around other cars.

But Johns was more worried about them being shot at by volunteers and lawmen than he was about Clyde's skilled driving. He directed Clyde through tiny towns, steering him away from the larger ones where they might be spotted.

They'd been on the road for a few hours when it started raining, turning the backroads into slippery, muddy trails. Clyde hit a huge, wet pothole at one point, spraying mud all over the windshield. Rather than stop, Clyde just stuck his head out the window to see, stretching to keep his foot on the gas as they revved along at 70 miles an hour.

Whenever they stopped for food, gas, or oil, Raymond and Johns were hidden in the weeds or trees while Bonnie and Clyde bought what they needed. Raymond kept a gun on the deputy the entire time, even when they were in the car.

After the sun went down, they stopped for a break. Clyde and Raymond took a nap while the woman Clyde only called "Honey" kept an eye on the cop.

"How do you like being a criminal?" the young woman asked him.

Johns chuckled a little. "It's my first experience."

"You've just had 24 hours of it," she replied. "We get 365 days of it every year."

That was a bit melodramatic, but that was Bonnie for you. So far, she'd only been on the outlaw trail for less than two months. Clyde hadn't been doing it much longer.

Later, Clyde joined in and told Johns that he'd tried to quit being a criminal, but the law wouldn't let him. "If we ever get caught, it's the electric chair for us," Clyde added.

They let Deputy Johns out of the car early the next morning, a few miles outside San Antonio. Clyde then searched for another Ford V-8 to steal. He wanted it for its powerful flathead engine that could outlaw law officers and for its reinforced steel body, which blocked most bullets. He found nothing in San Antonio but spotted one later that afternoon in Victoria, about 100 miles away.

It belonged to the wife of a refinery manager who watched as it sped away just minutes after she'd parked it in a garage. She alerted the sheriff's department, which soon had a report of a driver heading toward Houston, following a Ford coupe. Apparently, Clyde and Raymond figured two cars were better than one.

The sheriff's office quickly notified the surrounding counties. In Wharton, about halfway between Victoria and Houston, two officers set up an ambush and blocked a highway bridge. One of the lawmen ran a short distance up the road with a flashlight. When he saw the two cars, he'd turn on the light, alerting his partner that he should open fire.

As Clyde came speeding toward the bridge, he saw the light. On instinct, he slammed on his brakes and turned the car around, going back in the other direction. Raymond was much slower to respond. He hit the brakes, but by the time he made an ungainly U-turn, bullets were flying his way. Still, both cars escaped with only a few holes in one of them.

Up the road, the trio abandoned the car they'd driven from New Mexico. They left license plates and Deputy John's gun behind and took off in the Ford they'd taken in Victoria. They drove overnight to an abandoned farmhouse they used as a hideout west of Dallas.

On August 19, the Wharton County Sheriff sent a letter to the Dallas police asking for photographs of Clyde Barrow, Raymond Hamilton, and Bonnie Parker. "Some of our boys had a little fun with that bunch last evening. They took two shots at one of our deputies,' the sheriff wrote.

Bonnie wouldn't be widely known as a member of the gang for several more months, but after taking part in the kidnapping of Deputy Johns and the Wharton escape, she was on her way to becoming an outlaw.

AFTER THOSE CLOSE CALLS, BONNIE AND CLYDE needed a vacation. Raymond was also looking for a break, so they offered to drive him to Michigan, where his father lived. After staying for a week or two, they made their way back through the Midwest, stopping in Kansas City, where Bonnie got her hair done, and they ate in restaurants and went to shows. They returned to Texas in October because Bonnie missed her mother.

Or that's what their family claimed. Most – probably all – of it was untrue. Years later, piecing together newspaper reports and other sources, there's a more straightforward story of what Bonnie and Clyde did after the New Mexico trip – and it wasn't a vacation.

They did, however, take a trip. In early September, a bunch of members of the Barrow family traveled to Martinsville, Texas, which was close to the Louisiana border. Cumie went along, as did L.C. and Marie, and Clyde and Bonnie drove them to see Cumie's sister, Susie, and her husband, Jim Muckleroy.

The visit lasted for a few days and was mostly uneventful except for one thing – Bonnie shot herself in the foot.

Exactly why she'd been handling a gun is unknown, but when it went off, it took off the littlest toe on her left foot. Luckily, it wasn't serious.

After leaving Martinsville, they dropped Cumie and the kids off in West Dallas and kept going. They were not getting used to life on the road, making occasional trips back home to visit family. They used phony names, stayed in hotels and tourist courts when they had money or slept in the car when they didn't.

To pass the time, Bonnie wrote poems and read newspapers and detective magazines out loud to Clyde. They bought them in filling stations or stole them from mailboxes along the road. Later, when they became better known, they especially loved seeing their names in print, even when accused of crimes they didn't commit.

The money they scraped together came from robbing little stores, service stations, and occasional banks. They rarely had much cash. Living on the run could be expensive. Food came from cans or takeout sandwiches purchased from roadside cafes. They dropped their clothes off at a laundry when they could and circled back for them later. At other times, Clyde's family sent money for them to buy new things to wear.

In late 1932, when the US Bureau of Investigation first started trying to track the couple, federal agents who attempted to follow their trail found themselves hopelessly confused. They were all over the map, with no rhyme or reason to their travels.

Bonnie and Clyde

The Ford they'd stolen in Victoria, Texas, was later found in a cornfield outside Carthage, Missouri, about 700 miles from where they'd stolen it. Another car was stolen nearby, and it was found dumped weeks later in Southern Illinois. On September 2, a new Ford V-8 was taken from a doctor's driveway in Effingham, Illinois. It was found two weeks later in Pawhuska, Oklahoma.

The last Ford offered some clues to lawmen. It was left behind when "Mr. And Mrs. Roy Bailey" checked out of the Duncan Hotel in Pawhuska. They found clothing inside, including dresses, a lady's slip, two pairs of men's underwear, two dress shirts, and a pair of men's pants. All the clothing was dirty.

The search also turned up an empty prescription bottle with the name Susie Muckleroy on it. They'd eventually make their way back to their home in Martinsville, but Bonnie and Clyde never returned there.

As the pair roamed the Midwest, they managed to stay mostly out of sight until October 11. Around 6:30 that evening, Howard Hall and Homer Glaze were closing Little's grocery store in Sherman, Texas, a small town near the Oklahoma border. They had one last customer, a short man wearing a tan lumber jacket and a dark hat. He had a loaf of bread and asked a clerk for lunch meat and eggs.

But as the man started to pay Homer Glaze, he pulled out a pistol and snatched $50 from the register.

"Hey, you can't do that," Howard Hall protested. The older but much larger man started to rush toward the customer.

But the robber had that gun. He pointed it at Howard's face, and the bigger man stopped in his tracks. The bandit hit him in the face hard enough to knock Howard's glasses off his face. Angry, Howard rushed the man, and the bandit fired four times, hitting the man three times in the chest.

Then the robber turned the gun on Homer, but he didn't fire.

Instead, he ran outside and took off down the street, jumping into a waiting car.

Howard was taken to the hospital, but he died soon after he arrived there.

Homer Glaze described the thief as a small man, about five feet six inches. He was in his early twenties and had dark hair. Dallas police sent Clyde's photograph to Sherman, and Homer quickly identified him as the robber.

But was he? Clyde always swore he hadn't committed that robbery or killed Howard Hall. His family always believed him because, as his sister Nell later said, "He admitted so many crimes to us, often crimes that the law knew nothing about. Why should he lie to us?"

Clyde said he and Bonnie were far away when the robbery and murder happened – "They just hung it on us for luck," he said.

But it didn't matter. They were in enough trouble for the things they actually did. When the pair returned to Dallas around Halloween to see their parents, they discovered that a new $200 reward was being offered for Clyde's capture. They were soon back on the road again.

WHILE BONNIE AND CLYDE WERE ON THE LAM, Dallas County voters were doing one of two things that should have caused Clyde some concern.

The first was the election of Richard "Smoot" Schmid as the new Dallas County Sheriff. He was an imposing character, standing six feet five inches tall – not counting his ten-gallon hat – and had run on a promise to clean up the department and run it in a business-like fashion. He had no law enforcement experience and had never handled a gun, but he took the threat of outlaws like

Dallas County Sheriff Richard "Smoot" Scmid

W.D. Jones would become the youngest member of Bonnie and Clyde's "gang."

Clyde Barrow seriously. He hired new deputies, outfitted them with uniforms, and ensured they were all armed. He lobbied Governor Sterling to revoke Clyde's parole, guaranteeing that the bandit would return to prison – if he was captured alive, that is.

There was something else, too. Clyde's partner and pal, Raymond Hamilton, had run out of luck. He was arrested while roller-skating in Michigan and returned to Dallas. Clyde Barrow's name appeared in the newspaper as Raymond's partner for the first time.

As far as Clyde was concerned, he'd just made the big time.

AROUND CHRISTMAS 1932, BONNIE AND CLYDE gained a new partner in crime – William Daniel Jones, who went by the nickname of W.D. He was a friend of Clyde's younger brother, L.C., and was 19 years old. He had always idolized Clyde and had known him most of his life. The Jones and Barrow families had been close since coming to Dallas years before.

Like most West Dallas boys, W.D. Jones was already known to the police, but he'd never been in serious trouble. That may have been because he claimed to be just 16, which was too young to go to prison. Regardless, to him, Clyde's life was one big adventure, and he begged his idol to let him go on the road with him and Bonnie.

Clyde was mostly non-committal. He was home to celebrate the holidays with his family. He shared cash and presents with everyone, even giving little sister Marie a new book she'd always wanted.

But then Christmas Day turned ugly.

That afternoon, Clyde took W.D. with him to steal a new car he'd spotted sitting outside a house in Temple, Texas. It even had the keys in the ignition, so it should've been easy. Just as the engine roared to life, though, they caught the attention of the family in the house. Doyle Johnson, who owned the car, came tearing out of the front door. As they started to pull away, Johnson jumped onto the running board and tussled with Clyde. Both Clyde and W.D. pulled guns, and both fired at almost the same time. One of the bullets struck Johnson in the neck, knocking him onto the road.

The pair roared off. A few blocks away, they met up with Bonnie, who was waiting for them in their original car. Realizing the cops would soon be looking for Johnson's car, they abandoned it on the side of the road. Clyde stopped a mile up the road and ordered W.D. to climb a telephone pole and cut the wires. This would slow the police pursuit that was sure to follow.

Clyde had made a mistake. He hadn't planned on taking the young man along with them on the road. But now he had no choice. "Boy, you can't go home," he told W.D. "You got a murder on you. Now you're just like me."

AS IF CLYDE DIDN'T HAVE ENOUGH OF HIS OWN problems to worry about, he was also concerned about his friend, Raymond Hamilton. Raymond had been transferred to Hillsboro, Texas, to be tried for Clyde Bucher's murder. Clyde said this murder happened while he was outside in the car and when Raymond wasn't there at all.

Raymond was only 19 and was facing either a lengthy prison sentence or the electric chair. Clyde was determined to bust him out of jail.

On the night of Friday, January 6, Clyde, Bonnie, and W.D. stopped by the West Dallas home of Raymond's sister, Maggie, to discuss their plan to get him out of jail.

Maggie wasn't at the four-room house, but several lawmen were. Two sheriff's deputies, an investigator for the Tarrant County district attorney, a Texas Ranger, and a Dallas deputy had randomly chosen to stake out the house that night. They didn't even know Clyde was coming.

And Clyde didn't know they were there. He was unknowingly walking into a trap set for someone else – a bank robber who was a friend of Raymond's sister.

He walked straight to the door with a sawed-off shotgun hidden under his coat. Bonnie and W.D. waited in the car. He raised his hand to knock on the door and spotted a uniformed deputy through the window. He raised his gun and fired, shattering the glass.

The men inside the house returned fire, and W.D. began shooting from the car. Two deputies on the back porch heard the gunfire and ran toward the front of the house. One of the deputies, Malcolm Davis, saw Clyde and drew his pistol, but Clyde fired first, hitting him in the chest. As Clyde turned and ran for the car, W.D. provided cover. The motor was running, so Clyde jumped behind the wheel and sped away. None of the lawmen tried to follow.

Only Deputy Davis was hit during the gunfight. The quiet bachelor, known for his fresh catfish dinners, died before he got to the hospital.

Clyde Barrow's death toll continued to climb.

Over the next few days, deputies and police officers patrolled Dallas, Fort Worth, and the surrounding area, responding to an endless number of sightings from locals looking for the unidentified gunman. Armed officers raised one supposed hideout after another but found nothing.

More than a week later, the sheriff's office and Dallas police still weren't sure who the shooter had been. The residents of West Dallas were no help – they protected Clyde no matter what, just like his family did.

The only interesting information that trickled out came when Raymond Hamilton was transferred to the Dallas jail after he tried to escape from Hillsboro. A newspaper reported that a woman was often with Clyde during his robberies. According to the news reporter, Raymond told the cops, "She can handle pistols with either hand as skillfully as any young man."

An officer told the reporter that he knew a woman like that. "She is as tough as the back end of a shooting gallery, and she has been missing from these parts for some time."

It was not true, but it was the first mention of Bonnie Parker as an outlaw in print.

AS THE DALLAS AND FORT WORTH POLICE were chasing rumors about outlaws hiding out in the area, Bonnie, Clyde, and W.D. were somewhere far away. In fact, they'd been out of Texas before the sun came up on the day after Malcolm Davis was gunned down.

Little was heard from them until late January, when they popped up again in Springfield, Missouri. A motorcycle cop named Thomas Persell flagged them down after seeing them circle a parked Ford. When Clyde came to a stop, Persell rode up to the driver's door – and came face-to-face with Clyde's shotgun. Persell later said Clyde told him to "get my ass into the backseat, which I did."

They drove off as the police officer gawked at the array of heavy weapons and bags that he assumed were cash all over the backseat of the vehicle. The occupants of the car – who called themselves "Bud," "Sis," and "Boy" – had some foul words for him about law enforcement. Sis smoked all his cigarettes, and Boy was mainly quiet.

When the car's battery failed, they stole a new one and made Persell install it. Then, in an isolated spot near Joplin, they dropped him off. He wouldn't learn who he'd met that day until a week or two later.

When he did, he said he felt grateful to be alive.

BACK IN TEXAS, CUMIE BARROW WAS DOING all she could for her boys. She worked hard to come up with alibis for Clyde to prove he didn't do some of the things the police said he did, but she was also working hard to get Buck out of prison.

As she'd done for Clyde, she took a few liberties with the truth. She sent Clyde's wife, Blanche, to Austin to plead for a pardon for him, claiming she was pregnant with Buck's baby. She wasn't – Buck had been in jail for over a year – but they hoped no one looked too closely at the calendar. Cumie also petitioned every official she could find to write letters on Buck's behalf.

Her persistence eventually paid off, and shortly after his thirtieth birthday in March 1933, Buck was released from prison with a full pardon. He claimed his time behind bars had changed him for the better, and he wanted to settle down and stay out of trouble.

But he also wanted to see his kid brother. He worried about Clyde and told Blanche he wanted to try and convince him to turn himself in.

This was unlikely. It's more likely that Buck just told Blanche what she wanted to hear. He'd never worked an honest day in his life, and he wouldn't start now.

Blanche was completely against the idea of tracking down Clyde and his girlfriend, Bonnie. She sobbed and begged Buck not to go, but he wasn't listening. When he found out that Clyde was in Joplin, Missouri, Buck made plans to join his brother there.

On April 1, 1933, just days after leaving prison, Buck and Blanche set up housekeeping with Clyde, Bonnie, and W.D. in Joplin. Using the name "Callahan," Clyde rented an apartment from Paul Freeman at 3347 ½ Oak Ridge Drive on the south side of town.

Clyde's brother, Buck, and his wife, Blanche, after they met up with Bonnie, Clyde, and W.D.

The apartment was located over a two-car garage that faced Thirty-Fourth Street. It was just a couple of blocks from Main Street, situated on the edge of town. If there was trouble, the place offered an easy escape. Clyde parked the latest stolen Ford V-8 in one of the garage stalls. The other space was reserved for Harold Hill, a tenant in a nearby house. Because of this, Buck rented a small garage from another neighbor, Sam Langford, to park the car he had bought after he was released from prison. The car, a Marmon, was the vehicle the outlaws mainly used during their stay in Joplin.

They settled in quickly. Buck and Clyde bought quilts, bed linens, feather pillows, dishes, and silverware. Bonnie and Blanche made several trips to the local dime store, picking up glassware and picture frames. A few times, the girls went to matinee movies. The guys would often join them in the evenings.

Aside from that, they kept to themselves and didn't arouse much suspicion. Later, neighbors claimed to notice that they always kept their blinds drawn and stayed up very late at night.

Also, they always backed their cars into the garage so they would always be ready to leave in a hurry.

For the first time in months, Bonnie and Clyde slept in real beds and ate home-cooked meals. They idled away the time playing cards until the early morning hours. Bonnie used her spare time to write poetry, and Blanche played solitaire and worked crossword puzzles.

The garage apartment hideout in Joplin, Missouri

Clyde had promised to lay low, but when they ran short on money, he and W.D. slipped out and committed a few burglaries. One day, all three men returned late at night with a dozen or more new guns they'd stolen from an unguarded National Guard armory. They spent the next day out in the country testing them out. As their stay stretched into two weeks, W.D. stole another car: a Ford Roadster. Buck talked Harold Hill into letting the gang park it in the second space below the apartment.

But Bonnie was angry that they had added another car, sure it would draw too much attention. She and Clyde argued, and it got physical as it often did between them. Clyde knocked her down several times, but she always went after him, hitting him back and giving as good as she got. Clyde would always try to settle her down then, hoping to kiss and make up quickly.

By Thursday, April 13, they were all getting restless and bored. Blanche wanted to get on with her life with her newly freed husband, and Clyde was starting to worry about the attention they'd drawn a few nights earlier when a gun had gone off while he was cleaning it.

None of the neighbors had complained to them, but Clyde was right to be concerned – one of them had informed the Joplin branch of the Missouri Highway Patrol.

Around 4:00 P.M., Blanche was washing some clothes in the sink while Bonnie was packing. They were getting ready to leave Joplin the following day.

They didn't know it, but two Joplin police officers and two troopers from the Missouri Highway Patrol were on their way to the apartment in two cars. The highway patrolmen – G.B. Kahler and W.E. Grammar – had been joined by detectives Harry McGinnis and Tom DeGraff. J.W. Harryman, the Newton County constable, was also with them.

Suspecting that the people in the apartment were bootleggers or burglars, the lawmen arrived with nothing more than their service revolvers and a warrant to search for liquor and stolen goods that Harryman had picked up that day in Neosho.

Clyde and W.D. had just returned home when the police cars pulled up. The lawmen saw them standing inside the garage with the door partly open. Kahler pulled to a stop on Thirty-Fourth Street, but DeGraff whipped into the driveway and screeched to a halt just as the man standing next to the garage door tried to slam it shut.

"Just a minute! We want to talk to you," one officer called out.

Harryman sprang out of the passenger's seat while the car he was in was still moving, and he lunged toward the garage door to prevent it from closing. Tom DeGraff shouted to him, "Get in there as quickly as you can before they shut that door!"

But Harryman was too slow.

Gun in hand, he fired one shot, which slammed into the wooden garage door as it was closing. From inside, Clyde opened fire with his sawed-off shotgun, and W.D. blasted the nearly closed door with a Browning Automatic Rifle. The guns punched holes into the wood of the door.

Harryman went down on the other side of the garage door and was dead before he hit the ground.

As DeGraff came to a stop, Detective McGinnis jumped out of the backseat with a revolver in his hand. DeGraff exited the driver's side door. McGinnis squeezed off three shots at the splintered garage door, and one of his bullets winged W.D.

Clyde's shotgun roared again, and the detective was hit with a load of buckshot and stumbled backward. Crouching next to the police car, DeGraff fired several shots, making his way around to the rear of the vehicle just as McGinnis staggered past him and collapsed, mortally wounded. The shotgun blast had nearly severed his right arm, and he'd been struck in the left side and face.

The gunfight had already started by the time the highway patrolmen made it out of the car and onto the scene. Grammar ran toward the back of the garage, and Kahler quickly followed him, taking up a position at the corner of a nearby house, where he opened fire on the men he could see inside the garage.

Meanwhile, Detective DeGraff made his way around the east side of the garage, and when he saw Grammar at the rear of the building, he yelled at the patrolman, "For God's sake, run to that house and phone the station to send more men out here!" Grammar hurried to Harold Hill's home to telephone for reinforcements.

The situation inside of the apartment was as chaotic as the scene outside. When the shooting started, Buck, who had opened the garage door for Clyde and W.D. when they returned, ran upstairs and shouted to Bonnie and Blanche that they had to get out – the police were there.

Buck then ran downstairs and took W.D.'s weapon from him so that he could back up Clyde. W.D. stumbled up the stairs, clutching his wounded side and yelling for the women to hurry up and get to the car. Once downstairs, Bonnie jumped into the passenger's seat of the Ford. Blanche and W.D. – clutching his stomach and certain he was going to die – helped Clyde open the garage door

G.B. Kahler, now the only lawman in front of the garage who was not already dead or dying, continued to fire at the bandits with his revolver. A ricocheting bullet clipped Clyde, and a separate shot grazed Buck. From inside the garage, they returned fire. Kahler quickly retreated, tripping over a wire on the ground as he did. Clyde, thinking that the officer had been hit, turned around and started back inside. As he did, Kahler fired his last shot at him but missed.

The Ford's engine was racing, but the police car was blocking the way out of the garage. They released the parking brake but couldn't move it. Finally, Clyde decided to use the Ford to push the car out of the way and ordered everyone into the getaway vehicle. W.D. climbed into the backseat as Buck pulled Harryman's body clear of the path between the two vehicles. Clyde knocked up against the police car with the bumper of the Ford and managed to roll it out of the way. The police car now went careening down the sloped driveway toward the street.

In the commotion, Blanche's little dog, Snowball, had run outside, and Blanche, already hysterical over the gunshots and the sight of the dead police officers, chased after the dog. Clyde hit the gas and only slowed down enough for Buck to pull Blanche off the street and into the car. The bandits sped away with an armful of weapons but not much else.

As the car disappeared down the street, Kahler and DeGraff frantically reloaded their guns. Grammar raced over from the neighbor's house, too late to join the battle. Constable Harryman was dead, and McGinnis died a few hours later.

The bandits were long gone.

As additional police cars and ambulances were arriving at the Joplin apartment, the getaway car was speeding around corners, over hills, and in the general direction of Texas,

Inside the car, W.D.'s shirt was soaked with blood. Clyde was bleeding from a wound to the chest. In just minutes, everything had changed. Buck and Blanche would now be hunted for murder, just like the others, and W.D. wasn't sure he'd last through the night.

And then there was the evidence they'd left behind. Inside Blanche's bag, they found her and Buck's marriage license and Buck's recent pardon, so there was no doubt who they were. They also found a camera and several rolls of undeveloped film.

Investigators asked the local newspaper to develop the film, and they discovered the now-famous photos of Bonnie, Clyde, and W.D. clowning around and pointing guns at one another. When the photos, including one of Bonnie clenching a cigar in her teeth and clutching a pistol in her hand, went out on the newly installed newswire, the obscure outlaws from Texas became front-page news across America – and almost instant folk heroes. They weren't ordinary criminals – they were young, attractive, and well-dressed. They soon became a sensation.

But not everyone was thrilled with the photos. When they started appearing in newspapers and detective magazines, Bonnie was appalled. She sent numerous letters to every

Two of the undeveloped photos the authorities found in Joplin showing Bonnie and Clyde clowning around with guns and cigars.

publication she found them in to assure them that she did not smoke cigars. It had only been a joke.

All that press was more attention than the pair could have imagined. They soon became household names, with people all over the country recognizing the names and faces of Clyde Barrow and Bonnie Parker.

Clyde drove hard across West Texas, finally stopping for rest in the Panhandle. There, they bought rubbing alcohol and bandages to clean up their wounds. W.D. would survive. The bullet had passed clean through him. The bullet fragment lodged in Clyde wasn't deep. Bonnie popped it out with a hairpin. Buck thought he'd been shot, but it was only a bruise.

As their photos made the news, law enforcement from Texas to Missouri issued "shoot to kill" orders, and Dallas cops started staking out the Barrow home, expecting Clyde to make a trip home.

Despite what some might think, the reality of the couple's life on the run was far from glamorous. They often ate sardines from the can, bathed in rivers, and drove through the night, taking shifts sleeping and driving.

But Clyde wasn't that dumb. Avoiding the heat, the next two weeks became a blur for the fugitives as they sped across the middle of the country, from Texas to New Mexico to Kansas, Nebraska, Iowa, and Illinois, where they robbed another National Guard Armory. Then, they swung back down through Missouri, Arkansas, Oklahoma, and Louisiana.

They usually slept in the car or outdoors. It was a miserable experience for all of them, constantly on guard, guns close at hand. The stress made them all edgy.

Clyde and Buck both had bad tempers, but Buck was the worst. He was also drinking a lot, which made his anger flare even hotter. The brothers argued about whether to rob banks or stores, who was in charge, and who would drive while the others sat on top of each other in the hot, cramped car. Their bickering frequently escalated into fistfights.

Bonnie and Blanche were increasingly at odds, too. They had been close friends when their men were in prison, but now they'd become more and more competitive and critical of each other, especially when both were defending their partners.

And even when the group tried to lay low, they couldn't seem to avoid trouble.

They passed through Ruston, Louisiana, in late April, and Clyde spotted a new Chevrolet with its keys carelessly left in the ignition. He told W.D. to steal it, and the young man hopped in and hit the gas. The car's owner, Dillard Darby, saw the robbery happening and tried to stop him. Left in the dust, though, he called out to another renter in the boarding house where he lived, Sophia Stone. They jumped in her car and tried to chase W.D. but soon realized they couldn't catch him.

They turned around, but an angry Clyde cut off their retreat. He'd also lost W.D., and now he blamed Dillard and Sophia for ruining their plans to rob a bank. Clyde smacked Dillard in the back of the head with a pistol, and Bonnie dragged Sophia out of the car by her hair.

They ordered them into the front seat of their car, and Clyde drove around the area looking for W.D. but couldn't find him. Finally, he headed into southern Arkansas, still looking and only stopping for gas. W.D., it seemed, had decided to go home for a visit.

Clyde's mood blackened the longer he drove around, but Bonnie enjoyed the company, and she chatted with them and asked them questions. Sophia was a parish home demonstration agent. Her job was to teach rural women how to stretch their dollars by growing vegetables, canning, and making bread.

As they sped along the bumpy country roads, ammunition clips kept falling out of the glove box, so Clyde finally asked Sophia to hold them.

As the afternoon passed, Bonnie said they started to like the pair. Bonnie was especially tickled to find that Dillard was an undertaker. "I know we're going to get it sooner or later," she told him with a laugh. "I know you'd enjoy embalming us, so promise us you will."

Years later, Sophia recalled, "Clyde didn't see the humor."

Early that evening, they let the hostages out in rural Arkansas. Clyde started to drive off but stopped to give them $5 to help them get home. The pair got a lift into the nearest town and finally arrived home late that night.

As Dillard told the newspapers the next day, "Neither of us is much worse for the experience."

But for Bonnie and Clyde, life on the run was about to get worse – a lot worse.

ONE EVENING IN EARLY MAY, NOT LONG after W.D. took off, Clyde, Bonnie, Blanche, and Buck rolled into the Barrow filling station in Dallas. Without leaving the car, they chatted with Henry and Cumie. Clyde hoped to find W.D., but no one had heard from him.

Cumie begged Buck to stay and turn himself in. She believed that he and Blanche could blame Clyde for the carnage in

Joplin. That was Clyde's idea, and he offered to sign a statement saying so.

Buck shook his head. He told his mother there wasn't a chance in the world he could avoid the electric chair. He'd stick with his brother.

On May 12, they were back on the road, and Clyde and Buck tried their hand at bank robbing. They attempted to surprise the cashiers at the Lucerne State Bank in Lucerne, Indiana, but the employees grabbed their guns and drove them off. The would-be robbers quickly retreated to where Bonnie and Blanche were waiting in the car.

Their escape from town was almost as treacherous as the failed holdup. On the way out of town, a man threw a large piece of wood in front of their car, hoping to cause an accident. But Clyde swerved wildly into someone's lawn and kept going.

As they passed a church, they found the parishioners had flooded outside to see what was happening. With people in the street, Clyde had to slow down. He ordered Buck to fire some shots to scatter the crowd, but Bonnie forbade it.

Even so, a newspaper account published the next day claimed the bandits "literally shot up the town," resembling the "wildest escapades of Chicago gangland or tales of the wild and woolly west."

You can understand how Bonnie and Clyde captured the country's imagination at a time when people needed an escape from daily life during the Depression.

But there was gunfire that day – some coming from inside the outlaw's car and some from people on the street. As bullets plinked against the heavy metal of the motorcar, the occupants fired back. A bullet grazed the arm of a young woman. Two bullets tore through the wall of another woman's bedroom, and she was struck in the face by flying wood splinters. Bullets were later found lodged in telephone poles, trees, and sides of buildings.

Clyde and Buck were generally regarded as the shooters in the car – but were they the only ones? Witnesses reported seeing both a blond woman and a woman with brown hair in the car, and they were confident they had guns in their hands. According to one account, "Those who saw the bandits leave town were alike in their stories that the women did a large part of the shooting and probably all of it during the parting fusillade."

Clyde may have avoided the people in the street outside the church, but he didn't miss at least two pigs that wandered into the roadway just outside town. Those two were killed – the other 18 survived.

The following week, the two couples robbed a bank in Okabena, Minnesota, and made off with at least $1,400. Once again, a man and woman fired dozens of rounds from the rear window of the getaway car as it roared out of town, even threatening a school bus with more than two dozen children on board.

Not long after this heist, Blanche took a bus to Dallas to gather up the family for a reunion of sorts. Plans were made to meet Clyde, Bonnie, and Buck in a nearby town.

That wasn't usually how it was done. Most of the time, when Bonnie and Clyde wanted to meet with family members, they drove by the Barrow service station at night and tossed a Coca-Cola bottle with a note inside on the porch. The note included a time and meeting place. Then Cumie would call some of the other Barrow kids and Emma Parker and tell them she had red beans cooking. That was the code for an impending visit.

When the family gathered in May 1933, Clyde had some spending money for a change, and he spread it around – which was why it never lasted long. The two couples bought new clothes, and Clyde sent money for Cumie to buy new dresses for herself and his little sister, Marie. Bonnie loved Marie's dress so much that they exchanged clothing.

Clyde was generous with Marie, too. She was about to turn 15, and her brother gave her the money to buy her first bedroom furniture – a bed, a chest of drawers, and a dresser. It had been a hard year for her. Clyde and Buck were running for their lives, and all spring, one of her teachers welcomed her to school each day by asking, "Well, have they caught your brothers yet?"

The family was entertained with highly edited stories about their adventures on the road. Blanche had everyone laughing with her description of an argument between Bonnie and Clyde that escalated until Bonnie demanded Clyde stop the car. She threw her clothes in a sack and stomped off down the road, saying she was going home. Clyde thought it was funny – until

Even on the run, Bonnie and Clyde still managed to meet up with their families occasionally in Dallas.

Bonnie didn't come back. He followed her into a cornfield, pleading with her, but she ignored him. Finally, he threw her over his shoulder and carried her back to the car, kicking and screaming. The sack that held her clothes tore open, and Buck had to gather her clothing while Clyde tried to kiss and make up.

Even Bonnie was laughing at the retelling as they cleaned up after dinner, and the family tried once more to get Buck to turn himself in. Emma Parker pulled Bonnie aside and begged her to do the same. Both mothers believed time in prison would be better than what likely lay ahead for them.

But neither Bonnie nor Buck would budge. Buck said he was out of options, and Bonnie simply wanted to be with Clyde.

"I love him, and I'm going to be with him till the end," she told Emma. "When he dies, I'll want to die anyway, so let's don't be sad. I'm happy just being with Clyde, no matter what comes."

As the gathering broke up, Clyde left more money with the family -- $112 for Emma and a few hundred dollars for all the Barrows. It was a small fortune in those days.

The visit and the laughter had been a welcome respite for everyone. As Blanche would later recall, "We had to laugh to keep from crying."

SOON AFTER THE FAMILY VISIT, the two couples split up for a time. Buck and Blanche went to Oklahoma to see Blanche's father, and Bonnie and Clyde went to Dallas and found W.D., who hooked back up with them.

The Barrow brothers had arranged to meet back up at a bridge near Sayre, Oklahoma, on the far western side of the state. On June 10, Clyde, Bonnie, and W.D. were speeding to get to the rendezvous, flying down a new road near Wellington, Texas. It was dark, and he missed the detour sign to the old road – the new bridge hadn't been built yet.

Realizing his mistake, Clyde slammed on the brakes, but it was too late. Suddenly, the car was in the air, hurtling into the riverbed.

Two men eating ice cream on the porch of a nearby farmhouse saw the crash and came running toward them. Clyde and W.D. were banged up, bleeding, and shaken, but Bonnie was unconscious – and she was seriously injured. The car battery was shattered in the wreck, and the acid had sprayed onto her leg, badly burning her leg around and below the knee.

Clyde and W.D. gathered as many of their guns as they could, and Clyde asked one of the men who came to help to carry Bonnie to the nearby house. When they got there, the men's wives put Bonnie on a bed and began cleaning her up. They applied salve to her burn and washed the dirt and sand from her hair.

One of the men begged to call a doctor, but Clyde refused. "We can't afford it," he said, making an excuse to avoid the attention of law enforcement.

But while Bonnie was being cared for, one of the men had slipped out of the house to summon the sheriff – all the guns had made him uneasy. Clyde returned to the car to retrieve some of their things while W.D. stood guard outside.

Things were tense, and everyone was nervous.

One of the women in the house, with a baby balanced on her hip, walked over and latched the door, and the quick-triggered W.D. saw the movement from the corner of his eye and fired a shot at the window. Pieces of glass pierced her hand, and she screamed.

Clyde, alerted by the screams, ran back to the house. That was when he noticed that one of the men was missing. Knowing that he must have gone to the police, Clyde and W.D. took up positions outside. There was nothing else they could do – they had no car and couldn't run.

In town, County Sheriff George Corry learned that three people had been injured in a crash. He and town marshal Paul Hardy hurried to the house to help. He assumed they'd likely been drinking and gotten into a wreck, so he was surprised when he and Hardy walked up to the house and found themselves facing the barrels of two guns.

The lawmen were taken hostage, and Bonnie, awakened by the commotion, hobbled outside. After loading the men into Corry's car, Clyde shot out the tires of the family's truck so they couldn't follow.

Clyde didn't hold a grudge against the farmers for fetching the sheriff. He offered to pay them for the trouble, but the family declined. "If a man can't help another man, things are in pretty bad shape," one of them said.

Bonnie was initially in the front seat but soon moved to the back, lying down with her head in Paul Hardy's lap. She later said that Hardy treated her with unusual care and kindness, calming her and trying to protect her from the pain caused by the bumps along the road.

Finally, in the early morning of June 11, Clyde made it to the meeting place with Buck, who was waiting there with Blanche. Pulling Buck to the side, he told his brother about the situation – he thought Bonnie was dying, and he had two cops in his car.

"Are we going to kill those men?" Buck asked.

"No!" Clyde said firmly. "I'm beginning to like them." He had seen how kind the men had been with Bonnie and was determined to treat them well.

He and Buck used Sheriff Corry's handcuffs to link the men together and loosely tied them to a tree, so they'd be able to get free by morning. They left Hardy's car nearby so they could get home.

As they limped toward Buck's car, Blanche started to cry. She was convinced that Bonnie, Clyde, and W.D. would die. Bonnie was in terrible pain, and Clyde and W.D. were cut up and hurting, covered with blood. Bonnie was barefoot, and Clyde was missing one shoe.

As daylight spread across the horizon, the five headed to Kansas, where they rented a tourist cabin for a few days. Clyde and W.D. were recovering, but Bonnie was still in agony.

They moved on to a motel in Fort Smith, Arkansas, near the Oklahoma border, where Bonnie's condition got worse. She started running a high fever, became delirious, and called out for her mother. Her injury was gruesome. The acid had burned so profoundly through her flesh that bone was exposed in some areas. An infection had set in, and Clyde feared the worst.

Luckily, the motel owners were kind people. They did what they could, caring for Bonnie and helping Clyde find a local doctor who could treat her and provide medicine. He recommended hiring a skilled nurse if they refused to take Bonnie to the hospital.

Meanwhile, the police in Dallas had learned of the accident from Wellington officials and felt certain that Clyde would abandon Bonnie somewhere because her injuries would slow him down. That wasn't the case. He rarely left her side. He fed her and carried her to the bathroom and managed to find her Amytal, a powerful sedative. It made Bonnie irritable when it wore off, but when it worked, it dulled her pain and allowed her to sleep.

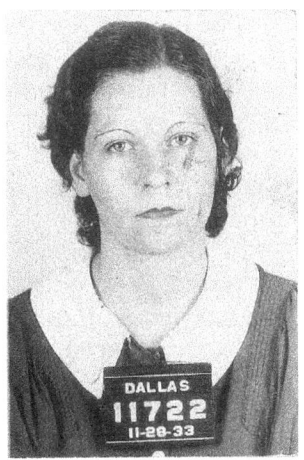

Bonnie's sister, Billie Jean

A week later, though, she hadn't improved much. Grieving and fearful she was going to die, Clyde drove all night to Dallas, even though he knew the police were watching for him. He was afraid to take Bonnie's mother because he was sure the cops were watching her, so Bonnie's sister, Billie, a single mother of two, agreed to go instead. They hurried back to Fort Smith right away.

While Billie nursed her sister, Clyde stayed nearby, only leaving for groceries and drug store items.

But he was running out of money. He needed more to pay for the bandages, the medicine, the nurse, groceries, the motel, and the money he'd been giving the owners to keep quiet. So, W.D. and Buck went out looking for a place to rob.

On June 23, they hit a small grocery store and snagged enough money to tide them over. With Buck behind the wheel, they were hauling down the highway at high speed when they topped a hill and crashed into a slow-moving car he couldn't see on the other side. He swerved just enough not to hit head-on, but he did knock the other car into the ditch, and Buck squealed to a stop.

The impact had left Buck and W.D. shaken and bruised, but once they calmed down, they grabbed their guns.

Town marshal Henry D. Humphrey and a deputy sheriff, Red Salyers, were driving in the opposite direction, looking for the bandits who robbed the grocery store. They had just passed the two cars, but when they heard the noise of the collision, they turned around.

As the policemen came to a stop and Humphrey got out, Buck and W.D. both opened fire, hitting him three times with enough force that the lawman was blown off the road. He survived for three days after the shootout before dying from his wounds.

Deputy Salyers got off a few shots but then hurried to a nearby farmhouse for cover. W.D. and Buck moved to steal the now-abandoned car as Salyers kept shooting. One of his bullets took off the tips of two of W.D.'s fingers, but he and Buck still managed to get away.

When they returned to the motel, Clyde realized they had to leave town immediately. They packed their things and took the motel's sheets and blankets, leaving behind $10 to cover the theft.

By the time the sun was up the next morning, they were all in Oklahoma. They couldn't wait any longer for Bonnie to get better. They were back on the run.

SOME WOULD SAY JUNE 1933 WAS THE beginning of the end for Bonnie and Clyde. It was undoubtedly a turning point, no matter how you looked at it.

Bonnie's terrible burns took a very long time to heal and had done so much damage that her leg never worked correctly again. As they moved on from Arkansas, she still needed help to perform some tasks and couldn't get in and out of the car by herself.

Their crimes had finally started getting national attention, and the U.S. Bureau of Investigation – which would later become the FBI – was stepping up its pursuit. The Bureau's interest was further heightened in June when a violent shootout between lawmen and unknown outlaws at Kansas City's Union Station, which left three police officers and a federal agent dead.

The "Kansas City Massacre," as it came to be called, led the new Franklin D. Roosevelt administration to declare a "war on crime" in response to the violent bank robberies and kidnappings happening during the Depression. Until then, the Bureau of Investigation had primarily been used to identify fingerprints and trace stolen cars that were taken across state lines. Eager to expand his power, the Bureau's director, J. Edgar Hoover, began beefing up his staff and angling for a more active role in pursuing criminals like John Dillinger, Pretty Boy Floyd, and Bonnie and Clyde. They were pawns to Hoover, serving as ways to raise his profile.

Clyde didn't care who chased them – he wanted to avoid everyone with a badge. Bonnie was finally improving and hoping to keep her sister, Billie, out of trouble. They dropped her off at a train station in North Texas with money to get home and some new clothes.

The bandits hid out in Oklahoma for a time after that. On July 7, Clyde and Buck raided another National Guard armory in Enid, bringing back so many weapons that W.D. said their hideout "looked like a gun factory." There were dozens of pistols, some rifles, several BARs, and cases of ammunition.

On July 18, they moved to the Red Crown tourist court in Platte City, Missouri. At the intersection of two highways, the spot had a popular dance hall and tavern nearby, a grocery store, and a filling station across the street. They rented two cabins with a garage between them for $4 a night.

Right away, the newcomers attracted attention. The two

The cabin at the Red Crown Tourist Court where the gang stayed until they started to draw too much attention.

couples and a friend began buying five meals at a time, paying as much as $10, which was more money than most people had around those parts. Clyde, Buck, and W.D. drank beer at the tavern until they started getting uncomfortable from the stares. They put newspapers over their windows to hide from prying eyes, but it didn't do much.

Blanche went into the local drugstore to buy bandages and syringes for Bonnie, which raised the pharmacist's eyebrows. Her "city clothes" got the attention of the locals who hung around the soda fountain.

By the next day, Sheriff Holt Coffey was pretty sure he had the Barrow gang in his county. Knowing they were dangerous, he put out the word for help from surrounding counties, including the sheriff in Kansas City. But from that direction, he received a chilly reply. "I'm pretty damn tired of every hick sheriff in the country coming in here and telling me they have a bunch of desperadoes holed up and want help," Coffey said the sheriff told him. But after some negotiations, the sheriff agreed to loan him a bulletproof car.

By evening, Coffey had pulled together a dozen lawmen, a couple of machine guns, the armored car, and a couple of metal shields for protection.

It would almost be comical if they hadn't been so serious about what they would try and do.

A little after 11:00 P.M., they made their move. A deputy pulled the armored car up near the garage. Then Coffey knocked on Buck and Blanche's cabin door and asked to talk to one of the men. He thought all five of the fugitives were in the same cabin.

Blanche agreed but said she had to get dressed first.

Hearing the conversation at the other cabin, Clyde looked out the window and saw the armored car and the armed officers. Sheriff Coffey was facing Buck's cabin, holding one of the metal shields.

Clyde cracked open a window and shoved the muzzle of a BAR outside. He pulled the trigger and sent a barrage of bullets into the armored car – which turned out not to be bulletproof. The bullets from the military rifle ripped through the vehicle, hitting the driver in both legs. Another bullet hit the horn, which began to blare loudly. A deputy in the car, seeing the driver hit, threw the car into reverse and stomped on the gas, jerking it across the parking lot. The other officers opened fire at the two cabins, although both machine guns jammed, rendering them useless.

Their service weapons were no match for the hardware being fired by the Barrows.

Locals gathered to watch the excitement suddenly found themselves too close to the action when the bandits returned fire. Clarence Coffey, the 19-year-old son of the sheriff, was watching from the front of the tavern with a waitress. When he saw his father get knocked off-balance after being grazed by a bullet, he tried to go and help. He only took a couple of steps before he was hit in the upper arm. A second bullet grazed his scalp, knocking him unconscious. The waitress managed to pull him to safety inside the tavern.

When the shooting started, Bonnie and W.D. grabbed as much as they could carry and got into the garage where the car was parked. Clyde opened the garage door for Blanche and Buck, but before they could get inside, a bullet struck the left side of Buck's head, exiting his forehead. He stumbled, and Blanche and Clyde had to lift him into the car.

As bullets from the cops' revolvers clanged into the car, Clyde whipped out of the garage and slipped past a truck that tried to block their exit. He slammed his foot on the gas pedal just as the car's rear window was shattered by gunfire. Some of the flying shards of glass pierced Blanche's eyes. Something else hit the side of her head. Bonnie's wounds were re-opened and bleeding, but Clyde and W.D. made it through with only a few scratches.

The assembled cops simply stood and watched them go. They had unloaded their weapons at the outlaws, but it hadn't done any good. The Barrows had outgunned them.

Clyde struggled to get away from the Platte City area. He repeatedly stopped the car to repair tires and care for the others' injuries. He tried to wash out Blanche's eyes and clean Buck's head wound. It was bleeding badly, but it wasn't fatal. Bonnie was in terrible pain. By morning, they were still near Kansas City – less than 10 miles from the scene of the shootout.

By Thursday, July 20, Clyde managed to get them into Iowa. He set up camp for them in a wooded area by an abandoned park near Dexter, Iowa, about 30 miles west of Des Moines. Before the Depression, the park had been home to a dance hall, ball field, and swimming pool. Buck's head wound was serious, but he was able to talk and eat. Blanche was more rattled. She had a piece of glass still stuck in one eye and was panicking about Buck's condition. She wouldn't leave his side.

At some point, Clyde and W.D. stole another car so they wouldn't have to explain the many bullet holes in the other one. Each day, Clyde drove into town for essentials. On Friday, July 21, he went into a shop owned by a man named John Love to buy two new shirts and a pair of shoes. Initially, Clyde seemed friendly and relaxed, Love recalled, but then he tensed up.

Clyde paid quickly and left – he'd gotten a glimpse of Love's deputy badge pinned to the shirt underneath his suit coat.

He then made a stop at a restaurant and ordered five dinners, and then he went to a pharmacy for alcohol, gauze, and burn ointment. Clyde returned on Saturday and Sunday for more meals and supplies, and by the end of the weekend, the shopkeepers were asking questions about the polite, pleasant-speaking stranger.

Out near the abandoned park, farmers had spotted the visitors, too. They were used to seeing down-on-their-luck travelers during the Depression, but they'd spotted some bloody clothing and used bandages and felt they ought to alert John Love. He came out to take a look and notified the county sheriff. They were convinced the travelers were the missing Barrow gang.

This sheriff also started assembling lawmen, including police officers from Des Moines and other towns and local volunteers who were good with guns. The men gathered on Sunday night, drawing an audience of dozens of thrill-seekers who wanted a front-row seat for what happened next. Most were drinking, and some had even brought dates.

When the sun rose on July 24, the posse began closing in on the camp. Love saw W.D. cooking hot dogs over a fire in the distance. They were about 100 yards away when Bonnie looked up, spotted the group, and alerted Clyde. Hoping to push them back, he fired a round from his BAR into the trees over their heads, dropping limbs and leaves onto the lawmen. When they kept coming, Clyde pulled the trigger again. One bullet grazed a deputy's forehead. Some of the officers hit the dirt and returned fire while others retreated.

W.D. stood up from his spot near the fire and was hit in the chest by a load of buckshot. He went down, and Clyde ordered everyone into the car. W.D. struggled to his feet and was hit again. He still managed to get into the car. Bonnie helped Blanche and Buck while Clyde returned fire. Finally, sliding behind the wheel, he hit the gas, and the car leaped forward – only to travel a short distance before hitting a dead end.

Clyde threw the car into reverse and was hit in the shoulder by a bullet. Unable to control the wheel, the vehicle went backward over a tree stump and got snagged. He tried to move it, but it was stuck, both back wheels off the ground.

The car doors were flung open, and they tried to get to their other, already damaged car, but by now, it had been demolished by the advancing lawmen and their weapons. Clyde shouted, and they ran for the woods. Shotguns blasted, and buckshot tore into the trees and brush. Two pellets hit Bonnie in her stomach, W.D. was struck again, and Buck was hit in the back.

Although bleeding badly, W.D. picked up Bonnie and carried her. Buck tried to get Clyde to leave him behind and take Blanche to safety. Blanche wouldn't hear of it, and neither would Clyde. He shoved them ahead of him through the brush until they reached a fence.

They managed to get over the fence and started climbing the hill on the other side. Buck couldn't go any farther, and he and Blanche fell behind. Clyde, Bonnie, and W.D. continued to a river. Spotting a nearby bridge, Clyde made them hide in some trees while he tried to run for a car. W.D. and Bonnie burrowed down among some briars and thorns while Blanche helped Buck hide behind a huge fallen tree.

Clyde stumbled toward the bridge and saw lawmen guarding it. He raised the BAR and tried to fire but couldn't control the heavy weapon with his injured arm. The shots went wild, and a deputy with amazing – or very lucky -- aim returned fire and knocked the BAR from his hands and clipped his neck. Clyde emptied his pistol toward the men on the bridge and disappeared back into the woods.

Bonnie was still crouched in the bushes with W.D. when she heard the yelling and shooting suddenly stop. She became convinced they'd gotten Clyde and started to cry. Then, suddenly, Clyde reappeared, crawling and covered with blood. They

Buck surrounded by officers and deputies as he lay on ground at edge of the park.

(Below) Blanche is taken into custodies by officers at the scene.

hugged and kissed, and then he explained they had no other options – they had to try and cross the river.

With Bonnie on W.D.'s back, they eased down a steep, heavily wooded hill and into the water. They waded across and climbed the hill on the other side. Clyde then pushed through a cornfield toward a barn with a wet, empty gun in his hand.

A farmer and his son were starting their day when a muddy, blood-spattered young man appeared from their cornfield and pointed his .45 at them. Clyde told them that he didn't want to hurt anyone – he just needed their car. The farmer handed over the keys.

After placing Bonnie in the back seat of the farmer's Plymouth, W.D. climbed in after her. Clyde slid behind the wheel, and they took off, looking for a new hiding place.

Meanwhile, some distance behind, the lawmen were carefully exiting the park and following the bandits into the woods. They didn't want to trigger any further gunfire from the people they were chasing. Finally, two hours after Clyde, Bonnie, and W.D. had escaped, the posse approached a large fallen tree that looked like a swell hiding place.

As the lawmen got closer, Buck raised his automatic at the two men in front of the group. His hand trembled as he tried to steady his aim. It didn't matter, though – two of the lawmen fired first. Buck was hit in the shoulder, and Blanche screamed and wailed as if she had been the one who'd caught the bullet.

The posse members moved in, and two lawmen carried the injured Buck back to the park. Another man led Blanche, who was barely able to see. She was beside herself with grief and terror. When they put Buck down, she rushed over to him. "Daddy, daddy, are you all right?" she cried.

"Sure, baby, I'm all right," Buck replied.

But he wasn't. The bandage was missing from his head, and brain matter was now seeping out of his wound. He had also been shot in the shoulder and the back.

When Buck and Blanche were taken away, souvenir hunters descended on the campsite and the two stolen cars. They took everything they could – a Bible, clothing, bandages, a magazine that had been stolen from a mailbox, bullets from the trees, anything at all. Luckily, the cops had already secured the guns and ammunition the Barrows had stolen, or the morbidly curious would have taken those, too.

Buck and Blanche were finished with the outlaw life, but somehow, Bonnie and Clyde managed to escape again. But now they were bleeding and wounded, and the future was looking very grim.

THE OFFICERS WHO NABBED BUCK AND BLANCHE first took them to see a doctor. Buck was examined, and the glass was removed from Blanche's eyes. She was then taken to jail, while Buck went to the local hospital.

Blanche was fingerprinted, weighed – a mere 81 pounds – and measured at just five feet one inch in her boots. She admitted that Buck was her husband but claimed that W.D. was "Jack Sherman," using a fake name because the police still hadn't figured out who the young man was. She wasn't going to help them.

Meanwhile, back in Dallas, Sheriff Schmid visited the Barrow filling station to tell Cumie and Henry that their oldest son was in the hospital with life-threatening wounds.

Cumie broke into sobs, begging to see her son before he died. Both parents asked about Clyde.

"Of course, I know you think they are bad boys," Henry said to the sheriff, "but they are our boys."

Schmid gave Cumie a letter introducing her as Buck's mother, so she'd have no problems getting into the hospital to see him. Later, Bonnie's sister, Billie, said that a deputy sheriff provided money that allowed her, Cumie, Emma Parker, and L.C. Barrow to drive to Iowa.

While his family was hurrying in his direction, Buck was being questioned in his hospital room by a parade of lawmen. Two officers from Alma, Arkansas, including Red Salyers, came to ask him about the recent murder of Henry Humphrey. Buck admitted to shooting the marshal, and he recognized Salyers. "You're lucky you got out of the way," he told him.

In an interview with a Bureau of Investigation agent and an Iowa sheriff, he denied raiding a National Guard armory – even though he had – but did confess to three service station robberies. The agent later wrote. "He seemed to be in good spirits. Even though he realized that he probably did not have long to live, he, on several occasions, laughed heartily at some of his escapades."

Doctors did not expect Buck to survive. His head wound had become infected and gave off such a foul odor that it was difficult for the lawmen to stand within a few feet of him.

By the time Cumie arrived on Wednesday, he had a fever of 105 degrees. She begged him to speak to her, and Buck groaned that he knew she would come. She kept a vigil at his bedside as he fell into a coma the next day.

Marvin "Buck" Barrow died on Saturday, July 29. He was 34 years old, and in the past four months, he had been involved in three murders, four shootouts, and the kidnapping of two people. He left behind a trail of more robberies than could be counted, along with a family who loved him, two children from two marriages, and a wife, Blanche, who was sitting in a Missouri jail on a bond of $15,000.

She'd later plead guilty to assault with intent to kill during the Platte City shootout in September. She received a 10-year sentence in a Missouri prison, where doctors operated at least twice to save the sight in her left eye, but they weren't successful.

A quiet funeral was held for Buck in West Dallas on July 31, after which he was buried. The Barrows held off on buying a gravestone – they figured they'd soon be burying another son.

When Cumie was in Iowa, she'd been asked if she would beg Clyde to turn himself in. She shook her head. "No, if he remains at large, officers will shoot him in their attempts to capture him. If he surrenders, he'll face execution."

Cumie walked past the reporters who anxiously awaited her statement, their pencils poised over notebooks.

She stopped and turned back to face them. Her eyes were sad and filled with tears. "So, I'm going to let him live his last few days as he wants to," she told them, "without any instructions or pleas from me."

WHILE BUCK WAS TAKING HIS LAST BREATHS in the Iowa hospital, lawmen were searching everywhere in the state for Bonnie and Clyde. Airplanes were flown over backroads and farmland, abandoned farmhouses were searched, and cops searched every outhouse, hen house, and doghouse, but the hunt didn't turn up anything but rumors.

Still locked up in Dallas, their friend Raymond Hamilton predicted that Bonnie and Clyde would be tough to catch. He told reporters that they were determined to avoid capture, even if it meant they had to kill each other if they thought their freedom was at stake. The pair were in love, and they'd do whatever it took for them to die together if they had to.

"They're all saying they'll catch them before the end of the week," Raymond added. "I say they're dead wrong."

And he was right about that.

Clyde was back behind the wheel of a fast car. After he, Bonnie, and W.D. escaped, they stole a Chevrolet from a filling station and kept going. Days and then weeks passed without new crimes, so some began to say they'd died from their injuries. In truth, though, they found quiet places to camp, stayed out of sight, and nursed their wounds.

But Clyde couldn't stand laying low for long.

In August, he and W.D. replenished their arsenal by stealing weapons from an Illinois National Guard armory that they'd robbed once before.

They went south to Mississippi, but after arriving there, W.D. had something important to talk to Clyde about – he was done with the outlaw life. Over eight months, he'd seen a lifetime of blood and violence, including five murders.

As he later said, "I'd had enough of blood and hell."

He said his goodbyes and headed for Texas, where he found work picking cotton.

Whether Clyde expected W.D. to leave is unknown, but this time, he didn't decide to go looking for him. He'd stay on his deadly course without his young friend and take the always loyal Bonnie with him.

Without W.D. to help, Bonnie and Clyde got by mainly on the take from small robberies and the food, blankets, and clothing their families provided. Bonnie was just 22, and Clyde was only a year older, but both were now thinner and older looking than they'd been only a few months before. They were living a tough life, but Blanche later said, "Bonnie wouldn't have done it if she hadn't loved Clyde so much."

Worried that they might not have much time left, the pair found ways to visit with their families despite being two of the most-wanted fugitives in Texas.

Hoping to go unrecognized in Dallas, they sometimes dyed their hair. Bonnie was a natural blond but was often a redhead, and at least once, so was Clyde. But there were likely other reasons – besides their bad disguises – why the police didn't bother them on their trips home. The Dallas police and county deputies were severely understaffed, poorly trained, or distracted by other crimes – those were the excuses for why they didn't stake out the Barrow and Parker homes. There's no proof that any officers took bribes, although police payoffs were common at the time. It's more likely that Bonnie and Clyde were left alone because no lawman in his right mind wanted to take on a gunman like Clyde – who didn't care about killing innocent bystanders and outgunned every lawman he came across – on his own.

So, even if Clyde had been spotted in Dallas, a cop would call for assistance before confronting him. By the time help arrived, Clyde would be long gone.

Still, Sheriff Schmid had not forgotten about the pair – or that he was up for re-election in 1934. He wanted nothing more than to capture Bonnie and Clyde. His closest men tried to convince him that capturing the two would be impossible, but the sheriff refused to hear it.

In mid-November, the sheriff's office got the break Schmid had been waiting for when a tip led them to W.D. Jones, who was now in Houston.

Under questioning, W.D. spilled his guts about Bonnie and Clyde to an assistant district attorney, albeit with several plot twists. W.D. claimed that whenever there'd been a shooting, he was either asleep or absent. He claimed Bonnie and Clyde had forced him into joining them and often handcuffed him to a tree to keep him from running away. If a second person ever fired a gun, it was Bonnie – not W.D.

He mapped out eight months of crime with the Barrow gang, state by state, robbery by robbery. He detailed the gun battles in Joplin, Alma, Platte City, and Dexter, though he never admitted to any shooting. He'd always participated against his will, he swore.

Most of the lawmen who heard his accounts didn't believe him, but it was a smart move. By refusing to admit to any real crimes and insisting that he was only 17, W.D. wouldn't face the harsh penalties that an adult would. Officials also sympathized with the young man's painful souvenirs from the road – the bullet wounds on his side and chest, the burns on his thigh, the scars on his face, and the buckshot still lodged in his body.

W.D. was playing the authorities for fools, and so far, it was working.

Sheriff Schmid insisted on keeping W.D.'s arrest a secret from the press. The sheriff's department knew Bonnie and Clyde were meeting with their families, and Schmid believed he could capture them. He didn't want them scared off by knowing W.D. had been caught.

On November 21, Bonnie and Clyde celebrated Cumie's fifty-ninth birthday with other family members on a deserted road west of Dallas. The pair were planning to leave town for a while, so they asked to meet the family again the next night in the same spot, something they rarely did.

An informant passed on the location and approximate time to the sheriff's office, and Schmid finally had the chance to be a hero. Edward Dowd, an agent for the Bureau of Investigation, offered to coordinate with Schmid to help him catch Clyde, but Schmid turned him down. "I prefer to work alone," the sheriff told him.

Ahead of the planned meeting, Schmid and three deputies – Bob Alcorn, Ted Hinton, and Ed Caster – parked their car a half mile from where Bonnie and Clyde would be. As the clock ticked closer, they crept forward and hid about 75 yards off the road in a ditch. They brought an arsenal with them – two Thompson machine guns, a repeating rifle, and a BAR.

A short time later, Marie Barrow's boyfriend, Joe Francis, drove the Barrow and Parker families to the meeting spot. They pulled over to the side of the road and got out of the car to wait. A few minutes later, another car approached them, barreling down the gravel road. Joe leaned into his car and turned on his headlights.

As the second car stopped next to Joe's car, Bonnie and Clyde greeted their family with smiles on their faces.

Before they could get out of the car, though, Schmid and his deputies emerged from hiding and opened fire. Its windows shattered, and bullets slammed into the steel exterior. Clyde raised a pistol and fired a few wild shots in the direction of the officers. In a matter of seconds, they were gone.

Most of the family had thrown themselves on the ground when the shooting started. Cumie cried and prayed at the top of her lungs. Once the guns fell silent, they hurried into Joe's car and sped away.

Clyde headed toward Fort Worth, running with one flat tire. A few miles from the ambush site, he saw another car coming toward him on the road, and he swerved to the side and cut it off. Gun in hand, he ordered the driver out of the car, but the man refused. Not in the mood to negotiate, Clyde fired one shot, blowing out the car's rear window. That convinced the driver to turn over his car.

Bonnie and Clyde grabbed as many guns as they could and drove off, leaving their bullet-riddled car. They also left behind about a dozen shell casings, an assortment of clothing, makeup, medicine, 11 license plates, and the December issue of *Master Detective* in the car. Clyde wasn't in that issue, but he was in the December issue of *Real Detective* as an example of the "New Bad Men of the Old Wild West."

The police would also find blood on the car seats, leading many to believe that one or both of the outlaws had been wounded.

Back at the ambush site, Sheriff Schmid was cursing his bad luck. They didn't have a car close by with which to chase Clyde. They hadn't planned for the bandits to escape. None of the cops had been hurt. However, a woman who lived a half-mile away was cut by broken glass when a bullet from one of their military rifles went through her window.

Rather than being celebrated as a hero, Schmid had to explain to the public and the press why he hadn't been better prepared and why he'd endangered the lives of innocent members of the Barrow and Parker families with his ambush.

He tried to steer the press toward his arrest of W.D. Jones instead, telling reporters, "Boys, it will take you until midnight to finish this story; it's so big."

His ploy worked, and Schmid's foolish decisions were barely questioned, helping him get re-elected three more times in his law enforcement career.

Even so, he never caught Bonnie and Clyde.

EVEN THOUGH NEWS REPORTS CLAIMED BONNIE and Clyde were badly wounded after the ambush, they weren't seriously hurt. A bullet had clipped both across the knee and leg. It managed to make Bonnie's limp even worse.

Retreating to one of their Oklahoma hideouts, they managed to get patched up by a nurse. Within a week, they were on their way back to Dallas.

Clearly, someone had snitched on them and revealed their plans to the cops. It was almost certainly a family member or someone close to one. Later, some family members would speculate that Joe, the other car's driver, was the informant, but this was never confirmed. Clyde didn't seem to blame him – Joe married Marie Barrow a few months later.

Clyde wasn't sure who'd crossed them, but his temper was boiling. He was even more angry at the police, who'd put his and Bonnie's mothers in danger so they could try and kill him. Once again, Clyde was looking for revenge, so when a former drug addict named Jimmy Mullins came calling a few weeks later, Clyde was primed for the most dangerous crime of his bloody and violent career.

JIMMY MULLINS HAD SPENT MOST OF HIS ADULT LIFE behind bars. Convicted of narcotics crimes and burglary, he served time in Illinois and Kansas before ending up at Eastham Farm in Texas.

At Eastham, he met Raymond Hamilton, who'd arrived in August filled with confidence and swagger. Raymond liked to brag that his friend, Clyde Barrow, would break him out. Of course, Raymond had been saying this since he'd been locked up, and no one took it seriously since Clyde still hadn't shown up. When Dallas County Sheriff Schmid warned prison officials that Raymond was a flight risk, they laughed at him. They told him that Raymond stayed out of trouble more than any other prisoner, and they weren't worried.

But Raymond had a plan.

He offered Jimmy Mullins a deal – if he'd help Raymond with his prison break, Raymond would give Jimmy $2,000 when he got out.

It was too good for Jimmy to resist. When he was paroled on January 10, 1934, he went to Dallas and found Floyd Hamilton, Raymond's older brother. He detailed a plan to bust Raymond out – the same plan that Clyde and Ralph Fults had put together a few years before.

Floyd, unsure about the plan, suggested that Jimmy talk to Bonnie and Clyde. The four met on a country road west of Dallas and discussed the plan, which called for two .45 caliber automatics hidden in some brush near where Raymond worked on the farm.

Clyde didn't trust Mullins. He could see how twitchy the man was. But he agreed to help if Mullins and Floyd were the ones who hid the guns on the prison property.

On January 13, Clyde, Bonnie, Jimmy, and Floyd drove to Eastham Farm. It was a mild winter evening, and as darkness fell, Floyd and Jimmy crept to the farm and tucked an inner tube containing two pistols and ammunition under a bridge near the woodpile where Raymond had been working.

They returned to Bonnie and Clyde without trouble, and the four of them headed north. That Sunday morning, Floyd picked up his wife in Dallas, and the couple went to Eastham to visit Raymond and tell him the plan was in place.

Meanwhile, Clyde, Bonnie, and Jimmy spent the nights prowling the area's roads, looking for the best escape routes. They took turns sleeping and keeping a lookout. Clyde still didn't trust Jimmy, so he didn't let him stand watch by himself.

Early on the morning of January 16, the inmates were forced to run from the barracks to where they'd been cutting and stacking wood and clearing brush. Raymond had quietly switched from his usual squad No. 2 to his friend Joe Palmer's No. 1 squad. Following standard procedure, guard Olin Bozeman wouldn't force him back to his proper squad until they reached the work site.

Once there, Bozeman called over to Major Crowson, the guard whose job was to hang back near the woods with a rifle to prevent escape. Sitting side-by-side on their horses, Bozeman asked him to tell another guard to come and get Raymond, who was out of place.

"Boy, you better watch out," Crowson told Bozeman. "That means something."

And he was right. Neither man even had a chance to react before they saw Joe Palmer aiming a pistol at them from a few feet away. He shot Crowson first. The bullet hit him in the stomach and ripped through his back.

Bozeman reached for his gun, and Palmer somehow shot it out of his hand. The guard's horse wheeled around, and the next shot caught Bozeman in the hip.

As Raymond Hamilton rushed to the scene, he tried to fire, too, but the clip fell out of the gun after the first shot.

Both guards went down, and Raymond, Palmer, and two other inmates ducked into a nearby ditch and began to run. Bonnie started honking the car horn to let them know which way to run while Clyde and Mullins opened fire into the trees, hoping to provide cover for the escapees and discourage anyone from following them.

The inmates followed the ditch all the way to the road, where they found the car waiting for them. They all jammed into the car, with two escapees hanging off the back.

Before an alarm sounded, Clyde was racing north, traveling along dirt roads, and cutting through fields to avoid roadblocks. Soon, reports of the escape were traveling by radio and telegraph. Near Hillsboro, about 150 miles away, Clyde stopped for gas, and the excited attendant asked them if they'd heard the news.

What news? Clyde asked him.

Well, the man said, Bonnie and Clyde had marched right into the Eastham dining hall and had broken Raymond Hamilton out of prison. The attendant was so chatty that Clyde finally had to ask when they would get some gas.

An early edition of the afternoon *Dallas Dispatch* also told a whopper of a tale – Clyde had driven up to the Eastham barracks alone, shooting three guards and rescuing Raymond Hamilton while he was having breakfast.

By morning, the prison break was national news, and the dramatic story raised the profile of the outlaw couple. The *New York Times* called it "perfectly executed" and added that the escape was aided by the "two-gun, cigar-smoking woman" Bonnie Parker.

The new gang – made up of Bonnie and Clyde, Raymond, Jimmy Mullins, Joe Parker, and the two extra inmates – almost immediately began robbing banks, primarily to raise the money owed to Mullins.

But living in a car and traveling from place to place daily was complicated, especially when Billie Parker joined them for a short time. They were all bickering within a week, and a couple of the escapees left on their own. One was quickly captured and spilled details to the cops.

On January 26, Bonnie, Clyde, and the remaining men returned to Dallas with plenty of cash. That night, Mullins later said, Raymond paid him $685 of the amount that he owed him for the prison break. He also gave $500 to his brother, Floyd, who'd bought new clothes for Bonnie and the men.

In mid-February, the group was joined by Raymond's new girlfriend, Mary O'Dare, who was married to one of his former partners who was now in prison.

Bonnie and Clyde disliked Mary, and they didn't trust her. They worried she might turn them in to get the reward money offered for their capture in several states. The rewards added up to hundreds of dollars, although Bonnie believed the woman would betray them for much less. She refused to let Mary out of her sight.

Mary didn't like them much either. She wanted to eat in nice restaurants and stay in nice hotels. She wasn't interested in greasy diners and sleeping on the side of the road. The tension between the two couples grew.

Once, after Bonnie and Clyde had a big fight, Mary suggested Bonnie should drug Clyde, take his money, and leave. Bonnie didn't appreciate the advice.

On February 27, the men robbed a bank in Lancaster, Texas, south of Dallas, getting away with more than $4,000. Raymond wanted his girlfriend to get a cut of the money, but Clyde refused. While driving later that day, Clyde saw Raymond in the rearview mirror, trying to pocket some additional cash. Clyde slammed on the brakes and pulled over. He frisked Raymond and found hundreds of dollars of extra money in his pockets.

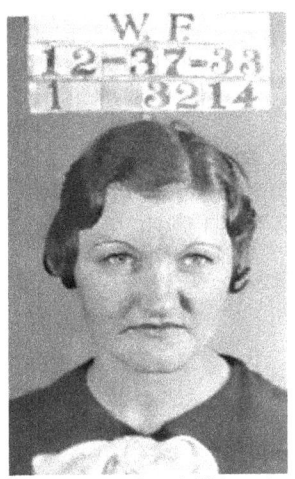

Raymond's girlfriend, Mary O'Dare. Bonnie and Clyde couldn't stand her – and their impression of her turned out to be right.

That was the last straw. The two couples parted ways a few days later – but the feud didn't end. Raymond was captured soon after and was back behind bars. In a newspaper interview, he insisted that Bonnie, not Mary, had demanded a cut of the money.

Bonnie and Clyde never formally responded to any mention of them in the newspapers, aside from when Bonnie wrote letters in response to comments about the photos found in Joplin.

But Raymond had gotten under their skin – especially after all they'd done for him.

The pair sent a scathing letter to the Dallas jail in late April. It was written in Bonnie's neat script, but the words were clearly from Clyde. After he had found the extra cash that Raymond had stolen, he said, "I should have killed you then."

THE PRISON BREAK HAD LEFT A LOT OF DAMAGE behind at Eastham Farm. The bullet that hit Major Crowson had torn apart his abdomen, and while in the hospital, he developed pneumonia. He died on January 27. He was only 33 years old.

One of the last things he said to Texas Prison Director Lee Simmons was that he hoped he caught Joe Palmer and "put him in the electric chair."

Outraged by the prison break and Crowson's death, Simmons was determined to seek justice. He wanted Palmer and Raymond Hamilton to pay for the murder, but more than anything, he wanted to end Clyde Barrow's seemingly endless crime spree.

In early February, he turned to legendary lawman Frank Hamer and asked him to hunt down Bonnie and Clyde.

Just shy of his fiftieth birthday, Hamer had a dangerous reputation as an old-school gunslinger. For years, he was acclaimed as a Texas Ranger, part of a small outfit charged primarily with defending the Texas border with Mexico. He had been called to control riots and investigate crimes and had been mixed up in more than 50 gunfights with criminals, smugglers, and Mexicans. He'd killed at least 20 men during his career.

When Texas governor Miriam "Ma" Ferguson took office in 1932, though, Hamer left the Rangers because he refused to work for a woman governor. He was between jobs when Simmons called him.

Simmons promised Hamer he'd have all the support he needed and assured him that Governor Ferguson had approved his appointment despite insulting her when she took office.

And he gave him one piece of unsolicited advice: "The thing for you to do is to put them on the spot, know you are right – and then shoot everybody in sight."

Hamer started the hunt on February 10, immediately trying to recreate Bonnie and Clyde's movements. While Clyde and Raymond were bickering, Hamer visited Louisiana, Oklahoma, Arkansas, and Dallas. In the last two weeks of February, he traveled 1,397 miles.

By March, he was in touch with the Bureau of Investigation, which shared all they'd learned after tracking the pair for over a year. Hamer found the couple's hideouts and makeshift shooting ranges and contacted Deputy Bob Alcorn, who was still chasing Bonnie and Clyde for Sheriff Schmid. Alcorn started working with Hamer, hunting the pair in Louisiana, where Clyde hadn't been accused of a serious crime yet.

Former Texas Ranger Frank Hamer and his posse of officers were tasked with tracking down Bonnie and Clyde. Hamer had a reputation for hunting criminals and bragged about killing 53 men when he was a Ranger.

Hamer was so confident in his skills that he fully expected to take Bonnie and Clyde alive. All he had to do was to catch them sleeping, he believed, tap each on the head, kick away their guns, and slap them in handcuffs before they were fully awake.

Hamer should have known better. It was going to take a lot more than that to catch the most lethal couple in America.

BONNIE WAS HOMESICK.

No matter what had been going on in the past, Clyde had always been able to get her home to see her mother occasionally. But now, things were just too hot in Dallas. After the last disastrous trip, Clyde was steering clear of home, even though he wanted to see his family just as much as Bonnie wanted hers.

Finally, she bothered him enough that he came up with a plan – they'd meet the family for a gathering on Easter Sunday, which fell on April 1. Bonnie had a special surprise for Emma – a white rabbit that she'd named Sonny Boy.

On that warm spring day, the couple parked on a hill near Grapevine, Texas, and waited for their families to arrive. Only

Henry Methvin

one of the Eastham escapees was still with the pair – Henry Methvin, a young man from Louisiana who was just short of his twenty-second birthday.

Henry was keeping a lookout, sipping some whiskey, while Clyde took a nap in the backseat of their latest stolen car. Bonnie was in the front seat, playing with the rabbit.

The car was parked about 100 yards off the road, but that was not far enough to escape the attention of two young state highway patrol officers on motorcycles. They saw the car and rode over to see if the occupants needed help.

Bonnie quickly alerted Clyde, but he knew immediately that the officers didn't seem to suspect trouble. "Let's take 'em," he said to Henry.

Barrow family members would later insist that Clyde only meant to disarm or perhaps kidnap the cops, as he had other officers who didn't mean any harm – but that's not what Henry heard.

He raised his gun and opened fire on the two officers.

One of the patrolmen went down right away. The other reached for shotgun shells in his pocket, and either Henry or Clyde – seeing he had no other choice – shot him, too. It was a brutal, unprovoked, and unnecessary murder.

And worse, there were witnesses.

Mr. and Mrs. Fred Giggal had been enjoying a Sunday outing when they saw the two patrolmen turn down the dirt road, and then they heard loud sounds, like a car backfiring. They hurried toward the sounds and saw two men. The taller one, they later reported, walked over to one of the fallen officers and shot him again. The two men then hurried toward a car parked nearby. The couple didn't remember seeing a woman in the car but saw two men as they sped toward them.

Mrs. Giggal told the authorities later that day, "I screamed at my husband to hurry – that they knew we had seen the shooting and would kill us."

But the outlaws' car swerved off in another direction and disappeared.

Another witness had a different story. William Schieffer was on the front porch of his nearby farmhouse and said that he saw a man and a woman shoot the officers. Then the smaller of the two – which he was sure was a woman – turned one of the cops over and shot him again in the chest.

You can imagine which story the police wanted to believe. They didn't even know that Henry was with the couple, and with Bonnie's reputation as a "gun moll," they weren't surprised she killed two officers. Besides that, they found a cigar stub that had been left behind – proof that Bonnie was there.

The cold-blooded murder on Easter Sunday shocked and angered the community. Patrolman Edward Wheeler was 26 years old, a sharpshooter, and a married four-year highway patrol veteran. The other officer, H.D. Murphy, was only 22, and it had been his first day of patrol duty. He was supposed to be married on April 13 and had already rented a small house where he planned to live with his new wife.

Though the Barrow family would always blame Henry Methvin for the murders, the public and the police blamed Bonnie and Clyde. Until then, she'd been a glamorous partner for Clyde, but now she was considered a vicious killer.

The Bureau of Investigation and Texas Highway Patrol publicly joined the many other agencies hunting for Bonnie and Clyde. Orders went out to stop and search any car that contained a man and woman. Sheriff Schmid ordered his deputies to circle the city with shotguns in pursuit of the couple. Behind the scenes, the Highway Patrol also made one of its men, a former Texas Ranger named Manny Gault, available full-time to Frank Hamer.

But none of the searches or the efforts to block the roads leading out of Texas got underway until Monday and Tuesday, which drew the criticism of newspapers across the state. The *Dallas Dispatch* wrote: "Where was the governor, where were the Rangers, and where was the state highway commission after two members of its force had been shot down?" The paper added that Bonnie and Clyde were "more merciless than rattlesnakes."

Of course, even with forces mobilizing against them and higher rewards offered, Bonnie and Clyde had slipped away.

CLYDE, BONNIE, AND HENRY METHVIN DIDN'T stay out of sight for long. They showed up less than a week later, on Friday, April 6, in Northeast Oklahoma. The area around the Oklahoma, Kanas, and Missouri borders had offered them refuge several times before.

They pulled over to the side of the highway to sleep, taking turns watching and dozing. When the sun came up, a passing motorist reported their suspicious car to the constable of Commerce, Oklahoma, Cal Campbell.

Campbell and Commerce Police Chief Percy Boyd – who was the entire police force – drove out to investigate the car, which seemed to be stuck in some mud. Figuring they could help out the stranded folks, the two lawmen got out of their vehicle and walked up to the car. When they saw a weapon inside, though, Campbell pulled his gun. By then, Clyde and Henry had seen them coming and drew their own guns. Both cops fired a few shots, sending bullets through the windshield. They passed so close to Clyde's head that he heard them buzz by.

Clyde and Henry returned fire. Boyd also claimed that Bonnie fired a shotgun. A bullet struck Campbell in the chest, and he died on the spot. Another bullet ripped across Boyd's head, and he went down, too.

After both men went down, the shooting stopped. Clyde and Henry scrambled from the car. Henry grabbed Boyd and hauled the bleeding officer into their vehicle – which was still stuck in the mud. Clyde ran to a nearby farmhouse, hoping to find a tractor to pull them out, but no one answered his frantic knocks on the door. He ran back to the road and flagged down a passing truck. Using his rifle for persuasion, he forced the driver to drag the car from the muck.

The bandits were soon on their way toward Kansas with Boyd as their wounded hostage.

Witnesses to the incident alerted the county sheriff's office, and deputies went in pursuit, but Clyde quickly lost them. As the morning turned to afternoon, many feared that Boyd had died from his wounds or had been killed.

But that wasn't the case. Like most of their other hostages, Boyd was treated as well as he could be under the circumstances. He conversed with Bonnie as she fed the white rabbit she'd wanted to give her mother. He gradually won her over and got some chuckles from Clyde with some of his stories. At one point, Bonnie cleaned and bandaged Boyd's head and then gave him a fresh shirt and necktie since his were bloody. They tried to provide him with a suit, but it was too small.

For a full day and into the early morning hours, they took Boyd on a long ride, looping through eastern Kansas and Oklahoma, sometimes at speeds of 90 miles an hour. Mud and dirt covered the car. A couple of times, they stopped for breaks, sending Henry to grocery stores for sandwiches and drinks.

They didn't know that Cal Campbell had died until they read it in a newspaper the following afternoon. Clyde told Boyd how sorry he was – and then he and Bonnie joked about the shooting all afternoon.

Boyd realized there was something not quite right about the otherwise friendly couple.

Finally, around midnight, they dropped Boyd off about seven miles from Fort Scott, Kansas. He was back home by 7:00 A.M. the following day with a story he would tell for years.

In the interviews that followed his adventure, he described the bandits' guns and ammunition and told reporters and lawmen that Bonnie and Clyde had no fear of being captured. They did, however, have messages they wanted to share.

"You can tell the officers anything you want to," Clyde said, "but be sure to tell them the truth. We would not have fired a shot if the old man – meaning Cal Campbell – had not come out of his car with a pistol."

Bonnie was still upset about the news reports that claimed she smoked cigars. Boyd laughed, "She told me she wanted me to tell her public that she does not smoke cigars. She is plenty mad about it."

On April 8, pursuers found the car that Clyde had been driving abandoned in Kansas. Inside was a collection of leftover food, men's socks, a loaf of sliced bread, chewing tobacco, a Boy Scout flashlight, a couple of newspapers, and a bloody blue-and-white-checked necktie. They also found some cabbage and partially chewed carrots, apparently for Sonny Boy.

Bonnie, Clyde, and Henry, though, were long gone.

BONNIE AND CLYDE'S CRIME SPREE continued to draw more and more attention. Law enforcement was doing its best to find them but wasn't making much progress. Dallas police and sheriff's deputies cruised by the Barrow filling station three or four times daily. Various agencies interviewed Raymond Hamilton and the Eastham escapees who had been caught, hoping they could point them toward the couple. The Bureau of Investigation contacted Clyde's former girlfriends and put a Barrow cousin on the payroll as an informant.

At the Dallas police station, a lieutenant had life-sized stand-ups made from photographs of the two outlaws. They were placed in the hallway coming into the station to remind the officers what the pair looked like – and to remind them they were still on the loose.

Despite the increased attention, Bonnie, Clyde, and Henry returned to Texas for another family visit in mid-April. Bonnie finally gave the pet rabbit to her mother, along with a humorous warning: "Keep him away from the cops. He's been in two gun battles, and he'll land in jail if the law finds out."

The Barrow and Parker family members knew Bonnie and Clyde couldn't stay lucky forever. They even urged them to leave the country and start over somewhere else. But the pair had been spending more time in Louisiana, near Henry's home, and were beginning to dream about finding a permanent hideout near his family, whom they were starting to trust.

In late April, the Dallas police finally tapped the Barrows' telephone. Over two weeks, handwritten versions of every conversation held on the party line the Barrows shared with their neighbors were recorded. The log was 69 pages long and included several conversations between Cumie and Emma about visits with "the kids."

Bonnie and Clyde probably called or visited during that time. On April 26, Cumie called her daughter Nell and asked her to come over, saying, "I've got a big pot full of beans and some cornbread," the family's code for a visit. Later that day, a friend called to report that he'd seen the police try to stop a Ford V-8 with a man and woman in it, but the driver shot at the cops and got away. The next morning, Cumie cut short a call, saying, "The Howards are out here in front, and I want to see them before they leave." Clyde used "the Howards" as a code for himself and Bonnie. It was the alias once used by outlaw Jesse James.

The Barrows were right to be cautious – a small group of lawmen was slowly and quietly getting closer to bringing down Bonnie and Clyde.

During an interview with Bureau of Investigation agents, Percy Boyd mentioned that the second man in the car during his kidnapping had been called "Henry." When he was later shown Henry Methvin's mugshot, he identified him as the third bandit.

Within days, Lester Kindell, a Bureau of Investigation agent based in New Orleans, and Henderson Jordan, the sheriff of Bienville Parish, learned that Methvin's family had recently moved from an isolated area in the country to a more populated area near Shreveport. Informants reported that Henry's father, Ivy, and one of his brothers "had shown signs of unusual and mysterious prosperity" after the move.

A raid was planned on a suspected Bonnie and Clyde hideout in Bienville Parish, but then it was called off because the place seemed abandoned. Even so, the plans leaked to the Shreveport newspaper, and soon after, Sheriff Jordan received a message that Ivy Methvin had something to discuss with him.

Ivy and his wife, Avie – the couple that Bonnie and Clyde had started to trust – told the sheriff they were terrified of the outlaw couple and were worried about the safety of their son, Henry. They claimed to be afraid that the couple would kill them or that Henry would be killed during a shootout with the law.

Sheriff Jordan suggested that Henry turn himself in, but Ivy said he believed Bonnie and Clyde would kill them all if he did. Clyde was "like a wolf, suspicious and smart," he told the lawman.

Ivy would betray the couple, but he'd only do so if Henry could go free. If his family put Bonnie and Clyde "on the spot," then his son shouldn't have to finish his jail time or face prosecution for the prison escape and any crimes he'd committed since then.

Ivy didn't just want a promise – he wanted it in writing.

The result of the meeting was passed on to Frank Hamer, who shared it with Lee Simmons. The Texas prison manager went to Austin to meet with Governor Ferguson and get her consent.

But he knew there was no way she'd turn it down – everyone wanted to get Bonnie and Clyde.

On April 28, the Methvins met with law enforcement officials again. Hamer brought a letter from the governor that made it clear that Henry's prison sentence would be wiped out if the family set up Bonnie and Clyde. But the state wouldn't make any promises about the crimes Henry had committed after his escape.

It was the best they could do, but it wasn't what the Methvins had hoped for. The family debated the offer at length and finally agreed to help the lawmen.

And they were given the letter from the governor, which might as well have been 30 pieces of silver.

IN EARLY MAY, BONNIE AND CLYDE WERE BACK IN Dallas. Bonnie went to see her mother, and they sat together one evening, sharing photographs and talking. Bonnie gave Emma a poem she'd written about her and Clyde's life on the run – "The Story of Bonnie and Clyde."

Bonnie made her mother promise she wouldn't say anything bad about Clyde after they died. She also asked her mother to bring her home for one last restful night with her family after her death rather than leaving her at the funeral parlor. Emma didn't like thinking about her daughter's death, but she agreed to her wishes.

She had no idea how soon she'd be asked to make good on her promises.

SOON AFTER THE TRIP TO DALLAS, THE OUTLAWS showed up in Louisiana for a visit with Henry's parents and brothers. Bonnie and Clyde felt comfortable enough to go into their home with only their pistols and to sleep for a few hours. Clyde told the Methvins it was the first time they'd slept in a bed in eight months.

Word of the visit leaked to the lawmen chasing the bandits. Agent Kindell was especially irritated when he learned Bonnie and Clyde had been at the Methvins, and the family hadn't alerted them. But Henry's brother had been worried about his wife and children and had been afraid of a shootout taking place.

But Kindell had a plan. On May 14, he informed Frank Hamer that he wanted him to stay in Shreveport or Monroe, the closest town to the Methvins' home. Kindell would also remain nearby. As soon as Ivy notified Sheriff Jordan of the couple's whereabouts, Hamer and Kindell would be contacted and waiting for Bonnie and Clyde when they arrived.

The Methvin house, where Bonnie and Clyde hid out in Louisiana – not knowing Ivy Methvin had already betrayed them.

Hamer liked the plan. In a letter mailed from the New Inn in Shreveport, he told the Dallas office of the Bureau of Investigation that while the outlaws might return to Dallas soon, "I feel certain we will sack the gang here."

OUTRAGE HAD CONTINUED TO GROW ABOUT the murders of the two young highway patrolmen on Easter Sunday. People in Texas and the surrounding states were terrified when they heard Bonnie and Clyde might be nearby.

The pair had once been folk heroes of a sort, but the murders of those particular police officers had turned people against them.

Newspapers couldn't write enough about the couple; stories appeared almost daily in Dallas. Unaware of Frank Hamer's secret hiring and pursuit, reporters were increasingly critical that more wasn't being done to catch them.

Finally, a few impatient lawmen took matters into their own hands.

On May 10, three officers arrived at the Barrow filling station and arrested Cumie Barrow. She had already been called before a Dallas County grand jury investigating whether family members and friends were illegally aiding the criminals, but this was different. Stuck in the backseat of the car between two lawmen, Cumie was driven to the East Texas town of Tyler, about 100 miles from Dallas. They didn't allow her a phone call or a lawyer, but they did feed her dinner before they locked her up in the county jail for the night.

In the lock-up, she saw Bonnie's sister, Billie, who'd been arrested and held since earlier in the week. Billie told her that Bonnie's aunt and her brother's wife had also been jailed.

In other words, they were arresting the Barrow and Parker women because they thought they'd be easily intimidated.

The next morning, the lawmen took Cumie to the courthouse for questioning before returning her to a cell. Then, that night, they took her home without any further explanation.

Though Cumie thought the men were Texas Rangers, they turned out to be two highway patrolmen and a deputy sheriff from outside Dallas who acted independently. Among other things, they wanted to know when she'd last seen Clyde. Had she seen him on Easter? Did she know where he was hiding out? Would he come to see her on Mother's Day?

No, no, and no, she told them. She said later, "They was nice to me all the time. I talked to them some, but I didn't tell them anything that would hurt Clyde. They oughta know a mother wouldn't tell nothing on her boy, even if she did know something."

Governor Ferguson lashed out at the actions of the three cops, saying that arresting and holding Cumie in another county was unlawful. Even Frank Hamer's brother, Texas Ranger Captain Estill Hamer, was sympathetic. "Those tactics are a mistake," he said. "I do not care how bad the badman is, there isn't any excuse for harassing his mother."

But harassing sisters was apparently okay. Billie was arrested on May 19, and she and Floyd Hamilton, who was already in jail, were charged with the murders of the highway patrol officers. William Schieffer, the farmer who lived near where the men had been shot, had been certain a woman had turned over one of the bodies and fired point-blank into it. But he couldn't identify Bonnie and Clyde from mugshots.

Instead, looking at other photos, he claimed the killers had been Floyd and Billie. Both were charged, even though the law knew there was nothing that linked either one of them to the murders.

They wanted to see if the charges would get Bonnie and Clyde's attention.

THE OUTLAW COUPLE DIDN'T KNOW ANYTHING ABOUT Billie's arrest, though. They were in Louisiana with Henry's relatives – who weren't telling the police they were there.

So, you can assume they weren't exactly "terrified" of the pair, as they'd told Frank Hamer and Sherrif Jordan, who were growing tired of waiting.

At some point during the visit, Ivy Methvin finally told his son that a deal had been made for his freedom in Texas. He stressed to Henry that he wouldn't have to return to prison and finish his sentence. However, he did fail to mention that Henry might be on the hook for the crimes he'd committed while on the run. Not knowing he was still neck-deep in trouble, Henry agreed to try and persuade Bonnie and Clyde to stay a little longer in the area.

On the evening of May 21, Henry told his parents he would find a way to separate from the couple the next day. If they did split up, Clyde knew he and Bonnie would find Henry at his parents' house.

The next morning, the three of them went to Shreveport. Around 9:00 A.M., Clyde sent Henry into a café to get some sandwiches. While waiting, Clyde spotted a police car and drove around while Henry was inside the café.

When the car pulled away, Henry bolted. He stole a car and had made it to his brother's house by mid-afternoon.

When Bonnie and Clyde didn't find Henry at the café, they headed toward his parents' home, arriving late in the afternoon. Ivy came into the yard to tell them Henry wasn't there. But, he said, they should come back the next morning. With a wave, Clyde drove off.

A few hours later, just after dark, Ivy told Sheriff Jordan that Bonnie and Clyde would be at his home the next morning.

The call sent the sheriff into action. He could not reach Agent Kindell, who was investigating a kidnapping in another part of the state. However, over the next few hours, the rest of the lawmen began to gather – Frank Hamer, Manny Gault, Dallas County deputies Bob Alcorn and Ted Hinton, and Jordan and his deputy, Prentiss Oakley. Bob Alcorn, they discovered at that point, was the only one who knew Clyde and what he looked like aside from his now outdated mugshots.

Hamer sent a message to Lee Simmons: "The old hen is about ready to hatch. I think the chickens will come off tomorrow."

The lawmen had already picked an ambush site along the narrow road leading to the Methvins' place. There was a hill on one side of the road where they could hide in heavy brush and remain invisible while still able to see cars coming from a distance.

During the early morning of May 23, 1934, the six men parked their cars and hiked to the site. They had an arsenal of weapons – shotguns, pistols, and automatic rifles. They took their places and settled down to wait.

Everything was finally falling into place.

Around sunrise, they were joined by a nervous Ivy Methvin. He drove up the road in his old truck, which he pulled to the side of the narrow road. He turned off the rattling engine and joined Sherrif Jordan, who'd come out of the brush to speak with him. The sheriff had ordered him to be there to keep an eye on him and use Ivy as a decoy. If Clyde was driving as fast as usual, he might speed past the officers in a few seconds. But if he saw Henry's father standing next to a broken-down truck, he'd likely stop to see if he needed help. As the sun rose, they jacked up Ivy's truck and removed a tire.

A few cars and a local school bus passed by and offered to stop and help, but Ivy waved them away. As soon as the bus left, Ivy pleaded with the officers to ditch the whole idea before they were all killed. He was shaking and trembling, but they sent him back to wait by his truck.

While the lawmen were waiting in the woods, being devoured by mosquitoes, Bonnie and Clyde were getting breakfast from a local café. They were eating sandwiches as they sped along toward the Methvin house.

Before they could see it, the lawmen heard the roar of the fast-moving car. A gray Ford V-8 quickly appeared, flying at 30 or 40 miles an hour along the rutted road.

Even from a distance, Bob Alcorn knew who it was. "That's them, boys," he called out.

ALL CLYDE SAW WAS IVY METHVIN, STANDING NEAR his truck, plus the one tire that was lying on the road next to it. He tapped the brake and slowed down, coming almost to a stop.

The men on the hill carefully aimed their guns.

Suddenly, a logging truck appeared, rumbling along from the other direction. Clyde rolled forward to make room for it to pass.

In the brush, Deputy Prentiss Oakley tensed up. Maybe he believed that Clyde was driving off, or perhaps he was overcome with nerves, or, more likely, Frank Hamer had made it clear that Bonnie and Clyde didn't need to be taken alive.

They were never given a chance to surrender.

Oakley fired first – two shots. One of them hit Clyde just in front of his left ear, probably killing him instantly.

The only sound for a moment was Bonnie's scream.

Then, the other lawmen opened fire. Bullets rained down on the Ford, shattering glass, punching holes in steel, and ripping apart the bodies of the couple inside. It was a continuous roar that went on for several minutes. Hundreds of bullets pounded into the car and made Bonnie and Clyde shake and jerk back and forth across the front seat. The screaming had since stopped, but the gunfire continued long after the outlaws were dead.

When it finally stopped, Clyde slid sideways, and his foot came off the brake pedal. The car rolled forward a short distance and slid into a ditch.

Bob Alcorn, worried they were still alive – or so he later claimed – came down the hill and fired more shots through the broken back window of the car. The bullets punched into the backs of the lifeless outlaws' heads.

The inside of the car looked like a slaughterhouse. Part of Clyde's skull was now missing. Bonnie's right hand was gone. Blood and tissue covered the car's interior.

The bullet-riddled car of Bonnie and Clyde.

Bonnie and Clyde's "Death Car." Bonnie can be seen slumped forward onto the dashboard. She was hit dozens of times.

Clyde's head was hanging out the window. After Alcorn's last shots, Bonnie slumped over with her head between her legs.

There were guns near them in the car, but neither had time to raise them or return fire. There had been no threat to the lives of the lawmen. In interviews after the ambush, some of the lawmen claimed they had yelled for them to stop or had told them to surrender, but these stories were outright lies.

After the smoke cleared, Ivy Methvin took off. Oakley, Jordan, and Hamer went into nearby towns to summon the coroner, get a tow truck, and make calls from a local gas station. Ted Hinton photographed and cataloged the scene before anyone else could get there and decide the story the lawmen told wasn't as accurate as they'd claim in the future.

Hamer let Lee Simmons know the job was done. He also called Sheriff Schmid in Dallas. Hamer asked if the sheriff had gotten a good night's sleep, and Schmid said he hadn't. "Well," he replied, "you can go home and sleep now. We just killed 'em both."

By the time the lawmen returned to the ambush site, locals who'd heard the gunfire or the rumors that quickly spread were already converging on the scene. They grabbed any kind of souvenir they could that would connect them to the outlaws. They tried to pry away pieces of broken glass and steal snippets of hair and clothing. Others picked up bullets and shotgun shells.

The tow truck didn't arrive for nearly two hours, but when it did, it took the bullet-riddled car – with its bloody occupants still inside – to a coroner in Arcadia, roughly 10 miles away. A caravan of at least 150 vehicles followed behind it. Thousands more gathered in Arcadia, hoping for a glimpse of the carnage.

Clyde's body was carried into Conger's Furniture Store on a stretcher as a crowd of the curious pressed in close, trying to get a souvenir from the body.

(Below) They reacted the same way when the "Death Car" was towed into town.

On the way, the truck passed a school in Gibsland, and students poured out into the street to see it, forcing the truck to stop. Bonnie and Clyde had been covered with a blanket by then, but one of the students pulled it away, revealing the slain outlaws.

In Arcadia, the bodies were placed on stretchers and taken in through the back doors of Conger's Furniture store, which doubled as a funeral home. The Ford was

locked behind a fence to keep curiosity-seekers away.

The coroner announced that Bonnie and Clyde had both been hit more than two dozen times, which would make embalming them a challenge. But there was someone who volunteered for the job – Dillard Darby, whom Bonnie had asked to embalm her when they'd kidnapped him a year earlier.

The coroner recorded their many wounds, cuts, scars, and tattoos in the small, hot, crowded room while a growing mob made rumbling noises outside. Eager to see the dead bandits, more than 500 people had jammed into the furniture store, ripping a door off its hinges, climbing on new furniture, and causing about $1,000 in damages. According to one story, workers sprayed the crowd with embalming fluid to keep them from charging into the back room. The streets outside were full.

Once the paperwork was completed, the bodies were covered by white sheets up to the necks and moved out into the store's showroom. The crowd passed by for a look over the next several hours.

While the coroner had been doing his job, the lawmen who'd arranged the ambush were being interviewed by reporters. They'd managed to coordinate the ambush but forgot to coordinate their stories.

Sheriff Jordan said they'd acted on a tip.

Ted Hinton and Bob Alcorn said they'd waited on the side of the road for two days and nights.

Frank Hamer claimed he'd set a clever trap as Clyde went to pick up mail from a hidden spot on the side of the road. He claimed there hadn't been any tipster, although the press would eventually learn that the Methvins had betrayed the couple when Henry received his conditional pardon from the governor. He was never tried for killing the two highway patrolmen near Grapevine.

As a result of the ambush, Frank Hamer used every opportunity to enhance his reputation as a legendary lawman, giving numerous interviews in which he took most of the credit for the hunt and the couple's death.

"I can tell you what happened that morning," he told one reporter. "We just shot the devil out of them, that's all."

He told another reporter that the hardest part of the whole thing was shooting Bonnie. But it was justified because she'd shot that highway patrolman at point-blank range. "I hate to bust a cap on a woman," Hamer said, "especially when she was sitting down. However, if it hadn't been her, it would have been us."

Frank Hamer died in 1955, and after the movie version of Bonnie and Clyde's story came out in 1967, his family sued the filmmakers for defamation, saying that the portrayal of him in the film made him look incompetent. The suit was settled for an undisclosed amount of money.

I guess it's a good thing the family didn't try to sue the studio for making Hamer out to be a liar. If they had, the filmmakers never would have spent a dime.

LET'S BE HONEST, THOUGH, LIES HAVE ALWAYS been a major part of the legend of Bonnie and Clyde. Lies – mostly about Bonnie – turned the couple into the anti-heroes they became. When it came to Bonnie and Clyde, real life was not as simple as the legend.

The public first learned of Bonnie's wish to be buried next to her Clyde when they read the poem that came to be called "The Story of Bonnie and Clyde" when it appeared in the *Dallas Daily Times Herald* after her death. The poem was the first time Bonnie received top billing in the Barrow Gang, although from then on, that's how the couple would be known.

But real life wasn't as simple as Bonnie's melodramatic poem. Emma Parker refused to allow the couple to be buried side by side. She had never approved of their relationship and blamed Clyde for Bonnie's troubles. She told this to reporters, failing to keep the promise she'd made Bonnie about not saying bad things about Clyde.

"Clyde had her for two years. Look what he did to her," she said to newspapermen. "Now she's mine. Nobody else has a right to her."

Emma hadn't been able to keep her other promise to Bonnie either – her wish to spend a final night at home. She'd fainted when a reporter first told her that her daughter was dead, but she did try to claim her body. However, there was no way to control the flood of curiosity-seekers. Crowds jammed the streets in front of both funeral homes before the bodies arrived in Dallas on Thursday morning. The police had to be called in to maintain order.

By that afternoon, close to 10,000 people packed the front yard of the Sparkman-Holtz-Brand Funeral Home downtown to see Clyde's remains. They shouted and demanded to see him, and when that didn't work, they made threats. When the doors still didn't open, they destroyed the landscaping in front of the business, pulling up flowers and shrubbery by its roots and

The funerals of the pair were held on opposite sides of town, but this was the scene outside the McKamy-Campbell Funeral Home, where Bonnie's service was held.

throwing them at the door. The police were called again, but there weren't enough of them to disperse the crowds.

Finally, Henry Barrow agreed to let them in. Clyde had been laid out in a casket and was wearing a light gray suit. The undertakers had done what they could with his damaged face, but it was still an unnerving sight. Hundreds of people pushed through when the doors were opened, but after hearing some gawkers remark they were glad Clyde was dead, Henry ordered the doors to be closed and locked again.

By then, the floors were scuffed and dirty, the rugs had been dragged into a heap, and cigarette butts littered the foyer and hallway.

Across town, an almost identical scene was taking place at the McKamy-Campbell Funeral Home, where another 20,000 people hoped to get a glimpse of Bonnie in a silky blue dress. There, the mob trampled the lawn and knocked down a fence in the frenzy that took place when the doors were opened to let the public inside. Up to 5,000 people per hour pushed and shoved through the funeral home, destroying their expensive carpets.

The scene was repeated on Friday until an estimated 50,000 people had viewed the outlaws.

Clyde was buried that evening with a short, private funeral with only family and close friends in attendance. The service was presided over by Reverend Clifford Andrews, a pastor who ministered to jail prisoners.

Reverend Andrews also conducted the private funeral for Bonnie on Saturday afternoon. Officials allowed Billie to leave jail, and she joined more than 150 others who gathered to say goodbye to Bonnie. The largest floral arrangement had been sent by local newspaper dealers, who had seen sales skyrocket after the couple had been killed.

As he had done with Clyde, the minister refused to pass judgment on Bonnie. He only asked for God to have mercy on her soul.

Emma Parker fainted as Bonnie's casket was lowered into the grave.

Clyde and Buck shared a gravestone in the other cemetery. Its only epitaph was "Gone but not forgotten." Bonnie's family was more expansive, choosing a rhyme that Billie said reminded her of how she used to be" "As the flowers are all made sweeter by the sunshine and the dew, so this old world is made brighter by the lives of folks like you."

For most, our story would end here, with Bonnie and Clyde forever in their graves, but we're not quite finished with the legend just yet.

THE WEEKS FOLLOWING THE DEATHS OF BONNIE and Clyde were eventful ones for the Parker and Barrow families.

By the end of May, ballistics tests on the guns found in the slain couple's car showed that two of them had been used to kill the highway patrolmen near Grapevine. A judge not only dropped the murder charges against Floyd Hamilton and Bonnie's sister, Billie, but he also apologized to Billie, saying she'd "been wronged" and that "the law made a mistake."

Both Emma and Cumie were grieving the loss of their children, but Cumie was nearly unhinged by a new film that was advertising only days after Clyde's death. Using film footage that Deputy Ted Hinton had shot while cataloging the interior of the "death car," the movie showed the aftermath of the ambush and all its gory details, along with highlights from Bonnie and Clyde's criminal career.

Barely a week after the funerals, Cumie charged into the theater where the film was showing and cried out, "You can't do that to my boy!"

Employees removed her, but that didn't calm her down. She ripped down a photo of Bonnie and Clyde from the theater's display, and staff called the police. She was taken to police headquarters, where she apologized and was released.

The next day, Emma sued the theaters showing the film, saying that it was causing embarrassment to family members who'd never been in trouble. After some arguing, the theaters ended the movie's run – in Dallas anyway. It continued to be shown in other cities.

At the end of 1935, 23 people with ties to Bonnie, Clyde, and Raymond Hamilton were charged with harboring or assisting criminals, including Cumie; her children, Marie and L.C.; Emma; her daughter, Billie; W.D. Jones; Henry Methvin; Floyd and Raymond Hamilton; and their mother and stepfather. At the time, it was one of the largest indictments of its kind in American history.

Oddly, Henry Barrow and his daughter, Nell, weren't charged.

Clyde O. Eastus, US Attorney for the Northern District of Texas, said the indictments were "highly important in the drive to stamp out crime and banditry." He made a point of saying that police officers had died because the accused had helped Bonnie and Clyde evade the law.

In truth, the charges were all for show – an effort to punish someone because Bonnie and Clyde had so easily escaped arrest for so long, making the authorities look foolish for not being able to catch them.

The case was rushed to trial in just three weeks. Not surprisingly, newspaper and newsreel photographers were allowed to set up their cameras to record the accused. The women entered the courtroom first, shielding their faces with handbags and handkerchiefs. The men, unnecessarily chained by the neck and legs, followed behind them.

Over three days, a jury heard details about Bonnie and Clyde's final year. There was testimony about the Eastham prison break and various robberies, and Billie spoke of how she had nursed her sister after she had been burned.

The star witness, though, was Cumie. Gray-haired and frail, she said she had visited with Clyde but never gave him food, clothing, or guns. She continued the secret meetings because, she said, "He was my boy. I loved him. I never knew whether it would be the last time I would see him."

She added that she had begged Clyde to give himself up many times and also defended her son L.C., saying he attended the get-togethers only so he could take her there since she didn't drive.

When cross-examined, Eastus asked why she didn't help the lawmen looking for Clyde, and she replied, "I couldn't do that, he was my boy."

Eastus berated and ridiculed Cumie on the stand and once waved a Browning Automatic Rifle in her face, asking her if Clyde had ever shown one of them to her. She managed to maintain her composure, but it was not easy.

During closing arguments, Cumie's lawyer argued that she should be acquitted. "The Constitution never intended to make it a crime for a mother to see her son," he said.

But Eastus retorted angrily that Cumie was the "ringleader" of the gang and ought to spend the rest of her life in prison.

She didn't – but she was sentenced to 30 days in county jail. Ultimately, five of the accused took guilty pleas, and the jury found 15 others guilty. Charges were dismissed against two women for lack of evidence. Emma Parker and the Hamiltons' mother were also given 30 days in jail. Billie, Mary O'Dare, and Blanche Barrow received a year and a day. The sentences for the men ranged from 60 days to two years, including 15 months for Henry Methvin and two years for W.D. Jones, which was in addition to his conviction for participating in crimes. Clyde's little sister, Marie, who was 16, was sentenced to one hour in custody.

Raymond Hamilton, although indicted, didn't go to trial with the others. He'd escaped from prison again and was on the run when the trial took place. He was finally caught, though, in April 1935. He and Joe Palmer had been sentenced to death for the murder of Major Crowson during the Eastham escape, and the state of Texas didn't waste any time carrying out that sentence.

Just after midnight on May 10, 1935, Palmer was executed in Old Sparky, the Texas electric chair. A few minutes later, Raymond took his place. He was given a chance to make a final statement, and then his arms and legs were strapped to the wooden chair. Copper electrodes were attached to him, a mask covered his face, and the switch was thrown. At 12:27 A.M., Raymond Hamilton was dead at the age of just 22.

It was the end that Clyde Barrow had done everything he could to avoid.

BONNIE AND CLYDE WERE OUT OF THE DAILY newspapers, but they appeared in many other places, namely the popular pulp detective magazines of the day. They took advantage of the couple's infamy and embellished and distorted their crimes to sell more issues. Every magazine with a Bonnie and Clyde story flew off the newsstands. For that reason alone, they started paying good money for write-ups about the pair, interviews, and first-hand accounts from people who encountered them during their crime spree.

W.D. Jones was paid for a two-part tell-all called "I Saw Clyde Barrow Kill Five Men," an embroidered and exaggerated version of stories he'd already told to the police in the past, blaming Clyde for everything and painting himself as a hostage.

"The Inside Story of Bonnie Parker" and the "Bloody Barrows" ran serialized over six months in *True Detective Mysteries*, written by Ed Portley, the Chief of Detectives in Joplin, Missouri, and Sheriff Jordan from Bienville Parish in Louisiana. Though some of the details in the six installments were true, most weren't.

More magazines followed, along with dozens of books, the worst of which was undoubtedly one allegedly written by J. Edgar Hoover called *Persons in Hiding*, which was supposed to tell the "true" stories of gangsters like Dillinger and Bonnie and Clyde. He promised to "tell the truth about these rats and their dirty, diseased women." He didn't.

A string of movies followed over the next few decades, usually painting Bonnie as some kind of "moll" who was the real brains behind the operation, dragging Clyde around like a second-rate crook. And then came the 1967 movie *Bonnie and Clyde*, starring a young Warren Beatty and Faye Dunaway as the title characters. It also starred Gene Hackman as Buck, Estelle Parsons as Blanche, Denver Pyle as Frank Hamer, and Michael J. Pollard as a made-up character named C.W. Moss, a combination of W.D. Jones, Raymond Hamilton, and Henry Methvin.

The bloody, sensationally violent movie was filmed in Texas, and the script took a lot of liberties with the facts. As it turned out, no one cared, and audiences loved it, laughing, cheering, and applauding to the end.

It was eventually nominated for 10 Academy Awards, including Best Picture and every major acting, writing, and directing category. It ended up winning two awards – for best supporting actress and cinematography. It became a bonafide hit and brought in $70 million at the box office – the equivalent of $500 million today – and brought fame for Beatty and Dunaway, two new actors who went on to have long and distinguished careers.

The real Bonnie and Clyde were back in popular culture again, too. The film made them more famous than they'd ever been in life, even though the onscreen characters were nothing like them. It wasn't long before actors and models, made up to look like them, started appearing in magazines and on television, pitching air travel and cars. Country singer Merle Haggard even had a hit single in 1968 called "The Legend of Bonnie and Clyde" from his album of the same name.

Of course, Henry and Cumie Barrow and Emma Parker were long gone before that. The new wave of attention opened up old wounds for the remaining family members. They'd tried to avoid the legacy the outlaws had left behind for years. Marie, L.C., and the oldest Barrow son, Jack, all had criminal records and were imprisoned in the 1940s. Only sisters Artie and Nell had managed to avoid trouble with the police.

Bonnie and Clyde were rarely discussed in Henry and Cumie's final years. They just wanted to let it all rest in peace. The movie – and the attention that followed – made that impossible. The press harassed family members, and no one was happy about the way they were all portrayed in the film. Buck's wife, Blanche, felt she had been portrayed as a "screaming horse's ass," and Billie, W.D. Jones, and Frank Hamer's widow were among those who protested about how they or their loved one appeared in the movie.

But there was a silver lining of sorts.

As interest in the outlaw couple grew, some of those still living – like Ted Hinton, W.D., Ralph Fults, Floyd Hamilton, Marie, and Blanche – became minor celebrities, appearing in television specials and documentaries and, in some cases, collaborating on books that told their stories.

Mementos, guns, and other Bonnie and Clyde artifacts – some owned by family, others by lawmen who kept them – soared in value.

Volunteers reenact the ambush yearly with a carnival and food in Gibsland, Louisiana, which has two small Bonnie and Clyde museums.

Other movies, documentaries, and specials about Bonnie and Clyde have appeared over the years, and there always seems to be an interest in them. Even people who know little about the bandits of the Depression era can name at least two outlaw gangs – Dillinger and Bonnie and Clyde.

They were prominently featured in country songs for years but recently appeared in rap and hip-hop music. These artists – like their country counterparts – identify with the pair as outsiders who feel mistreated by the law, and they portray Bonnie and Clyde as kindred outcasts trying to survive, only getting by because of their undying love for each other.

BONNIE AND CLYDE. Romanticized or vilified, hated or admired, they remain legends after all these years. But is it for who they were? Or is it for who we want them to be?

> *Someday they'll go down together;*
> *They'll bury them side by side;*
> *To few it'll be grief –*
> *To the law a relief –*
> *But it's death for Bonnie and Clyde.*

"THE GHOST IN THE ATTIC"
The Story of Dolly and Otto

THIS HOUSE HAD GHOSTS, TOO.

That's the only thing Fred Oesterreich could imagine would explain the strange sounds he'd heard at night – the creaking of the floorboards, soft footsteps, and rustling in the ceiling. There seemed to be someone – or something – with his wife and himself in their two-story Los Angeles home. He couldn't imagine what else it could be besides a resident specter. Had the same ghost followed them here from Milwaukee?

Fred was convinced he was losing his mind. The wealthy German businessman, who had made his fortune by manufacturing aprons in Milwaukee, had recently moved to Los Angeles to get away from the ghosts. To think the spooks had followed him to the West Coast didn't frighten him – it made him angry. The rich, loud, and overbearing man was determined not to be run out of this new house by a denizen of the spirit world.

He'd get to the bottom of what was happening this time if it was the last thing he ever did.

THE STORY OF WALBURGA OESTERREICH TRULY begins in 1903, nearly two decades before her husband, Fred, began hearing strange sounds in the attic of their California home. At that time, Walburga – better known by her nickname "Dolly" – was 36 years old but looked much younger. She was of average height but had a trim, voluptuous build, sultry smile, and eyes that managed to get her in a lot of trouble. When her story eventually became known, she was often described as a "nymphomaniac," which may or may not have been accurate because there was one man that Dolly was not passionate about – her husband, Fred.

Fred and "Dolly" Oesterreich

Fred owned a factory that made aprons in their hometown of Milwaukee. A few years older than Dolly, Fred was the epitome of a German businessman who had fought his way to the top from immigrant beginnings. By 1903, he was worth at least $250,000, and while he prospered, he watched every cent and devoted nearly every waking moment to his business. He was loud, crude, cruel to his employees and wife, and often intoxicated.

Otto Sanhuber

Dolly could have dealt with all that. What she could not tolerate was that Fred was clumsy and unsatisfying in bed. Dolly had appetites, and her husband failed to meet them. She often berated Fred so loudly and violently about his conjugal failures that neighbors were sometimes compelled to call the police.

It was not surprising that Dolly would find a lover. What was a shock was that he was a worker in her husband's factory, a small, frail-looking young man named Otto Sanhuber.

Otto had been a foundling, left at a Milwaukee orphanage with no idea who his biological parents were and when he had even been born. He was quiet, painfully shy, friendless, and barely five feet tall with a sallow complexion, receding chin and hairline, and weak blue eyes that looked out from cheap spectacles. In the summer of 1903, he was thought to be 17 years old, so he applied to apprentice as a sewing machine repairman at Oesterreich's factory.

For whatever reason, Otto caught Dolly's eye, and she saw many hidden possibilities. She later said that he reminded her of her late son, Raymond, who died before he could reach Otto's age.

Which makes everything that happened even creepier, in my opinion.

At first, her interest in the boy was motherly, and Otto admired how she stood up to her domineering husband, who terrified most of the factory workers. Soon, though, he stopped seeing her as a mother figure, and Dolly began to realize that Otto had a hunger that matched her own.

According to most accounts, she summoned Otto to her home to "service a sewing machine" one day. When he arrived, he found the lady of the house wearing nothing but a silk robe. She led him off to her bedroom to inspect the damaged appliance.

Otto serviced it – and then he serviced Dolly.

Dolly, to her delight, discovered that her instincts were correct. Between the sheets, the boy was much more of a man than her husband.

All went well for some months. Otto continued to sneak over to the Oesterreich home whenever the husband was away. They took a "weekend" trip to St. Louis that lasted nine days and never left their hotel room. Dolly was satisfied by the odd young man. Fred continued to work and drink, and everyone seemed to be happy.

But then, in 1907, the first signs of trouble appeared. A busybody neighbor informed Fred that his wife seemed to be having a suspicious amount of trouble with her sewing machine. Fred confronted Dolly about her visitor, but she calmly asserted that such stories were all lies. She put on such a convincing display of wounded outrage that Fred backed off, apologizing for even bringing it up. He drank more and put the whole idea out of his mind.

Dolly was torn. She couldn't risk the loss of her marriage – or at least Fred's money – and she couldn't lose Otto either. If only she had a place where she could keep Otto where he could be entirely out of sight, still come and see her, but not be spotted by anyone else.

She suddenly thought of the perfect place – the attic of the house.

A small cubbyhole in the attic, conveniently above the primary bedroom, could only be entered through a small trap door in the ceiling. Dolly decorated it with a cot, a table, a chair, a chamber pot, and other household items. She told Otto to quit his job at the apron factory. And when the day came that they were sure Fred was safely out of the way, she installed her lover in his new place, which was right above the Oesterreich bed.

Otto obediently settled into his new life. When Fred was away at work, Otto would come downstairs and take care of everything that needed tending to in the house. He took great pride in his talent for washing floors, preparing food, doing laundry, and, of course, taking care of Dolly's many physical needs. When Fred returned home in the evening, he huddled in his attic room, reading by candlelight.

Otto spent his time devouring adventure novels that Dolly got him from the local library. After reading hundreds of cheap

A newspaper photo of the Oesterreich house with an illustration showing where Otto lived in the attic.

novels and pulp magazines, Otto decided to try some writing of his own. Dolly got him a post office box, and, using a pen name, he scribbled stories of excitement, adventure, and sex, often set in the Orient. Dolly typed them up and mailed them to the pulp magazines, and they started selling. Dolly opened a bank account for the attic dweller, who now had a career in pulp fiction.

Otto was perfectly happy in his bizarre life. So was Dolly.

On the other hand, Fred became sure that he was losing his sanity. Often at night, he heard strange noises coming from the ceiling. Food he could swear he had seen just a short time before would suddenly be gone. His cigars began disappearing. Once, when he was in the backyard, he swore he saw a face in the attic window.

Dolly sighed and suggested that her husband consult a doctor. He was slipping, she told him, after too much work, too much drink, and not enough sleep. The only entrance to the attic was over their bed. No one could be up there. She even let him pull on the door, which Otto had locked from the inside. It didn't budge, she told him, because no one had been up there for years.

Fred didn't see a doctor, and after that, when he heard a cough from the ceiling, noticed footsteps, or saw that some leftovers had vanished from the refrigerator, he kept silent. He was convinced their house was haunted, but he knew no one would believe him.

The odd sounds continued until Fred became so rattled that he insisted they move to a new house, so Dolly found one with a large attic. When the Oesterreichs moved, so did Otto.

At first, Fred thought he was safe from the ghosts, but soon, they returned. He heard soft noises at night, and his food and cigars continued to vanish. Dolly's hints about his drinking and his need to seek medical help ensured that he kept his complaints to a minimum.

In 1913, the Oesterreichs moved again. Otto came along, much to Dolly's delight and relief, setting himself up in another attic room. The three might have remained in Milwaukee for good, except one night in 1918, Otto got careless. While Fred and Dolly were out with some neighbors for the evening, Otto came downstairs for dinner. He was sitting in his underwear in the kitchen when Fred and Dolly returned unexpectedly early.

Fortunately for Otto, Fred was drunk. He escaped with only a beating before Fred stumbled off the bed, convinced he had surprised a peculiarly dressed burglar. Still in his underwear, Otto was locked out of the only home he had. He hid in a park and returned the following day after Fred had left for work.

Otto came up with a new plan. World War I had started, and Otto told his lover he would join the army and serve his country. But Dolly had her own plans – she needed Otto's services more than Uncle Sam did. Dolly gave him the money he had earned as a writer and told him to use the money to go to Los Angeles. They would keep in touch via a post-office box, and she would persuade her husband to move there as soon as possible.

As always, Otto did as he was told. He took the next train to L.A. and got a job as a porter in a hotel, staying in touch with Dolly through his old post office box in Milwaukee. Rather than enjoying his new-found freedom, though, Otto missed his quiet, safe place in the attic and the private little world he had built with his writing and with Dolly.

In a few months, true to her word, Dolly convinced Fred to sell his holdings in Milwaukee and expand to Los Angeles. Otto was so excited that when he learned the arrival time of their train, he watched it approach Union Station with binoculars from the Elysian Street Bridge.

Within a short time, Fred had bought a controlling interest in a garment factory downtown, and Dolly had found a charming home on a small hill overlooking Sunset Boulevard. It had an attic above the primary bedroom, and Otto worked nights for two weeks, creating a comfortable and secure spot there.

Life went on, just as it had in Milwaukee.

That is until the night of August 22, 1922. Late that night, neighbors reported ominous crashing noises coming from the Oesterreich house. When several gunshots followed these sounds, they called the police.

At Fred and Dolly's house in Los Angeles, Otto moved right back into the attic. But it would be here where everything would go wrong.

Officers arriving at the scene found the body of Fred Oesterreich on the living room floor. He had been shot several times with a .25-caliber revolver.

They could hear knocking and crying coming from the hall closet, and they opened it to find Dolly inside. She seemed frightened but was unhurt. She told them that she and her husband had come home and surprised a burglar in the house. The intruder shot her husband and then locked her in the closet to prevent her from calling for help. As far as she could tell, the only thing missing seemed to be Fred's diamond-studded watch.

Detectives seem to have sensed from the beginning that there was something a little off about Dolly's story -- not to mention something a little off about Dolly herself -- but without any evidence to show she was involved, Fred's murder went unsolved.

Meanwhile, Dolly had Fred's complicated estate to settle. She needed an attorney and chose Howard Shapiro to sort things out. Their relationship soon went beyond attorney and client, and they became lovers. To show her appreciation for Shapiro's hard work, Dolly presented him with a gift – an expensive diamond-studded wristwatch.

"It had been my dear husband's," she said. This watch was previously presumed stolen, but Dolly claimed that she found it under the couch cushions in the living room a week after the murder but was too distraught to tell the police. An attorney who sleeps with his clients doesn't have many rules, so Shapiro started wearing the watch.

As you might imagine, this was a bad idea.

Dolly put her home up for sale -- too many bad memories and all that -- and bought a smaller one on Beachwood Drive. It had a lovely attic, which made Otto happy, and he soon moved into it.

One day, Dolly gave a large envelope to another of her gentlemen friends, an actor named Ray Bellows. When he looked inside, he saw that it contained a .25-caliber revolver. Dolly explained that she kept the gun for self-protection, but since "dear Fred" was killed with a similar weapon, it might be awkward if the police found it in her possession. She asked him to get rid of it for her.

The door leading into the attic where Otto lived. The space was only waist-high, reports said, but Otto stayed hunched over to avoid bumping the ceiling.

Bellows asked no questions and obediently dropped the weapon into the La Brea tar pits, where he thought it could never be found.

Dolly had gotten away with everything – or so she thought.

CHIEF OF DETECTIVES FOR THE LAPD, HERMAN Cline, had never forgotten about Dolly Oesterreich. He felt in his bones that she had something to do with her husband's murder, but he couldn't prove it. He kept the case open, even as it became colder and colder over the following year.

There were little things that ate at him. For one, there was a gap between the floor and the bottom of the closet door where Dolly had been locked. The gap was wide enough to easily accommodate a large key – like the one found several feet in front of the locked door when the cops arrived. He theorized that Dolly had shot her husband, locked herself in the closet, and then slid the key across the floor. Cline was sure she'd done it for the money. He had discovered Fred's estate was worth more than $1 million.

Cline thought it was a simple motive, never realizing just how complicated it would turn out to be.

Cline took a trip to Milwaukee to snoop around on his own dime, where he found several witnesses who recalled that Fred and Dolly argued and bickered constantly and had a terrible marriage.

LAPD Detective Herman Cline

He still didn't have enough to make an arrest – but he soon would.

About a year after the murder, Cline bumped into Dolly's lawyer, Herman Shapiro. He noticed Shapiro's wristwatch and asked him about it. Shapiro stated that Dolly had given it to him, repeating Dolly's story about finding the watch in the couch cushions. Cline didn't say much, but he filed the information away.

A few weeks later, it came back up when Ray Bellow decided to talk to the police about the gun. He and Dolly had quarreled and broke things off. Now, he felt obliged to tell the police about the weapon he had tossed into the tar pits. The police carefully searched the edge of the tar pits and, by incredible chance, found the envelope with the gun inside. It had landed just a few inches short of the pits. The weapon was rusted by recognizable.

Detective Cline went straight to the house on Beachwood Drive and arrested Dolly for murder. Even so, he still didn't have the whole story. That wouldn't be revealed until Dolly demanded to see her lawyer a few days later. When Herman Shapiro arrived, she begged him to go to the bedroom closet of her home, find the trap door in the ceiling that led to the attic, and knock softly three times.

She tearfully claimed that her mentally challenged half-brother was hiding there, and without groceries, he would starve. Shapiro was supposed to tell him she had to go away on a business trip, but she would see him soon.

Confused, Shapiro did as he was asked. When he rapped on the trap door, Otto's thin face emerged. When he heard Dolly's message, Otto sighed and commented, "It's too bad that she has been so upset over something that I did."

Otto, desperate for a conversation with someone other than Dolly, prodded Shapiro with questions. The attorney eventually admitted that Dolly was in jail. Otto wept, telling the attorney she was only there because she had been protecting him.

Once he started talking, Otto couldn't stop.

While Shapiro sat in astonished silence on the floor of Dolly's closet, staring up at the man who had lived in six different attics, Otto poured out the details of his 20 secret years with Dolly, including what happened on the night of Fred's death.

The Oesterreichs had come home drunk and, as usual, arguing violently. This time, though, it seemed worse than expected. Otto feared for his lover's safety and decided he'd had enough of Fred Oesterreich. While still upstairs, he heard a crash and then a thump as Dolly hit the polished wood of the living room floor. Truthfully, she had merely slipped on a throw rug, but Otto didn't know that. He assumed that Fred had knocked her down. He grabbed Dolly's gun and rushed into the living room with this belief. Like a hero straight out of his adventure stories, he confronted Fred, "Unhand this lovely woman!" Otto cried.

Unimpressed by Otto's gift for dramatic dialogue, Fred lunged at him. Otto panicked and, without thinking, shot him in the chest.

Otto and Dolly realized their only hope was to make the murder look like a robbery. Dolly took Fred's watch and hid it in some couch cushions. Then, she locked herself in the closet and shoved the key through the crack underneath the door while Otto fled the house.

Shapiro was fascinated – and out of his depth. He was a civil attorney and realized that this case needed an expert. He helped Dolly hire Frank Dominguez, one of the best criminal lawyers in the city. Shapiro told Dominguez to go to Dolly's house and tell the guy hiding in her attic to get out of town – fast.

Once again, Otto did as he was told. He left town, changed his name to "Walter Klein," and eventually settled in Vancouver. Dominguez then went to the district attorney and demanded Dolly's release. He claimed that with no witnesses, no confession, and a weapon that was too corroded to be traced to the murder, there was no case against his client.

Dolly was released from jail. She settled into a life without Otto but with the money from Fred's substantial estate to ease the pain.

Otto married and eventually returned to Los Angeles. He got a job as a night janitor in an apartment house, which suited him. After spending all those years in an attic, Otto had a distaste for being out in the daylight. He and Dolly had parted ways, and their story seemed over.

But with a story like this, could it really end so easily?

In 1930, Dolly and Herman Shapiro had a falling out. He had learned, among other things, that she was cheating on him with her business manager, Ray Hedrick. Angry, the attorney wanted revenge.

One day, he walked into the district attorney's office and filed a complaint against Dolly for threatening his life. Because of that, he wanted to file a formal affidavit about the death of her husband. He told everything he knew about Dolly, which was plenty, and she and Otto were both indicted for murder when he finally finished.

Not content with simply informing on his old flame, Shapiro also filed a lawsuit against Dolly, alleging that she had violated an agreement to assign some of her insurance claims to him. Ray Hedrick's wife, Geneva, brought her own legal charges against Dolly for alienation of affection.

In front of a grand jury, Dolly denied everything but was nevertheless indicted for murder. Her defender was Jerry Geisler, who managed to get separate trials for Dolly and Otto.

Otto told the grand jury the same story he told Shapiro years before. Perhaps he felt nostalgic for his attic and figured a closed-in jail cell would be the next best thing.

He rambled on about being Dolly's love slave, and she would threaten him with punishment if he didn't make love to her. When he was too tired or too sick to have sex, she starved him until he agreed to do so. In addition to sex, he also cleaned the house, cooked, and did Fred and Dolly's laundry. He spoke in a quiet, sobbing voice, and jurors strained to hear every juicy detail.

He was charged with murder, which had no statute of limitations, and went on trial first. His lawyer persuaded him to retract his confession, so the only evidence against him put before the jury was Shapiro's account of the murder. The defense could scornfully dismiss this account as a fantasy that Dolly's disgruntled ex-boyfriend invented.

Even so, Otto was found guilty of manslaughter. This left everyone with an interesting legal problem on their hands. Fred had been shot eight years before Otto went on trial. The statute of limitations for manslaughter ran out after three. Thanks to the delay, Otto had to be released.

Once he was out of jail, he disappeared for good. There are no records of what happened to him next. With any luck, he found a comfortable attic and spent the rest of his days there.

Dolly at the courthouse during her trial. The story of the sex slave "ghost in the attic" became such a sensation that the jury was unable to reach a verdict.

THE DISTRICT ATTORNEY HAD BEEN UNABLE to build a case against Dolly for murder, so she had been indicted for conspiracy instead. The defense presented by Jerry Geisler was simple: Otto was to blame for everything. After Fred's death, she had not come forward with the truth because explaining her unconventional private life might have been embarrassing.

Dolly Oesterreich was just too much for the jury. They found themselves unable to reach a verdict. The district attorney, hoping new evidence might someday come to light, kept the case against her open for six more years until he finally gave up and dropped the charges.

Dolly lived uncharacteristically quietly in Los Angeles until she died in 1961. She had married Ray Hedrick just two weeks before her death, leaving him with what was reported to be Dolly's multi-million-dollar estate.

The story of the "Ghost in the Attic" had finally ended, but what lesson it can teach us is anyone's guess. An old radio show used to assure us that "crime doesn't pay," but, in this case, it certainly did.

"THE DUMB-BELL MURDER"
Ruth Snyder and Henry Judd Gray

THE SNYDER-GRAY MURDER OF 1927 IS one of those killings that has been portrayed in the seediest way possible over the years. It happened during those thrill-hungry days of the Roaring 20s, when the public was devouring every sordid detail of even the most mundane crimes, turning the people involved into infamous celebrities, whether they deserved to be or not.

One crime writer called the murder "a cheap crime involving cheap people," while another called it "the dumb-bell murder" because the whole thing just seemed so stupid – as was the response to it by the public. I'm not sure that either of those phrases was the best way to put it, especially when it involved the murder of a man who probably didn't deserve it, but it certainly gives the reader an idea of what was making headlines at the time.

MOST WOULD SAY THAT THE EVENTS that led to Albert Snyder's murder began in 1925 when Ruth, a discontented housewife, met a corset salesman named Henry Judd Gray while having lunch in New York City. I would say that the roots of the murder can be found much earlier than that – when two utterly incompatible partners got married in 1915.

Albert was born "Albert Schneider" to a close German family in 1998. His father, Charles, ran a bakery in Brooklyn until he retired and moved the family to Bedford-Stuyvesant. Albert attended nearby Pratt Institute, where he studied art and graphic design, using his leisure time to pursue "real" art and devoted himself to boats, automobiles, and mechanics. He was an enthusiast of outdoor sports, especially swimming, but also spent many weekends hiking, fishing, and camping.

After the move to Bedford-Stuyvesant, Albert fell in love with a young woman named Jessie Guischard, whose family lived nearby. She was a schoolteacher, and her father was a printer at a publishing company. The pair were together for years – although it's unknown if they were ever formally engaged – but tragically, Jessie died of pneumonia in November 1912. Albert was at her bedside until the end.

Albert Snyder

Albert's life moved on, and in 1913, he took a job working for *Motor Boating Magazine*, which combined his work skills as a graphic designer and his love for boats and the outdoors. He thrived in his role at the magazine and, by 1914, had recovered from his grief over losing Jessie to begin seeing a secretary named Ruth Brown, who claimed to be 19 but was actually 23.

The story of their meeting is right out of a romance magazine story of the era. One morning, when a call was misdirected to Albert at the magazine, he gave the secretary who had placed it a piece of his mind and slammed down the receiver. A few moments later, regretting his behavior, he called and apologized, and they started chatting. Ultimately, he invited her to come and see about a job at the Hearst Corporation, which published *Motor Boating*.

Ruth Brown – whose parents had immigrated to America from Norway and Sweden – was born in 1891. Her family had lived in Manhattan for years and then settled in the Bronx. They were well-off, but Ruth always maintained that she'd had a hard life. Her father, Harry, had epilepsy and was often in poor health. His carpentry contracting business was troubled, and her mother, Josephine, had to supplement the family's income as a nurse. In Ruth's story, she never missed out on food, clothing, or necessities – she just didn't get the fancy dolls and parties other girls in the neighborhood had.

Ruth Snyder, despite her poor health, turned a lot of heads when she was young. When they met, Albert immediately began romancing her.

But she was a sickly child. When she was six, she underwent intestinal surgery and, at nine, suffered severe sunstroke. When she was 12, she underwent a botched appendectomy and then had more surgeries to correct that one. She tired easily and could not keep up with other girls at play and in sports. She fainted often, which she blamed on epilepsy she'd inherited from her father, although that wasn't the case.

Ruth left school after eighth grade and went to work for the New York Telephone Company. She was hired as a nighttime relief operator, working the graveyard shift and turning over her $15-a-week salary to her family without opening the envelope. She did this for two years before leaving to learn typing, stenography, and other secretarial skills. After that, her jobs improved, and so did her salary, allowing her to help her parents while keeping a little money for herself.

Despite her poor health, Ruth turned heads with her looks. She was tall, blond, and slim, with high cheekbones and bright blue eyes. She met a few boys, but none were serious. She spent most of her time working, watching movies with her friends, and reading romance novels.

It was during this time that Ruth placed a call to the wrong number and met Albert Schneider. By the end of that day, she'd been hired as a proofreader and copyist in the pool that served *Motor Boating, Cosmopolitan, Heart's Weekly*, and several other publications in the same building.

Almost immediately, Albert began romancing her, asking her out on dates and to dances and parties. A few other girls in the pool warned her away from dating him – he had a reputation as a lothario – but she finally agreed to have lunch with him.

When Albert good-naturedly tried to take things further, Ruth turned him down. He didn't seem to mind, and her respectability made him more interested in her. When Ruth left Hearst for a higher-paying job downtown at a lithograph company, Albert was always there to take her to lunch, dinner, and the theater. He turned into a serious prospect. He was well-read, artistic, attentive, and much more established than other men Ruth knew. He also had money and loved to go out on the town as much as he did.

At Christmas 1914, Albert proposed, but Ruth turned him down. But then, at her "20th birthday" party in March 1915, he arrived with a box of chocolates, somewhat disappointing the birthday girl who'd hoped for something more expensive. However, she found a solitaire diamond engagement ring inside when she opened the box.

That did the trick, and on July 24, 1915, she and Albert were married at her parents' apartment. The family-and-friends-only ceremony was followed by cold sandwiches, salads, cake, and coffee prepared by Ruth and her mother. Unfortunately, Ruth was having her period at the time and felt terrible. Albert reacted by losing his temper and going home to his parents' house for the night.

Things were not off to a good start.

The newlyweds rented a house in the Bay Ridge neighborhood of Brooklyn. Gone were the days of the attentive boyfriend. They had been replaced by the husband, who wanted to return to his days of boating, fishing, and working around the house. He spent his time tinkering and doing handyman jobs, and between his outdoor pursuits, the garden, and the garage, Ruth hardly even saw her husband on weekends.

They never went to restaurants or the theater like they used to do. Albert's idea of entertainment was going out on his boat, which he berthed on Long Island, spending entire days on the water with family and friends. The boat was still called the "Jessie G" when he and Ruth were married, but Ruth convinced him to re-christen it the "Ruth."

She also thought the name "Schneider" looked too foreign and convinced him to change it to "Snyder," which her in-laws never forgave her for.

It was almost as if the step of changing their family name was what cemented the differences between them. Albert had no desire for children, but Ruth had dreamed of having a family since she was a small child. A medical condition prevented this, however. But after two years of marriage, without her husband's knowledge, she had a minor operation and was soon pregnant. Albert was angry initially but accepted the idea, convinced he'd have a son to keep him company. When a daughter was born in November 1917, though, he was inconsolable. Worse, baby Lorraine was difficult and sickly, always crying and causing trouble.

The Snyders moved several times in the following years, first next door to Albert's grandmother so she could help with the baby and then next door to a rental house he'd purchased. Friction developed with the tenants, and they moved again. Their last home was in a new housing development in Queens.

Life with Albert could be difficult. He could be compulsive about neatness and order, wanting everything in a particular way. He yelled at Lorraine for normal childish behavior and complained constantly about the family's expenses – even though he made good money. They had a lovely home that had nearly been paid off by 1927, and he planted roses, created a garden, built a garage on the side of the house, and an elaborate birdhouse in the backyard. At Ruth's insistence, he bought a top-of-the-line, seven-passenger Buick sedan, and he was free-spending when it came to renting summer bungalows at Long Island resorts.

Ruth did her part for the family. She cooked, cleaned, canned fruits and vegetables, and sewed curtains for the kitchen and living room windows. She decorated with frilly cushions, knickknacks, and family photographs and made sure a large, eight-volume edition of the Bible dominated the small book collection in the living room. On the walls were prints, pictures of pastoral nature, and three oil paintings done by Albert himself. She also furnished the sunroom with white wicker and filled it with carefully tended plants.

Albert made $155 per week and gave $85 of it to Ruth for household expenses. By all accounts, she made her budget stretch. Ruth seldom went shopping in retail stores and always became acquainted with salesmen who sold to friends at wholesale prices. She was well-known around the community of

Queens Village, where the Snyders lived. She knew most of the tradesmen by their first names.

Years later, a neighbor said it was no accident that Ruth knew every man in town. "She wasn't interested in women," the neighbor said. "She'd hardly ever speak to a woman on the street, but every man in the neighborhood was on speaking terms with her. She made it a point to nod to every strange man she saw and soon would establish a casual friendship with him."

Her sister-in-law and neighbor, Mamie Thake, was a little harsher. "She was man crazy. She's married above her station. We knew none of her friends. She and there were on a different social plane from us, and they weren't our kind of people. We tolerated her Albert's sake."

At the best of times, there was an uneasy truce at the Snyder home, although there would occasionally be outright battles that left the couple refusing to speak to each other for days.

And Albert's temper, never good, became ugly. When a neighbor boy accidentally sent a baseball through a kitchen window, he pursued the terrified boy down the street and into the boy's home, where he proceeded to whale on him until he screamed for help. Once, in a fit of rage, after Lorraine refused to finish her oatmeal, Albert ran upstairs and threatened to kill himself with a pistol. The little girl, weeping uncontrollably, ran after him, threw her arms around him, and brought him to his senses. On a rare occasion dining out, Albert complained all through dinner that they could have eaten the same meal at home for half the cost, and when he exchanged words with the waiter about it, he swept his arm across the table and sent plates, glasses, food, drinks, and silverware crashing to the floor.

When the marriage first started to deteriorate, Albert would try to interest his wife in sex, and she'd refuse. Soon, he began forcing himself on her. Eventually, things got to the point that he stopped bothering her altogether.

As if all that wasn't bad enough, Albert became a heavy drinker. He made his own beer and wine in the cellar and consumed bootleg whiskey with his friends – also heavy drinkers – on most evenings. Ruth liked it when he got drunk at parties because, at least then, she could let loose, too. She had to watch out, though, because a bit of alcohol could send her off the deep end. After a skinny-dipping party on Long Island, she passed out naked and dripping wet in someone else's bed. And once, after a bridge party, she had to take the wheel from her drunk husband and was pulled over by a traffic cop. Ruth was tipsy herself, and things looked bad for a moment since she'd been speeding, had no driver's license, and Albert was unconscious. But her gift for gab paid off, and the officer let her go with a warning. Albert was still so drunk when they got home that she had to drag him out of the car.

At some point that evening, he'd lost his wallet with $75 inside. The next day, hung over, he complained loudly in front of Ruth's brother, Andrew, and his wife, Margaret, that one of Ruth's "card-playing friends" had stolen it. "Nice crowd she runs around with," he growled and proceeded to complain about the missing wallet for weeks.

By the 1920s, divorce wasn't common, but it had finally become more acceptable in American society, and Ruth began to consider it. But she didn't just want a divorce -- she wanted alimony and, most of all, custody of Lorraine, too. Under New York law, though, the only way she could sue for divorce was to prove cruelty or adultery.

Albert was the kind of guy who slapped her around on occasion, but in the 1920s, cruelty meant the really depraved kind. He was bad, but not that bad.

As for adultery? Maybe. Her husband seemed to dress better and come home later on Wednesdays, and she once found a pair of theater matinee ticket stubs in his pocket, which really made her mad since he never took her out anymore. She suspected he might be running around with girls from the office but could never catch him at it. She thought about framing him for adultery. She and her best friend, Ethel Pierson, constantly hatched schemes to get her out of her marriage, but for one reason or another, Ruth never went through with any of them.

After ten years of dealing with Albert, Ruth was starting to lose her mind. She suffered fainting spells, heart palpitations, hot flashes, headaches, and stomach pains. After a doctor diagnosed her with anemia, she tried being a Christian Scientist for two weeks, but that didn't help either. Once, things got so bad that she went across the street and sobbed to a neighbor that she was going to kill herself. She just couldn't be with Albert anymore.

Then, in June 1925, Ruth was having lunch with her hairdresser friend Kitty Kaufman and Harry Folsom, a stocking and hosiery man who used to sell items to Ruth and her friends, when another man walked in the door of the restaurant. Folsom had known him for years and called him over to their table.

The man's name was Henry Judd Gray.

Henry Judd Gray

JUDD GRAY WAS BORN IN 1892 INTO A very different family from Ruth's. His father, Charles, came from early American stock, dating back to the founding of the Connecticut colony. Charles was the co-owner of a prestigious jewelry firm, the Gray-Howes Company, in Newark, and his mother, Margaret, was the daughter of a man who had made his fortune with the Empire Corset Company.

Judd grew up with money but, like Ruth, was a sickly child. He had trouble keeping up with other children, including his sister, Margaret, and when he was 11, he suffered a bout of pneumonia that almost killed him. A few years later, when a handful of sand was tossed in his face on the playground, he nearly lost an eye and was left with permanently impaired sight.

Aside from being constantly sick, three things made up Judd Gray's life – he was very religious, adored his mother and sister and desperately wanted to be considered one of the boys. He worked hardest to achieve the latter, becoming president of his fraternity in school, chairman of the Dance Committee, manager of the basketball team, and, even with his poor eyesight and small size, football team quarterback.

At 16, Judd met the woman he'd later marry – Isabel Kallenbach, the daughter of esteemed lithographer Ferdinand Kallenbach. But even his need for love was to be "part of the gang." His sister was already engaged to Harold Logan, an officer manager for a Newark stamping and stove firm, so Judd needed a fiancée, too.

Judd's move into the business world was a rocky one. His father wanted to take him on as a salesman for the jewelry company, but his mother put her foot down. She said he needed to start on the factory floor if he was going to learn the business. Judd began spending long, hot, dirty, noisy days in a workman's apron, standing at a jewelry press making blanks for earrings.

It was a miserable experience, so he was thrilled when he finally was able to start as a traveling salesman for the company. Even though he missed Isabel and his mother, the salesman's life was not without charm in those days.

In 1914, though, he made a big decision. After his maternal grandfather collapsed and died at the Gray family Christmas dinner, the Empire Corset Company offered Judd his grandfather's sales position with the company. After conferring with his father, Judd accepted.

The differences between selling jewelry and ladies' undergarments could not have been greater. The jewelry business was quiet, understated, and meant dealing primarily with men. Selling corsets meant dealing almost exclusively with women. Strict rules forbid drinking and socializing when carrying jewelry samples, often worth thousands of dollars. But now, wining, dining, and parties were a huge part of Judd's new job.

In November 1915, Judd and Isabel were finally married, and they moved in with Isabel's mother in East New York. Judd was uncomfortable there, especially after Isabel announced she was pregnant, and Mrs. Kallenbach disapproved. When their daughter, Jane, was born in August 1916, the couple had been apartment hunting for several months. They found nothing suitable in the city, so they rented half a two-family house in Orange, New Jersey, not far from Judd's family.

During World War I, Judd wanted to enlist, but Isabel and his mother objected, so he volunteered with the Red Cross and helped with bond drives. His failure to serve would always be his greatest regret. What better way to be "one of the boys" than to serve in the army?

In 1921, Judd took a new job with the Benjamin and Johnes Company, which made the Bien Jolie line of women's underwear. This was a big step up. In addition to being a prominent manufacturer, the company had outlets in Paris, London, and New York. Judd and Isabel were able to buy a much larger home in a better neighborhood, which was close to their daughter's school. Judd joined the Elks and sang in the choir, which gave concerts at churches, schools, hospitals, and prisons. He also taught Sunday School at the local Methodist Church.

Although life seemed perfect, their marriage was far from it. Because of Judd's constant traveling, he and Isabel rarely saw each other before marriage. Then Jane was born, and they moved to New Jersey – it all happened so fast they hardly knew one another. Isabel objected to Judd being on the road and disliked the "fast crowd" she mixed with in his business. Judd tried a few times to include her in trips to nightclubs and the theater with which he entertained his customers, but she was upset that he paid more attention to his buyers than he did to her. When Judd came home from entertaining in New York, she complained about the smell of liquor on his breath. While on the road, Judd sent postcards and telephoned often, but when he came home, he felt like a visitor. When he finally had the chance to spend time with Isabel, he'd find she had scheduled a trip to the country club to play tennis with friends or an outing with her mother.

At the age of barely 30, Judd Gray felt like a man who was lost and unappreciated, but all that was about to change. His life would take a direction he never could have imagined.

JUDD JOINED THE LITTLE PARTY AT THE RESTAURANT that day, where quite a few highballs were consumed, and the meal stretched into mid-afternoon. He and Ruth hit it off so well that they lingered over their drinks after Harry and Kitty had left.

Judd finally left around 4:00 P.M. and insisted that Ruth stop by his office one day for free undergarments. The next day, he telephoned her and asked her to write to him while he was on the road.

When Judd returned to New York in late July, the stories of what happened next varied slightly. According to Judd, Harry Folsom invited him to a nightclub for dinner one night and found Ruth among the other guests. According to Ruth, Judd called her at home on August 4 after a particularly nasty fight between the Snyders and asked her to dinner with Harry and another woman.

However it happened, they all ended up out on the town one night when cocktails were freely flowing. Harry and his date left early, but Judd and Ruth stayed behind. When they left for Penn Station, Judd asked her to stop by his office. When Ruth complained about having sunburned shoulders, Judd offered to apply some ice. She slipped out of her dress, and one thing led to another.

It was love at first... let's say "sight" for the unusual pair. Judd was short, and Ruth was tall. He usually wore bookish, round-framed, tortoiseshell glasses that gave him a look of perpetual surprise, a white silk shirt, silk tie, suit with vest, gloves, hat, silk scarf, and overcoat. Ruth was loud, blond, and wore cheap, flashy wholesale dresses. She completed her overall look by chewing gum incessantly. But Judd, practically smothered by his respectable mother, sister, wife, and mother-in-law, had discovered the most exciting, uninhibited woman he'd ever met in Ruth. Ruth, alternately ignored and abused by Albert Snyder, found in Judd a man who listened to her dreams, bought her flowers, and made love to her with tender touching instead of crude groping or outright rape.

Judd often referred to her by the wildly Oedipal terms of "Momsie" or "Mommy," while the nickname Ruth used for Judd was one she picked up from his close friends, the decidedly neutral "Bud." In a few letters, she addressed him as "Lover Boy."

Ben Hecht, one of the wittier journalists of the 1920s, referred to their love affair as "peculiarly uninteresting," but for Ruth and Judd, it was all-consuming. They became inseparable. Judd stayed in New York on business as much as he could, and Ruth would use the excuse of visiting friends to be with him. They checked into hotels, and when Ruth had no one to watch Lorraine, she'd bring her along and let her amuse herself in the lobby while she went upstairs. On Thursday nights, when Albert went bowling, Ruth and Judd would chat on the telephone for hours. Soon, she invited him to Queens for lunch while Lorraine was at school and Albert was at work. They met as often as possible and never seemed to be able to get enough of each other.

In September 1925, things between Ruth and Albert became especially volatile. Ruth managed to get through it, but there was one thing she insisted on: getting Lorraine out of the house and into a good convent school. She had even worked a little selling stock in a dental supply firm to save up for the tuition.

But Albert exploded at the idea. Ranting and raving, he refused even to consider sending their daughter away to school. He forbade Ruth even to bring up the subject again.

Shortly after the argument, Ruth became interested in insurance. She discovered that Albert only carried a measly $1,000 life insurance policy on himself, which seemed much too small considering his enjoyment of the outdoors and the fact that he'd had a couple of accidents working on cars in the garage over the summer. His policy was through an agent named Leroy Ashfield, who worked for Prudential. When he came to make his regular monthly collection rounds in November, Ruth discussed with him the idea of increasing Albert's life insurance. Ashfield was happy to make his sales pitch and convinced Albert to sign a blank policy application form that said he would consider purchasing higher insurance at a later date.

Apparently, though, Albert made that decision very quickly. The next day, Ruth called Ashfield at his office and said that her husband had made up his mind and wanted a $50,000 policy, with Ruth as the beneficiary and double indemnity in case of death by misadventure. He wished to pay for it on the "Modified Life Plan" – which was "Buy Now, Pay Later" – and premiums would be at half-rate for the first five years and then correspondingly greater after that.

Ashfield wrote up the policy using the form Albert had already signed, but then he ran into trouble. Because of the size of the double indemnity policy, the company balked at paying more than $500 a month in disability based on Albert's income. But Ashfield, being the ambitious salesman he was, decided to work around the problem and not bother the Snyders with it. He wrote one $45,000 policy with double indemnity and one $5,000 policy without it. Then, he traced Albert's signature onto the new form.

Ashfield hand-delivered the policies to Ruth, who asked him to follow the same practice with the payment receipts. She also took aside her postman and told him that, like letters to her from Mr. Gray and telephone bills, all mail from the Prudential Life Insurance Company was to be given to her only. The postman – friendly with Ruth, of course – happily agreed.

Albert Snyder, an annoyance at best when alive, was now worth ten times his annual salary when dead – and 20 times that amount if he happened to die by misadventure.

ACCORDING TO THE STORY THAT RUTH TOLD later, things became unbearable in the Snyder home in February 1927 when her husband threatened to "blow her brains out." She wrote this in a letter to Judd, who asked her if she thought he was serious. Ruth replied that he was certainly capable of it during one of his fits of temper. To this, Judd said that they should get Albert before he got her.

The house in Queens where Ruth lived with Albert and their daughter, Lorraine.

Ruth had slowly been trying to convince Judd that her life was in danger for months. Initially, Judd dismissed her worries, but Ruth continued to pester him with hints, suggestions, and, finally, outright demands that something should be done about Albert. Judd became so unsettled by her demand that he often drank too much to settle his nerves. But even that didn't help. Ruth would beg, argue, and threaten, but he refused until he finally gave in.

On Saturday, March 5, the couple met for lunch, and Judd gave her a window sash weight – an iron bar about 18 inches in length, a bit smaller than a rolling pin in diameter, and weighing about five pounds – and told her to take it home with her. Ruth later said that Judd came to the Snyder home on Monday, March 7, planning to hit Albert on the head with it while he was sleeping and then chloroform him. But they didn't go through with it. Both got "cold feet and cried like babies," she said.

"Go home," Ruth told Judd, "You're not going to do it."

On Saturday, March 12, there was another terrible fight at the Snyder home. Albert told his wife that if she didn't leave the house, he'd kill her. Once again, Ruth wrote to Judd, and he again asked her if she thought he'd really do it. Of course, she replied, he was capable of anything. That was the last straw, Judd told her on March 19 that they would "deliver the goods."

When Ruth received this note, she told Judd that she and her husband would be away at a party that night and that he should hide in the house and wait for them to return. She left the cellar and kitchen doors unlocked for him when she, Albert, and Lorraine went to the party. After they returned, Ruth put her daughter to bed, undressed, and got into bed. About 10 minutes later, Albert did the same. After about half an hour, when she was sure her husband was asleep, she got out of bed and went to Judd.

He was waiting for her. Judd had spent most of the day drinking, trying to summon the courage to go through with the murder. He and Ruth had cooked up a plan that had him traveling by train to New York from Syracuse and then by bus to Queens Village. After arriving, Judd walked around for an hour, stopping under streetlights to take drinks from his flask. It was almost as if he hoped to be spotted and arrested for breaking the law. No one paid any attention to him, though, and finally, he had to enter the Snyder home.

As planned, Ruth had left the sash weight in the spare bedroom. Judd had brought the chloroform in a brown medicine bottle, some cotton rags, and a blue bandanna handkerchief.

Ruth left her bedroom and opened the door to the spare room. "Are you in here, Bud, dear?" she whispered.

Judd soaked one of the rags with chloroform and wrapped it in the bandana. There was a brief, whispered conversation in which Ruth told him it was either her or her husband. They kissed, and then Judd grabbed the window sash weight. Ruth led him to the primary bedroom, where Albert Snyder slept with the blankets over his head. The room was dark, except for the glow from a streetlight in front of the house.

The pair stood on opposite sides of the bed, and then Ruth saw Judd raise the sash weight. He brought it clumsily down on Albert's head. The man groaned twice while Judd tied his hands behind his back, pressed the chloroform-soaked cloth over his mouth, and jammed his face into a pillow. Then he tied Albert's feet together.

"I guess that's it," he commented as he left the bedroom, peeling off his gloves. He entered the bathroom and discovered blood spatters on his shirt, so Ruth found a shirt for him to change into. Together, they took the stained shirt and the sash weight down to the basement, burned the shirt in the furnace, and placed the murder weapon in a toolbox, sprinkling it with ashes so it looked like it had been there a long time. They sat down in the living room to rest when they finished.

The pair then set about faking a robbery by knocking over some chairs and emptying all the drawers in the house, except for the ones in Lorraine's room. Ruth removed the wallet from Albert's pants and gave the money to Judd. They scattered pages from an Italian newspaper around the bedroom to support the burglary story, removed Albert's pistol from its holster, and put it on the floor next to the bed.

Judd left about two hours later after tying up Ruth with a clothesline and leaving her on the bed in the extra room. She stayed there until close to dawn when she got tired of waiting to be discovered, wriggled off the bed, and down the hall to her daughter's bedroom door.

A few minutes later, Harriet Mulhauser, the Snyders' next-door neighbor, was awakened by a call from Lorraine. "Come over to our house quick. Mama is very sick!" she cried.

Harriet opened the front door of the Snyder home and stepped inside. She heard moaning sounds from upstairs, so she climbed the staircase. She found Ruth sprawled on the landing in a short green nightgown trimmed with lace. Her feet were bound loosely with thin rope, but her hands were free. On the floor next to her was more rope and a loosened gag.

Harriet quickly untied Ruth's feet and was told she'd been hit on the head. Lorraine was sent over to the Mulhauser house while Harriet telephoned the police. She also called her husband,

Ruth and Albert's daughter, Lorraine, who discovered her mother tied up and went next door to alert a neighbor.

Louis, to come over and look around the house.

It was Louis who discovered Albert's bloody and beaten body under a heap of blankets in one of the twin beds in the primary bedroom. He was tied up, face down, on a pillow that was smeared with blood. Looped around his neck and digging deeply into the flesh was a length of picture wire, cinched at the back, its loose ends sticking out at odd angles. Next to the body was a revolver, broken open. Louis pulled a sheet over the corpse and left the bedroom.

He placed a call to another neighbor, George Colyer, and the two men carried Ruth into Lorraine's room and put her to bed. They said nothing to her about her husband, nor did she ask. Another neighbor, Dr. Harry Hansen, was summoned, examined her, and found no evidence that she had been hit in the head, as she claimed.

That was the first lie that Ruth had been caught telling – it wouldn't be the last. Celebrated newsman Damon Runyon later wrote that Ruth and Judd were "inept idiots" and called the whole mess the "Dumb-Bell Murder because it was so dumb."

Even though the pair were convinced that they'd planned everything down to the letter, the "robbery" was far from convincing to experienced police investigators – and many of them were on the scene. The first patrolman to arrive on the scene quickly called the precinct house to ask for detectives and medical personnel. Murders simply didn't happen in middle-class Queens Village, and NYPD Deputy Commissioner James Leach was soon on the scene, along with 60 detectives, who were quickly crawling all over the property.

Dr. Howard Neail of the New York Medical Examiner's Office – the highest-ranking forensic pathologist in Queens County – examined the body. None of the wounds seemed to make sense, especially based on Ruth's story. He also checked her for any signs of attack and found none. He could find no explanation, other than fear, for the time she claimed to be unconscious. Her wrists didn't bear the marks of having struggled free from tight bonds, nor any of the bruises she'd have if she laid on the floor for an extended time. He laughed when a detective told him that Ruth maintained she had been senseless for five hours.

"Five hours?" he chuckled. "It's more like five minutes."

Ruth told detectives that the family had returned from a bridge party around 2:00 A.M., and Albert quickly fell asleep. A few minutes later, Ruth heard a noise and thought it might be Lorraine, awake from having eaten something that didn't agree with her at the party. When she passed the spare bedroom, a huge man appeared in the doorway. He grabbed her and dragged her into the room. She said that her assailant was "swarthy, had a black mustache, and looked like an Italian." Then came the blow to the head, and she was out cold for the next five hours. It must have been the robber – or maybe more than one robber – who had ransacked the house, looking for valuables, she told the police.

The detectives did not give Ruth's story even the slightest bit of credence. First, it was clear that she hadn't been struck and knocked unconscious for five hours. She also couldn't have fainted and remained senseless for so long. Second, since her hands were free, why hadn't she untied the ropes around her ankles?

And those weren't the only glaring inconsistencies in her story – there were plenty of others. Burglaries, especially professional ones, shunned low pay-off risks. They wouldn't bother with a modest home like the Snyder house. The only item that seemed to be missing was the money in Albert's wallet. They left behind his watch and other jewelry in the house.

The ransacking of the house itself was suspicious. Burglars entered homes, knew where to look for what they wanted, took it, and left. No thief, no matter how meticulous, would bother searching under sofa cushions and inside kitchen cabinets as the Snyder home invaders allegedly did. Detectives knew that no burglar would bother with the kitchen.

Why wasn't Lorraine's room searched? These burglars wouldn't have cared if the young girl had been awakened, yet her room was undisturbed. What kind of burglar carried chloroform, rope, and picture wire? Ruth surely knew that Albert had a loaded pistol, so why hadn't she called out when she was first grabbed?

Ruth's answers to these questions – and others – were evasive and unsatisfactory. She claimed that jewelry worth at least $200 was missing, but in the early afternoon, the supposedly missing items – three rings and a silver bar pin – were found wrapped in a cloth under Ruth's bed. The pillowcase on her bed appeared recently changed and had never been slept on. Police found a bloodstained pillowcase thrown in a dirty clothes hamper in the basement. A squirrel coat that Ruth claimed was stolen was found on a shelf in her closet.

A small calendar with many names on it was found. When asked about these, Ruth flushed and stammered when the police questioned her about an entry for H. Judd Gray from East Orange, New Jersey. The detectives' interest in Mr. Gray increased when a pin bearing the initials "J.G." was found on the floor of the primary bedroom, along with several canceled checks made out to Judd Gray.

Other canceled checks to the Prudential Life Insurance Company were found, suggesting that Albert's life had been heavily insured. When asked about this, Ruth lied again. "It's only for $1,000," she said. When pointed out that this was not nearly enough to explain the checks, she quickly replied, "Well, it was for $1,000, and now it's $25,000." So yes, she lied once again.

After collecting accounts from Lorraine – "Mommy and Daddy had fights because Mommy stayed out all night long" – as well as friends and neighbors, who told police about fights between the Snyders, heavy drinking, late-night parties, Ruth was taken to the local precinct house for more questioning.

It didn't take her long to crack. Surprisingly, she gave up everything and confessed to the murder of her husband. Not surprisingly, though, she blamed everything on Judd Gray.

He was found hours later, hiding in his Syracuse hotel room. He shrieked his innocence and insisted that he had not been in New York. When confronted with the train ticket stub that he had carelessly tossed in the trash can of the hotel room, he broke down and confessed. Like Ruth, he blamed everything on his accomplice.

By the time the case went to trial, the two former lovers were at one another's throats, each blaming the other for the deadly deed. The trial became a media frenzy. Celebrities attended in droves, including mystery writer Mary Roberts Rinehart, director D.W. Griffith, author Will Durant, evangelists Billy Sunday and Aimee Semple McPherson, and many others. McPherson even received a large sum from the *New York Evening Graphic* to write up a piece on the sordid case. Sister Aimee, who would be involved in a scandal of her own a year later, used her column

By the time Ruth helped kill her abusive husband, she probably didn't fit the "Red Hot Cutie" nickname.

(Below) But then, "Lover Boy" Judd Gray wasn't exactly inspiring love letters anymore either.

to encourage young men to say, "I want a wife like mother -- not a Red Hot cutie."

Both defendants had separate attorneys arguing for their innocence. Ruth's lawyer stated that her husband "drove love out from the house" by longing after a departed sweetheart. He also said Gray had tempted her by setting up a $50,000 double indemnity insurance policy on Albert Snyder. Her attorney insisted she was a loving wife and the conditions in her home were not her fault. He then put the "wronged woman" on the stand, wearing a simple black dress. She played the role of the suffering wife, describing how her husband ignored her most of the time, except when taking her to the occasional movie. It had been she who had read from the Bible to daughter Lorraine and had made sure the little girl attended Sunday school. Her lawyer glossed over the Gray romance, and Ruth justified their affair by saying that Judd was also unhappy at home. The affair had turned horrible as "Lover Boy" dragged her to speakeasies and night spots, where she had watched him drink himself senseless. Ruth swore she rarely touched a drink and never smoked. Then she testified that Gray insisted that she take out the heavy insurance policy on her husband. She also told the court that he had once sent her poison and told her to give it to her husband.

At this, the excitable Judd Gray began whispering to his lawyers. A short time later, he also took the witness stand, and his attorney described Judd's situation as "the most tragic story that has ever gripped the human heart." The lawyer claimed that Judd was a law-abiding citizen who had been duped and dominated by a "designing, deadly conscienceless, abnormal woman, a human serpent, a human fiend in the disguise of a woman." He then added that he had been "drawn into this hopeless chasm when reason was gone, mind was gone, manhood was gone, and when his mind was weakened by lust and passion."

Judd played the victim when he took the stand, nervously glancing over at his elderly mother, sitting in the courtroom next to the actress Nora Bayes, who had come to watch the show. He testified that Ruth had tried to kill her husband several times, once putting knockout drops in his drink and, when they failed, trying to gas him. He also testified that she had once given Albert Snyder poison as a cure for the hiccups. It made the man violently ill instead. Judd said innocently, "I told her she was crazy. I said to her that it was a hell of a way to cure hiccups."

Finally, Judd stated that it had been Ruth who had taken out the insurance policy on Snyder, and it had not been his doing or his idea. He also described how she had struck the death blow on the night of the murder. At this, Ruth began to sob loudly in the courtroom, and even the judge glanced in her direction. The jury was out only 98 minutes before returning with a guilty verdict. Both defendants were stunned and then shocked even further when they learned the sentence for their crime was death.

Judd Gray was executed first on January 12, 1928. He sat smiling in his cell when the warden came for him. He had received a letter from his wife forgiving him. He told the warden that he was ready to go. He said, "I have nothing to fear."

Ruth Snyder followed her former lover just minutes after she watched the prison lights flicker, signaling that the switch had been thrown for the electric chair. Reporters remembered that, as she was being led to the death chamber, she had said days before that God had forgiven her and that she hoped the world would.

A clever *New York Daily News* reporter smuggled a camera into the death chamber by strapping it to his ankle. He clicked

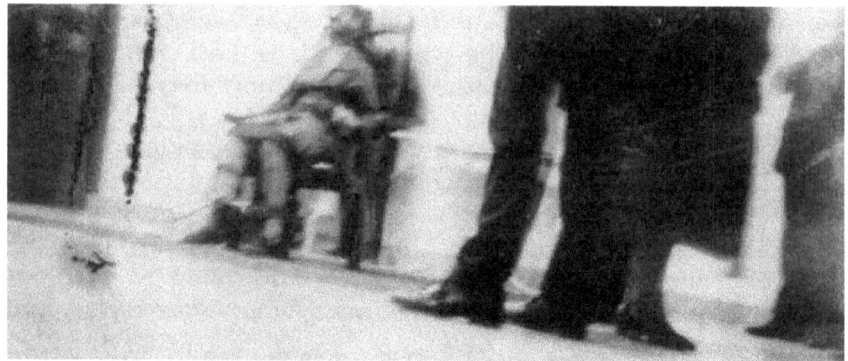
The last photograph of Ruth Snyder

off a photo just as the current entered Ruth's body and snapped her against the chair straps.

The photograph ran in the next day's edition of the paper, but soon, the lurid tale faded into history. What was once the largest attended "celebrity trial" of 1927 is barely a footnote in American crime history today.

THE "LONELY HEARTS KILLERS"
Raymond Fernandez and Martha Beck

"LONELY HEARTS" ADVERTISEMENTS DIDN'T START WHEN the infamous case of Martha Beck and Raymond Fernandez began being splattered across the pages of detective magazines in the late 1940s – and they didn't end there either.

For decades, people had been advertising for love in newspapers and magazines, leading thousands to meet, court, and marry partners they met through the mail.

Gradually, those advertisements evolved into "lonely hearts clubs," which provided names and addresses for a fee. The clubs rose in popularity as it became difficult to meet people in bars and clubs during Prohibition in the 1920s, and people had to look for other ways to meet people. The clubs seemed to break down into two categories – middle-aged people looking for love and young people anxious for the "joys of marital life." In 1920s speak, "marital life" meant sex, so the clubs became the era's version of a hook-up app.

But it seemed most club members were those with limited social options, particularly widows, single women, and men past a certain age.

Whatever their reasons, they flocked to the lonely-hearts bureaus. The love-starved sent hundreds of thousands of letters through various services, hoping to meet the perfect person each year. Advertisements that attracted as many as 500 letters per day included things like "Rich Widows... Wealthy Widowers!" and hinted at the possibility of landing someone with a six-figure bank account.

The cover charge for most clubs was 25 cents, the price of a four-page brochure containing a snapshot and brief biography of clients looking for spouses. For $3, a client could receive a yearly subscription. The rest was up to the correspondents who exchanged letters – or, as they called it, "engaged in postage stamp flirtation."

It all seemed innocent enough, but as some would discover, the person writing the letters wasn't always what they appeared to be. There are numerous accounts of men and women corresponding with a dozen or more people at a time, accepting gifts, money, and marriage proposals, which suddenly disappeared, ending the scam. People lost their fortunes, their hearts, and, inevitably, their lives.

Terrible tales of misfortune, robbery, and death haunted the lonely-hearts clubs and sometimes resulted in investigations and temporary injunctions against some of the most popular groups. But efforts to close them down permanently met with failure. New ones popped up in the classified ads of newspapers and magazines like weeds and became fixtures in the back pages of romance and detective pulps.

The "Lonely Hearts Killers," Raymond Fernandez and Martha Beck

More scandals followed, and when federal authorities did manage to make a case against some devious con artist, the story was always given front-page headlines. Even so, the exposure still failed to slow down the business end of matchmaking. Lonely hearts simply ignored the cautionary tales of robbery – even murder – and continued to look for love among the ads.

But, of course, that wasn't all they found.

RAYMOND FERNANDEZ WAS A BRAIN-DAMAGED Latin lover who was already luring lonely, wealthy women through lonely hearts ads in romance magazines before meeting the woman who sent him entirely off the rails.

They became a match made in hell, and their lives would end together in the electric chair, still professing their undying love.

The woman who managed to catch Raymond was Martha Beck, a lonely single mother from Florida who responded to one of his ads. She soon had him completely under her spell. As for Martha, she was head over heels for Raymond. Together, they would unleash a kind of horror their victims had never imagined.

Martha would later say that her life began on December 9, 1947 – the day she met Raymond Fernandez – but in truth, she was born Martha Jule Seabrook near Pensacola, Florida, on May 6, 1920.

Allegedly due to a glandular problem – a common explanation for obesity in those days – Martha was an overweight child and went through puberty early. She later claimed that her brother had raped her, and when she told her mother what happened, she was beaten because her mother told her she was responsible. She ran away from home as a teenager and spent some time with a traveling carnival.

Regardless, Martha finished school and became a registered nurse but had trouble finding a job because of her weight. She worked as an undertaker's assistant and prepared deceased women for burial. Later, she moved to California and worked as a nurse at an Army hospital during the early years of World War II. While living in California, she became pregnant by a soldier stationed at a nearby base. After failing to convince him to marry her, she returned to Florida – single and pregnant.

Martha told people that her baby's father was a serviceman she had married and that he had been killed during the Pacific campaign. The town mourned her loss and even published a story about his tragic death in the local newspaper.

Shortly after her daughter was born, Martha became pregnant again by a Pensacola bus driver named Alfred Beck. They quickly married, but it was a disaster, and they were divorced six months later. Soon after that, Martha gave birth to a son.

Unemployed and the single mother of two young children, Martha escaped into a fantasy world, buying romance magazines and novels, and seeing romantic films at the local theater. In 1946, she found work again at the Pensacola Hospital for Children.

For months, Martha had been poring over the lonely-hearts ads she found in the back of the magazines she read, dreaming of finding the perfect man. So, in 1947, she placed an ad of her own – an ad that the man of her dreams answered, Raymond Fernandez.

RAYMOND MARTINEZ FERNANDEZ WAS BORN to Spanish parents on December 17, 1914, in Hawaii. When he was three, his parents moved to California and eventually to Bridgeport, Connecticut. As a teenager, he worked hard on his family's farm but moved to Spain to work for his uncle after a confrontation with his father. There, he married a local woman, Agnesia Robles Alonaso. After the birth of their first child, Raymond returned to the United States, already bored with married life. He stayed until 1935 when his son became ill. This prompted a return to Spain, but he didn't plan to stay long. He saw his future in America and wanted to return as soon as possible.

But that chance didn't come until 1947. Thanks to the Spanish Civil War, he remained with his wife for the next decade, and they had three more children. He eventually abandoned all of them.

During World War II, Raymond served in Spain's Merchant Marine and later claimed to have been a spy for British Intelligence. It's possible this was true. He would have been well-suited for this kind of work with his considerable charm and charisma.

In 1947, Raymond finally decided to return to New York. Shortly after boarding a ship for the United States, a steel hatch fell on him, fracturing his skull and injuring his frontal lobe.

This injury would be used to explain Raymond's change in behavior – and his turning to a life of crime, which began with committing burglaries of homes and stores after he was released from the hospital.

He was arrested after stealing some clothing and spent a year in prison. While there, he allegedly learned magic and voodoo from one of his cellmates and began using his so-called magical powers on the women he started meeting through the lonely-hearts ads. He later claimed that black magic gave him his irresistible power and charm.

One of his victims - Jane Thompson - traveled with him to Spain. He talked her into changing her will, making him the sole beneficiary. She then died under mysterious circumstances. He told one person that she had a heart attack, then told Jane's mother that she had been killed in a train accident. Whatever happened, Raymond wound up with her money.

His schemes continued, preying on other lonely women before writing to Martha Beck after seeing her ad in a romance magazine.

Jane Thompson

Martha would describe meeting Raymond as knowing they were a perfect match for one another. After a brief but torrid exchange of letters, Raymond traveled to Florida on December 9, and the lovers spent the weekend together. Three days later, before returning to New York, Raymond proposed marriage, and Martha gladly accepted. Martha stayed behind in Pensacola, preparing for the wedding.

Martha, unable to think about anything but Raymond, lost her job, so she took her two children and followed him to New York. Raymond loved being suffocated by her, and he spilled the details of the times he'd already defrauded lonely women. And he told her the plans he had to defraud many more.

Never realizing that she had originally been one of Raymond's targets, Martha decided that it was her duty to join in the fun. She even gave her children away so she could devote herself to Raymond full-time. She dropped them off at the Salvation Army one day and never looked back.

Raymond then laid out a new scheme that would involve Martha. She would pose as his sister while he seduced other women through the lonely-hearts ads. Then, they would rob the women before going on to their next victim.

Martha agreed, but only if the scheme would remain business, not pleasure. Raymond belonged to her and her alone. Raymond couldn't do anything but agree.

And the violent string of matrimony and murder began.

WITH MARTHA SITTING AT HIS SIDE, RAYMOND began writing to five or six women, including Esther Henne, a teacher from

Pennsylvania. Around Valentine's Day 1948, "Charles Martin" -- the name he'd decided to adopt -- and his "sister," Martha, traveled to Pennsylvania, where Raymond began wooing the unsuspecting woman. The two got "married" in Virginia, and the three of them returned to New York. The marriage didn't last long. Esther got suspicious and went home. With help from a lawyer, she got back most of the money the pair had stolen from her.

While recovering from this failure, Martha and Raymond took a trip, stopping in Miami and Havana and landing in Chicago in May 1948. They both got temporary jobs while Raymond swapped letters with an Arkansas widow named Myrtle Young.

With Martha standing by as his "sister," he married Myrtle in August. The marriage only lasted a few days, ending when Myrtle left Chicago to cry on her sister's shoulder in St. Louis. The affair was profitable for Martha and Raymond, netting them about $4,000.

After this, Martha and Raymond traveled to North Carolina, where Raymond romanced another woman on his list. When that relationship didn't work out, the pair drove to Vermont and met with another target, Irene De La Point.

Martha was starting to question Raymond's devotion to her at this point. She decided to teach him a lesson and wrote a letter to Irene, warning her of Raymond's intentions. And then Martha walked out, leaving her lover stranded in Vermont. She first went to see her mother in Florida and then visited a sister's house in North Carolina on November 1. Two days later, Raymond finally tracked her down. He begged for her to come back. After a suitable amount of groveling, she agreed, and they rendezvoused in New York to patch things up.

Raymond already had another victim on his list, and this time, things would get ugly.

ON JANUARY 1, MARTHA AND RAYMOND traveled to Albany, New York, so that "Charles Martin" could meet a 66-year-old widow named

Janet Fay

Janet Fay. While Martha remained at the hotel, Raymond met Janet for dinner, still attempting to figure out how much money she had. Convinced of her wealth by the large diamond ring that she wore, he invited her to stay with him at a house that he had rented in Valley Stream.

The building in Queens where Raymond hid Janet Fay's body in the basement. His sister lived in an apartment upstairs.

During a trip with Janet to New York City, Raymond introduced her to his "sister." The three of them were staying in a hotel when Martha began to get suspicious about what Raymond was doing. Though she encouraged Raymond to keep preying on the lonely woman, Martha continued to insist that he never have sex with any of them. When she found him in bed with Janet, Martha lost her mind.

She hit Janet's head several times with a hammer, shattering her skull. When that didn't kill her, Raymond finished her off by strangling her with a silk scarf. They placed the body in a trunk and stashed it in the basement of Raymond's sister's building in Queens. It stayed there until January 21, and then Raymond buried the trunk in the basement and covered it with fresh concrete.

With the body hidden, Martha and Raymond fled New York and traveled west to Michigan, where they committed the murders that would send them to the electric chair.

ON JANUARY 12, 1949, A 31-YEAR-OLD WIDOW named Deliphene Price mailed a letter that eventually led to her death.

It was written to a wealthy New York man named Charles Martin. The two had first made contact the previous month through a lonely-hearts ad. Thrilled to receive correspondence from an affluent Manhattan businessman, Deliphene thought nothing of fulfilling Charles' request for a recent photo and a lock of her hair.

Hoping to make herself seem attractive to a man from the big city, she presented herself as a woman of means, mentioning that she soon hoped to buy a new car and described her two-stall garage and her nice home in the suburbs. She also hinted that she was eager to find love. Perhaps a little too eager. She even mailed a second letter to Charles before he received her first one.

That would be the biggest mistake of her life.

Widowed schoolteacher Deliphene Downing

Born November 4, 1917, Deliphene Price grew up alongside her older sisters – Zora, Zella, and Esther – on her father's 3,000-acre ranch near Palisade, Nebraska. She attended the local high school and graduated in 1934. Her senior photographs showed a cute girl with curly brunette hair worn just over her ears and parted on the side, a wide, mischievous grin, and smiling eyes. Friends and relatives always described her as "old-fashioned," seldom using makeup or wearing pantyhose, stockings, or garters.

After graduating, Deliphene took a job teaching at a small school near home. In the summer of 1942, during a visit with a sister living in Los Angeles, she met and fell in love with a dashing soldier named Rolland Downing. They corresponded for almost two years before marrying during one of Rolland's furloughs in 1944.

After the war, the newlyweds moved to Rolland's hometown of Grand Rapids, Michigan. They lived with his parents while house hunting and then moved into a five-room bungalow on Byron Center Road in Wyoming Township, a small suburban community. A machinist by trade, Rolland worked as a truck driver until he could save enough money to start his own business. On June 6, 1946, the couple welcomed a daughter named Rainelle.

But Deliphene's life was shattered on a gray November morning when a passenger train struck Rolland's truck, killing him instantly. Rainelle was only 17 months old when her father died, and Deliphene was left to raise her alone on a monthly life insurance payment of $125.

A year after her husband's death, the widow joined a lonely-hearts club -- a fact she kept hidden from family and friends. She was still young and pretty and ached to find someone to spend her life with.

So, she was thrilled on January 23, 1949, when Charles and his sister arrived at her bungalow on the southwest side of Grand Rapids.

Raymond and Martha would offer two different accounts of what happened after they arrived at Deliphene's house, and Raymond began trying to work his "magic" on the woman.

Deliphene's young daughter, Rainelle

Raymond said he'd liked "Dela" – as he called her – more than any other women he'd met through the lonely-hearts ads and contemplated bringing her back with him to New York City. But then an incident occurred that changed everything.

They had started arguing on a Saturday afternoon. Raymond claimed there were two reasons for the fight. The first involved money Deliphene wanted to withdraw from her bank account to send to her sisters. "But what about us?" he'd asked, trying to manipulate her into not giving away what he saw as his windfall.

The second reason for the spat involved the $150 hairpiece that Raymond had purchased in downtown Grand Rapids. Deliphene didn't like how it had changed his appearance – or so Raymond later told the police.

It likely had more to do with Deliphene's sense that something fishy was happening with her new lover and his sister. She had already refused to move her savings into a joint account that he'd suggested they open, and the hairpiece seemed to be one more reason to doubt the man's sincerity.

Deliphene's home in Grand Rapids.

Deliphene allegedly became hysterical during the argument, and Raymond said she began hurling dishes and silverware at him.

As Raymond later recounted this story to the police in his confession, he decided to throw his accomplice, Martha, under the bus. He said that Martha was an unwanted hanger-on that he didn't seem to be able to get rid of.

"I liked her – but she wouldn't go away," he stated. "She said when I was settling down, she would go away, but she didn't. This last one, Deliphene, was the nicest. She was really a very nice woman. She was the one I wanted. But I didn't love Martha. I couldn't get her out of my system. I tried to make her go away, but whatever she wanted she would whimper and cry and make me do what she wanted."

Jealous of Raymond's attention to Deliphene – and fearful she might be replaced – Martha, the trained nurse, convinced the young woman to take some medicine to help her calm down. She convinced her to swallow 14 phenobarbital tablets. The dose wasn't lethal, but it did put her into a deep sleep.

Seeing her mother unconscious, Rainelle began to cry. Unable to get her to stop, Martha nearly strangled the girl, finally letting go of her when Rainelle's face started to turn blue. But then, realizing that no amount of smooth-talking would keep Deliphene from going straight to the police about the argument, sleeping pills, and bruises on her daughter's neck, Raymond decided to kill Deliphene before she woke up. Using Rolland Downing's army-issued .45, he shot her in the head while Rainelle watched the whole thing.

But is that really how it happened? Martha offered a slightly different version of Deliphene's death.

She agreed that the breaking point came that Saturday afternoon when Deliphene reacted badly to the new toupee that Raymond was sporting. A heated argument followed. According to Martha and John Bossler, the shop's proprietor where he'd purchased it, the wig made Raymond look much younger, which must've raised Deliphene's suspicions and triggered the argument.

Martha told the police that the sleeping pills had been Raymond's idea, not hers. Raymond shot Deliphene when she became restless that night, trying to wake up. He had wrapped the pistol in a baby blanket to muffle the sound, but he worried that a neighbor might have heard something, so he wanted to get rid of the body right away. Raymond went to the basement and started digging a hole in the floor. He had tools and leftover concrete from a project he had recently worked on in the house.

He told Martha to wrap the body up in a blanket. "I tried tying her, but the rope kept slipping," she recalled. "He, in the meantime, had gone into the basement to dig a hole. The hole kept filling up with water, and I don't believe he dug it as deep as he had planned."

Together, they carried Deliphene's body downstairs, and Martha bailed two buckets of water from the hole before they placed the body into it. Once it was covered, Raymond filled the hole with cement.

After burying the body, Raymond and Martha took Rainelle out for dinner and a movie. By the following day, though, they were unable to pacify her. She cried continually, begging for her mother so loudly that the couple feared the neighbors would be alerted. Trying to calm her, they took her for a drive and promised her a puppy. They stopped at a local pet store and purchased a cocker spaniel, but when the dog accidentally scratched her, Rainelle began screaming, and they returned it.

The next day, the crying continued, and they began to talk about "putting it down with its mother."

While deciding what to do next, Raymond and Martha went to the bank and withdrew all but $500 of the money in Deliphene's account. When they returned to the house, Martha had decided what to do about their "problem."

Martha later claimed that she initially decided to keep Rainelle and take her back to New York with them. But then she realized they would have problems with the child's grandparents. There would also be explanations that had to be created for Raymond's family in New York. So, unable to develop a credible story, Martha decided Rainelle would have to join her mother.

Raymond told the police, "When we came back, Martha said she was going to drown the baby and took her down into the basement."

Martha undressed Rainelle in the basement and thrust her head into the muddy water that filled the hole where Deliphene had been buried. She leaned forward, holding the child's heels, using her body weight to keep the thrashing little girl from coming up for air. "The baby struggled so much I could hardly hold her," she admitted.

Before she had shoved Rainelle's head into the water, Raymond heard the girl crying in the basement. He told detectives, "I ran down and said, 'Let her be! Don't let her suffer anymore!'"

The sight of Martha holding the girl by the legs and forcing her head down into the murky water allegedly unhinged Raymond, and he ran back upstairs.

Martha cruelly called after him, "What's the matter? Why don't you come back down?"

After Rainelle stopped struggling, Martha pulled her out of the water. To be sure she was really dead, Martha battered the little girl's head with a heavy object.

She was dead. Rainelle never moved again.

After calming down, Raymond returned to the basement. While he mixed another batch of cement, Martha wrapped the dead little girl with wire, placed her in her father's footlocker, and shoved it into the hole next to her mother's corpse. Raymond dumped a thin layer of wet cement over the whole thing.

And then they went out to the movies.

They returned to the house around 10:00 P.M. and started packing, planning to leave in the morning. They were nearly finished when they heard a knock on the front door. They had planned to flee the area but weren't fast enough.

It was the police at the door.

BOTH RAYMOND AND MARTHA BEGAN CONFESSING to everything at the jail, initially putting most of the blame for their crimes on the other. Reporters quickly filed their stories, and the two killers soon became known coast-to-coast as the "Lonely Hearts Killers."

The police searched Deliphene Downing's home and recovered the bodies of her and her daughter from the basement. Detectives were sickened by their confessions. One of them, John Vanderband, balled up his fists tightly and muttered to one of the other lawmen, "It makes me want to smash them."

Raymond was prodded to reveal the location of Janet Fay's body in New York. He was convinced he would face the most serious charges in Michigan, not New York, so he decided to cooperate with detectives back east. He directed them to his sister's house and told them how to find the body under the basement floor.

Using pickaxes, two officers broke through the recent cement patch and dug down four feet to reveal Janet Fay's body, clad in a bathrobe and with her knees trussed up to her chest, just as Raymond had left her. Her hair was covered in sticky red blood, and it was apparent a hammer had bashed in her skull. Bruising around her throat showed that she'd been strangled from behind.

Raymond and Martha made their first court appearance on March 2, 1949. Each of them faced separate warrants for the murders of Deliphene and Rainelle.

Eager to catch a glimpse of the infamous killers, a standing-room-only crowd of mostly women packed into the small courtroom. They craned their necks to see the woman who admitted holding a toddler's head under muddy water until she drowned and saw Martha in a black dress with her lips pursed in irritation.

Raymond looked utterly dejected – and he had cause for concern. The Michigan Attorney General, Stephen J. Roth, had asked for a delay in court proceedings to give New York time to extradite the two killers. Michigan didn't have the death penalty, but New York did. If they were sent there and convicted, it would mean the electric chair.

They spent only a few minutes before the judge that day, but it was enough for reporters. By the following day, Martha and Raymond's photos were plastered across front pages all over America.

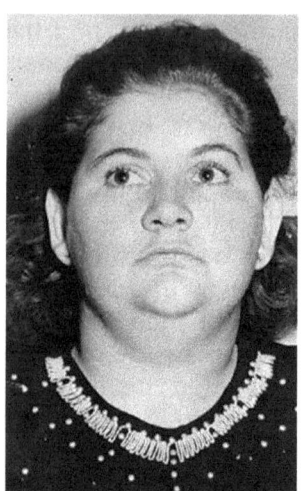

The press loved to hate Martha Beck, but it was difficult to feel sorry for a woman who was clearly a monster.

The confessed killers became overnight media sensations – especially Martha. Depicted as a monster, Martha's weight becomes a theme of the stories and is always mentioned prominently in the text, even if it has little or no relevance to the rest of the story. Of the two killers, writers pegged Martha as the one with the bloodiest hands and the dominant to Raymond's submissive. Her fits of insane jealousy, it was agreed, ultimately led to the murders of Janet Fay, Deliphene, and Rainelle.

A reporter for the *Chicago Daily Tribune* wrote:

Twice in two months, her jealousy flamed into murderous rage. Twice she took preliminary steps in murder and twice she forced her shrinking consort to finish the job. She was an iron woman, coldly and implacably demanding bloody proof from her lover that his attentions to another had after all only been play acting. He could and did atone – on each of these occasions – by killing the woman for whom his protestations for love had been too realistic for his co-conspirator.

The press loved to hate Martha Beck.

And so did everyone else. The unflattering photographs made her situation worse. Her blank expression and her vacant stare as she focused on nothing in particular – the product of exhaustion more than apathy – became the face of a malignant force that would kill an older woman, feed an overdose to a single mother, and drown a child in a muddy puddle, all for the love of a man.

And then there was Martha's smile – in reality, a nervous tic that pulled up one corner of her mouth. The odd effect led reporters to conclude that she felt no remorse for her horrific deeds and smirked whenever she discussed them.

There was one photograph that showed a very different Martha Beck, however. It was taken after her first interrogation, and it revealed her overcome with emotion and her face buried in her hands. The picture was largely ignored by those who wanted to see Martha as cold and devoid of feelings. Reporters all agreed that she seemed "too human" in that one.

But she wouldn't have looked "too human" to anyone if they had looked closely at the three ringers on her fingers in the photo – Martha had taken them from the dead fingers of Janet Fay and Deliphene Downing.

WHEN THE "LONELY HEARTS" CASE HIT NEWSPAPERS across the country, inquiries began pouring in from other law enforcement officers who were trying to track down missing women. Authorities from Chicago, Denver, Minneapolis, St. Louis, and other cities wanted to know if Raymond and Martha had hunted in their towns, too.

When Raymond was arrested, he carried a list of names – reportedly numbering 100 – in his jacket pocket. There were 17 entries check-marked on the list. The first name on the list had been Janet Fay, which led the police to fear that 16 other women lay undiscovered in concrete basement tombs somewhere.

The names on the list contained ages, addresses, and perhaps most telling, a dollar amount after each one. Of course, the figures – money that Raymond expected to steal – suggested that he had engaged in at least some correspondence with the women. But had he and Martha killed them, too?

The police began contacting the women on the list, and luckily, they all seemed to be alive. Of the 17 names, only Janet Fay was under a basement floor.

But if Martha and Raymond hadn't been caught, any – perhaps all – of them could have been next.

RAYMOND AND MARTHA WERE EVENTUALLY extradited to New York, where they were put on trial for the murder of Janet Fay.

Their trial opened on June 9, 1949. It produced a flood of sensational testimony as both defendants, apparently anxious to prove they were insane, unleashed lengthy obscene descriptions of their intense love life. What the court stenographers recorded couldn't be printed even in New York City's most sensational papers.

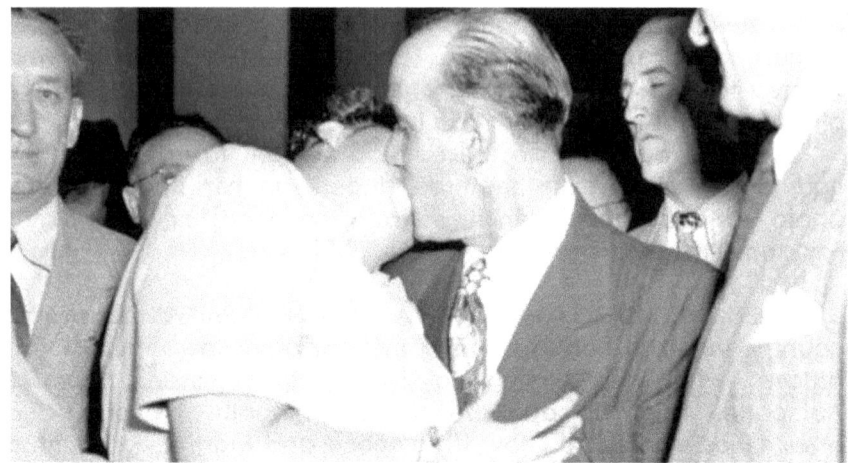

Before the guards could stop her, Martha approached Raymond and kissed him on the mouth. The press ate it up.

But the news reporters could describe how Martha Beck strode forward when called to the witness stand – clad, of course, in a "massive silk dress" –and then suddenly detoured across the courtroom to Raymond. Catching his face in her hands, she pulled it toward her, kissing him on the mouth and, as the guards dragged her away, leaving him with a grin of bright red lipstick.

Following the prosecutor's straightforward presentation of the chilling facts, the defense tried to prove the couple's shared insanity. Martha testified to four suicide attempts, said her mind was blank during the actual killings and denied trying to shield Raymond from legal consequences. A hired psychiatrist declared her mentally unsound and noted that, even if she participated in the killing, she had no idea what she was doing. Defense attorney Herbert Rosenberg, claiming that Martha had killed Janet Fay in a fit of insanity inspired by jealousy, tried to prove that Raymond had no part in the crime.

The jury deliberated for just over 12 hours before returning with first-degree murder verdicts against both defendants.

The death sentence was mandatory.

The pair was packed off to Sing Sing Prison, and their dates with the executioner fell on the same day – March 8, 1951.

Both killers filed multiple appeals, but all failed. The New York State Court of Appeals denied the pair a new trial. Governor Thomas E. Dewey turned down a plea for clemency. The U.S. Supreme Court refused to review the case. Raymond, claiming he received cruel treatment in Sing Sing, was denied a habeas corpus order. At one point, Martha even offered to donate her corpse to science if officials would agree to commute Raymond's sentence. The offer was turned down.

Any animosity between the two of them, when they were blaming each other for the murders, had melted away by the time they landed in prison. Although banned from writing to one another on Death Row, they had found a way to send each other a final love note of sorts on the eve of their executions. They were allowed to make public statements, and each declared their undying love for the other.

They ate their last meals at 5:00 p.m. – Martha had fried chicken, French fries, and a dinner salad, while Raymond had an onion omelet, sliced tomatoes, and almond ice cream. Then they changed into their "death suits." Raymond was given a white shirt and black pants, and Martha wore a house dress. One hour later, a bald patch was shaved into Martha's hair.

Raymond was first into "Old Sparky." When he sat down in the chair, he pulled up the legs of his pants to maintain a crisp crease in his trousers. It took only three minutes to strap him into the seat, and his body jumped slightly when the first surge of electricity went through his body. Three shorter bursts followed, and he was dead just four minutes after entering the death chamber.

Martha walked into the execution chamber just five minutes later. The press couldn't resist one last jab about her weight. "The electric chair was a tight fit," wrote *Daily News* reporter Martin Kivel. A fellow reporter added that "Martha had to wriggle slightly to get her more than 200 pounds between the fatal arms."

A reporter then described her final moments:

Her eyes drifted around the room, and she glanced up as the death mask was lowered. At that moment, a ghostly smile played at the corner of her mouth. She looked to her left where the matrons who had attended her during her long imprisonment

were standing. Two matrons, Mrs. Nellie Evans and Mrs. Bessie Irving, were near tears, fighting for control. Martha seemed to sympathize. Her left eyelid dropped in an unmistakable wink.

A smile and wink? Or were the expressions caused by the facial tics that went with Martha's frayed nerves? The press chose to assume the worst.

Unlike Raymond, Martha's death did not occur quickly. She struggled and strained against the straps as the first jolt hit. Again, at the second shock, she jerked forward. Two more followed before she was finally still.

"I pronounce this woman dead," the prison doctor finally announced.

And the "Lonely Hearts Killers" case silently came to an end.

BADLANDS
Charles Starkweather and Caril Ann Fugate

HE WANTED TO LOOK LIKE JAMES DEAN.

No, that's wrong, he wanted to BE James Dean.

After he saw Rebel Without A Cause, Charlie became obsessed with the actor. He started styling his hair like Dean and dressed like Dean's character in the movie. Charlie related to the character he saw on screen, the troubled, rebellious teenager who couldn't stay out of trouble. Charlie believed the character was a kindred spirit of sorts, someone who had suffered from the same things that Charlie had.

He was a born loser and a no-good delinquent, but James Dean's character in the movie wasn't the kind of kid that would go on to create the kind of horror story that Charlie would. He didn't go on a murderous road trip through the badlands of Nebraska and Wyoming that ended only after 11 people were dead.

No, that was all Charlie. He terrified the public in 1958 by introducing them to a kind of rampage like nothing America had ever seen before.

CHARLES RAYMOND STARKWEATHER WAS BORN IN Lincoln, Nebraska, on November 24, 1938. He was the third of seven children born to Guy and Helen Starkweather. They were an ordinary, working-class family, and there was nothing about them to suggest that one of the Starkweather children would grow up to be a killer.

Charlie's father, Guy, was by all accounts a mild-mannered man. He had been a carpenter all his life but was often unemployed because of severe rheumatoid arthritis in his hands. During times when Guy couldn't work, Helen supplemented the family income as a waitress.

Charlie attended Saratoga Elementary School, Everett Junior High, and Lincoln High School – but his school years were a time of torment for him. He was born with a mild defect that caused his legs to be misshapen, and he also had a speech impediment. These things led to constant teasing from his classmates. Desperately unhappy, he refused to apply himself to his studies, leading to him being labeled a slow learner. Worse yet, he was diagnosed with myopia, which drastically affected his vision for the rest of his life. He walked funny, talked funny, and had to wear glasses – all ammunition for the bullies who preyed on him at school each day.

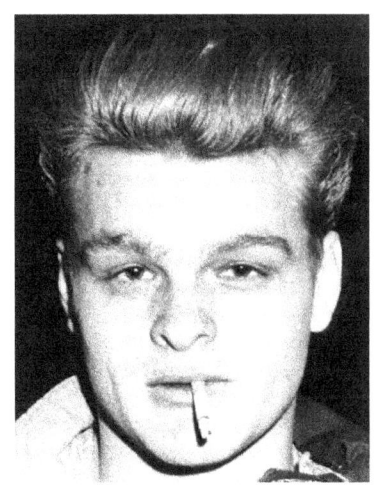

Charles Starkweather

But then Charlie found something that he excelled in – gym class. There, he found a physical outlet for the rage growing inside him. Charlie used his newfound physicality to fight back against those who had bullied him for years. They quickly found the tables had been turned, and Charlie went from someone they teased to someone they feared. Charlie soon went from being considered one of the best-behaved students in school to one of those most in trouble. Students – and even faculty members – were afraid of him.

A high school friend, Bob von Busch, later recalled: "He could be the kindest person you've ever seen. He'd do anything for you if he liked you. He was a hell of a lot of fun to be around, too. Everything was just one big joke to him. But he had this other side. He could be mean as hell, cruel. If he saw some poor guy on the street who was bigger than he was, better looking, or better dressed, he'd try to take the poor bastard down to his size."

Around this time, Charlie attended his first showing of *Rebel Without A Cause* and became obsessed with modeling himself after James Dean, as well as other "rebels" he saw in the movies. He sported a black leather motorcycle jacket, black and white cowboy boots, and sometimes darkened his naturally red hair with black shoe polish.

In 1956, Charlie, then 18, met a 13-year-old named Caril Ann Fugate, a petite, pretty girl whose older sister had been the girlfriend of one of Charlie's friends. He developed a fixation on Caril Ann, and she returned his attention. She swooned over the older, rugged, and handsome boy and spent every minute she could with him.

Caril Ann Fugate

So that he could be closer to Caril Ann, Charlie dropped out of Lincoln High School in his senior year and started working at the Western Union newspaper warehouse. It was the perfect job for him since it was located near Whittier Junior High, where Caril Ann was a student. Being close by, he could visit her every day after school.

Charlie was a lousy worker. His employer later recalled that he had to be told two or three times before getting it right. But being stupid wasn't what made Charlie bad at his job – it was his obsession with Caril Ann.

Caril Ann inadvertently caused Charlie to be kicked out of his family home after she crashed his 1949 Ford into another car. He was trying to teach her to drive. Guy Starkweather, the legal owner of the car, had to pay the damages, and an altercation between the two erupted, ending with Guy forcing Charlie to move out.

Charlie quit his job at the warehouse and started working as a garbage collector. Angry, unhappy, and belligerent, he used the garbage route to scout out homes for robberies. He decided that he wanted to become a criminal and developed a personal philosophy that stayed with him for the rest of his life – that dead people are all on the same level.

Charlie Starweather had no respect for life or death. It was all the same to him.

Finally, his antisocial behavior turned murderous on the evening of November 30, 1957. Robert Colvert was a 21-year-old young man recently discharged from the U.S. Navy. Bobby had married his childhood sweetheart the previous year, and they were now expecting their first child. He worked nights at the Crest Service Station in Lincoln, pumping gas and dreaming about bigger and better things. Everyone who knew him described him as a kind man and excited father-to-be who, like his father, enjoyed carpentry. He was easygoing and always quick to laugh. Unfortunately for Bobby, though, he crossed paths with a loose cannon.

Charlie stopped at the service station with plans to buy a stuffed animal for Caril Ann on credit, but Bobby refused him. Angry, Charlie stomped out of the place but returned around 3:00 A.M. with a shotgun. He demanded the money from the register – around $90 in bills and loose change – and then took Bobby with him. Charlie drove him to an isolated spot along Superior Street, where some kind of altercation occurred. Bobby, probably believing that Charlie was going to kill him, began fighting for his life and was injured in the fight. Charlie put the shotgun to his head and pulled the trigger. Then, he drove off, leaving Bobby to die in an empty field.

Later that Sunday, December 1, Charlie went into a thrift shop where he bought shoes, a jacket, shirts, undershirts, and jockey shorts. He paid for all of it with $10 in loose change that he pocketed from the robbery.

Charlie found himself empowered by committing his first murder. He had a new existence, he believed, and a new purpose in life – to kill the unworthy with impunity.

Although Charlie confessed the murder to Caril Ann, the police had no suspects. They suspected that Bobby had been killed by a transient, and, as a result, they didn't spend much time investigating it.

On December 12, 1957, Bobby was laid to rest in Beaver Crossing Cemetery after a service at the United Methodist Church.

THE THRILL FROM CHARLIE'S FIRST KILL lasted until January 1958, when he lost his job. On Tuesday, January 21, he went to Caril Ann's house, supposedly looking for his girlfriend, although he must have known she was at school. His knock on the door was answered by Caril Ann's stepfather, Marion Bartlett. He was home with his wife, Velda, and their two-year-old daughter, Betty Jean. Neither of Caril Ann's parents cared for the moody and troublesome young man, and since Caril Ann wasn't around to interrupt, they took the opportunity to tell Charlie to stay away from the young girl.

Charlie offered a response – he shot them both to death.

Even worse, he killed Betty Jean, too.

Marion was shot in the head, and Velda was shot in the face and then bludgeoned with a rifle. It's unclear where Betty Jean was killed. Some believe she was initially spared, but her crying got on the nerves of both Charlie and Caril Ann, so she was stabbed to death. Others say that Charlie beat, stabbed, and strangled the little girl before Caril Ann got home from school.

Regardless of when they were killed, all three bodies were placed in outbuildings around the home – Marion in the chicken coop, Velda in the outhouse, and Betty Jean in a trash barrel.

Years later, Caril Ann would claim she had broken up with Charlie on Sunday, January 19. She would also claim that her family was dead when she arrived home, and that Charlie told her that she would be killed too if she didn't cooperate with him. That was her story,  anyway, although based on many of her actions, this was decided long after the events.

The teenage couple lived in the house together for the next six days. The proximity of the three dead bodies didn't seem to bother them. Caril Ann turned away visitors and concerned family members, including her grandmother, sister, and brother-in-law, claiming the entire family was sick with the flu. She posted a "sick note" on the front door, allegedly signed by her mother, asking that the household not be disturbed.

It was only when Caril Ann's grandmother threatened to call the police to check on the family that the couple decided to go on the run.

In Charlie's car, they drove 15 miles out of Lincoln to the small town of Bennet, where a friend of the Starkweather family named August Meyer lived. They turned into the long driveway when Charlie's car bogged down in the mud. He and Caril Ann had no choice but to march to the farmhouse on foot.

August Meyer was a lifelong bachelor, a quiet and friendly man who lived simply on his farm. He offered his horses to assist Charlie in pulling his car out of the mud, but Charlie killed him anyway. The two teenagers were following August to his barn when he raised the shotgun and killed the longtime family friend with both barrels in the back. When August's faithful dog tried to defend his owner, Charlie beat the dog to death, breaking the stock on the shotgun.

Caril Ann later claimed the brutality of August's death – along with the beating of the dog – convinced her that her only option was to go along with whatever Charlie told her to do.

She helped him ransack the farmhouse for food and money, and then, with the car still buried to its axles in the mud, they started walking along the road, hoping to catch a ride.

And they did, later that same night. A kind and unsuspecting couple -- Robert Jensen, 17, and Carol King, 16 – stopped when they saw the pair walking down the highway. Charlie was charming when they first got into the car but soon turned vicious. He ordered Robert to drive to an abandoned storm cellar in Bennet, forcing the couple out of the car and into the cellar. In that dark underground chamber, Charlie shot Robert six times in the head and then tried to rape Carol, stabbing her once in the abdomen as she struggled. She managed to get free, but Charlie shot her down – or did he?

Later, Charlie confesses to killing Robert Jensen, but he claims that it was Caril Ann who, in a jealous rage over seeing Charlie's reaction to the pretty young woman, shot and killed her. Caril Ann claimed that she stayed in the car while Charlie did all the killing. Who was telling the truth?

The couple fled from Bennet in Robert's car and returned to Lincoln. The plan was to find a suitable house where they could hide out. Caril Ann chose the house on January 28 while driving near Lincoln's Country Club. It belonged to C. Lauer Ward, a wealthy industrialist. He and his wife, Clara, had one son, Michael, and thankfully, he was away at school. Like Caril Ann, Michael was only 14.

They slipped into the house and tied up Clara and her hearing-impaired maid, Lilyan Fencl. Charlie and Caril Ann took turns sleeping so that one of them would always be standing guard. At some point, both hostages were stabbed to death, and Charlie also snapped the neck of the family dog. Clara was stabbed in the neck and chest, and Lilyan was tied to a bed and stabbed.

Charlie later admitted to stabbing Clara once, but he accused Caril Ann of inflicting the rest of the wounds on her body. He also claimed that Caril Ann had stabbed Lilyan, too.

When Lauer Ward returned home that night, Charlie was waiting. He shot him in the head and killed him instantly.

Then, with Caril Ann's help, he gathered up all the cash and jewelry he could find, and they loaded it into the Wards' 1956 Packard. They fled Lincoln, leaving victims eight, nine, and ten behind them. They planned to head for Washington state, where one of Charlie's brothers lived.

It was the murder of the wealthy businessman, his wife, and their maid that created outrage in the community. Every law enforcement agency in the region began a house-by-house search for the killers. Governor Victor E. Anderson contacted the Nebraska National Guard, and the Lincoln police chief called for a block-by-block search of the city. Frequent sightings of the two were often reported, but the teenage killers stayed one step ahead of the law.

Charlie realized that the Wards' Packard was too high profile, and they needed to find a new vehicle. They got lucky about 10 hours outside Lincoln when they saw a traveling salesman named Merle Collison sleeping in his Buick outside Douglas, Wyoming. Charlie tapped on the window to wake him up, then demanded he leave the vehicle. The salesman did everything Charlie told him to do, but the couple killed him anyway. Charlie later claimed that his gun jammed and that it was Caril Ann who finished Collison off.

Charlie climbed behind the wheel of the Buick and tried to start it. But the car had a push-pedal emergency brake, something new to Charlie. He managed to start the car, but it stalled as he tried to drive away.

Seeing two cars stopped, a passing motorist named Joe Sprinkle pulled over to help. Charlie, confused by the new parking brake, asked Joe for assistance. But then Joe noticed Collison's body stuff in the car – and the gun that was pointed at his face. But Joe Sprinkle wasn't afraid of much. Outweighing Charlie and standing at least a head taller, Joe decided to put up a fight, and he managed to wrestle the gun from the teenage killer.

At that same moment, Natrona Deputy Sheriff William Romer arrived. As he was stepping out of his vehicle, Caril Ann suddenly jumped out of Collison's car and ran toward the deputy, screaming, "He's going to kill me! He's crazy! He just killed a man!"

Charlie, now unarmed, jumped into the Packard he'd tried to abandon and roared away, heading toward Douglas. After being told by Caril Ann that the escaping man was Charles Starkweather, Romer stayed behind and radioed for help. A

Charlie's last stolen car – the police filled the Packard full of holes.

roadblock was immediately set up at the Douglas city limits. Charlie blew through it, leading the authorities on a 100-mph chase through the town streets. Officers fired shots at the Packard, punching holes in the metal body. Just east of town, a shot shattered the back window, and Charlie slammed on the brakes, coming to a screeching halt. He sat motionless behind the wheel for a few stress-filled moments as officers called out threats and fired warning shots, and then he surrendered.

Flying glass from the shattered back window had nicked Charlie's ear and right hand, leading him to believe he had been shot. The cold and brutal killer, who had no value for the life of anyone else, apparently valued his own enough to give up when death he might die. Converse County Sheriff Earl Heflin later told the press, "He thought he was bleeding to death. That's why he stopped. That's the kind of yellow son of a bitch he is."

Charlie later claimed he only gave up because he was out of ammunition.

THE NEXT DAY, JANUARY 29, 1958, CHARLIE appeared before a Wyoming justice of the peace to be charged with the murder of Merle Collison. Governor Milward Simpson had already publicly announced that if Charlie were convicted and sentenced to death by a Wyoming jury, he would commute the sentence. Simpson was opposed to the death penalty. Faced with this dilemma, the Wyoming state's attorney let it be known that he would defer to Nebraska prosecutors. Governor Simpson, as anti-death-penalty as he was, quickly signed extradition papers to send Charlie back to Nebraska, a state whose governor had no aversion to using the electric chair.

Two days later, Charlie was back in Nebraska. He stayed in jail until May, while the trial began. Against his wishes, his attorneys attempted an insanity defense, but the jury didn't buy it. On May 23, 1958, he was found guilty and sentenced to death for the murder of Robert Jensen.

Caril Ann's entanglement with the legal system would be much more complicated. Nervous, upset, and said to be in a state of shock at the time of her surrender, she had to be sedated at the jail in Douglas. The following morning, she cried for her mother and wondered why she couldn't call her parents. Sheriff Heflin – whose shot had shattered the back window of Charlie's car – initially believed that Caril Ann had no idea her family was dead. He was present on January 31 when Caril Ann was told her family was dead and saw her break down.

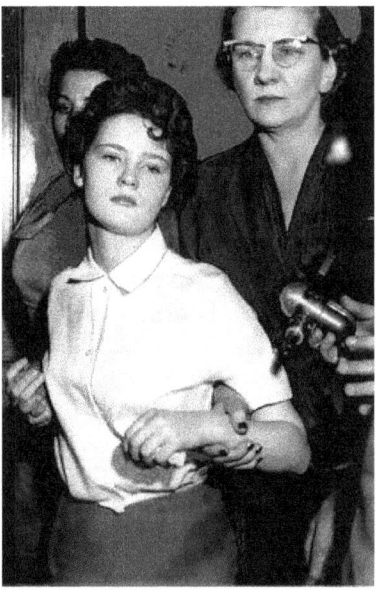

Caril Ann under arrest. Her experience with the legal system was much more complicated than Charlie's. **Was she a victim, a hostage, or a willing accomplice?**

Even Charlie first insisted that Caril Ann was a hostage and had nothing to do with the crime spree. However, Natrona Deputy Sheriff William Romer – the officer Caril Ann surrendered to – disputed this. He said that Caril Ann told him that her parents were dead and that she had watched them die. When Sheriff Heflin found this out, he searched through the items taken from Caril Ann when she was arrested and discovered newspaper clippings about her family's death had been in her pockets. Nebraska prosecutors responded to this information by charging the young woman with murder.

By the time Caril Ann went to trial, Charlie had changed his story, clearly stating that his girlfriend had played an active role in the murders and had personally slain some of the victims herself. When her trial began in November 1958, she became the youngest woman in U.S. history to be charged with first-degree murder.

In the courtroom, Caril Ann's attorneys continued to claim that she was held hostage by Charlie. He threatened to kill her family, and she was unaware they were dead. But Judge Harry A. Spencer – and the jury – didn't believe her. She'd had too many chances to escape, yet she never did. Caril Ann was convicted of murder and sentenced to life in prison.

Charlie wasn't even that lucky. At 12:04 A.M. on June 25, 1959, he was executed in the Nebraska electric chair. Half an hour before the execution, the doctor who was supposed to pronounce Charlie dead, B.A. Finkel suffered a fatal heart attack.

Charlie was indifferent towards his execution. He offered no last words but wrote in a letter from prison to his parents: "Dad, I'm not real sorry for what I did for the first time me and Caril had more fun."

He was unrepentant to the very end.

Charlie was buried in Wyuka Cemetery in Lincoln along with five of his victims – the Bartlett family and the Wards.

Caril Ann was considered a model prisoner during her years behind bars, but her role in Charlie's killing spree remains controversial even today.

WHILE IN PRISON, CARIL ANN WAS CONSIDERED a model inmate. She was paroled in 1976, after serving nearly 18 years, and left Nebraska for Lansing, Michigan. She changed her name and lived a quiet existence as a janitorial assistant at a local hospital. Except for a 1996 radio appearance that she made after the state refused to pardon her, she never spoke about the events of 1958. She married in 2007 but was widowed after an auto accident only six years later.

The murder spree of Charles Starkweather and Caril Ann Fugate was the first of its kind in post-World War II America. It was also the first major crime incident of the television era. Reporters and journalists flooded Wyoming and Nebraska, broadcasting to viewers the horrible details of the violence left in the couple's wake. Thanks to the sensational reporting, the people of Nebraska and the surrounding region lived in a state of terror while they were on the loose.

Unlike many other murderers that have been glamorized over the years, Charlie wasn't all that interesting. He wasn't particularly smart, and he struggled with his own feelings of inferiority, evidenced by his romancing of a 13-year-old girl. Starkweather killed out of anger and envy and a demand to be noticed. He despised the normal lives of the people he killed because their normality was what he wanted for himself. He wanted to be seen as a tough guy, but he was just a bully who enjoyed causing pain for others.

Caril Ann's role in the murder spree was much more complex. She was barely 14 when the rampage began, but she'd been involved with Charlie for months. She could have left Lincoln with him as a desperate means to stay alive after seeing her family slaughtered – or she could have also been a willing participant until it seemed their capture was inevitable.

If what she claimed about being manipulated and held captive by Charlie was true, then how do we explain what happened before her family was killed? She claimed she broke up with Charlie on January 19, 1958, but she knew he had killed service station attendant Bobby Colvert almost two months earlier. She'd later say that she only knew that Charlie robbed the service station. She didn't know about the murder. This is impossible, however. The murder was covered in newspapers and talked about around town. So, why did she wait so long to break up with him – if she actually did? And why didn't she go to the police then? She could have saved ten lives if she had.

The biggest issue with Caril Ann's story is one that confused investigators then and now – why didn't she escape when she had the opportunity? According to her version of events, she waited in the car while Charlie killed Robert Jensen and Carol King in the abandoned storm cellar. If the keys were in the car, why didn't she leave? If Charlie took the keys, why didn't she escape on foot? When they returned to Lincoln, they slept in shifts at the Ward house. Why didn't she run – and possibly save the lives of Clara Ward and Lilyan Fencl – while Charlie was asleep?

In 2012, a copy of an investigative file was discovered that had been compiled by a Lancaster County deputy sheriff in Nebraska named Robert G. Anderson. In the report, he stated that Charlie and Caril Ann had stopped at a service station near Roca, Nebraska, on January 27, 1958, around 1:00 P.M. While Charlie was talking with a mechanic about repairing a tire, Caril Ann had gone into an attached diner and ordered four hamburgers for the road.

According to the waitress on duty, she sat down at the counter and was very calm and nonchalant. She waited about 10 minutes for the burgers to be cooked and never once indicated that she had been kidnapped or was in any kind of distress. The waitress added that three men were sitting at the counter, too, and she didn't say anything to them either.

By the way, that was the same morning that August Meyer had been murdered. Soon after leaving the diner and service station, the couple would also murder Robert Jensen and Carol King.

Caril Ann always insisted that she never played a part in the murders, but there is no one left alive who can confirm or deny her statements. There seems to have been good reason – in my opinion – why the judge in her case, law enforcement officials, prosecutors, and jury at her trial didn't believe her side of the story.

Do I think that Caril Ann Fugate would have been involved in a multi-state murder spree if she hadn't been influenced and manipulated by Charles Starkweather? No, I don't.

But do I think she had a role in the murders? Yes, I do. She was a very young and impressionable girl, and Charlie knew precisely how to make her do what he wanted.

But there's one more question worth asking – would Charles Starkweather have gone on a rampage across Nebraska and Wyoming if he didn't have Caril Ann – the love of his life – at his side? Maybe, or maybe not.

I sometimes wonder what would have happened if the two of them had never met, if Charlie hadn't tried to buy that stuffed animal at the service station, or if....

Well, there's no sense in continuing. They did meet, and 11 people died for their love -- a reckless, terrifying, utterly destroying kind of love that manages to ruin the lives of everyone who came into contact with it.

THE SHOE FETISH KILLER'S WIFE
Jerry and Darcie Brudos

"HOW DID YOU KNOW I WOULD BRING YOU BACK HOME AND NOT TAKE YOU TO THE RIVER AND STRANGLE YOU?"

That was the question the strange little man asked his prospective date in 1969. When she was shocked, he pretended it had been a joke, but the young woman didn't think it was funny. When she made the man leave, she called the police, and a short time later, a search warrant was obtained for the home of Jerome "Jerry" Brudos and his wife, Darcie.

When police investigators opened the door to the secret, locked workshop he had built onto his house, Jerry was arrested, and the murders of the "Shoe Fetish Killer" – a serial murderer that no one knew existed at the time – came to an end.

JERRY BRUDOS WAS BORN IN THE SMALL SOUTH DAKOTA town of Webster in 1939. Times were hard for everyone in town, including the Brudos, who had suffered from the Great Depression for nearly a decade. Not long after Jerry was born, they gave up their farm and moved to Oregon, but the move didn't change much. Jerry's father, Henry, was forced to work two jobs and had little time to spend with his family.

And this left Jerry mostly with his mother, Eileen. He had been born the youngest of two sons – something the stern and overbearing woman never let him forget. She had hoped for a girl and was disappointed when she got Jerry instead. Throughout his childhood, she constantly reminded him what a burden he was. When she wasn't berating him about not being a girl, she neglected and ignored him, leaving the imaginative young boy to his own devices.

Jerry Brudos

One day, while exploring a local junkyard, Jerry found a discarded high-heeled shoe. Fascinated, he took it home with him – the start of something he would do many times in the coming years. He began wearing them secretly around the house, but when his mother caught him, she flew into a rage and insisted he get rid of them. When she discovered he didn't, she burned the shoes and made Jerry watch as they went up in flames.

The incident created Jerry's obsession with the forbidden, and by the time he started elementary school, he was sneaking into neighbors' homes and stealing women's shoes and underwear. He even attempted to steal his teacher's extra pair of classroom shoes at one point. He was eventually caught and punished, but it did nothing to discourage his fetish.

And if it had just remained a fetish, several lives would have been saved. Unfortunately, though, it didn't.

By 1955, the Brudos family had climbed out of poverty and had moved into a pleasant middle-class neighborhood. Jerry had just turned 16 and found himself living next door to a family with three teenage daughters. He not only spied on the girls through the windows of their home, but he began stealing their underwear from the clothesline.

After the theft of the underwear was reported, Jerry convinced one of the girls that he was working to solve the crime with the police, and he invited her over to discuss the case. When she came over, Jerry left her alone momentarily and returned wearing a mask with a knife in his hand and forced her to undress.

With her clothing on the floor, Jerry took photographs of her before leaving the room. He quickly returned just as the girl was ready to flee. Before she could raise the alarm, he quickly told her that a masked man had broken into the house and locked him up. Was she okay? It was a ridiculous story, but the young woman was so ashamed about what happened that she refused to talk about the incident.

Emboldened by this event, Jerry soon attacked another young woman, physically forcing her to strip for him before being interrupted by a couple out for an evening walk. The police were called, and the investigation led to a search of Jerry's room, where the shoe collection, stolen underwear, and nude photos of his neighbor were found.

Jerry was sent to the psychiatric ward at the Oregon State Hospital, where he described his fantasies to psychiatrists. He most often returned to one that involved an underground prison where he could keep captive girls that he could have any way he wanted, any time he wanted.

None of the doctors were concerned by what they heard. They believed that Jerry's dark sexual fantasies would pass as he got older, but they did diagnose him as borderline schizophrenic. They also blamed his mother's mistreatment for his resentment of women. He was confined at the hospital for nine months, and when he turned 18, he was released.

This would prove to be a fatal mistake.

Jerry returned home, graduated high school, and enrolled at Oregon State University with plans to be a mechanical and electrical engineer. He missed so many classes, though, that he was kicked out. After that, he joined the Army, but after revealing his sexual fantasies to a military psychiatrist, he was discharged due to "bizarre obsessions."

Back home, Jerry returned to his old habits of stealing shoes and underwear and assaulting young women. When he tried to abduct one girl, she fainted, and he stole her shoes instead.

In 1961, Jerry became an electronics technician and started working at a local radio station. It was there where he met his future wife, an attractive 17-year-old named Darcie, who liked the idea of dating a man who was five years older. The two of them soon began dating, and Jerry finally lost his virginity at the age of 23. And then Darcie became pregnant.

Darcie's parents disapproved of their daughter's relationship with Jerry but reluctantly agreed to their marriage in the spring of 1962. They settled down in a suburb of Salem, Oregon, and

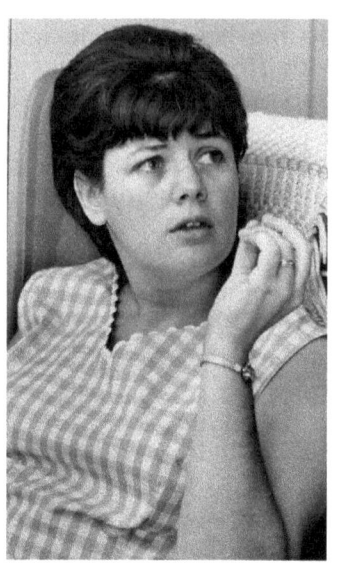

Darcie Brudos

soon, the couple had two children together. Jerry seemed to stay out of trouble at the beginning of the marriage but began making requests from his wife that seemed a little odd -- like having Darcie clean the house nude except for a pair of high-heeled pumps. Darcie agreed, flattered by the attention and by Jerry's constant need to take nude photographs of her.

Darcie knew that he was printing the photos because he'd built a darkroom in his workshop. He had added an extra room to the house during their first year of marriage and called it his workshop. She wasn't allowed inside, however. Jerry demanded his privacy and would disappear into the room for hours. She had no idea what he was doing in there – not at first – but she was sometimes startled by the strange noises from behind the locked door.

Jerry had started complaining of migraine headaches and "blackouts," and the only thing that seemed to help was for him to go on nighttime prowls around the neighborhood. Darcie wasn't sure where he went, but he'd always vanish into his workshop when he returned. She wasn't yet aware that he would spend his time behind the workshop door putting on the high-heeled shoes that he stole and wearing the lacey underwear that he'd found hanging on clotheslines.

Then, one night, soon after the birth of his and Darcie's second child, Jerry spotted an attractive young woman walking down a street in Portland. He followed her to her apartment and then stood and watched her through the windows. Hours passed, but Jerry did nothing until he was sure that she was asleep. His plan was only to steal her used underwear, but when she was startled awake by an intruder, he attacked and raped her.

She wasn't the only one. Other reports from the area came in about women being attacked, sexually assaulted, and robbed of their shoes and underwear. There's no record to say this attacker was Jerry, but everything about the crimes seems to fit his pattern.

Meanwhile, Jerry was still convincing Darcie to take part in his sexual fantasies. As things escalated with other women, they escalated with Darcie, too. Jerry would often dress in his wife's underwear when they had sex and had become increasingly rough with her. The photographs that he took of her became more explicit, but Darcie still wasn't allowed to see the finished prints that were displayed in her husband's workshop.

Linda Slawson

And then, on January 26, 1968, Jerry committed his first murder. A 19-year-old woman named Linda Slawson was making college money selling encyclopedias in the neighborhood and made the mistake of stopping at the Brudos home. Jerry acted interested to get her inside, and then he knocked her down and strangled her to death.

There is no record of where Darcie was when this incident occurred – no one has ever really asked – but it seems likely that she and the children were home. Darcie didn't work outside of the house once she and Jerry were married, so she had to be there, where Jerry led Linda Slawson into his workshop. She had to have noticed that the young woman didn't come back out.

And there's no way she didn't notice that Jerry spent an inordinate amount of time in his workshop over the next few days.

Jerry dressed Linda's corpse in the lingerie that he'd been stealing for years and placed high-heeled shoes on her feet. He took numerous photographs of her in a variety of outfits while also repeatedly having sex with her body. Before he was finished with her, Jerry cut off one of Linda's feet with a hacksaw and placed it in the basement freezer – the same freezer from which Darcie removed meat and vegetables that she'd prepare for dinner. There's no way that she could've missed it – and yet, she remained silent.

From time to time, Jerry would take Linda's foot from the freezer, place a shoe on it, and then masturbate. The rest of the young woman's body was thrown from a bridge into the Willamette River.

Once Jerry had killed, he couldn't stop, but he did wait several months before claiming another victim. In the meantime, he had moved his family to Salem, Oregon, and into a new house. It was a rundown, unattractive place, but it did have a ready-made location for Jerry's new workshop – a detached garage that was located a dozen or so yards from the house.

Jan Whitney

But Jerry did kill again. He took his second victim, University of Oregon student Jan Whitney, on November 26, 1968. She was traveling home for Thanksgiving when her car broke down. Jerry happened to be driving by at the time and pulled over to help. Unable to get the car started, he offered her a ride to the nearest telephone. But once she was in his car, Jerry strangled her and then had sex with her corpse.

Then he took her home to where Darcie and the kids were.

For the next five days, Jan's body hung from a meat hook in Jerry's garage workshop. He dressed her corpse, took photos of her, and had sex with the body.

Then, he took a break so that he could go on a Thanksgiving weekend holiday with the family. While they were away, a traffic accident occurred on the street where they lived. A car sped out of control and crashed into the garage with such force that it caused a large split in the wooden wall. Several police officers were on the scene but never looked inside the garage. If they had, they would have spotted Jan's corpse hanging there, and Jerry's secret life would have come to an end.

But they didn't, and Jerry kept killing. The close call seemed to embolden him, and he started to think he was too clever to get caught. Soon after his return from the holiday trip, he disposed of Jan's corpse in the river. Before he did, though, he cut off her right breast, intending to use it as a mold for making paperweights.

When Jerry had killed Linda Slawson, she'd accidentally shown up at his house. He'd found Jan Whitney by chance. Now, Jerry was ready to go out and hunt down his next victim. Hanging around in a Salem department store parking garage on March 27, 1969, he grabbed his next victim, 19-year-old Karen Sprinker, and brought her home to his workshop garage. He didn't kill her right away. Instead, he forced her to model various items from his undergarment collection so he could photograph her. When he got bored of that, he put a noose around her neck, raised her a few inches off the floor, and went into the house to join Darcie and the kids for dinner. When he returned, Karen was dead. He had sex with her corpse, cut off both of her breasts and then dropped the body into the Long Tom River.

Karen Sprinker

There had been something unsatisfying about Karen's murder, and within a few weeks, Jerry was looking for another victim. Darcie had noticed his growing agitation but kept silent. She was even more curious about the garage than she'd been about her husband's original workshop. She knew it wasn't normal to have a garage where the family car was never parked, but she never spoke up. Darcie knew about Jerry's sexual fantasies, but he no longer bothered her with the photos and unusual requests that he'd made of her in the past. She had to have known that something was going on in the garage that Jerry spent so many hours in. Perhaps she just assumed he was having an affair and didn't care.

Or maybe she knew that something much worse than an affair was happening but feared for her life – or perhaps she was just happy that Jerry wasn't pressuring her anymore with his sexual demands.

We'll probably never know.

LESS THAN A MONTH AFTER KILLING KAREN, Jerry attacked another woman in another parking garage. Sharon Wood, though, didn't go down quietly. She fought back, and after managing to bite Jerry's thumb so badly she drew blood, the would-be killer ran off.

A few days later, he tried again, this time choosing a much younger target – 12-year-old Gloria Smith. She was walking to school when he approached her with a fake gun and started marching her to his car. But Gloria acted quickly and ran to a woman that she saw working in her garden. Jerry fled the scene.

Linda Salee

After failing twice – even being outwitted by a young girl – he decided that a fake pistol wasn't enough, so he purchased a police badge. He'd use the badge to fool his final victim, Linda Salee. He approached her in a Portland shopping center parking lot and accused her of shoplifting. For whatever reason, Linda went along with it, and Jerry shoved her into the backseat of the family car and told her she was going to the police station. Instead, though, she was taken to his garage workshop, where she was bound and gagged while Jerry went into the house for dinner with the family.

As soon as he finished eating, he returned to the garage and discovered that Linda had managed to untie herself but hadn't been able to escape the locked garage. Jerry quickly overpowered her, tied her more tightly, and then suspended her from the ceiling. After removing her clothes, he photographed, raped, mutilated, and strangled her, then tossed her body in the Long Tom River.

Linda was Jerry's fourth victim, and yet the police hadn't linked any of the murders together for one simple reason – they didn't even know the women were dead. So far, each had been reported missing, but their bodies had not been found. However, the final two girls would prove to be Jerry's undoing.

On May 10, 1969, a fisherman near Corvallis, Oregon, found a body floating in the Long Tom River. It turned out to be Linda Salee. Two days later, police divers found the body of Karen Sprinker near the same spot. Both women had been tied to auto parts to weigh them down, but it hadn't worked.

Jerry was unconcerned when news of the murders spread through the community. He was convinced the police had nothing that could link him to the bodies – but he was wrong.

When he'd tied the women up, he'd used an unusual knot, one that was often used by electricians when they pulled wiring through a house.

THE INVESTIGATION INTO THE MURDERS OF LINDA AND KAREN began with detectives questioning Karen's fellow students at the University of Oregon. Several of them revealed that they had received phone calls from a man claiming to be a lonely Vietnam veteran looking for a date. Only one student had accepted his offer. She told detectives that the man acted strangely and asked her, "How did you know I would bring you back home and not take you to the river and strangle you?"

Detectives asked her to set up a second date with the man so they could question him, and she gave Jerry Brudos – the mystery date – a call. When he arrived for the date, he didn't find a pretty college girl waiting for him. He found the police instead. Jerry denied knowing anything about any murders, and detectives decided to release him – for now. Something bothered them about the man, though, and they decided they needed to look a little closer. Meanwhile, other detectives were looking into cases of women who had been attacked in the area and called in one of them to look at photographs of possible suspects. Almost by accident, she picked out Jerry Brudos as her attacker.

A background check revealed not only Jerry's occupation as an electrician but also his teenage record of harassing young women. They decided to pay a visit to the Brudos' home when they noticed a piece of rope that looked very similar to the rope that had been tied around the bodies found in the river. Seeing the investigators' interest, Jerry offered them a sample of it to take with them.

It would later turn out to be a perfect match – and all the cops needed for a search warrant of the house and Jerry's garage workshop.

But before the warrant could be served, Jerry, sensing the police were finally closing in, decided to make a run for the Canadian border. Next to him, in the passenger seat of the car, was his wife, Darcie, who was more than willing to flee the country with him. I believe that anyone who thinks she knew nothing about what was going on is sadly mistaken. I don't believe that Jerry could've gotten away with his macabre hobbies for as long as he did without a silent Darcie at his side.

Unfortunately for the couple, they were spotted by the Oregon State Police and taken into custody. At first, Jerry was charged with the relatively minor charge of armed assault against 12-year-old Gloria Smith, but he would eventually become very talkative while in custody.

On May 25, 1969, detectives searched the Brudos' home, and in his garage workshop, they found evidence that would put him behind bars for the rest of his life – photos of the dead women, shoes, bras, underwear, and, of course, the gruesome trophies that he kept.

Confronted with the evidence, Jerry confessed to the murders on the spot. He took great pleasure in providing detailed accounts of the murders he'd committed, showing no remorse for anything he'd done. He compared the women he'd killed to candy wrappers. As he told one detective, "Once you're done with them, you just discard them. Why would you not discard them? You don't have any more use for them."

On June 27, he entered a guilty plea in court, and he received three life sentences. While in prison, Jerry often wrote to shoe companies and requested catalogs. Prison authorities could do nothing about it. Women's shoe catalogs were not on the list of banned materials – but maybe they should have been.

When Jerry was not perusing his catalog collection, he was busy filing appeals to regain his freedom – but none of them worked. He became eligible for parole in 2005, but as the date grew closer, it became increasingly clear that he'd never be a free man again.

He died in prison in 2006 of liver cancer at the age of 67. But the memory of his crimes lives on, leaving a permanent mark on the town of Salem, Oregon. The community was stunned by heinous murders committed by the "Shoe Fetish Slayer," and they still serve as a reminder that evil can lurk in even the most unassuming places.

AND PERHAPS IN THE MOST UNASSUMING PEOPLE, TOO.

Jerry Brudos was obviously a monster, but what about his wife, Darcie? On the surface, she appears to be another victim of her terrible husband, but was she really? She was aware of Jerry's fantasies and desires and had to know that his hours alone in his secret workshop could lead to something horrific. But she never spoke up, and when Jerry tried to flee the country when he knew the police were closing in, she happily fled with him. Was this the actions of an accomplice or a woman so brainwashed that she refused to see the truth?

Darcie Brudos photographed in her delight at being cleared of being her husband's accomplice in the murders.

On one hand, we have Darcie being manipulated by her husband. There are reports that Jerry installed an intercom system so that Darcie would ask his permission before she entered the garage. When questioned by the police, she claimed she never heard anything unusual coming from either of Jerry's workshops.

If that's true, then we have to believe that Darcy wasn't just manipulated but naïve and likely stupid. She ignored some very obvious warning signs about her husband's activities, including the time he brought home a woman's breast, cast in resin, to use as a paperweight. And let's not forget the severed foot that she couldn't have missed in the family's freezer. She knew that Jerry often left their home late at night and returned with women's clothing and shoes. She also knew about the darkroom, where he developed photos of nude women – including pictures of Darcie herself. However, she claimed not to have been bothered by any of this unusual behavior and never suspected it would lead to anything criminal.

Do you find her innocence as hard to swallow as I do?

If so, we're not alone. Darcie was arrested along with Jerry and charged as an accomplice. A neighbor claimed she saw Jerry and Darcy carrying an unconscious woman, but a defense attorney shredded that testimony at trial. Had it been a lie or just clever lawyering? It wouldn't matter. With no other evidence against her, the case against Darcie was dismissed.

But, as we know, that doesn't make her innocent.

Freed from custody, Darcie filed for divorce, changed her name, and took her children across the country, far away from their father. Her new name has never been released to the public, so it's unknown at the time of this writing if she is alive or dead.

Frankly, I'm not sure it matters. No matter how you look at it, I believe that Darcie Brudos should have been charged as an accomplice after the fact. It's hard to argue against the fact that she got away with murder.

THE "SUNSET STRIP KILLERS"
Doug Clark and Carol Bundy

ON JUNE 23, 1980, A MAN WALKING PAST AN ALLEY in the Los Angeles neighborhood of Studio City spotted a well-made pine box lying abandoned near a dumpster. Curious, he lifted the lid and looked inside – something he would regret for the rest of his life.

Wrapped in a stained t-shirt that was printed with the words "Daddy's Little Girl" was the head of a 20-year-old woman named Exxie Wilson.

The terrifying discovery would shock the city of Los Angeles and send the police department on a frantic hunt for a serial killer who was stalking the fabled Sunset Strip. But it wasn't just one killer they were looking for – it was two.

The manhunt would further add to the chaos of the summer of 1980 in L.A. – a season of record-high temperatures and rampant crime that had punk fans fighting with motorists as they spilled out of the clubs on the Strip.

In the middle of this, a man with strange eyes and a plump, unassuming woman were driving around Hollywood, looking for their next victim.

THE MAN WITH THE STRANGE EYES WAS Douglas Clark, who had been born in Pennsylvania in 1948. From a well-to-do family, he was the third of five children born to a retired Navy Admiral turned international Naval Intelligence officer. His father moved frequently during Doug's childhood, and he later boasted of living in 37 countries. In 1958, his father left the Navy and took a civilian position as an engineer with the Transport Company of Texas, but the family continued its nomadic lifestyle.

Douglas Clark in a photograph from the Culver Military Academy

Doug was sent to the exclusive International School of Geneva and later attended the Culver Military Academy while his father continued working overseas.

However, beneath the veneer of a comfortable life, Doug began exhibiting signs of disturbing behavior, even as a young boy. When he was a teenager, he reportedly recorded having sex with girls at school without their knowledge and began developing fantasies about rape, murder, mutilation, and necrophilia.

After graduating in 1967, Doug enlisted in the U.S. Air Force and was stationed in Colorado and Ohio. After being discharged, he drifted for the next decade, sometimes working as a mechanic. He eventually ended up in Los Angeles. His first job was as a steam plant operator for the Los Angeles Department of Water and Power, but he got bored and quit one day. He then became a boiler operator at the Jergens soap factory in Burbank but was fired for making violent threats against co-workers.

While living in L.A., Doug spent his nights in local clubs and bars, searching for lonely, older women he could seduce out of their money. He was a charismatic man, and he used his charm to manipulate his victims. He dubbed himself the "king of the one-night stands" and immersed himself in the nightlife scene around the Sunset Strip. Through these places, he became acquainted with sex workers who operated in the area, allowing him to seek out the kind of sex that he couldn't get from the women he was using for money and a place to sleep.

Then, on Christmas Day 1979, he noticed an awkward, solitary woman in a bar called Little Nashville. He began making small talk and was soon getting to know Carol Bundy, a vocational nurse at the Valley Medical Center in Van Nuys and an overweight mother of two who had left an abusive husband earlier that year.

She was at the bar that night to watch singer and apartment manager John Robert Murray, her on-again, off-again married boyfriend.

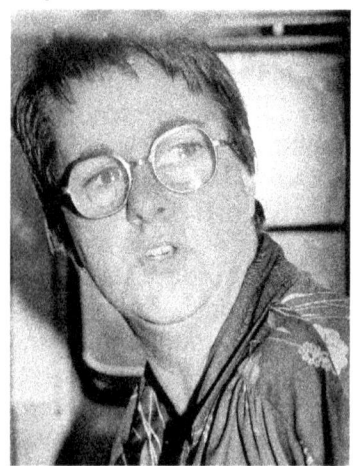

Carol Bundy

But Doug Clark knew an easy mark when he saw one, and he began drawing Carol into what would become one of the most horrific killing sprees in the city's history.

CAROL BUNDY'S LIFE HAD NEVER BEEN ANYTHING but traumatic. Her tragic cycle of abuse began at a young age. She was born in August 1942, and her parents were both violent alcoholics. Her mother died when she was a child, and her father began raping her when she was 11. After Carol's father remarried, he put her in various foster homes, and even after she escaped from that nightmare, the cycle of trauma continued. When she was just 17 years old, she married a 56-year-old man, who subjected her to physical brutality, perpetuating the cycle of abuse that had plagued her from childhood.

By the time Carol met Doug at the age of 37, she had recently escaped a third marriage to an abusive man with whom she'd had two sons. She was also involved in an affair with Jack Murray, the part-time country singer, and had been so taken with him that she'd once tried to bribe Murray's wife into leaving him.

It was during Murray's Christmas show at Little Nashville that she met Doug Clark. Carol was smitten with him, and a short time later, Doug moved into her Van Nuys apartment.

AS THE RELATIONSHIP BETWEEN THEM deepened, Doug began disclosing his most disturbing and violent sexual fantasies to Carol. Rather than recoiling in horror from what she heard, she embraced and supported his desires, cementing the bond between them and creating a sinister partnership.

And if it had only been shared fantasies, kept between the two of them, there would be no story to tell – but it wasn't.

Together, Doug and Carol began molesting an 11-year-old girl who lived in the same apartment complex, photographing the abuse. This became the start of their deviant acts, but it would not be the end of them.

How their fantasies progressed into dark reality remains unknown – since Doug and Carol were both pathological liars – but it seems that Doug first began trolling the Sunset Strip area on his own. His first victim was a teenage sex worker named Marnette Comer. Then he murdered teenage stepsisters Cynthia Chandler and Gina Marano, who were known for running away from their Huntington Beach home and hanging around the Sunset Strip neighborhood.

Marnette Comer

After describing this double murder to Carol, she decided to join him on his next deadly outing.

Together, the two of them cruised for a vulnerable prostitute and finally found one on Highland Avenue in Hollywood. She got into the front seat, and Carol was sitting behind her with a pistol

Teenage stepsisters, Cynthia Chandler and (Left) Gina Marano

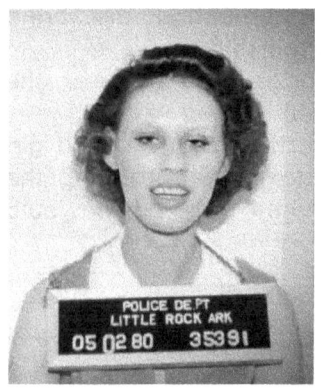

Exxie Wilson

in her hand. When the time came, though, Carol couldn't pull the trigger. She claimed she gave the gun to Doug, who shot the girl in the head. Carol undressed the body while Doug drove along the Hollywood Freeway until he came to a grave road. When they were finished with her, the prostitute's body was dumped under some bushes.

Now, with a taste for blood and danger, Carol began accompanying Doug on every hunt. The rampage claimed several young women – mostly sex workers – who were lured into their vehicle, sexually assaulted, and killed. The depravity of their acts extended into Doug's desire for necrophilia.

But the harrowing number of victims – and the careless way they were disposed of – could only continue for so long before someone noticed.

On June 12, the bodies of Cynthia Chandler and Gina Marano were discovered by a highway worker who was picking up trash near the Forest Lawn Drive on-ramp to the Ventura Freeway.

A few days later, the torso of Exxie Wilson, who had recently come to L.A. from Arkansas and became a sex worker on the Sunset Strip, was found near a dumpster in the Valley. The body of her friend and fellow prostitute Karen Jones was found behind a steakhouse in Burbank.

Then, Exxie's head was found in that handmade wooden box.

The LAPD was sure it had a serial killer on its hands – and it's no surprise they thought so. During the 1970s, L.A. had become a city gripped with fear as more than 20 serial murderers were operating simultaneously within a five-mile radius. Killers like "The Hillside Strangler" and "The Freeway Killer" became household names as their crimes created panic among the city's residents. As body after body turned up around the city, Los Angeles became known as the "serial killer capital of America."

And now it looked like they had one more.

A chilling pattern had emerged that revealed that the six latest victims had been sexually assaulted and were each killed by a fatal gunshot to the head. The scattered dumping of the victims around different parts of Los Angeles posed a significant challenge for law enforcement, and multiple press conferences were held seeking information from the public. Numerous detectives were assigned to the case, including California's first female detective team -- Helen Kidder and Peggy York.

But that didn't stop the discovery of more bodies.

On June 30, the remains of Marnette Comer were found by hunters off the Golden State Freeway, which put teenagers and sex workers who frequented the Sunset Strip on high alert.

By now, detectives had discovered that many of the victims had either been picked up or were last seen around the Strip. This helped them to narrow down the geographic focus of the investigation, linking the murders to that infamous stretch of L.A. roadway.

A task force was created and began to try and dissect the crimes, which involved multiple victims, locations, and a significant degree of brutality that shocked even veteran investigators. They brought in profilers – a relatively new idea at that time – to try and create a psychological portrait of the offender and analyzed the geographical pattern of the crime to identify potential areas of interest and potential suspects. It was a new kind of police work that was designed to narrow the pool of suspects, gather vital information, and, hopefully, help close the case.

But as it turned out, the break in the case didn't come from police work – it came from an unexpected confession.

BY MID-SUMMER OF 1980, CAROL BUNDY WAS completely unraveling. Unable to mentally deal with what was happening, she called the police and tried to tip them off about the murders, but the call wasn't taken seriously.

Carl Bundy's off-and-on boyfriend, country singer Jack Murray. His headless was discovered sitting in his van on a residential street.

She also confessed to her ex-boyfriend, Jack Murray, and then changed her mind about it and became terrified that he would tell the police. To silence him, Carol lured him into his van with the promise of sex and then shot and stabbed him multiple times. Worried that the police would be able to identify the gun by tracing the bullets she'd fired into his head, she decapitated him. According to a news story that was later written about this incident, Carol had called Doug and told him that she was bringing Murray home with her. When he got angry, she clarified that she was only bringing home his head.

Murray's head was later dropped into a random trashcan, and it was never found. His body was left in his van, where it was discovered on August 9 on a residential street in Van Nuys. People living nearby had been complaining about the smell coming from the vehicle.

It was Murray's death that finally drove Carol over the edge. She broke down in front of co-workers and admitted that she had "taken lives." She told them, "I can't take it anymore. I'm supposed to save lives, not take them."

Carol's co-workers quickly called the police, and when she was taken to the station, she spilled everything. She offered details about the murders and even offered detectives photos of the 11-year-old girl that she and Doug had molested. She agreed to testify against him in court, solidifying the case against the couple. The subsequent trials relied heavily on Carol's testimony, physical evidence like the murder weapon Doug still had in his possession, and forensics that linked the victims to the murderous pair.

Doug was quickly arrested – initially for child sex abuse – but he denied killing anyone. He said that Carol and Jack Murray had committed the murders. He hadn't had anything to do with them.

Detectives didn't believe his story, especially since the interviews they were conducting with Carol were chilling them to the bone.

She offered intimate details about the crimes and admitted they had kept Exxie Wilson's head in a freezer. Doug had used it sexually while Carol was "having fun," putting makeup on the dead girl's face, and "making her over like a big Barbie doll."

Doug Clark during his arrest for the murders.

She also added, "I don't know if you guys have ever in your life shot anybody, but it's really fun to do it. It sounds terrible, but it is."

THE TRIAL OF DOUGLAS CLARK BECAME one of the most notorious in the history of L.A. crime. It began in 1981 and quickly became a media spectacle thanks to the gruesome nature of the murders and Doug's erratic behavior. He maintained his innocence throughout the proceedings and, at one point, insisted on representing himself. The judge denied his request.

The prosecution was assisted by forensics and physical evidence but really hinged on Carol's testimony and the explicit details she offered about the murders. Her version of events painted Doug as the mastermind behind the killings, describing how he picked up young women, raped and tortured them, and then executed them.

The defense, though, tried to portray Carol as the real killer, arguing that she was twisting events to save herself. The attorneys also questioned her credibility, pointing out her involvement in the murders and mental health issues.

Despite the defense team's efforts, the jury found Doug guilty on six counts of first-degree murder in February 1983. He was sent to death row at San Quentin.

Carol had agreed to testify against Doug in return for a deal, and on May 2, 1983, she pleaded guilty to killing Jack Murray and handing a gun to Doug to kill a sex worker. In her plea, she called herself a "reluctant partner" who had been in the hands of a maniac who manipulated and overwhelmed her. Carol claimed it had been a "fantasy that had just got badly out of control."

But Carol Bundy was no innocent victim. It was true that she'd lived a difficult life marked by abuse, but she was colder, darker, and much less sympathetic than she appeared on the surface. Journalist Mark McNamara – who interviewed her later in jail – said, "She seemed motivated by a true sociopathology, as well as a desire to manipulate people. She wouldn't talk to me unless I bought her a typewriter."

Carol tried to use her past as a way to garner sympathy, but the authorities saw her as an accomplice to the brutal crimes, not another victim. She was sentenced to life in prison without the possibility of parole.

She died of heart failure at the Central California Women's Facility in Chowchilla in 2003.

AS FOR DOUG CLARK, HE SPENT THE NEXT 40 years on Death Row, still insisting that he was innocent. He continued to be his charming, manipulative self, even behind bars, managing to convince some crime experts of his claims.

But Doug seemed to accept the idea that he was never getting out. "I don't think I'll ever live long enough to get out of here," he said in 2015. "But you get by. I've always been a very Zen person."

He was right about never getting out. He died of natural causes in San Quentin in October 2023.

His death was certainly no loss to humanity.

DOWN ON THE FARM
Ray and Faye Copeland

THE ANONYMOUS CALL CAME INTO Crimestoppers in August 1989. It was a man's voice on the other end of the line, insisting that he'd seen human skulls and bones buried on a farm near Mooresville, Missouri. He used to work on the farm as a hired hand, he claimed, and he'd nearly ended up buried in the field there, too, but he'd managed to get away.

The caller would eventually be revealed to be a man named Jack McCormick, a transient with a record of writing bad checks. This fact didn't convince the police to take him seriously – not at first, anyway. Besides that, the owners of the farm where he claimed the bodies were hidden were an elderly couple who'd never caused trouble for anyone.

But that wasn't entirely accurate. Apparently, Ray Copeland, one of the owners, had been in some trouble in the past. Maybe it wouldn't hurt to take a look after all. So, the authorities got a search warrant and paid Ray and his wife, Faye, a visit. When they handed over the paperwork that authorized the search, Ray laughed at them. "You'll find nothing on my place," he said.

That, also, wasn't entirely accurate. During the two-week-long search that followed, police found five bodies and a quilt made from the bloody clothing of the victims.

There was certainly something very strange happening on the farm.

RAY COPELAND WAS BORN ON DECEMBER 30, 1914, in Oklahoma. His family moved around a lot and eventually settled in the Ozark Mountains of Arkansas. Like many others who fell victim to the Great Depression, Ray had to drop out of school in the fourth grade to work and help support the family. This left him mostly illiterate for the rest of his life.

Filled with anger and resentment, Ray committed his first crime at age 20, stealing hogs from his own father's farm and selling them in another town. His father refused to file charges, and Ray was released, but he never stopped stealing and

Ray and Faye were married just six months after they met in 1940.

cheating people. He finally got jammed up with his first serious crime in 1936 when he was caught forging government checks in Harrison, Arkansas. He was sentenced to spend one year in the county jail.

Then, in 1940, he met his match. Her name was Faye Della Wilson, and she was 19 years old. She had been raised in a dirt-floor cabin in Harrison and came from a very religious family. Ray made her his bride just six months after they met. In 1944, they moved, along with their first two children, to California, where they had another child. The pair would go on to have five children altogether: four sons and one daughter.

Ray struggled to support the family. With no education, he had limited skills and supported the family through theft and schemes, which often landed him in trouble and behind bars for short periods of time.

Ray's frustrations led to him being violently abusive toward his family, often beating his wife and children with anything he could lay his hands on, including cast-iron skillets. Faye, raised as a fundamentalist Christian, believed the husband was the head of the household and that divorce was a sin, so she wouldn't leave Ray. She took his abuse and worked a few jobs outside the home to pay the bills.

The year their youngest child was born, Ray was accused of stealing horses from a local farmer. No charges were filed, but he decided to move the family back home to Arkansas. Less than a month after their return, he was arrested for selling stolen cattle and ended up behind bars for another year.

When he got out, the Copelands moved to Missouri – where Ray was arrested for cattle theft again. The family moved once more. Finally, in 1966, after multiple jail stints, arrests, damaged reputation in various locations, and financial problems, the Copelands managed to buy a humble 40-acre farm in

Mooresville, just outside Chillicothe, Missouri. Faye helped make ends meet by working in a local factory and, later, as a motel housekeeper.

Ray Copeland made very few friends in Mooresville. Neighbors and town residents suspected he verbally and physically abused his family. He mistreated the waitresses in the café and once even purposely ran down a dog in the street. One local referred to him as a "menacing oddball."

That would prove to be an understatement in time.

By the 1980s, Ray was in his seventies, and his children had grown up and fled the farm as soon as they could. Ray was hard of hearing, old, and slow-moving. He needed help on the farm. Plus, due to his history of fraud and writing bad checks, most cattle auctions refused to sell cattle to him. Ray decided to hire some men to help on the farm. Most of them were transients drifting through the area, but Ray and Faye paid them a modest salary along with room and board.

He also now had fall guys to take the blame when Ray gave them forged checks to use at cattle auctions. By the time the checks bounced, Ray would have sold the ill-gotten livestock, and the drifters would be long gone. When the cops showed up to look into the situation, Ray blamed the farmhands, claiming they'd written him back checks, too. The police had no reason to suspect that anything was amiss until one of the drifters got caught and pointed the finger at Ray. He was arrested again and spent another year in jail for forgery.

Ray was arrested a number of times for cattle theft and writing bad checks. He had a violent temper and was known around town for abusing his family. He was not well-liked.

When Ray got out of jail this time, he knew he needed a better way to continue his scheme – he'd get rid of the evidence, quite literally, eliminating the witnesses who might rat him out.

Ray now started recruiting homeless men from shelters and missions in nearby towns, offering them $50 a week plus room and board to help around the farm. For many of them, it seemed like a deal too good to be true.

And, of course, that's because it was.

The new farmhand would then open a checking account in his own name with $200 Ray would front them, using a post office box as an address. He would then ride along with Ray to cattle auctions, and Ray would signal the man which cattle to bid on and how much to offer. When they purchased the cattle, the man would pay with one of his checks, which would clear – the first time. They would sell the cattle and come back and do it again, but this time, the check would bounce. While it worked its way through the banking system of the 1980s, Ray had plenty of time to sell the cattle. Meanwhile, the homeless man would disappear.

Dennis Murphy was one of these men, and in 1986, he was sought by the police for writing bad checks at cattle auctions. The only lead they had was that the cattle had been taken away in a trailer owned by Ray Copeland. The police questioned Ray, and even with his sketchy history, they believed his story when he said that Murphy had up and skipped town. Murphy was a drifter. That's what drifters do, the cops said, and they apologized for bothering the Copelands as they drove away.

A month later, in November 1986, a deputy from a different county showed up looking for another man, Wayne Warner. The Copelands gave him the same story – just as they would about Jimmy Harvey in October 1988, John Freeman in December 1988, and Paul Cowart in May 1989. Eventually, there would be seven men who were wanted for forged checks at cattle auctions throughout central Missouri.

All the men were missing.

And all had a connection to Ray Copeland.

THEN, IN 1989, CAME THE TIP TO CRIMESTOPPERS that cracked the case open. Jack McCormick called the Missouri authorities from Nebraska. He told them that he'd seen human bones on the

Copeland farm – but he lied about that. He just wanted to get the cops' attention.

When he did, he told them all about the check-writing scheme – and how afraid he was of Ray Copeland. One night, he said, Ray had asked him to couple out to a neighbor's barn under the pretense of shooting a raccoon that had gotten inside. Ray had a .22 bolt-action Marlin rifle with him. Ray told Jack to poke a stick under a horse stall and get the raccoon out, but when he turned around, he saw Ray had the rifle pointed right at his head.

Jack had to talk him out of shooting him with the promise that he would leave town and keep his mouth shut. He didn't keep that part of the promise, but he certainly left town.

By the time Jack had come clean about the human bones part of his story, the police had already searched the Copeland farm, and as Ray had promised when they showed up with the warrant, they didn't find anything. But they knew that something was going on – they had seven missing men who were all wanted for writing bad checks at cattle auctions, and all had worked for the Copelands.

Soon, they discovered the list. It was a handwritten list that was hidden in the house. Since Ray couldn't even write his name, it was clear Faye had written the list. On it were the names of the seven missing men, plus five more men the authorities knew nothing about.

All seven of the missing men had a large X next to their names.

They also discovered a large quilt that had been made from discarded men's clothing. None of the clothing belonged to Ray, and some of it was found to be spotted with blood that didn't match either of the Copelands. Faye had apparently crafted it using clothing that belonged to some of the missing men.

But where were those men? Had they simply left town, as the Copelands claimed? The police search hadn't turned up any human remains on the farm. Had the cops missed them? Or were they never there at all?

While police officials debated what to do next, a tip came in from an unnamed local man who said that Ray had often worked on a neighboring farm – the same farm where Jack McCormick had been taken to look for a raccoon. The tipster

Ray and Faye were both charged with five murders and while her children and attorneys claimed Faye was unwilling accomplice, the just didn't buy it.

added that one of the barns on that property smelled like an animal had died inside.

Another search warrant was obtained, and the search shifted to the other property. The first place they checked was the barn, and inside, they found a shallow grave that contained the skeletal remains of three men. A .22 bullet to the head had killed all of them. In a separate barn, they found another body and then discovered another in a well on the property. That last man was wearing a belt with the name "Dennis" burned into the back of it.

Unfortunately, identifying the bodies was difficult. Since they were transients, any medical or dental records were old or non-existent, and many had gone years without proper dental care. The odd shape of his jawbone identified Dennis Murphy. Forensic scientists were also able to identify Paul Cowart, James Harvey, John Freeman, and Wayne Warner.

All of them had x's next to their names on Faye's list.

RAY AND FAYE COPELAND WERE BOTH charged with the five confirmed murders, though authorities were convinced there were others that they didn't find, primarily thanks to the list that Faye had written.

In November 1990, Faye's defense painted her as a victim, an abused wife who had no idea what her husband was doing. A defense psychologist stated that she suffered from textbook battered woman's syndrome, a kind of learned helplessness where the victim becomes unquestioningly compliant. She stated over and over that whatever Ray did or said, she never asked questions for fear of being beaten.

At the start of the trial, Faye was offered a plea deal by the prosecution, but she didn't take it because she insisted that she had no information to give them – she hadn't known about the murders, and she didn't know where the bodies were buried.

The testimony about battered woman's syndrome was deemed inadmissible during the trial. So, no testimony about the abuse she suffered from Ray or how he controlled her was allowed in her defense. Even without that, the evidence against her was flimsy – just the list and the quilt.

It's possible – maybe even likely – that Ray had dictated the list. In their marriage, any reading or writing was left up to Faye. He could have told her to put X's next to specific names and never told her why. She could have believed the men had just left. Making a quilt from the clothing of the missing men – although it seems macabre – could have been just a "thrifty" idea for a farm wife without much money to make something from discarded clothing.

Or the answers could just as easily be what the prosecution believed – that she was a willing accomplice to the crimes that her husband committed, a greedy, cold-hearted killer, and not a beaten-down wife. There was no question that Faye often spoke with the farmhands, fed them meals, handled bank transactions, and later told the banks that she didn't know who the men were when their checks bounced. Besides, Ray couldn't have written out his fraudulent checks over the years – he'd have needed help – and who better but his wife? There was plenty of evidence that Faye was aware of Ray's fraudulent schemes and the murders.

The jury may have felt she was a battered woman when they reached their verdict, but they still thought she was guilty and needed to be held accountable for the murders. Faye was convicted on five counts of first-degree murder and sentenced to death.

When Ray went to trial, he initially tried to enter an insanity plea, but prosecutors were unwilling to deal with him. He was also convicted on the same five counts of first-degree murder and sentenced to death.

At 69 and 76 years old, they were the oldest couple ever sentenced to death in American history.

Neither would be executed, in any case. Ray died in prison from natural causes in 1993, and in 1999, Faye's sentence was commuted to life with no possibility of parole. Despite support for her claims of abuse, she was never exonerated.

On August 10, 2002, Faye suffered a stroke that caused her left side to be paralyzed, and she lost her ability to speak. She was given medical parole and sent to a nursing home in Chillicothe, Missouri. She died there on December 23, 2003, at the age of 82.

Ray and Faye seemed to be unlikely serial killers, and yet five men – or more – were murdered on their Missouri farm. Many still question Faye's knowledge about the depravity of her husband, while some insist she was a willing participant in his crimes.

But if Faye Copeland knew anything about the other men whose names she had written on a list and placed an X next to, she took that secret with her to the grave.

THE "TOY BOX"
David Ray and Cindy Hendy

THE NAME OF THE TOWN USED TO BE "HOT SPRINGS." That was a name that lured people to that part of New Mexico for hospitality and relaxation. They came to soak in the Geronimo Springs at John Cross Ranch, the first of several dozen spas that opened to take advantage of the heated water that still bubbles up from under the small town.

In 1950, though, the name of the town was changed to Truth or Consequences when the popular radio quiz show of that name offered to broadcast from the first community to rename itself after the show. No one could say that this little place in New Mexico didn't know how to have fun.

But the good times of yesterday were darkened in 1996 when the crimes of the so-called "Toy Box Killers" came to light. While typical murder cases usually involve shocking acts of violence, these crimes extended well beyond that into the realm of the unimaginably horrifying and included abduction, sexual torture, and murder.

The kidnappings, cruelty, and murders committed by David Ray and his accomplices – Cynthia "Cindy" Hendy and his daughter, Glenda "Jesse" Ray -- shocked the state and the nation, exposing a level of brutal inhumanity seldom seen, even in the darkest corners of American criminal history.

DAVID PARKER RAY WAS BORN IN NEW MEXICO in 1939 and spent his childhood living in poverty on a small ranch with his younger sister, Peggie, and his strict grandparents.

How much his mother, Nettie, was around remains unclear, but it is known that his father, a troubled alcoholic, would occasionally

David Ray

breeze into David's life, bringing him the sinister gifts of discarded pornographic magazines that were filled with haunting, sadomasochistic photographs. They would shape David's sexual fantasies from a young age and lead to unimaginable horror for many women.

David's adolescent years continued to be turbulent. He was an introvert in high school, which made it nearly impossible for him to talk to girls. Other students took advantage of his shyness by taunting him, so he followed in his father's footsteps and took refuge in drugs and alcohol.

According to David's later statements, his assaults on women began when he was still a teenager. He claimed the first attack occurred in 1957 when he abducted a woman and tied her to a tree. He said that he tortured her and killed her.

It will never be known how many women David abducted and raped over the decades because the women were drugged. He often met them at the Blue Waters Saloon, which was located in the small town of Elephant Butte, about 150 miles south of Albuquerque and just north of Truth and Consequences. David lived on the edge of this rural town and frequented the dimly lit tavern, which drew in wanderers and the handful of locals that lived nearby. A drug slipped into their drink would ensure that his victims didn't remember anything that happened to them when they left the bar.

Although, of course, some of those who were abducted were never seen again. How many women did David kill? That remains a mystery to this day.

Some of his victims may not have been women, either. Billy Ray Bowers was 53 years old, and in 1986, he opened a used car business in Truth or Consequences called Canal Motors. David worked there for a while as a mechanic, but he and Bowers never got along. Finally, on September 25, 1988, Bowers was reported missing. Four years later, almost to the day, a body was found wrapped in a blue tarp by some fisherman. There was no identification on it. Years later, in 1999, thanks to dental records, it was confirmed that the body belonged to Billy Ray Bowers.

Ray's daughter, Glenda, who went by "Jesse." She was a willing accomplice to her father.

Jill Troia was 22 years old when she decided to go to a bar with some friends on the night of September 30, 1995. Later in the evening, she and another friend, Glenda "Jesse" Ray, decided to split off from the group and get some supper. According to witnesses, the two women argued, and that was the last anybody ever saw of Jill. Glenda later told the police that, after the argument, she had left with her father, David, and Jill had gone to the Elephant Butte Reservoir with another friend.

But the first real police involvement – as lackluster as it was – with David's crimes occurred on July 26, 1996. That night, the sheriff's office in Truth or Consequences received a call from a worried husband. He said that on the previous day, he'd argued with his wife, Kelly Van Cleave, and he hadn't seen or heard from her since.

But there was nothing deputies could do. His wife had been gone for such a short time, he was told, that she couldn't be considered a missing person. The officer told the man not to worry – based on his years of experience, she'd turn up soon.

And he was right. Kelly returned home the next day. She was dropped off at home by an employee of nearby Elephant Butte State Park – named for the shape of an island created by the Rio Grande River – where she had been found wandering in a dazed and incoherent state.

Kelly could only recall a few of the hours she had been missing. After the argument with her husband, she remembered going to a friend's house, followed by a trip to several local bars, the last of which was the Blue Waters Saloon. When they arrived, Kelly ordered a beer, her first drink of the evening.

Within a minute or two, she started to feel dizzy. She knew she couldn't be drunk from a few sips of beer, but she definitely didn't feel right. After that, there wasn't much she could remember, though she was sure that an old friend, Jesse Ray, had offered to help her.

The missing hours brought an end to Kelly's marriage. Her husband refused to believe she was telling the truth about her disappearance and was convinced she was having an affair. Jesse could have told him the truth, but she never answered any of Kelly's calls.

Kelly never saw Jesse again. Soon after she and her husband separated, she left Truth or Consequences – but was unable to forget the place. She began suffering from horrifying nightmares that were always the same. In each, Kelly saw herself tied to a table, her mouth covered with duct tape, and a knife at her throat. It didn't make sense to her, but she couldn't exactly report bad dreams to the police.

At that point, the sheriff's office in Truth or Consequences had nothing on file but a worrisome phone call from a jealous husband. They couldn't have known that the woman who came into the station on July 7, 1997, would bring them information that would be connected to Kelly's missing hours.

The woman had come to report that she hadn't heard from her 22-year-old daughter, Sylvie Marie Parker, for the last two days. Although the two were estranged, she frequently heard from her daughter, especially when she needed money. Sylvie lived in a tent on town property, and she'd had issues with cocaine and meth.

This time, the police investigated, and it wasn't hard to track the young woman's movements. Sylvie was last seen on July 5 at the Blue Waters Saloon, drinking with Jesse Ray. Jesse told the authorities that Sylvie had been drinking heavily, so she had driven her home, but she hadn't seen her since.

But Jesse was not the only person that Sylvie had been hanging around with on the night she disappeared. She'd also met up with an old boyfriend, Roy Yancy, who was also a well-known troublemaker in town. As a child, he'd roamed the streets with a group of other boys who strangled cats, poisoned dogs, and knocked over tombstones in the town cemetery, acts that led the city to cancel that year's Halloween celebration. Forced to choose between jail and the military, Roy enlisted in the U.S. Navy but was soon dishonorably discharged.

The investigation into Sylvie's disappearance was predictably short. She was a homeless drug user, hung around disreputable characters, and was part of the region's transient population. When someone came forward with a hazy recollection of a girl who hitched a ride out of town, the cops stopped looking for her.

Cynthia "Cindy" Hendy

Around the same time that Sylvie vanished, a young woman named Cindy Hendy came to Truth or Consequences. She had a history that drew David Ray to her like a moth to a flame. A victim of sexual abuse, she had been molested by her stepfather before being kicked out of the house at age 11. She became pregnant as a teenager but turned the baby over to foster care. When she arrived in town, she was on the run from drug charges after supplying an undercover cop with cocaine. She was a violent woman with a short fuse, and it was inevitable that she ended up in the local jail. She was freed into a work-release program that brought her out to Elephant Butte State Park, and it was there she met David Ray.

By then, the quiet, approachable man lived in a run-down bungalow near the park. He'd settled there in 1984 with his fourth wife and worked to support them as an aircraft engine mechanic. By 1995, his wife had left him, and he'd taken a job as a New Mexico Parks Department employee, which is how he and Hendy met.

Somehow, David recognized her as a kindred spirit, and in January 1999, Cindy moved into his house. It didn't matter that he was two decades older than she was. The 38-year-old Cindy was convinced she'd met her soulmate – a man who shared her obsession with sexual torture, pain, and, eventually, murder.

CINDY HAD BEEN LIVING WITH DAVID FOR less than a month before she lured her first victim into their lair. On February 16, 1999, she invited Angie Montano over for a visit. Angie, a single mother, was new in town and wanted to make friends – but she definitely came to the wrong house.

Angie was blindfolded, stripped, tied to a bed, and sexually assaulted, but David and Cindy's tastes went beyond just rape. Angie was tortured, stunned with cattle prods, whipped, cut, and traumatized with devices that David had made himself.

After five days, Angie convinced David to let her go. He drove her to the nearest highway and left her there. As luck would have it, she was picked up by a passing off-duty police officer. She shared her story with him but refused to press charges or make an official report. Angie quickly left Truth or Consequences and never returned.

After Angie was released, Cindy had other things on her mind. She was about to become a grandmother at the age of only 39. The daughter she reconnected with lived in her old hometown of Monroe, Washington, and Cindy planned to be there for the birth. Before she could leave, though, she was determined to find a sex slave for David, so he'd have someone to meet his needs in her absence.

On March 18, they drove to Albuquerque in David's RV, hunting for their next victim. It was there they found Cynthia Jaramillo, a 22-year-old prostitute, who was easy to convince to get into their vehicle.

Cynthia had been selling drugs and sex on the streets of Albuquerque since she was only 13. Once David and Cindy got her into the RV, she was handcuffed and shocked with a cattle prod.

As they drove toward Elephant Butte, Cynthia unscrewed the cabinet to which she was handcuffed and waited for the RV to slow down, but just when she was about to make a run for it, David hit the brakes, and she tumbled to the floor. Cindy shocked her with the cattle prod again, rendering her unconscious.

When the couple got her to the bungalow, she was collared, chained, blindfolded, and gagged. When she woke up, she heard David's voice echoing in the room they were holding her captive in. It was a pre-recorded tape that he played for all his victims after they woke from their drugged state. The tape was a cold, clinical list of all the things they were about to experience and was designed to instill maximum fear in their captives. "The gag is necessary," his voice said, "because after a while, you're going to be doing a lot of screaming."

But the chilling audiotape was just the beginning. For the next three days, Cynthia was tortured and raped using an extensive collection of torture devices, which included a gruesome assortment of pulleys, whips, and a host of sexually perverse contraptions.

The house was a chamber of horrors that was only rivaled by the semi-truck trailer that was also parked on the property. Luckily for Cynthia, she escaped before she could be subjected to what awaited her there.

During those three days, David assaulted Cynthia only when he wasn't at work. On the morning of the fourth day, he put on his state park uniform as always and drove away. Cindy was in charge of keeping their prisoner under control – a task at which she failed.

As David and Cindy had been taking Cynthia from room to room during her captivity, she'd studied her surroundings. After David left, she finally got her chance to escape. Cindy left her alone to make lunch and carelessly left the keys to her chains on the coffee table.

Cynthia scooped up the keys and tried to unlock herself, but Cindy rushed in and started hitting her with an empty bottle. Cynthia was cut by broken glass, but she had grabbed two vital things – the telephone and an ice pick. With one, she dialed the police; with the other, she stabbed her captor in the neck.

It wasn't a fatal blow, but it was enough to give Cynthia time to get out of the house. She bolted -- naked except for a dog collar and covered in blood -- down the road. The first car that drove past her stopped, but the woman driving wouldn't let her inside. Cynthia ran to a nearby trailer and, fortunately, received help from an elderly couple whom she later called her "guardian angels."

Cynthia's first call to the Sierra County Sheriff's office had been cut off, but her second one went through. When deputies arrived at the trailer, they were stunned by her story of torture and rape. As Cynthia was transported to the hospital, the sheriff's department decided to call in the state police. This was a case they weren't equipped to handle.

More than a dozen officers converged on David's bungalow, but they found that Cindy had fled.

The empty house was a mess. It was filthy, with garbage littering the floor. If there was any order, it was found in the couple's instruments of torture, which were arranged on hooks hanging from the walls. Books were stacked everywhere and included volumes of violet pornography, torture, and the occult. There were also piles of medical books, which apparently informed David of the best places to apply his torture devices.

The hunt was now on for David and Cindy, but it was a short chase. The couple hadn't fled the area – instead, they were driving along nearby roads, searching for Cynthia. The police caught up with them just two blocks from their home. They quickly admitted they had been looking for the young woman, but the two sadistic rapists desperately tried to paint a picture of innocence. They alleged that Cynthia was a heroin addict and insisted their actions were merely attempts to wean her off the drug.

But no one was buying their story. The cops uncovered the chilling collection of torture paraphernalia that starkly contrasted their story and, instead, corroborated Cynthia's harrowing account.

The pair were arrested and taken into custody. As the investigation of David's property began, the state's law enforcement officials realized they didn't have the resources to deal with what they were finding either.

David had meticulously documented his violent acts in diaries, noting details like the time and place of the kidnappings. However, his journals offered no insights into the events that

The detached semi-trailer that David Ray had styled into his horrifying "Toy Box"

(Below) The interior of the "Toy Box" was so shocking it chilled the blood of hardened FBI veterans. Ray had dubbed it "Satan's Den."

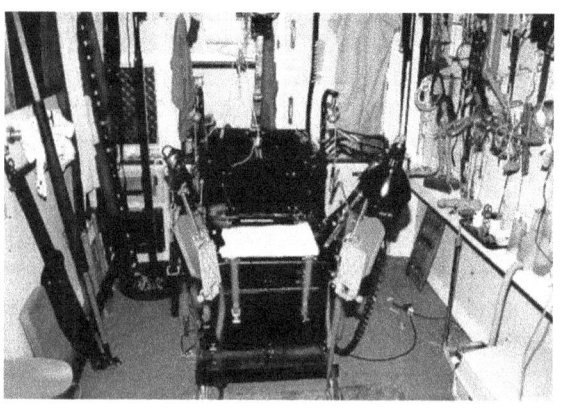

followed the brutal rapes, leaving out what became of the victims – and whether they were alive or dead. Law enforcement could only speculate about his victim count at this point, as well as how many of his victims had crossed state lines, making his offenses federal crimes.

Just as over their heads as the local sheriff's department was, the state police pulled the FBI into the case – and that's when the ugliest aspects of the case were finally revealed to the country.

They were discovered inside of the semi-trailer that was kept locked outside of the house. David called it his "Toy Box." He had managed to funnel a reported $100,000 into the collection of torture devices that he kept there. Many of the instruments were purchased from specialty dealers, and others David made himself.

FBI agent Jim Yontz led the search of the "Toy Box" and created the stomach-churning report of what his team discovered there. After gaining entrance to the trailer, Agent

Yontz entered the main room. A door over the entrance read "Satan's Den."

It proved to be an accurate description.

Just past the entrance was a tall tripod with an expensive RCA camcorder pointing toward a black leather table that was set up with metal stirrups on it, electrodes, and red plastic straps. A leather-topped stool was placed at the foot of the table, just between the stirrups. Above the stool was a television. It hung from the ceiling so that a woman on the table was offered a clear view of what David was doing to them.

On the left side of the chamber was a coat hanger with a long black robe hanging from it. On a clipboard hanging next to the robe was a list of the women that David had kidnapped between 1993 and 1997. Yontz read through the list and later said that he tried not to let his emotions get in the way of the investigation, but it was very hard to do -- especially when he noticed the cork bulletin board next to the clipboard. It was covered with color and black and white photographs of the women he'd tortured and raped. Above the gallery of photos were the block-printed words "THE LURE OF SATANISM," as if this justified the brutality shown in the images.

The photos showed David's victims in different stages of bondage. There was a red-headed woman who was naked with her hands tied behind her back. A red bandana was tied over her mouth, and her frightened eyes looked straight into the camera. Another photo displayed a woman's naked torso, but she was wrapped so tightly with the white rope that her flesh bulged due to obvious pain. There was a nude woman with old-fashioned wooden clothespins clipped to her nipples and eyes that were filled with terror. A woman with blood all over was shackled to a bench. Another woman was bloody and battered and had bruises all over her body, particularly on her inner thighs.

And there were more. There were too many more.

On the wall next to the photos were a series of drawings that explained the stages of torture to which David subjected his captives. In one illustration, a woman clung to a table with her wrists and ankles tied together behind her back, twisted up in pain. Written above the drawing was the label "New Table for Church Rituals." David had also drawn a woman tied to something he called his "doggie frame." She was down on her hands and knees. There was also a drawing of a man-resembling David - standing beneath a woman's open legs as she hung from the ceiling by her hands. The man in the drawing had a reversed pentagram hanging around his neck.

The drawings - along with the black robe, skulls, and occult books found in the trailer and the house - implied that David was assaulting, raping, and torturing women as some sort of "devotion to Satan." However, his knowledge of the occult was about as authentic as a teenage boy spray painting "666" on a highway overpass. It was nothing more than a way to make himself look more menacing to his victims.

The wall on the right side of the room was covered with the various tools he used for torture -- chains, whips, paddles, leather belts, saw blades, harnesses, handcuffs, ropes, wires, needles, pins, nipple clamps, breast suction cups, metal bras, sandpaper, dildos of all sizes made from metal, wood, glass, and plastic, a branding iron, a soldering iron, an assortment of hooks, and more.

There was a large yellow metal box sitting on the floor. It had a top handle, a motor, and a motorized jackhammer arm that had a massive, bulging, flesh-colored dildo attached to it that was so thick that a man couldn't hold it with a closed fist. It had three switches that controlled the speed of the device.

The agents also found another gynecological table that was wired to a voltage meter, with electrodes that could be attached to a woman's breasts and genitalia. A pedal controlled the position of the table that changed the elevation, foot position, back angle, and, if necessary, the tilt of the entire body tied down by red nylon straps to the D rings that served as wrist and ankle stirrups. There was also a large light bolted at the end of the table so the torturer would have a clear view.

Finally, Yontz also documented a medicine cabinet that contained latex gloves, forceps, rolls of cotton, lubricants, bottles of chloroform, ammonia poppers, and hypodermic syringes.

There were white candles mounted on the top of a human skull standing next to a hand-carved wooden dildo. There were anatomy books and two naked baby dolls, one with a big patch of blond pubic hair and the other with a big patch of black pubic hair.

Behind a plastic curtain was a makeshift dressing room that contained nightgowns, shampoos, body lotion, baby powder, baby oil, mouthwash, perfume, and lipstick.

And finally, there was another set of drawings, horrible drawings, which were numbered from 1 to 13. One of them was a drawing of a naked woman, strapped down by her hips, belly, and chest, with a hood over her face. Rubber-lined clamps were attached to her nipples and connected to a machine. Beneath the drawing were explicit instructions on how best to send hundreds of volts of electricity through the unfortunate woman who found herself in David's clutches.

Jim Yontz, shaken and pale, stumbled out of "Satan's Den" and fled the fresh air outside. He hoped never to see anything like David Ray's "Toy Box" ever again.

VIDEOTAPES THAT WERE TAKEN FROM THE HOUSE and trailer turned out to be valuable evidence against David and his accomplices. They linked Jesse Ray to her father's crimes and helped the authorities determine some kind of number when it came to David's victims. It was an incomplete list, but it was a start.

Testimony from Kelly Van Cleave and Cynthia Jaramillo turned out to be crucial to the investigation, but the most damning information came from Cindy Hendy.

Withing days of her arrest, she had turned on her boyfriend. She told investigators that David had been abducting and torturing women for years – and that his fantasies had often ended with murder.

Searches of Elephant Butte Lake and the surrounding countryside didn't turn up any bodies, but the police and FBI were convinced that David had killed in the past.

Cindy also confirmed that Jesse Ray had participated in some of the abductions and that she often did so with the help of Roy Yancy, the man last seen with Sylvie Parker before she disappeared.

Although Ray tried to appear tough around town, he broke down immediately after he was arrested. He told police that he and Jesse had drugged Sylvie and had taken her to David, who tortured her. When David was tired of her, he'd tell Roy to get rid of her. He told the police where to find her body, but it was never found. Even so, he was charged with second-degree murder and sentenced to 20 years in prison.

Jesse – after pleading guilty to kidnapping Kelly Van Cleave and Sylvie Parker – received a nine-year sentence. But that would soon be greatly reduced.

Cindy was convicted of numerous charges and faced the possibility of a 197-year prison sentence before agreeing to cooperate with prosecutors. She was sentenced to spend the next 36 years behind bars, but in 2019, after serving about two-thirds of her sentence, she was granted parole and released. It was a controversial decision made by the prison board, but Cindy quietly disappeared to Montana, where she still lives today.

At the time of Cindy's release, Cynthia Jaramillo stated that she had forgiven Hendy for what she'd done. "I think," she told the press, "there was a part of her that was David Parker Ray's victim, too."

Initially, David Ray refused to cooperate with the authorities. He claimed that while he had many sexual fantasies, he had never abducted, raped, or murdered anyone who hadn't consented to it. They were volunteers, he claimed, not victims.

But that story changed after his daughter, Jesse, received her lengthy prison sentence. He ultimately pled guilty to the charges against him to spare his daughter. As a result of that deal, Jesse was only forced to serve two-and-a-half years of her original sentence. When she got out, she vanished. Her location remains unknown today.

On September 30, 2011, David Ray was sentenced to 244 years in prison for the rapes and abductions of Kelly Van Cleave and Cynthia Jaramillo.

But he served less than a year.

On May 28, 2002, he had a massive heart attack and died in his cell. If only the Devil had taken him sooner, then fewer lives might have been ruined.

Part Two
"LOVE YOU MADLY"

THERE'S NO QUESTION THAT, IN THIS era of true crime podcasts, books, and television shows, we are fascinated by murder. And among those murders, there are none we find more intriguing than crimes of passion.

We find them compelling for many reasons, not the least of which is the fact that crimes of passion are offenses not usually committed by criminals – but by ordinary people who only become criminals by these acts. Both men and women commit these murders, as do those from every level of society. Those who commit them are blue-collar workers, celebrities, socialites, and everyone in between.

Crimes of passion have inspired not only legends and literature, including the works of great playwrights, but also novels, symphonies, operas, and works of art. In fact, it's hard to imagine art, literature, or music without the violent outpouring of passion and the stories of human depravity that gave birth to them.

Ana Freud once said, "A crime of passion is an action committed without the benefit of ego activity. The term means the passion, the impulse, is of such magnitude that every other consideration apart from its fulfillment is disregarded."

That's an eloquent way of saying that the mental functions of an otherwise sane person are shut down until they can act on the impulse to kill the person who has driven them crazy.

And the feeling that drives a person insane may not be love, but let's be honest, it usually is.

It's love that can drive a man or a woman to do the unthinkable. Simply put, they reach the end of their rope. It doesn't usually happen for financial gain; there's no reward, only release. They are crimes that are direct responses to betrayal, broken hearts, ruined lives, injured pride, jealousy, and probably all the rest of the Seven Deadly Sins.

It can even happen when someone can't have something – or someone – they desperately want.

ON NOVEMBER 18, 1905, a young woman named Lizzie Kaussehull was murdered at a Lincoln Avenue streetcar stop on the north side of Chicago.

Her killed was a man named Edward Robhaut, who had been pursuing her for nearly three months. During that time, he had unsuccessfully tried to win Lizzie's heart by following her, writing her letters, sending her flowers, and refusing to accept her rejection. He waited for her each day at the corner of Lincoln and Carmen, waiting for the streetcar that would bring Lizzie home from her job at a grocery store.

When she stepped off the streetcar each night, she tried her best to ignore him, but it was not easy to do because he followed her all the way to her door each evening.

As Edward became more persistent, he became more unhinged, once telling Lizzie that he would kill her if she refused to marry him. She became so fearful for her life that her family reported Edward's behavior to the police. He was arrested, and a restraining order –

called a "peace bond" in those days – was filed against him on November 11, but it had no effect on his actions. He continued to follow her home from the streetcar stop each afternoon, begging her to marry him and threatening to kill her if she did not.

On the afternoon of November 18, Lizzie finished her shift at the grocery store and, as she always did, she rode the streetcar north on Lincon Avenue toward home. When she reached her stop, she stepped off with several girlfriends, all of them laughing and talking.

Then, she saw Edward leaning against the wall of a nearby storefront. Lizzie's friends froze, and Lizzie shakily put up a hand and stammered in his direction that the peace bond was still in place against him. He wasn't allowed to come any closer.

But he did – and Lizzie began to scream.

Edward sprang on her and plunged a knife into Lizzie's chest. She staggered away from him, but Edward pushed forward once more, stabbing her three more times. At last, she fell to the sidewalk at his feet, covered in blood.

Edward looked down at the woman he claimed to love so much that he had to kill her because he couldn't have her, drew a revolver from his coat, placed the barrel in his mouth, and pulled the trigger. The back of the young man's skull blew apart, and blood sprayed across the brick wall behind him.

His body collapsed on top of Lizzie's. They were finally together – in death.

But this was not the end of the story. According to legend, Lizzie's ghost has haunted the intersection at Lincoln and Carmen for more than a century now. The stories claim that, on nights of the full moon, Lizzie returns to the former streetcar stop and can be heard screaming – just as she did when she saw Edward Robhaut coming toward her on the day that he ended her life.

A CRIME OF PASSION.

That's what they call it when an otherwise sane and normal person is driven by panic, love, or jealousy to kill a spouse, a lover, or a rival. Some say it's not exactly murder – it's insanity instead.

But whatever you want to call them, history is filled with these kinds of crimes and stories that never – not ever – end well.

THE CASE OF THE "RAGGED STRANGER"
Killing Ruth Wanderer

ONE OF THE STRANGEST AND MOST colorfully solved murder cases of the 1920s was undoubtedly the Chicago case of the "Ragged Stranger." Over the years, it's been re-told in books, detective magazines, and even in one Hollywood movie. Many different people took credit for solving the case – both the press and the police department – but whatever really happened, an unlikely killer was brought to justice.

But this is a story with a twist. The killer was eventually convicted of his crime, but according to the legend in the neighborhood where he lived, his victim refused to leave the place where her young life was cut short.

And her ghost still walks today.

CARL OTTO WANDERER WAS BORN AND raised on the North Side of Chicago. His parents, German immigrants, taught him the value of a dollar at a young age, and he became a thrifty young man. He never drank, never smoked, never gambled and never chewed gum. He worked in his father's butcher shop, and the customers all liked him.

But his strict upbringing and frugal ways left Carl feeling more unhappy and restless than anyone knew. Adventure was calling his name. The newspapers were recounting the raids by Pancho Villa into the southwestern United States, and there was a call for volunteers to help pursue the Mexican bandit and his men. Carl couldn't resist, and he joined the Army in 1914.

Carl Wanderer

He left around the time that he said his mother started acting crazy. She had a vision that wouldn't let her rest, he said. She claimed she'd seen Carl lynched, hanging from the limb of a tree. One of Carl's sisters said that the vision made her "despondent" and surmised that this might have been why she killed herself. She slit her own throat.

By then, though, Carl was on his way to New Mexico to serve under "Black Jack" Pershing as a cavalry officer. The Army made him a machine gunner, then it made him a sergeant, then it promoted him to second lieutenant. He was respected, and his experience with the First Illinois Cavalry made him valuable when he was in one of the first units sent to France when the United States entered World War I. He saw action on the western front and returned home with medals for bravery in 1919.

In October of that same year, he married his sweetheart, a chubby, attractive 20-year-old named Ruth Johnson. They'd known each other since they were kids, and Carl had never even kissed another woman besides Ruth. She'd been singing in the choir of the Holy Trinity Lutheran Church for eight years, but when Carl enlisted in the Army, she quit the choir. She said she didn't want to give any other man the opportunity to ask to escort her home after practice.

The couple moved into an apartment shared by Ruth's parents, and it was here that the affection he'd had for Ruth

The butcher shop where Carl worked with his father.

began to die. The claustrophobic flat became unbearable, thanks to Ruth's neediness and his nagging mother-in-law, who berated Carl about the fact that he didn't have enough money for the couple to get a place of their own.

Carl's restlessness once more got the better of him, but he didn't go on an adventure this time – he started seeing a 16-year-old typist named Julia Schmitt. He often met her at the Riverview Amusement Park while his wife was otherwise engaged.

And then, shortly before Christmas, Ruth happily announced to her husband that she was pregnant. Carl would become a father the following summer. He was dismayed to learn the news and fell into somber, sullen moods. He rarely spoke while working in his father's butcher shop but also avoided coming home. He pondered his options, and as it turned out, he bided his time until a plan to rid himself of his problems slowly came to mind.

THE REASON THAT CARL AND RUTH HAD been living with her parents was so that the couple could save their money to buy a home of their own. By June 1920, they'd saved up $1,500, the equivalent of nearly $24,000 today.

By then, Ruth was eight months pregnant. She'd been buying little things for the baby, marking them off a list she kept in her dresser. One day, she told Carl that it was time to get their savings from the bank so they could buy a house.

Or that's what Carl later said, anyway.

According to Carl, they went to the bank and withdrew all but $70 from their savings. They took the money home with them, and Ruth put it in her dresser, next to the baby list.

The next day was Sunday, and Carl stayed home all day, guarding the money and watching over Ruth. Why Ruth? Carl said that she had told him that she noticed a strange man – a "raggedy stranger" – eyeing her suspiciously. Carl started carrying his sidearm from the Army, a .45 automatic.

On Monday, June 21, Carl went back to work. He and his father went shopping for new knives for the butcher shop, and then Carl spent the rest of the day behind the meat counter.

That night after dinner, though, he and Ruth thought it might be nice to go to a movie. They attended an early evening showing of *The Sea Wolf*, a

Carl and Ruth Wanderer

rousing Jack London adventure story, at the Pershing Theater (now the Davis) at Lincoln and Western Avenues.

As they strolled home afterward, Carl later reported seeing a sinister-looking man – a "raggedy bum," he called him -- lurking near Zindt's Drug Store on Lawrence Avenue. According to his story, the man crushed a cigarette as they passed by, and then he followed behind them at a distance.

"Ruth went up ahead of me when we reached the house. She opened the outer door, and I heard her fumbling with her keys to the inner door of the hall," Carl later told the police. Ruth reached up for the chain dangling from the overhead light so that she could find the right key. Carl asked her if she was having trouble, and she laughed.

Neither of them noticed the man who followed them into the dark vestibule. The "Ragged Stranger," as this man would come to be known, stepped forward with a gun trained on Ruth. "Don't turn on the light," the man said. "Throw up your hands!"

Before Ruth and Carl could comply with his order, the stranger shot Ruth two times. Carl claimed that he heard the man shout out a string of obscenities, and he continued to fire. Carl jerked out his own Colt .45 service revolver and emptied his clip in the direction of the dark figure. It was later discovered that 14 bullets had been fired in the small vestibule in only a matter of seconds.

When the smoke cleared, Carl could see the stranger was down. But so was Ruth. Carl went to where she was lying on the floor of the vestibule in a spreading pool of blood.

Ruth's mother rushed down to the door to find her daughter had been shot. Carl had gone berserk with rage, smashing his gun and his fists against a man who was lying on the floor. Ruth lived just long enough to utter a few tragic words: "My baby.... My baby is dead."

The murder scene today – the apartment where Carl and Ruth lived with Ruth's parents.

And so was Ruth, along with the Ragged Stranger. The police lieutenant who first interviewed Carl said, "I thought he was entitled to a medal for bravery after I listened to his version."

He would eventually change his mind.

Detective Sergeant John Norton arrived on the scene just minutes after the shooting. Around the time that Carl Wanderer had been mustered out of the Army, the Chicago Police Department had established its first Homicide Bureau, made up of the best and brightest detectives on the force. John Norton had been the man chosen to head the squad.

By the time he arrived on the scene, neighbors and onlookers had started to gather around the scene. The detective saw Carl, covered in the stranger's blood, and Ruth's mother, holding her daughter's lifeless body in her arms. Norton pushed his way through. The bulky detective was well known in the neighborhood, having been shot four times during his celebrated career, and everyone knew that he would get answers quickly in the case. He started with just one question: why was Carl Wanderer carrying a gun?

Carl had a quick answer: There had been a robbery attempt at his father's butcher shop a short time before, and Carl was carrying his service revolver in case it happened again. He suggested to Norton that perhaps this man could have been involved. He hadn't yet mentioned the money he and Ruth had taken from the bank or that Ruth told him she'd seen a "raggedy man" eyeing her on the street – but he would.

Detective Norton searched the dead man's pockets and came up with just $3.80 and a meal ticket from a traveling circus. There was nothing else on the body, which was taken to Ravenswood Hospital for a check of fingerprints and the inquest.

During the questions that followed, Carl decided to embellish the interactions with the stranger a little further. He looked familiar to him, Carl said and believed the man had flirted with Ruth a few nights earlier. She had come home and reported the news to Carl in a near panic, terrified that the "raggedy man" was following her.

Neighbors thought Carl was a hero, and newspapers thought so, too, printing headlines like WAR HERO IN DEADLY BATTLE. "I got him, honey, I got him," the papers wrote that Carl whispered as he cradled Ruth's body.

The papers wrote of Carl's heroics in battle and exemplary military record, touting his service in New Mexico and during the war. He was a brave soldier who had fought to protect America from her enemies, they said, and now this same man had been forced to endure the cold-blooded murder of his wife and unborn child. It was a heartless and horrible crime, and the public reacted with shock and outrage.

Carl had valiantly defended the honor of his wife and should be celebrated, reporters and the public believed, even though the result had been tragic. It was expected that he might be charged with nothing more than justifiable homicide or self-defense in the murder of the "Ragged Stranger." He deserved to be left alone to grieve for his family, and that should be the end of the story.

But little did they know, the story of the "Ragged Stranger" was just getting started.

A WEEK PASSED AND LIEUTENANT CARL WANDERER – the heartbroken hero – went back to work behind the counter of his father's shop. The newspapers had found other stories to tell.

Detective John Norton read the papers like everyone else. Even so, he had some questions about the case that he wanted answered.

If Carl Wanderer was the hero, who was the dead man?

The dead man also had a gun, a heavy-duty Army Colt .45. Two big guns were blazing away in that vestibule. Two bullets in Ruth, three bullets in the bum, and a lot of holes in the wall. But not a scratch on Carl Wanderer.

They'd found no name for the bum. He'd been in his twenties, the same age as Carl. He was frail, dirty, and dressed in rags. Oddly, though, he'd just gotten a haircut and a manicure. And his gun had been an expensive weapon., A man down on his luck could have easily hocked it and made a decent amount of money. That would have been much easier than risking a street robbery.

But first, Norton decided to run down the meal ticket that he'd found in the man's pocket. He traced the ticket – a pass that allowed employees to get meals – to a circus in Kansas City. It had belonged to a man named Masters. He sent a photo of the dead man to the circus, and the commissary agent identified the dead man as a roustabout named Mahoney. He had disappeared soon after stealing Masters' meal ticket. Norton then discovered that Mahoney had killed a man in New Hampshire – beat him to death in a bar fight – but had since been released. However, it turned out that Mahoney was 20 years older and six inches taller than the "Ragged Stranger." It wasn't him.

People began visiting the morgue to see the body. More identifications of the dead man were made. An elevator operator at a theater said he was a man she'd met in a military hospital in England during the war. He was Canadian and told her his father was a wealthy New York businessman. Norton's squad contacted the cops in New York City, but the businessman didn't exist.

The head of a Catholic Orphanage was sure he'd seen the dead man before. He even brought some of his boys to the morgue with him. All were convinced he was a former resident but couldn't recall his name.

A copy whose beat was the city's West Side "Skid Row" thought the dead man was a homeless veteran named "Snuffy."

A man named Pryor thought the dead man was a childhood friend named Bill whom he hadn't seen in eight or nine years when he'd run off to join the circus – and the list went on.

Norton then turned his attention to the dead man's gun. The Army Colt .45 had a serial number of C2282. In 1920, ballistics in an investigation relied on cartridge calibers and weapon serial numbers. Using the marks left by firing pins and the rifling or barrels wouldn't come into use until later in the decade.

The Colt company told Norton that it had sold the weapon to the Von Lengerke & Antoine Sporting Goods Store in Chicago in 1913. A check with the store revealed that the gun had been sold to a man named John Hoffman, a telephone repairman who lived on Crawford Avenue.

It was soon discovered that Hoffman had sold the gun to his brother-in-law several years earlier. The brother-in-law's name was Fred Wanderer --- he was Carl's cousin.

When Fred realized that he'd loaned the pistol to his cousin Carl on June 21 – the day Ruth had been killed – he was so shocked by the realization that he fainted.

DETECTIVE NORTON HAD CARL BROUGHT in for questioning. For two days, Norton, Lieutenant Mike Loftus, three men from the state's attorney's office, and two men from the coroner's office, including the coroner himself, confronted Carl Wanderer with what they'd found.

They showed him photos of his dead wife, reminded him that she was looking down from heaven, accused him of killing her because he wanted to keep the house money for himself, and claimed that he'd murdered her because she was sleeping with someone else. They yelled at him, shook their fists at him, pushed him around, slapped his face, talked to him quietly, man-to-man, with their arms around his shoulders, and asked him to describe the scene in the vestibule of the apartment building over and over again.

Carl shrugged it all off. He smiled little smiles at them and spoke calmly when he spoke at all. He told them several different versions of the same story. His favorite one seemed to be how the dead man managed to have a gun from Carl's cousin.

He had been carrying Fred's gun, he told detectives. The other one, which had been used by the "Ragged Stranger," was mistakenly identified as his. As it turned out, this was a possibility. A check with the Colt Company revealed that the other gun had been part of a massive shipment of weapons sent to military training camps during the war. The whole thing, Carl assured them, was all an innocent mistake.

But the cops and prosecutors were not convinced.

As for the $1,500 that had been taken out of the bank, sometimes Carl said he didn't know anything about it, sometimes he said it was his idea, and sometimes he claimed Ruth had done it secretly and he hadn't known about it until his mother-in-law found it in Ruth's dresser after she did. And then he'd wonder out loud why they were making such a fuss about the money because it was his, and he'd brought it home from the Army.

At 2:00 A.M. on the third day, Carl was shaken awake in his cell to start what became 16 hours of what was then called "the third degree." In addition to more demands for the truth, accusations, and sympathy, he was also shouted at, slapped, punched, kicked, and knocked down, only to be hauled back up into his chair again. Then, the prosecutors would rush into the room and pretend to throw the cops out, bringing Carl water and even a big steak for lunch.

Around 6:00 P.M. that night, Carl leaned over to one of the men from the prosecutor's office and told him that if he could get cleaned up, he'd tell him the whole thing. Carl hadn't been allowed to wash or shave for three days. He was given soap and a razor, and then someone tracked down a police stenographer. Since whatever confession Carl made would first be heard by a coroner's jury, Coroner Peter Hoffman, a middle-aged man with a proper gray mustache, asked most of the questions.

His confession was 20 pages long. Some of what he said sounded strangely matter-of-fact, hollow, and uncaring. Other parts were bizarre, the reasonings of a crazy man. Most of it, though, was cold-blooded, clear-minded, and very sane. As one of the inmates who later shared space with him at the county jail said, "Wanderer's either innocent or crazy, or he's not human. And he doesn't seem crazy."

Carl said that it took a week for him to make up his mind to kill his wife. He decided that he needed to do it quickly while he wanted to, or he'd lose the idea of doing it. "A man's place is with his wife," he told them, "and I was always home. I was always kind to her but see, I was just tired of her. I didn't want her anymore. I killed her so no one else would have her."

He explained that the thought of killing someone didn't bother him as much as it would most people. He'd put a lot of time in at his father's butcher shop, and the idea of shedding blood didn't offend him. "Besides that," he added, "there's my Army experience. That taught me not to mind killing."

He told Hoffman and the police officers gathered in the interrogation room that he wanted to be hanged. "I want to join my wife in death," Carl said. "Her lying in the vestibule after I shot her haunts me. I wonder if she will forgive me. I loved her too much to let another man have her."

Carl explained that he'd had two guns that night. The "Ragged Stranger" wasn't even armed. He'd borrowed his cousin's gun because he wanted it to look like a stick-up job. He planned to leave the second gun to make it look like it had belonged to the bandit. It hadn't occurred to him that his cousin's gun could be tracked. Carl had feared that his own gun could be traced since the military issued it, but he'd overestimated the efficiency of the federal government.

The longest – and most unnerving – part of the confession concerned his hunt for the man who would take the blame for the murder and, as the newspapers called him, "the poor fool who hired himself out to be killed."

After shopping with his father for blades on June 21, Carl went to check out some of the seedy saloons on West Madison Street's "Skid Row" but found his fall guy hanging out in front of a cigar store on a corner nearby. The man was young and hungry, and Carl offered him a job driving a truck for his father's business for $25 a week, which was a good wage in 1920.

Carl said he'd put him to work that night. He just needed to meet him at the corner of Logan and Western at 6:00 P.M. – one block from the Wanderer's butcher shop. He gave him a quarter for streetcar fare and sent him on his way.

The man showed up at the time Carl gave him and was instructed to follow him onto a streetcar. The man didn't ask any questions. Soon, they left the car, and Carl told him to wait on a corner and said he'd be back.

Carl walked to his cousin's house and asked to borrow the gun. Fred asked why, and he told him he needed it for a bet – a bet to show how quickly he could take it apart and reassemble it. Fred believed him. Carl walked back to the waiting men with the gun in his pocket. They boarded another streetcar – it was too crowded for them to talk – and at Lawrence and Lincoln, they climbed off. They were just two blocks from where Carl and Ruth lived with Ruth's parents.

Carl now gave the young man some specific instructions. He was going to give him some money, and to get it, he just needed to come to the vestibule of Carl's apartment building, ask for the money, and wait for Carl to give it to him. He was supposed to take it from Carl as fast as he could and then leave.

"How will I know when to be there?" the man asked.

Carl explained that it would be between 9:00 and 9:30, that Carl would return to the corner where they were standing, and that he should follow him. Then, Carl gave the man $1 for supper and left him there.

He went home and had supper with Ruth, and then they decided to go see the movie. On the way to the show, Carl made sure they didn't walk the route that would take them past the man. On the way home, though, he steered them toward the rendezvous spot.

At the corner, by the drugstore, the two men spotted each other. Carl nodded his head to him, and the man began following them. At times, he was right behind them, which undoubtedly unnerved Ruth, who had no idea what was happening.

In the vestibule, Ruth fiddled with the key and started to turn on the light. The man then said what Carl had instructed him to say, warning Ruth not to turn on the light and demanding money.

Carl whipped out a gun and was so nervous that the first shot was fired into the floor. Then, he drew the other weapon and started firing in two directions. He wanted both of them dead. The plan had been to kill Ruth, but the man had to die "just to make it look like he'd done the job," Carl said.

After they had fallen, he fired several more shots to make sure they were dead and then went into his "avenging husband act" for Ruth's mother, who he knew would rush to the scene.

After everyone was satisfied, Carl ordered pork and beans for supper, and he was taken back to his cell.

The newspapers now had a new story to run – the vicious "Ragged Stranger" had been a victim, too. The noble war hero was really an ice-blooded killer. No one said it, but everything thought it: a man who'd kill his pretty, young wife and the child she carried in her womb had to be crazy.

THREE DAYS AFTER THE NEWSPAPERS PUBLISHED Carl's confession, a pretty young stenographer named Julia Schmitt came to see Detective Norton. She lived with her family across the street from the Wanderers' butcher shop, and that's how she'd first met Carl. They became friends, and soon, it was more than that. They went to dinners and visited the Riverview amusement park, but she'd never known that Carl was married until she'd read about his wife's death in the newspapers.

Julia gave Norton some of Carl's letters, and the detective suddenly realized the case finally made sense. He finally had a real – and all too familiar – motive. Detectives searched Carl's room and found a single letter that he'd written to Julia. It began, "Sweetheart, I am lonesome." He'd torn it up, but he'd kept it.

Carl's father and sisters

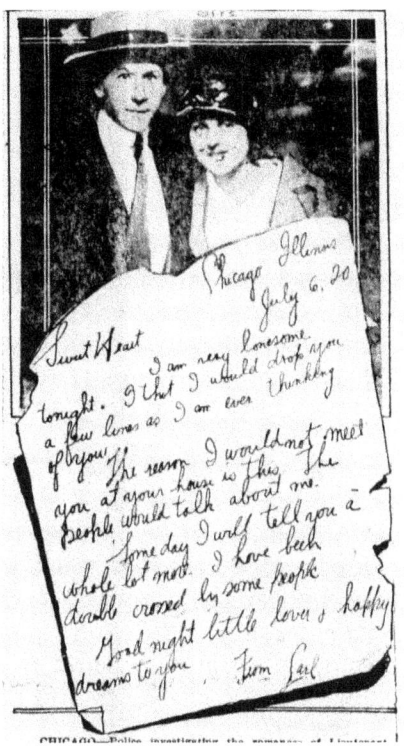

Julia Schmitt was a young stenographer that Carl had been seeing on the side. The police found a letter he'd written to her during a search. It was published in the newspaper.

came to see him. They brought him a Bible and a prayer book. They prayed with him, and they wept. Even the guards were moved, but Carl wasn't. "A man's got to take his medicine," he said. "I'll ask them to hang me as soon as possible."

Detective Norton was impressed. Carl Wanderer seemed to have a spine after all.

A week passed, and one of Carl's guards tipped off a reporter. Wanderer had changed his mind and decided not to plead guilty. He'd told the guard, "They'll have to fight to hang me. I've got a swell lawyer and we'll beat the case yet."

Three months passed, and on the day before his trial, Wanderer gave an interview to reporters. They asked the obvious – why was he denying his own confession? Wasn't he denying everything he'd told everyone – press, police, and family – for months?

"Life is sweet and I'm fighting," he answered. When he walked away, one reporter heard him whistling a tune called "There's a Long, Long Trail A-Winding."

Carl Wanderer had told a lot of different stories before he'd confessed, but now he had a new one.

The trial began on October 4, 1920. There were no women on the jury – the nineteenth amendment, the one that allowed women to vote, had just become law, and it was too soon to get them into jury pools – but the courtroom was crowded with women every day of the trial. They came early and stayed late and brought sandwiches to eat so they could keep their seats during the recess. The judge didn't like it – growling that it wasn't a lunchroom and told them to eat in the corridor. They did as they were told, but they stayed, and more women came with each passing day. Ruth was young, pretty, innocent, and pregnant. Sitting through a lengthy trial and eating in the hallway was a small price to pay to see justice done.

The prosecution spent two weeks presenting its case – Fred's gun and its serial number, the money and the timing of the withdrawal, and finally, Carl's lengthy confession.

The defense had their own strategy. They argued that Carl was insane, that his so-called confession was coerced, and that even if Carl did shoot his wife, it was an accident. They mixed reasonable doubt with mental incapacity.

On October 20, the defense called a string of Carl's family and friends to testify about his mental health. He was the son of a mother who was insane for five years before committing suicide. When Carl was a boy, he tried to kill himself after he contracted scarlet fever. In France, he'd been hit in the head by a baseball and had been unconscious for three hours. Another time, he'd been knocked out after falling off a horse and spent three weeks in the hospital.

The next day, Carl took the stand. The defense attorney began by asking him if he'd shot his wife. Carl denied it and claimed that his confession had been bullied and beaten out of him. He even claimed that Detective Norton had come into his cell while he was still in his underwear and had beaten him up. Even Coroner Hoffman, he claimed, had punched him in the head several times.

"It was all forced out of me!" he exclaimed. And all that talk about him "taking his medicine" and wanting to be hanged – he'd never said any of it. Anything the press, his family, or the police said – he denied it all.

The prosecution called five people to rebut the defense's claims of insanity, including Ruth's parents. The prosecution pressed on, asking about Julia Schmitt, but Carl said that if he'd written her love letters or taken her to amusement parks, he didn't recall any of that.

"Kisses for Julia, bullets for Ruth!" the prosecutor shouted during his closing arguments.

Carl's attorney applauded the prosecutor for his drama, but he said the facts remained – Carl didn't kill Ruth. His confession had been forced. If he had shot her, her death was an accident. Most important, Carl was insane.

The jury took 23 hours to make up its mind. The foreman later said that they believed the confession had been forced out of Carl by Detective Norton and that the state didn't provide enough evidence to prove that Carl had both weapons – at first. They initially had difficulty deciding whether Carl had them both or the stranger did, but eventually agreed on Carl. He admitted that some members of the jury were afraid that if Carl was found insane, he might be committed to an asylum for a year or two and then released. They didn't want that, so they decided he was sane. The foreman added, "Some thought 14 years would be sufficient. Some wanted life. We compromised on 25 years."

Carl cheered the verdict. "I knew they wouldn't crack me! I knew I'd never swing!"

His attorneys were a little surprised that he was grateful for 25 years behind bars. Wasn't this the man who wanted to join his wife in death?

The prosecutor was even more surprised. He'd been telling reporters throughout the trial that he was certain Wanderer would hang. He was stunned by the jury's decision. "What absurdity!" he said. "What fallacy! What foolishness!"

Even the judge weighed in. "You have erred," he said to the jury. "You told me that you believed him insane but that an insanity verdict would not keep him locked up. Now you find him sane! Why, men, I would have sent him away for so long a time that he would never again kill. A grievous error. A regrettable error."

Detective Norton had his own ideas. "They should have had a woman's jury try that wife killer. Women would certainly have done no worse and chances are they would have done much better. That bird should wing, if ever a man should."

THE JURY'S OFFICIAL VERDICT HAD BEEN "manslaughter," and if Carl behaved himself at Joliet prison, he could be released in a little less than 14 years. The state decided not to let that happen. They may have gotten an unsatisfying verdict when they tried him for killing Ruth, but Carl had killed two people.

The prosecutors could still try him for John Doe, the man the newspapers had been referring to as "that poor boob."

Well, maybe. No one had ever prosecuted a John Doe case in Cook County before. No one was even sure that it could be done, but they were willing to try.

Prosecutors decided that the best chance they had of hanging Carl was to prove him sane and then convict him for killing John Doe. In truth, it wasn't the stranger they cared about – the public wanted revenge for the murder of Ruth Wanderer.

The governor appointed a "special board of experts from the Public Welfare Department to evaluate Carl and testify about his sanity. The new trial judge ordered the experts to conduct their exams in the presence of both the defense and the prosecution.

Although the state's specialists hadn't released their findings by the time Carl's subsequent trial began, his attorney told the jury that results showed conclusively that Carl had the mentality of a child of 11. He had been insane for some time, he added. "We will not ask you to acquit him," the lawyer said, "but we shall ask you to send him where he belongs – to a hospital for the criminally insane."

State hospitals were notoriously overcrowded and understaffed at the time. Their escape rates were at around 25 percent. The first jury had voted him sane to keep him locked up for more than a few years. But how could a man be sane and do what Wanderer had done? On the other hand, if sane men were crazy enough to fight in the Great War, then a man like Carl – the war hero – might be judged as normal. If Carl was sane – then who was crazy?

The courtroom was as packed as the first trial. The new judge, Joseph David, quickly intervened in the situation. He stated that no men were to be admitted to the room until all the women who wanted to see the trial had been seated. For those women who came to see the state take a second shot at hanging the man who'd killed poor Ruth, this must have been a relief.

On the second day of the trial, as both sides were presenting their opening arguments, two women arrived at the city morgue to identify John Doe. They joined the dozens who had come before them, attracted by the continuing newspaper coverage. These women, mother, and daughter, announced he was Joseph Ahrens, their missing son and brother. Twelve men, including Joseph's old boss at a tannery, signed an affidavit attesting to that.

A week later, Joseph Ahrens himself came to the morgue to look at the body. He agreed that the dead man resembled him. "I can see how the mistake occurred," he said. "There is a resemblance in the eyes and hair. I'm going to buy the poor fellow a wreath."

He left the morgue, assuring everyone that he wasn't dead.

Meanwhile, back in court, the criminologists and psychiatrists were in a heated debate. Dr. William Hickson, head of the city's Psychopathic Lab, offered the same diagnosis that he'd made public on the very day that Carl had been arrested – he suffered from Dementia Praecox Catatonia, a disease he'd had since birth. It meant he was the insane son of an insane mother. During cross-examination, Dr. Hickson added something else. It was his belief, he said, that 90 percent of all criminals were insane.

A state psychologist from Evanston followed Dr. Hickson to the stand and testified that standard tests showed that Carl had the mental capacity of an 11-year-old.

The judge interrupted. "What do you mean by standard tests? Are they the same for everyone? Suppose a man has lived in the mountains all his life. Would you ask him the same questions you asked Wanderer?"

"Yes," the psychologist had replied.

On the first day of questioning, the defense caused a rift in the courtroom over the question of inherited madness and standard tests that were not actually standard.

The prosecution countered with its experts. The superintendent of the state's psychiatric hospital testified that Carl was sane. Dr. Singer, the Department of Public Welfare's staff psychiatrist, stated that Carl told him that his wife visited him every night in his dreams – that didn't make him crazy, though, just feeling guilty. Finally, Dr. Krohn, the only specialist in private practice on the government's board, took the stand and said that he believed Carl was faking his insanity. Faking required cunning, the prosecutor told the jury, and cunning implied sanity.

The prosecution followed up with two more witnesses, Julia Schmitt and Lieutenant Lester Atkins, Carl's senior officer in France. Both agreed that Carl was sane.

The defense called its last two experts – Dr. James Whitney Hall, president of the Cook County Insanity Commission, and Dr. Florence Fowler, a colleague of Dr. Hickson at the city's Psych Lab. She just reaffirmed Dr. Hickson's diagnosis, but Dr. Hall stated that Carl had been hearing voices since he was a child.

No one cared.

The jury took 12 minutes to reach a verdict, and they'd spent part of that time electing a foreman. Their second ballot decided Carl was sane. The third ballot agreed he was guilty. The fourth ordered that he be hanged. Carl tried to smile as a flashbulb went on in his face as the foreman announced the verdict. "I hope my mother-in-law is satisfied," he said. "If she is, I am."

But, of course, that wasn't true.

Back at Joliet prison, Carl frantically paced his cell. One of his guards told a reporter, "He's been extremely nervous since the verdict was returned. He's been morose and terrible and irritable and won't talk to anyone. He stops his pacing once in a while to listen for his wife's ghost."

The warden placed Carl under suicide watch.

Two months passed, and now Carl said that the Devil – and his wife's ghost – had been visiting him. The judge ordered a Chicago psychologist named William Herschfield to reevaluate Carl, who deemed him insane – again. The judge was skeptical, however. Just because spirits visit him doesn't make him crazy, he argued. It was 1921, and all sorts of people believed in spirits. Sir Arthur Conan Doyle – grieving the loss of his son during the war – was the most public of them, but many widows, mothers, sisters, and brothers had lost men in the war and now contacted the spirit world. "Does that mean Arthur Conan Doyle is insane?" asked Judge David.

"No one knew the truth of such things," Herschfield replied.

Judge David waved him away. Now Carl Wanderer was insane again.

Agreement about Carl's sanity seemed to change as often as the identity of the still unidentified John Doe that he'd shot. Doubts, possibilities, and certainties about the two men were constantly shifting. The public watched and waited for the next shoe to drop in the strange drama.

State law required Judge David to order a sanity trial, complete with more lawyers, more expert witnesses, and a brand-new jury. If that jury decided that Carl was, indeed, insane, he had to be hospitalized. If the jury decided that he was, for better or worse, sane, then according to a recent State Supreme Court ruling, he had to be hung within 48 hours.

Another ten days of debate played out in front of a jury. The only surprise was when Dr. Singer, a member of the governor's original "special board," changed his diagnosis. Three months before, during the John Doe trial, he'd pronounced Carl to be sane. But now, he claimed, Wanderer was insane.

The jury took less than an hour to reach the verdict of "sane." Carl rubbed his face and yawned.

Carl was scheduled to be hanged on July 29, 1921 – but not so fast. The Illinois Commander of the American Legion appealed to the governor to grant Carl a 60-day reprieve. The commander asked the governor to appoint a "new commission of alienists" to determine – again – if Carl was insane. The commander said that Dr. James Whitney Hall had presented new information to him, saying that the "horrors of war" had deranged Lieutenant Wanderer's mind.

"Horrors of war?" Carl asked, confused. "I was happy in the Army."

The governor granted the American Legion's request.

Carl smiled when he heard the news. "I guess my wife will just have to wait a while before she sees me." That night, guards reported, he started acting crazy again.

At this same time, Carl's attorney announced that he had new information that would reveal the true identity of the "Ragged Stranger." He was a notorious gunman, and the lawyer could prove it – but he never had the chance to prove anything.

On August 6, 1921, a homeless washerwoman named Nellie Ryan finally revealed the identity of John Doe – he was her son, Eddie. Mrs. Ryan and her two daughters, Agnes and Marie, had believed it was Eddie for months, but it was only when they came to the morgue that they discovered the truth.

She hadn't seen him in years. Eddie's father had died when he was very young, and Nellie had been too poor to support her six children. Eddie had been sent away to a farm named Alexander Anglin in South Dakota, and the other boys were given to other farmers. The two girls had stayed with Nellie.

"I used to write to Eddie often," she said. "He stayed on the farm until he was 16 and then went off to see the world. I heard he was in Chicago, but it's such a big city. I looked for him everywhere but never could find him."

She read about the homeless man killed by Carl Wanderer, and she became determined to get to the morgue and see him. "I went, and it was Eddie. I knew him at once. He looked so much like Marie, so much like myself," she told a reporter.

At least one mystery in the case was finally solved.

THE GOVERNOR NEVER GOT AROUND TO APPOINTING that new sanity commission. The 60-day reprieve came and went, and Carl was once again scheduled to hang.

While he waited in jail, he continued to be visited by doctors who tried to decide if Carl had been sane when he planned Ruth's murder. No consensus was ever reached.

He was also frequently visited by reporters, who never got tired of milking a good story. Two of Carl's favorite journalist visitors were Ben Hecht and Charley MacArthur, two of Chicago's most famous writers from the colorful and sensational journalism era of the early 1900s.

They were covering Carl's story for their respective newspapers and visited him often, playing poker with him and becoming quite chummy. They even convinced Carl to read two letters that they had written, hilariously attacking their bosses from the gallows. The newsmen didn't remember until the last minute that Carl's hands and feet would be bound when he was executed, so he couldn't read the letters.

So, they asked him to croon a rendition of the song "Old Pal, Why Don't You Answer Me?" moments before the drop instead.

On the day of his hanging, Carl was brought to the gallows, and to the surprise of everyone present, save for Hecht and MacArthur, Wanderer began to sing.

Old pal – old pal
You left me all alone.
Old pal – why don't you answer me?

The hangman stepped forward after the first chorus, but Carl warned him away with a shake of his head. After the second chorus, even though Carl was still singing, He got impatient and placed the black hood over his head. When the song finally finished, he was asked if he had anything to say.

"Christ, have mercy on my...." Carl began but never finished his plea. The trap sprung open, and Carl shot downwards until the rope snapped tight and instantly killed him.

Charley MacArthur had the last word. He turned to his friend Ben Hecht and said with a sigh: "You know, Ben, that son-of-a-bitch would have been a hell of a song plugger."

THAT LAST, INTERUPPTED PLEA FOR MERCY was the last thing ever heard from Carl Wanderer, but the same cannot be said for his wife, Ruth. The legends of Chicago's Lincoln Square neighborhood say that the building where the ill-fated couple once lived and where Ruth died remains haunted by her spirit to this day.

This apartment building, located at 4732 North Campbell Avenue, is just a half block from Lawrence and two blocks west of Western Avenue. The place has changed much since 1920. It's been remodeled several times, and the number on the building is no longer visible, which is likely an intentional oversight. These days, a wooden gate protects the vestibule where Ruth was heartlessly gunned down.

For many years, the crime that occurred here was widely discussed, and few could pass this house without pointing out, often with trembling hands, the place where the murders occurred. As time passed, though, and the tale of the "Ragged Stranger" slipped from the public consciousness and took its place among the many other murders in the city, the story of Ruth Wanderer began to fade.

Soon after, stories of the haunting began.

Sources state that in the years after World War II, regular accounts appeared about the sounds of a woman's screams that came from the vestibule of the North Campbell Avenue house. The screams, neighbors claimed, were those of Ruth Wanderer, perhaps re-living her final moments --- perhaps just as she realized that her husband intended to kill her. These same sources say that the screams are still heard occasionally, even today.

According to her husband, Ruth's ghost had quite literally haunted him into the grave. Was Carl's story true, or was he pretending to see her ghost to lend credence to his claims of insanity? We may never know, but some of his guards said they were convinced that he genuinely believed Ruth was waiting for him on the other side.

But if Ruth stalked Carl at Joliet prison, why does her spirit still haunt this place? And why did she wait until more than two decades after her death to make her spirit known?

Perhaps the answer to this is that she wants people to remember her story, to remember that she once lived and died, and most heartbreaking of all, to remember the life of her child, who was never allowed to live at all.

"BLACK WIDOW"
The Murderous Career of Louise Peete

I DON'T THINK THAT LOUISE PEETE WILL EVER be mistaken as a woman who killed for love or committed a "crime of passion." She was many things – refined, elegant, charmingly feminine, callous, cold-blooded, and a master manipulator of men – but she never acted out of passion.

Louise never showed an ounce of remorse for her crimes or her victims, and her reign of terror lasted nearly four decades before she was apprehended. Incredibly, four of her husbands died suspiciously or by suicide before anyone noticed. But she eventually paid the price for her lifetime of deceit and murder, holding the dubious distinction of being one of only four women executed in California's gas chamber.

No one mourned her when she was gone.

She was born Lofie Louise Preslar on September 20, 1880, in Bienville, Louisiana, the daughter of a wealthy, socially prominent newspaper publisher. She lived a life of privilege and attended the best private schools. At age 15, her parents enrolled her in an upscale New Orleans boarding school, but her stay there turned out to be short-lived. Within a few months after the start of the semester, she was shockingly caught stealing and engaging in sexual escapades with male students. The story goes that Louise left Louisiana and moved to Boston, where she allegedly worked as a high-class call girl, although I've seen no proof of this.

What we do know is that in 1903, she married a traveling salesman named Henry Bosley. Although his job kept him away from home most of the week, he had no reason to think that his wife wouldn't be faithful to him – until he found out she wasn't. After catching Louise in bed with another man, Henry became profoundly depressed and eventually committed suicide.

Or at least that's what Louise always claimed.

Soon after his death, Louise emptied his bank accounts, sold all his belongings, and returned to Louisiana. She purchased a large home in Shreveport but soon found her finances strained.

Louise Preslar – later to be Louise Peete. She was not conventionally attractive but had a way of attracting desperate men.

Anxious to make money, she started her own business as an independent prostate. It boomed, with Louise charging high prices for her regular customers and using her sexuality and talents of seduction to charm unsuspecting men out of even more money. Unable to get enough money to satisfy her needs, she emptied customers' wallets and sold their stolen watches and jewelry. But when she fleeced one customer too many, she decided to skip town and wound up in Waco, Texas.

In Texas, Louise continued her scams, cozying up to wealthy men who paid for her clothing, jewelry, and apartments and made sure she had cash. It was the beginning of the oil boom in Texas, and there were a lot of rich men around, including Joe Appel, a flashy, newly minted millionaire who drove big cars, wore diamond rings, and even sported a sold gold belt buckle. He was a prize just too big for her to resist.

Within a week of their meeting, Joe was shelling out all kinds of cash to keep Louise around, and then suddenly, he ended up dead – shot in the head and his wallet and jewelry missing. The police went looking for a suspect, and soon, they had Louise. Called before a special grand jury, she tearfully admitted that she had shot Joe, but she'd done it in self-defense. She told the all-male jury that he'd become violent and tried to rape her. Fearing for her life and her honor, she'd be forced to defend herself with fatal results. The jury ate it up and openly applauded her when the police set her free.

Joe's missing wallet and jewelry were never found.

By 1913, she was running out of luck and needed more cash, so she moved to Dallas, Texas. Not long after she arrived, she became acquainted with a man named Harry Faurote, who worked as a night clerk in one of the city's finest hotels. Less than a month later, they were married.

Harry seemed unlike Louise's other victims – he was young, uneducated, and didn't have a lot of money. Louise also didn't marry him for his sexual prowess either since she openly flaunted several affairs during the two years they were together.

It turned out, though, that there was something Louise wanted from him. One night, while Harry was at work, more than $20,000 worth of guests' jewelry vanished from the hotel safe. As the person on duty that night, he became the prime suspect, but after a police investigation, he was cleared.

Spouse of Murderess Believed Suicide. Mr. and Mrs. R. C. Peete, in happier times. She is in San Quentin for Denton murder and he was reported yesterday to have committed suicide. (Times photo.)

Louise and her husband, Richard Peete. After the next murder she was accused of, he committed suicide.

No one bothered to check out his wife.

Harry, thoroughly embarrassed at being suspected by the police – and likely aware that his wife wasn't innocent of the crime –became deeply depressed and committed suicide by hanging himself.

Again, or so Louise claimed.

Soon after Harry's death, Louise moved to Denver, Colorado, where she met and won the heart of a door-to-door salesman named Richard Peete. The couple married bought a small, modest home, and welcomed a daughter named Elizabeth the following year.

If it sounds to you like Louise finally settled down and put her wicked ways behind her, you'd be mistaken. She quickly tired of her boring domestic lifestyle, and she and Richard began to bicker about everything. After another year in this now toxic marriage, the pair decided to part ways. Louise abandoned her husband and daughter in 1920 and went to California.

OCTOBER 28, 1920.
Held for Denton Murder
Louise Peete

The good news is that at least they both survived their time with her. Most people couldn't say the same.

While looking for a place to live in Los Angeles, Louise met Jacob Denton, a wealthy and recently widowed mining executive with a teenage daughter. Quickly winning him over, Louise moved into his Wilshire Boulevard mansion as both his lover and housekeeper. After several weeks of torrid sex, Louise abruptly asked Jacob to marry her, but still grieving the death of his wife, he politely declined.

This proved to be a fatal mistake.

In May 1920, Jacob Denton disappeared. When asked, Louise explained his absence as a sudden business trip. At first, everyone, including his daughter, believed this story for nearly a month. During that time, Louise – after forging his signature – began withdrawing money from his bank account and valuables from his safety deposit box. Though the bank teller had noticed the signature to be suspicious, she believed the lie that Louise had told her -- that a mysterious Spanish woman had got into their mansion and shot Jacob in the right arm. He was using his left to write until his other was healed.

As time passed, friends, neighbors, and business associates became more insistent about speaking to Jacob. Louise, always with an explanation, concocted wild stories about his continued absence, many of which contradicted each other.

It would be Jacob's daughter who finally sounded the alarm. After weeks of her father not returning or communicating with her, she went to see his attorneys and explained the situation. One of the lawyers from the firm came to the house and asked Louise to provide helpful information about Jacob's business trip and his whereabouts. As usual, excuses were given, but surprisingly, she offered to provide the lawyer with access to his financial and business documents once she managed to get hold of them.

That same night, Louise packed up and fled Los Angeles. She returned to Denver and her husband, convincing him to give her another chance.

Meanwhile, back in L.A., Jacob's attorneys had contacted the police, and a search was conducted of the Denton home. On September 23, his body was discovered buried in a shallow grave in the basement. He had been shot in the head.

Louise was, of course, the prime suspect. She was arrested in Colorado and brought back to Los Angeles for questioning. She once again offered a number of excuses and even tried to claim that Jacob was alive. The body in the basement, she claimed, was an intruder that Jacob had accidentally killed, and now he was hiding out, fearing his story wouldn't be believed.

But this time, it was Louise's story that no one believed. The body had already been positively identified, and she was charged with first-degree murder.

Her trial began on January 21, 1921, and thanks to the lurid details of the case being splashed across the front pages of newspapers, it became a circus. Thousands of people lined the downtown streets, hoping to catch a glimpse of Louise.

From the start, her defense attorneys tried to plant the seeds of reasonable doubt in the minds of the jury. Louise was too small to have murdered Jacob, they said, and then dragged his body all the way down to the basement. She couldn't possibly have committed the crime. But the prosecution managed to discredit every witness, finally forcing Louise herself to take the stand. She proclaimed her innocence and insisted that she had no idea who killed Jacob.

On February 5, unmoved by her story and after only deliberating four hours, the jury found her guilty. As the verdict was read, Louise showed no emotion. Two weeks later, Judge Frank R. Willis sentenced her to spend the rest of her life in San Quentin.

But things wouldn't work out that way.

Sadly, Richard Peete was greatly affected by the guilty verdict and the prison sentence. He truly believed his wife was innocent. He wrote letter after letter to her while she was behind bars, but Louise never answered any of them. Finally, in 1924, he could stand it no longer and ended his own life.

It was reported that while she was in prison, Louise loved to tell the story of how Richard had killed himself because he couldn't have her. It was proof, she claimed, that she was so appealing to men that they'd rather die than be without her.

A LIFE SENTENCE FOR LOUISE PEETE turned out to be just 18 years. Thanks to good behavior and her work inside the penitentiary, she was granted parole in 1939 and released into the care of Jessie Marcy, a woman who had lobbied for her release. The court allowed her to change her name to Anna Lee to avoid publicity, and she found employment as a housekeeper for several wealthy residents of Los Angeles.

Three years later, Jessie was found dead from an apparent stroke, but oddly, her home had been ransacked, and all her valuables were missing. With no place to live, Louise – we're not going to refer to her as "Anna" – moved in with her parole officer, Emily Latham. Then, on September 14, 1943, Emily died from an apparent heart attack.

In what could have only been a careless or inept investigation, the police seriously studied neither of those two deaths. It turned out they were unaware that Anna Lee used to be the "Black Widow" Louise Peete.

Again, with no place to live, Louise turned to Margaret Logan and her husband, Arthur. Louise and Margaret had met behind bars and formed a close friendship. Since Margaret was released before Louise was, she had even cared for Elizabeth, Louise's daughter, after her father committed suicide. Louise agreed to help the couple with housework in exchange for room and board at their home in Pacific Palisades.

In May 1944, though, Louise found another man with a hefty bank account. His name was Lee Judson, and he was a former advertising executive who was oblivious to the fact that he had married a convicted killer.

Later that same month, Louise's friend, Margaret Logan, mysteriously disappeared – or so anyone who didn't notice the fresh mound of earth with the flowerpots on it in the Logans' yard thought. She explained to Arthur that his wife was in the hospital and was unable to receive visitors. Within days, Louise had convinced the authorities that Arthur was mentally unbalanced, and he was committed to the Patton State Hospital, where he died on December 6, 1944.

With the Logans now out of the way, Louise moved into their home with her new husband. Louise forged Margaret and Arthur's signatures and started withdrawing money from the bank.

It was impossible for Lee Judson not to notice money was appearing, which he knew nothing about. He also discovered a bullet hole in one wall in the house, that strange mound of dirt in the garden, and an insurance policy that named his wife as Margaret Logan's sole beneficiary.

Despite his suspicions about the missing Margaret, Lee said nothing, which is probably what kept him alive.

TWO EVENTS OCCURRED AT ALMOST THE same time that finally stopped Louise Peete.

The first was the checks that continued arriving at the bank in mid-December 1944, made out to cash and signed by Arthur Logan. One of the bank tellers, knowing he had recently died, reported the checks to the police.

The second problem was Margaret's parole officer. She hadn't been checking in as she was supposed to, so the police were sent to her house to check on her.

When the officers arrived looking for Margaret – both on behalf of her parole officer and to inquire about the checks – Louise told them that Margaret was away, having surgery. She should be back soon, she said.

A few days later, the police returned, but this time, they had a search warrant in hand. The search finally forced Lee to open his mouth about his suspicions, and soon, Margaret's body was discovered in a shallow grave under an avocado tree.

Once again, Louise had a story. She claimed that Arthur Logan had shot and killed his wife in a fit of rage – he was insane, after all – and frightened that her criminal history would make her a suspect, Louise agreed to help hide Margaret's body. Then, worried that Arthur might kill her too, she got him committed to an asylum.

It was actually one of Louise's better stories, but the cops didn't believe her. She was arrested on December 20 and charged with Margaret's murder.

'GUESS I WAS PRETTY GULLIBLE'—Thus Lee Borden Judson, husband of Louise Peete, explained why he's in jail over alleged slaying of wife's friend.

Louise Peete's Husband Sobs Out Story in Jail

Lee Judson narrowly escaped prison as an accomplice to Louise's latest murder. He was another husband who committed suicide.

Lee was also arrested, and he was charged as an accessory to her crime. He maintained that he knew nothing about the murder, and on January 12, charges against him were dismissed for lack of evidence, and he was released.

The next day, though, Lee climbed to the ninth floor of the Spring Arcade Building in the city's financial district and leaped to his death.

When Louise was informed of his suicide, she was devastated by the news. She wept hysterically and blamed herself for his death. It was a strange reaction from a woman who once gloated that a man couldn't stand to live without her.

After all those men and all that crime, had Louise Peete actually been in love this time?

HER SECOND TRIAL FOR MURDER BEGAN on April 23, 1945. Once again, the defense tried valiantly to confuse the jury and get them to doubt the prosecution's story, but the district attorney argued that Louise had killed Margaret Logan to gain control of her finances.

The trial – which unearthed Louise's identity and revealed her former crime – lasted for five weeks. On May 28, the case was handed to the jury, and they deliberated for only three hours. She was guilty – again – of first-degree murder. And once again, Louise didn't seem all that interested as the verdict was read.

On June 1, Judge Harold B. Landreth passed down a death sentence for the twice-convicted killer. She now had a date with the gas chamber.

On April 11, 1947, after numerous appeals, delays, and stays of execution, Louise finally went to her death. She met her fate with the same resignation with which she'd listened to the verdicts in her trials. She showed no remorse for her crimes. She became the second woman to die in California's gas chamber. Her body was cremated, and she was buried in an unmarked grave at Angelus-Rosedale Cemetery in Los Angeles.

Clinton Duffy, the warden of San Quentin, once described Louise as a woman with "an air of innocent sweetness, which masked a heart of ice." When she died, she left a string of murders and suicides behind her that are nearly unrivaled in the history of American crime.

Louise looked like a harmless old woman at her final trial – but she was far from harmless.

She serves today as proof that -- even though most will claim the opposite – men are far more naïve and easily fooled than those we often call the "weaker sex."

"THE MURDERING MINISTER"
Lawrence Hight and Elsie Sweetin

THERE IS AN INSCRIPTION ON THE TOMBSTONE of a coal miner named Wilford Sweetin, who is buried in the Kirk Cemetery, just north of the small Southern Illinois town of Ina. The epitaph reads:

Earth has no sorrow that heaven cannot heal.

It seems a pleasant and forgiving sentiment to place on the marker of a man who was murdered. And once you know what happened to him, "solace" and "forgiveness" are not the first words that come to mind.

But Wilford was not the only victim of the two killers whose identities shocked the small town in 1924.

Rev. Lawrence Hight and his wife, Anna, with whom he had three children.

LAWRENCE HIGHT WAS THE PASTOR OF THE local Methodist Church in Ina. He had been married to his wife, Anna, for 26 years, and together, they had three children.

Lawrence had grown up on a farm in Metropolis, Illinois, where he took an early interest in the racehorses his father owned. Although his family encouraged him to continue his education at the country grammar school he'd attended, he was only passionate about horses. Eventually, he relented, attended two years of high school, and then went to work. He was saving his money for one thing – to buy his own racehorse.

Within a few years, he had two horses in his stable and was spending the summers traveling around Illinois and the Midwest, attending fairs and entering races, making a decent name for himself in horse racing circles. Many stated that he could have made a good living as a jockey, riding in more important races, but his ambitions never took him that far. He just continued traveling from county fair to county fair and returning home to the family farm in the winter. His father was well-off and always made sure his son knew that he was welcome to return home.

Over time, Lawrence acquired more horses and was seen on tracks throughout the summer, making money by winning purses and gambling on the races in which he rode.

But then his life changed in 1911 when he was 27 years old, and he attended a Methodist prayer meeting in Golconda, Illinois.

Those who knew him before the prayer meeting considered him a carefree, devilish young man, always looking for a good time, a drink, and a pocket filled with cash. They assumed the only reason he'd attend a prayer meeting would be to scoff and heckle. However, Lawrence actually became interested in the words of the minister, and by the time it was over, he was thoughtful and reflective. He thought about what he'd heard that night for the next several days and would later call it "the turning tide of my life."

He said that he was standing in a pasture with his horses, and he felt "deeply burdened by sin." He added, "Suddenly, a great light broke on me as I stood there. My sins dropped off me, and I knew I was cleansed. It was the great awakening."

Then, 13 years later, he was the pastor at the Methodist Church in Ina. His wife, who'd grown up in Mount Vernon, had always encouraged him and helped him to get started in the ministry. Everyone in town knew Reverend Hight. Although considered a little on the eccentric side, he was respected in the community and was well-liked even by those who didn't attend his church.

This was likely why people were so shocked and surprised when gossip began to spread around town about what Reverend Hight was doing when he wasn't behind the pulpit.

The gossip concerned the minister and an attractive member of his church, a woman named Elsie Sweeten. The pretty young woman caught Hight's eye shortly after she began attending Sunday services. Her husband, Wilford, was a coal miner and the father of her three sons. Everyone acknowledged Elsie to be very beautiful, and she entranced Hight. One resident later testified that Hight had commented, "Mrs. Sweeten is the best-looking woman I ever saw." He also reportedly told another minister that Elsie "walked down the church aisle, and a power came over me that I could not resist."

The attraction that Hight felt for the woman was apparently mutual, and the two began an illicit affair. As it developed, there were stories told of clandestine trysts following prayer meetings and church services. At one point, when Hight was conducting a

10-day camp meeting in a rural area, Elsie was secreted away in a small cabin next door to his own on the campgrounds. During this time, Anna Hight, oblivious to the affair, wrote a number of affectionate letters to her husband.

They were later found among her belongings after her mysterious death.

ANNA MAY HAVE BEEN UNAWARE OF what her husband and Elise were up to, but few others in town were as clueless. The minister and the member of his flock poorly concealed their relationship, and as their passion became more heated, more and more people started to talk.

By early summer 1924, the lovers decided they couldn't stand to be separated any longer and began making plans to be together forever. Since divorce was out of the question because of Lawrence's position in the church, they concocted a plan to murder their spouses instead.

Murder was, apparently, less of a sin to Reverend Hight than divorce.

Elsie Sweetin and her husband, Wilford, who she was accused of murdering.

Wilford Sweeten was the first to die. In confessions that she later made, Elsie said that Lawrence provided her with the arsenic used to take her husband's life about two weeks before Wilford was slightly injured in the mine where he worked. Off work on the day after the accident, Wilford and Elsie went to Benton, Illinois, stopped at a drug store, and bought ice cream, candy, and Coca-Cola. When they got home, Elsie gave her husband the first dose of the powder that Lawrence had given her. He became very sick but seemed to get better, so a few days later, she mixed some into his morning oatmeal. She continued giving him the poison three times each day. When she ran out, Lawrence would visit the Sweeten home – under the guise of a pastor visiting a sick member of his congregation – and leave her with more of it.

Wilford suffered intense agony for nine horrible days, receiving the last dose of poison on July 25, 1924, shortly after being visited by Dr. S.J. Thompson. He died just three days later.

Wilford's cause of death was said to be ptomaine poisoning, supposedly traced to spoiled ice cream. Reverend conducted an outstanding funeral service for Wilford, even going as far as to boast that he had converted the man to the Lord and had "saved him" while the miner was on his deathbed.

SIX WEEKS LATER, ANNA HIGHT BEGAN TO suffer an unknown illness. She was in terrible pain after succumbing to paralysis and then death on September 12, 1924.

At first, the Jefferson County coroner also believed she had died from ptomaine poisoning. In her case, it was thought that a batch of spoiled ham had killed her.

By now, though, the rumors about Reverend Height and Elise Sweeten had become a full-blown scandal. The coroner decided to take another look at the case and ordered an analysis of the contents of Anna's stomach from a laboratory in Chicago. He also had Wilford Sweeten's body exhumed and examined. The results of both tests were identical – death had come from acute arsenic poisoning.

The authorities wasted no time in arresting Reverend Hight. At first, he pretended to be shocked to learn that his wife had been poisoned. He said that he honestly believed that his wife had died from the spoiled ham, which had also made his children sick, although they had recovered. But then he tried to blame the poisoning on "gangsters," claiming that bootleggers had attempted to murder the family as revenge for Reverend Hight's crusade against them.

Regardless, he claimed to be completely innocent of the crime – at first.

He soon changed his mind, though. Whether it was an attack of guilt or that he just saw no way out of the mess he'd created, he admitted his role in the murders and took full blame for both deaths – although, even then, he continued to lie. He claimed that both victims had been suffering from severe illnesses, and he had only administered the arsenic "to put them out of their misery."

When that didn't work, he changed his story once again. This time, he implicated Elsie as his partner in both murders. She was arrested, and then she also began offering several different accounts of the crimes. In the end, she admitted her guilt, even if she did blame the whole thing on Lawrence.

The heartless and cold-blooded murders -- as well as the sorted nature of the love affair -- captured the attention of newspaper readers across Illinois and, later, throughout the country. Locals clamored for a trial, and as reporters from papers all over the Midwest descended on the small Southern Illinois town, residents soon became semi-celebrities for their headline-grabbing quotes about the case.

"Reverend Hight should be taken out and hanged like any other criminal," said Reverend R. Keene Ryan of the Ina Congregational Church during an interview that went out on the *United Press* wire. "No mercy should be shown him. Minister or jockey, it makes no difference," he added, referring to Lawrence's earlier days on the racetrack.

Reverend Ryan went on to say that Hight's actions could not be construed as a blow to religion any more than one faulty automobile can be held against all the automobiles in the country. "Hight does not represent the Methodist Church, and the church should not suffer. He should hang."

It was eventually decided that the pair would be tried together at the courthouse in Mount Vernon for the murder of Wilford Sweeten. Despite detailed and often confusing confessions, both defendants pleaded not guilty. The trial that followed became a lurid sensation in Southern Illinois.

The witness stand offered one shocking story after another. Many of the residents of Ina had something to say about the coal miner's wife and her minister lover. Witnesses described how the pair arranged their romantic trysts, when and where they had met, and how Reverend Hight had purchased the arsenic.

When Elsie Sweeten took the stand, she offered a dramatic -- and not entirely accurate -- version of events. She now claimed to have only feelings of contempt for her former minister, who was said to have repeatedly fallen asleep during her testimony. Elsie continued to claim that Lawrence was the one to blame for the murders – that he had pressured and manipulated her into poisoning her husband. She'd had nothing to do with Anna's death.

When it came time for Lawrence to offer a defense, his attorney tried to portray him as insane, suffering from "pre-senile dementia." His daughters testified that he often saw strange visions and lights and heard messages from unseen beings. They also claimed that he sometimes suffered from extreme and uncontrollable rages. One of these spells even led him to inflict a nasty bite on a mule's nose when it angered him. Members of his church, those few who did not feel betrayed by his affair with Elsie Sweeten, stated that he would sometimes run up and down the aisles of the church laughing uncontrollably.

The prosecutor delivered a scathing attack on the minister. He scorned the insanity claim, charging that the defense wanted a "nice, pleasant stay in the asylum for Brother Hight." He also described Elsie Sweeten as "a cold-blooded murderer… who administered dose after dose" to her devoted and clueless husband. The prosecutor had one fierce charge for the jury, which he shouted at them, "Hang them! Hang them both!"

The jury took 11 hours to reach their verdict, and while they quickly concurred that both defendants were guilty, they were unable to agree on the proper sentence to impose on them. After more deliberation, they finally voted for life imprisonment for Reverend Hight and 35 years for Elsie Sweeten.

An editorial that appeared in the *New York Times* in the wake of the verdict and sentencing stated that the results illustrated a growing resistance to capital punishment because "if any murderers deserved to go to the gallows, those two did."

Lawrence seemed unconcerned about the verdict. He shrugged and announced, "I ain't mad at nobody." He was taken by train to Menard Prison in Chester. As it traveled through small towns, Lawrence stood near the window so the crowds that gathered to see him would be able to get a better view.

Unlike her former lover, Elsie was visibly upset by the verdict. She wasn't the only one. Her father-in-law, Columbus Sweeten, was also in the courtroom and had reluctantly testified against Elsie during the trial.

"My own father is sending me to prison," Elsie had muttered after his testimony. "It is his testimony that is taking me away from my children and leaving them motherless. But I don't blame him. He did what he thought was right. He told what he thought was the truth. They all misunderstood me, and I am the one to pay the penalty. What can I say but that I am innocent."

After the verdict was read and Elsie was taken out of the courtroom, reporter Sonia Lee from the *International News* noted that old Mr. Sweeten watched as she was led away. "She made her bed – she is lying on it," he sighed.

As he started to get up from his seat, he said one more thing to the reporter, "I love her – loved her as a daughter, and now half of the heart which was hers when she married my son is dead. The other half is down in the grave with the boy she murdered."

ELSIE WAS ORDERED TO SPEND HER SENTENCE at the state prison in Joliet, but just two years after the verdict was read, she was able to secure a new trial after the Illinois Supreme Court ruled that she should have been tried separately from Lawrence Hight, the first time. Despite copious amounts of damaging evidence, including her confession, the jury deliberated for only five minutes before finding her not guilty.

They blamed the minister – who obviously led her astray – and believed she had been punished enough.

Following her release, she and her sons moved to Chicago, where she remarried and lived out the rest of her life.

Lawrence Hight was released from prison after serving 27 years of his life sentence. He returned to the Mount Vernon area and died there in 1959, his earlier notoriety completely forgotten.

Only the solitary tombstone remains in the town of Ina as a reminder of what happened there in 1924. If you ask just about anyone you might see on the quiet streets of town, they would be as unaware of the murders committed by Lawrence Hight and Elsie Sweeten as those thousands of travelers who pass by Ina on the interstate each day.

The story of the murderous minister is a piece of history long forgotten but a dark secret that, thanks to the grave of Wilford Sweeten, will always be stitched into the secret history of this little town.

THE DOCTOR, HIS WIFE, AND THE OTHER WOMAN
Betrayal and Forbidden Love in Roaring 20s Detroit

THE FIRST BLOW KNOCKED GRACE LOOMIS to her knees and opened a gash on her head, just above her left temple. When she fell to the floor, her killer raised the wooden club to strike again and sent a fine spray of blood onto the wallpaper and window drapes.

Then, the club fell again. The wood collided with Grace's skull and made a dull, thudding sound. Her breath whuffed from her throat. More blood. She fell onto the floor of the sunroom between two wicker chairs. Her body shook and convulsed.

The killer hit her again - once, twice - and she finally lay still. Blood flowed away from her body, making a halo around her battered skull.

Grace Loomis

The attack had taken her completely by surprise, and the silence of it - a whispered cry, a muffled wail, the shuffling of feet - had not awakened her two children, who were asleep upstairs.

Grace Loomis, only 34 years old, the mother of two and the wife of a prominent Detroit doctor was dead. Her murder remains unsolved to this day. Even the best detectives in the city -- veterans who traded bullets with gangsters and bootleggers - couldn't crack the case.

But that didn't mean they didn't know who'd probably done it.

IT WAS FEBRUARY 22, 1927, AND IT WAS AN ordinary night at the Loomis home at 13901 Marlowe Avenue in Detroit. Frank Loomis

The Loomis children – Frank, Jr., and Jeannette – who were home when they mother was murdered.

came home at the usual time and had dinner with his family – wife, Grace, son, Frank, Jr., who was eight, and daughter, Jeannette, who was six – around 6:00 P.M.

After dinner, the couple talked for a little while, and then Frank announced he needed to go back to his office for a bit. When he returned at 8:00 P.M., the children had been put to bed, and Grace was reading a book. He remembered that she had asked him for money to buy a new coat and he gave her $100 for it.

An hour later, just before 9:00, Frank announced that he was going out for a walk. This was his usual habit. He took regular strolls in the evening. He liked the exercise and wanted to take care of himself. The evening air always seemed to relieve the stress that had built up over the course of the day.

This evening wasn't terribly relaxing, though. It was chilly – it was mid-winter in Michigan, after all – and a light but steady rain was falling. He usually walked for about an hour in the neighborhood, but on this miserable night, he decided to cut things short and go home. He arrived back home around 9:30 P.M.

Frank stepped inside and brushed the rain from his coat. He thought about calling out to Grace but remembered the children were asleep, and he didn't want to wake them. He took off his rubber overshoes and then went into the sunroom, looking for his wife.

And he quickly found her. She was lying on the floor in a pool of blood, her head bashed in by some blunt weapon.

He let out a cry, rushed across the room, and fell to his knees next to Grace. He frantically searched for a pulse but found nothing. He hurried to the telephone, but when he lifted the receiver, there was no sound. It wasn't working, so he went to the back porch of the house and began yelling toward the home of his neighbor, Mildred Twork.

Up to this point, the only account we have of Frank's movements that evening came from Frank himself. No one could verify them but Grace, and she was dead.

Mrs. Twork picked up the story from there.

She was just getting ready for bed when she heard Frank calling her name. She opened a bedroom window and looked out to see what was wrong. He yelled up to her: "My wife has been murdered! Please call the police and come right over?"

Dr. Frank Loomis

Then, even though he had just asked Mildred to call the police, Frank left the house and ran down the street to the nearby Schoolcraft police station. He arrived about 9:50 P.M., and after slamming through the front door, he cried out, "Please come quick, there's been a murder! Someone has murdered my wife!" With Sergeant Milford Harrison and Officer Elijah Wasson closed behind him, Frank ran towards home.

As soon as the officers entered the house, they noticed how hot it was inside. Harrison later described it as a blast of heat to his face. The furnace in the cellar was blazing, turning the house into an oven. A little later, when Harrison checked the furnace, he found that someone had recently stoked it, raising the heat levels, but it had been such a short time before that much of the coal that had been fed into the furnace remained unburned.

For now, the cops were more concerned with the battered body of Grace Loomis in the sunroom – and with the woman who then walked through the front door. It was Mildred Twork. She'd gotten dressed and come over, as Frank had asked her, too. But when she walked into the house and got a glimpse of the bloody scene in the sunroom, she became hysterical. Crying and wailing, she collapsed into a chair. One of the officers comforted her, and in a few minutes, she calmed down. Once she had, she asked the question that Frank hadn't bothered to think about, "Are the children all right?"

Frank let out a choking gasp, "You don't think..." He and Officer Wasson ran up the stairs to check the children's rooms. They found both Jeannette and Frank, Jr. fast asleep.

It was the last time the children would sleep soundly for a very long time.

WITHIN AN HOUR, SIX HOMICIDE DETECTIVES were on the scene, led by Detective Lieutenant Frank McNally. When the men stepped into the overly warm house, they quickly shed their coats and started searching for evidence.

The scene in the sunroom suggested a violent struggle. An overturned chair was on its back. Blood was spattered on the walls and curtains near Grace's body. A window had been shattered, and pieces of glass were scattered on the front lawn, indicating that it had been broken from the inside. Detectives surmised this might have happened during the struggle. The telephone in the room was on the floor, and, oddly, its receiver was in place.

Grace was fully clothed, and later, a postmortem would show that she hadn't been raped. But she had fought her attacker. She had defensive wounds on her hands, scrapes on her knuckles, a contusion over her left eye, and scratches across her jaw. This would explain the state of the room, Detective McNally thought admiringly. She didn't go down without a fight.

Once the red-hot coals in the furnace cooled down, detectives sifted through the ashes and found two scorched pearl buttons, suggesting that the killer had taken the time to stoke the fire and burn any incriminating evidence, like a bloody shirt.

Detectives also discovered a syringe that was filled with morphine, although at the time, this didn't raise too many questions since Frank was a doctor.

McNally quickly eliminated two possible motives – Grace hadn't been raped, and robbery also seemed out of the question. Except for the $100 that Dr. Loomis claimed to give his wife for a new coat, nothing was missing. Grace habitually wore three rings, and all of them were still on her fingers.

Frank Loomis, though, spoke up and suggested that the $100 he gave Grace might be to blame. What if someone outside the house had seen him give his wife the money through the open blinds of the sunroom? When he left for his walk, the perpetrator might have entered the house and attacked her.

I don't know if Detective McNally rolled his eyes at this suggestion, but I'd like to imagine that he did.

McNally was no sucker. He was a veteran detective who'd worked his way up through the ranks to the top of the Homicide Bureau. He'd dealt with gangsters and stone-cold killers, and he knew that when a wife was murdered, the number one suspect is *always* the husband.

This time around was no different, no matter how prominent the doctor might be. So, McNally allowed Dr. Loomis to search the house for clues alongside his men, although he made sure that Frank was never out of sight. During the search, McNally peppered the doctor with casual questions about his movements that night. At some point, though, Frank caught on. "Gentlemen," he said to the group of detectives," I am telling you everything. I wish I could tell you more. I am more eager than you to clear up the slaying."

McNally was no wet-behind-the-ears rookie detective, but during the investigation to come, Frank Loomis would prove that he was no ordinary suspect.

As the night progressed, McNally's team spoke to several eyewitnesses who provided information about the timeline of the murder and the events that surrounded it.

Florence Nellis, who lived two houses away, said she heard glass breaking at almost exactly 9:05 P.M. She knew this because she heard her clock strike nine – she even counted the chimes, she said – and she was sure five minutes passed before the glass shattered. When she heard it, she called out to her 14-year-old brother, Harold Simms.

Harold had also heard the breaking glass. He added that he had seen Grace Loomis standing by her sunroom window at around 8:30 P.M., which, aside from her husband, made him the last witness to see her alive.

At approximately 9:00 P.M., Charles Blockson and Ethel Bell were walking past the Loomis house and heard muffled screams followed by moaning and breaking glass from the sunroom. The blinds were closed so that they couldn't see anything. Ethel, who said she was less than 15 feet from the house, told detectives, "I felt inside of me that someone was being murdered."

What did they do? Nothing.

Ethel said she wanted to go to the police, but Charles believed that the sounds came from one of Dr. Loomis' patients – a convincing argument since neither of them heard a man's voice – or there was a family squabble going on. Either way, it was none of their business, and even though they waited a few minutes to see if they heard anything else, they kept walking.

Ethel later recalled, "We remained outside the house for at least three minutes, but nobody ran out while we were there. Whoever killed Mrs. Loomis stayed inside there with the body for at least that length of time after the murder."

A telephone operator named Doris McClure said she received two calls that night from the Loomis residence. The first was between 7:00 P.M. and 8:42 P.M. When Doris asked what number the caller wanted to be connected with, a woman's voice on the other end of the line responded, "Never mind, the telephone fell over."

The second call was at 9:05. When Doris asked for the number this time, there was no response. A few seconds later, she heard a scream, and the line went dead.

DETECTIVE FRANK MCNALLY WAS STUMPED. He knew what to do – look at the husband first – but he couldn't seem to find a reason why Frank Loomis would want to kill his wife, even if the evidence seemed to point in his direction.

Frank Loomis and Grace Burns had met while he was doing his internship at New York's Metropolitan Hospital. Grace was a young nursing student who had grown up on a farm near Sussex, New Jersey. As a native of Brooklyn, Michigan, Frank was a small-town boy in the big city. They discovered how much they had in common and fell in love.

Their whirlwind romance led to the altar on October 1, 1915. A few years later, the couple moved to Michigan, where the doctor first practiced in his hometown. They relocated to Detroit in 1924, and within three years, Frank had established a sterling reputation as a skilled anesthetist.

They seemed to have a fairytale romance with two children and a beautiful house in the suburbs. Neighbors never heard them argue, and Grace adored her husband. "They seemed like the perfect couple," one neighbor told detectives. "Grace was the perfect wife and mother."

And then this happened.

McNally knew there had to be more to the story, but nothing at the scene suggested a break-in. Grace kept all the doors and windows locked at night. It would have been possible for an intruder to reach in through the milk chute – kind of like a "dog door" but for deliveries from the milkman – and unlock the exterior door, except Grace had latched the milk chute both outside and inside the house. None of the doors or windows had been jimmied, and the only broken window was in the sunroom, which had been broken from inside.

Frank's overcoat had been streaked with blood, but he explained that by saying that he'd held his wife's lifeless body in his arms while he looked for her pulse. Oddly, though, his shirt didn't have any blood on it. The clean shirt, along with the pearl buttons found in the furnace, led McNally to consider an alternate scenario than the one that Dr. Loomis described.

What if Dr. Loomis had returned from his walk, removed his coat and overshoes, and met Grace in the sunroom? He lowered the blinds, and when she turned her back to him, he slugged her in the head with a club or piece of wood like a section of two-by-four. He then burned his bloody shirt and the wooden club in the furnace, put on a fresh shirt, put his coat back on, and then "discovered" his dead wife.

This seemed like a solid possibility to the detective, but there was one small problem – Frank Loomis had an alibi. Well, sort of an alibi. At the time his wife was killed, Frank was strolling around the block on his evening walk. Or so he said. Detectives hadn't found anyone who'd seen him that night, and his walk hadn't put him very far away from the crime scene. Even so, they needed to find a way to break it.

Throughout that night and into the early morning hours of February 23, McNally, Detective Lieutenant John Navarre, and Assistant District Attorney Paul O. Buckley questioned Dr. Loomis, attempting to poke holes in his alibi. For nearly 20 hours, they grilled him about the previous night's events, but Frank didn't waver. His story never changed. "I am as innocent as a man can be," he said several times during the interrogation.

He repeated his movements of the night at least a dozen times, always ending with his discovery of her body. When McNally asked him if either he or Grace had been involved in anything "on the side," Frank became heated. He accused the detective of dishonoring his wife and vehemently denied the existence of an "other woman." He did, however, acknowledge that he'd recently driven a former patient named Gertrude Newell downtown, but she was only a friend. The police interviewed Gertrude Newell but were convinced the association between them was just as Dr. Loomis presented it and dismissed her.

Prosecutor Buckley was bothered by the way Loomis handled himself with the interrogation. "I have never seen a man cooler under cross-examination than he has been," he said, but he did remark that Frank's alibi seemed a little too neat. "The imperfection of the doctor's story is the perfection."

The police were frustrated. They had absolutely nothing to indicate that Frank had murdered his wife, but they also had nothing to suggest that someone else had. There seemed to be simply no motive for Grace's murder.

But the District Attorney's office wasn't prepared to let Frank Loomis go. The exhausted suspect was taken from the interrogation room to a jail cell.

Locking Frank up sparked a courtroom scrap between Buckley and Frank's attorney, Louis Colombo, who demanded that his client be released. The police had nothing on him, he insisted, so they had no right to hold him.

The drama played to a full house of mostly women who stood in line for over two hours to catch a glimpse of the handsome doctor as he entered the courtroom.

Circuit Court Judge Joseph A. Moynihan listened to the arguments and gave the authorities 24 hours to present compelling evidence of Frank's guilt. If they failed to find anything substantial, he would be released.

The judge's deadline came and went with no new evidence in the case, but he decided to delay the doctor's *habeas corpus* hearing until Monday, which gave investigators a little more time to gather evidence. But Frank got out on Saturday afternoon anyway. A friend supplied the $10,000 bond set by Judge Moynihan, and Frank was out.

Throughout the weekend, investigators combed through the evidence recovered from the scene. They interviewed witnesses again and re-canvassed the neighborhood. Even after more hours spent on the case, though, they found no murder weapon or anything that solidly linked Dr. Loomis to the crime scene or revealed a viable motive for the murder of his wife.

On Monday morning, February 28, Judge Moynihan returned the $10,000 bond money, and Frank walked out of his courtroom a free man. He promptly took his wife's body to her hometown of Newton, New Jersey, for burial. Grace Morris was finally laid to rest.

But there was no rest to be found for the detectives investigating the case. For the next five weeks, McNally's team, along with reporters and private detectives from the Burns Detective Agency, continued their relentless search for new evidence. They dug into Frank's life, retraced his steps leading up to his wife's murder, and interviewed everyone who knew the doctor.

At first, they still found nothing, but then Frank returned from New Jersey, and the detectives began tailing him every time he left the house. One night, he got in his car and drove to a small house on the other side of town. He got out, knocked on the door, and waited until the door was opened by a woman, who let him inside.

The cops had finally found the person the doctor swore didn't exist – Frank's "other woman."

THE MYSTERY WOMAN – WHO FRANK OFTEN referred to as "G"– was none other than his platonic friend, Gertrude Newell. Considered nothing more than a casual acquaintance and released after a brief round of questions, detectives now realized that Gertrude was more than just a former patient.

She was an attractive 29-year-old divorcee who couldn't be less like Grace Loomis if she tried. While Grace cooked, cleaned, and took care of her children, Gertrude put on a party dress and high heels and danced the night away in downtown speakeasies. Grace wore very little makeup, while Gertrude wore her bright red hair in a fashionable bob and covered her plump lips with

Frank's mystery woman – Gertrude Newell – who he referred to often as "G."

bright-colored lipstick. The magnetism of her physical beauty combined with her exotic lifestyle and the forbidden nature of their relationship proved to be irresistible to the upstanding Dr. Loomis.

Gertrude's marriage to a real estate agent named Ritter ended in 1922 because, according to Ritter, his wife "took no interest in their home." Gertrude's nine-year-old daughter, Purnesse, went with her father.

Freshly freed from married life, Gertrude quickly found her way into Detroit's high life on the arms of wealthy men. Two prominent surgeons – who only talked to the cops after hearing promises that their names would be left out of the case – each told of being entranced by the red-haired siren. Detectives also learned a great deal about her from the son of an affluent business and community family whose mistress was a close friend of Gertrude's.

She was simply a "sugar baby," seeking out wealthy men for money, nice clothes, cars, and a place to live and giving them sex and excitement in return.

Frank Loomis probably wasn't the only man she was seeing at the time, but she certainly made him feel that he was. He'd tried in vain to keep their relationship a secret, but the couple often went to public gatherings together, which begs the question – why did it take the cops so long to find out about her?

In fairness, though, the gatherings they attended undoubtedly weren't the kind with invitation lists or with people who'd want to talk to the police.

But some of them did.

Investigators found witnesses who talked about Gertrude's strange behavior after Grace's murder. She and a friend, Bessie Fraser, were drinking with two male friends in a speakeasy when

Gertrude spotted a newspaper with a front-page story about Frank's arrest. She started to sob and buried her head in her hands.

The woman who ran the place noticed the paper on the table, laughed, and sarcastically commented, "Dr. Loomis could throw light on that murder."

One of the men tailed her to the kitchen, told her not to say that, and added that Gertrude "is Dr. Loomis' sweetie."

Once the cat was out of the bag about their relationship, Gertrude apparently felt the heat. According to a neighbor, when she saw a headline that read "Woman Sought in Loomis Case," Gertrude packed a bag and skipped town for a few days. Even more suspicious was the telephone operator's report that the voice on the call placed from the Loomis residence on the night of the murder was a woman.

The police found Gertrude at Bessie Fraser's house and brought her in for questioning. At first, she denied that she even knew Frank but then admitted to seeing him once or twice. Eventually, she confessed to an ongoing relationship that stretched back to months before Grace was killed.

Things had started innocently. She'd first met Dr. Loomis the previous November when he treated her for a cold, but things soon became heated. Checking the doctor's bank records, it was easy to see when the two became an item – the longer he was with Gertrude, the more his finances suffered. According to bank statements, more was going out than coming in as the doctor fed his and Gertrude's alcohol- and drug-fueled lifestyle. Detectives now had a lot of questions about the syringe filled with morphine that was found at the crime scene.

When Frank was confronted with his mistress, he tried to convince the cops that she was just a friend, but they didn't buy it. He'd been tailed several times to Bessie's house after the police discovered his interest in Gertrude, and they knew he'd been spending hours with her. Not only that, but they'd bugged her bedroom. What they heard on that listening device was never made public, but it likely contained sounds that suggested more than a casual friendship.

In the speakeasies downtown, Frank and Gertrude had been talking about moving away together. Gertrude suffered from tuberculosis and wanted to move out west, where the air was dryer and more hospitable. Soon after, Frank contacted the Colorado State Board of Medicine about obtaining a license to practice there.

When McNally learned that piece of news, the motive seemed complete. He envisioned a scenario where Grace learned of his affair with Gertrude and confronted him on the evening of February 22. The argument turned violent, and Frank bludgeoned her to death.

But this scenario was missing one thing – none of the witnesses within earshot of the house heard shouting or a man's voice.

It seemed a tough sell to the jury, but it wasn't McNally's problem –District Attorney Robert Toms would be the one dealing with them.

McNally had just locked them up, and on April 12, he arrested Dr. Loomis for the second time at his office.

THE LOOMIS TRIAL BECAME THE BIGGEST SHOW in town – and the tickets were the hardest to get. When the trial opened on May 27, 1927, a reporter described a "tidal wave of spectators" who rushed into the courtroom when the bailiff opened the doors. The room would only seat 100 people, and yet at least 300 had pushed and shoved their way inside.

Once everyone had gotten into their seats, Judge John V. Brennan called things to order, and the attorneys made their opening statements.

Of course, every eye – from the spectators to the reporters crowded into the press section – was on Dr. Loomis. The six weeks that he spent in jail awaiting trial had not been kind to him. His face was pale and gaunt, his eyes were shadowed, and he sat at the defense table, showing almost no emotion at all. He smiled when he had to – an arrogant grin that suggested a mix of disdain and amusement – and turned it on whenever normal human behavior required it.

Ethel Bell was the first to take the stand. When she passed him, Frank smiled. And then it was gone. He repeated this motion throughout the trial.

Ethel was the witness who claimed to hear the screams coming from the Loomis' sunroom around 9:00 P.M. on the night of the murder. This would have been at the same time – or even slightly before – the defendant claimed to have gone out for a walk.

During the cross-examination, Frank's lawyer, Louis Colombo, drove Ethel to the point of a nervous collapse with a series of relentless questions. Trying to discredit her testimony and shatter the timeline the prosecution established for the murder, he managed to show that the beautiful and very married young woman was stepping out on her husband that night with Charles Blockson.

Ethel had little choice but to reveal her secrets in court and admit to a long-term affair with Charles, who owned a local butcher shop. But she did explain to the courtroom that during the time between the murder and the trial, she had divorced her husband and had married Charles.

Even though Ethel's love life had nothing to do with whether she was telling the truth in court, the damage had been done as far as the jury was concerned.

Dorothy McClure, the 18-year-old telephone operator, took the stand and described the calls from the Loomis house that night. She didn't know for sure what time the first call came in but knew it was between 7:00 P.M. and 8:42 when she took her 15-minute break. The second call, though, was at 9:05 P.M. and, as Dorothy said, "No one answered but a scream." When Louis Colombo asked her to imitate the scream, she refused, saying only that it was a "lady's scream."

An assistant city engineer testified about retracing the path of Frank's walk that night and concluded there was a 10-minute gap in his timeline – a gap that the district attorney hoped the jury would see as a time when he could have come home and murdered his wife.

Strangely, neither Robert Toms nor Louis Colombo had Gertrude Newell on their witness lists. It was an odd omission for the prosecution since she represented the only known motive in the case. Learning of their affair was the reason for Frank's second arrest, and yet, if anything, Toms downplayed the doctor's illicit relationship.

A reporter later tried to explain this by saying that since Gertrude was considered a hostile witness to the prosecution and because of the testimony of Dr. Loomis, Gertrude could only be used as a rebuttal witness. For that reason, the D.A. didn't put

Frank Loomis on trial. He was found "not guilty" but he later committed suicide.

her on the stand, although she was held for several weeks under high bail as a police witness against her lover.

The district attorney called a few witnesses who testified about the blood on Dr. Loomis' coat, but the state's case really rested on the telephone operator and the young woman who was cheating on her husband. Their testimony established a timeframe for the murder as five minutes before Frank supposedly left on his evening stroll.

If that seems like a fragile case to you – it is. Toms failed to present a compelling motive, couldn't link Frank to the crime scene with any physical evidence, and his murder timeline didn't implicate the doctor at all.

It was almost as if he was trying to lose.

After Toms rested his case, Colombo made a motion for a directed verdict of "not guilty," but the judge denied it. The trial would continue.

Then, it turned into a real spectacle when Frank Loomis took the stand in his defense. No one noticed what Frank was wearing until he stood up and walked to the witness box – it was the overcoat that was stained with his wife's blood.

The spectators were further shocked when Colombo, playing the part of Grace's dead body, lay down on the courtroom floor. Frank then re-enacted finding his wife's body, taking Colombo in his arms, and searching for a pulse. This was to show that the blood could have easily been only on the coat and not on his shirt. When Toms cross-examined Frank later, he and his attorney replayed the scene, undoubtedly to the spectators' delight.

While on the stand, Frank repeated the same story he'd told when the police first arrested him. He also denied anything more than a friendship with Gertrude Newell, which was an obvious lie.

The trial lasted for several weeks and was marked by odd happenings and calamities – the extra, thirteenth juror unexpectedly died, the court reporter had a nervous breakdown, Ethel Bell was hospitalized for nervous exhaustion, and another juror was rushed to the hospital for surgery.

Finally, the case went to the jury in late June, and the carnival-like proceedings ended with a verdict of "not guilty."

It was over for everyone, but Grace Loomis – her murder was now officially unsolved. But suspicions remained about some of the parties involved, and some might say that Grace would eventually have her revenge.

Once the trial was over, Frank continued – or, more accurately, flaunted – his affair with Gertrude. They frequented restaurants, theaters, and speakeasies and eventually moved to a rented apartment together.

In May 1928, their landlady spoke anonymously to a reporter and described their situation, suggesting that as Frank's money ran out, so did Gertrude's interest in the doctor. Gertrude constantly wanted to go out and party, and Frank let her, but he was "insanely jealous" when he stayed home. On several occasions, there had been violent arguments when Gertrude stayed out all night. On one occasion, he'd smashed dishes, and on another, he'd burned underwear that had been given to her by another admirer.

Gertrude usually quieted things down by threatening to leave him for another man or return to her ex-husband, which then caused Frank to respond with profuse apologies. She packed her bags and left once after one argument and told the landlady "that she was afraid to be alone with the doctor because of his temper."

Frank apologized, she moved back in, and the whole cycle started again. By the time of the interview in May 1928, he had started spending nights on a cot in his office.

Then, on May 18, a shouting match occurred that everyone in their apartment building witnessed. An upstairs neighbor, who heard the whole thing through the floor, recalled one provocative comment: "I know as much about you as you know about me!" Gertrude screamed, followed by the slamming of the apartment door.

The arguments, it was later revealed, usually began because Gertrude wanted Frank to marry her, and he refused because he didn't believe she was faithful to him.

Gee, I wonder why?

Frank's office became a sanctuary of sorts for him, although by the spring of 1928, he was on the verge of losing it. His acquittal hadn't saved his reputation. One by one, his patients left and started seeing other, less notorious doctors. Everywhere he went, people looked at him and whispered. He received threatening telephone calls at all hours. He was running out of money, and he needed what he had to support his children, who were now living with relatives in New York.

Some might say that Dr. Loomis could have used a warning when he started looking for something more exciting in his life – a warning that told him to "be careful what you wish for."

ON MAY 19, THE MORNING AFTER THE TERRIBLE fight with Gertrude, a janitor in Frank's office building discovered the doctor dead on the couch in a fellow physician's office. A rubber tube had been inserted into his mouth. It was connected to a pump that had discharged a lethal dose of gas.

Before Frank had taken his own life, he wrote two suicide notes – one for the press and once for his best friend, Victor Kolar, the assistant director of the Detroit Symphony Orchestra. The notes were placed in an envelope and left in the appointment book of his colleague, Dr. C.J. Kirwin, along with directions about what to do with them.

Frank then scribbled a third note. It was addressed to the Detroit Police Department and noted, "A newspaper article will be published in 24 or 48 hours explaining this action on my part. Please be patient until then."

Dr. Kirwin discovered the letters later that day and, after consulting with some other doctors, decided to follow Frank's instructions to the letter.

Any hopes of a deathbed confession from Frank were dashed when the *Detroit News* published his suicide note. Instead, he criticized District Attorney Robert Toms for grandstanding during the trial and making a fool of himself. He also went on to complain about all the untrue things that had been printed about him in the newspapers over the past year and the gullibility of the public for believing everything they read.

"Many have never learned the lesson which I have had," he wrote. "So long as the paper continues to print articles which they know to be untrue, many innocent people will have to suffer along with those whom the paper is trying originally to hurt."

There were many, Frank said, who could be blamed for the fact that Grace's murder was never solved, but he was not one of them.

After the letter was published, Gertrude was again splashed across the front pages of newspapers. To both the police and the press, she downplayed the troubles that damaged their relationship. "We were the best of friends right up to the end," she claimed. There had been no argument on the night Frank killed himself. She had no idea why he'd done it.

After wrestling with his conscience – which he said involved 50 sleepless hours – Victor Kolar decided to go public with his letter from Frank. He turned it over to the police, but someone in the department leaked it to the press.

He started out by thanking Victor for his friendship and then tried to explain his actions, starting with the line, "G. drives me

> **Several Love Deaths.**
>
> Several who were in love ended their lives. A suicide that attracted nation wide attention was recorded May 19 when Dr. Frank R. Loomis, took his life in his office on West Grand River avenue.
>
> Dr. Loomis' wife, Mrs. Grace Loomis, was beaten to death in her home on Marlowe avenue the evening February 22, 1927.

crazy." He described their final argument, which occurred after she made an overnight trip with another man, and it escalated from there.

"My god, how I love her!" Frank wrote. "Perhaps we will meet again when both of us will be more reasonable."

He said goodbye to his friend, thanked him for all he had tried to do for Gertrude and himself, and asked him to try and protect her if he could. "Bid G. good-bye for me and tell her I love her," he concluded. "And if anything should happen to G. in the near future, try to have her placed in my grave."

The letter created a complication for Gertrude, whose denial about a screaming match between them – one witnessed by a dozen or more people – was proven untrue.

Investigators also wondered if the line about "if anything should happen to G." indicated that the pair had planned some kind of suicide pact. That seems unlikely, but if any type of agreement like that existed, then I'd be willing to bet that Gertrude told Frank she'd go along with it without any intention of doing so.

But that wasn't what got the attention of Detective McNally with this whole mess. He was intrigued by the report of Gertrude shouting, "I know as much about you as you know about me," which convinced him that Gertrude knew a lot more about the Grace Loomis murder than she'd admitted.

When detectives went to interview her about the Kolar letter, they found her on the verge of a breakdown, unhinged by constant demands from the press. She had left the apartment she'd shared with Frank and had taken refuge at the Seville Hotel.

Even the tough-as-nails detective didn't want to be responsible for the woman's further unraveling and decided not to ask her any questions about Frank's suicide. He decided that the case could end with the doctor's death, which he felt was as close to a confession as he would ever get.

Detective John Navarre agreed. He always believed that Frank had killed his wife, and for good reason – he was convinced that the doctor had partially confessed to him.

In the interrogation room after Frank's arrest, Navarre had pointed out the difference to the doctor between first-degree murder and manslaughter. He said that if Frank had killed his wife in a heated argument when he was out of control for just a moment, he likely committed manslaughter. First-degree murder meant that he'd carefully planned it out.

"Now, doctor, don't you want to clear your mind once and for all of this terrible affair?" Navarre asked him. "You'll feel better if you do."

Frank considered this for a moment and then replied, "Give me a little time to think it over, will you?"

Navarre agreed and left the interrogation room, and then Louis Colombo, Frank's attorney, came along. Later, during a break in the trial, Navarre approached Frank outside of the courtroom and reminded him of that conversation. "What about that matter we were discussing?"

But this time, Dr. Loomis responded, "You'll have to talk with my lawyer."

Navarre believed that Frank had thought about it, and he gave his real answer when he wrote his suicide note on May 19, 1928. The first line of it read, "I am not guilty of murder."

Navarre was convinced it could also be read as "I am guilty of manslaughter." He said that the natural expression would have been "I did not kill my wife" or something like that, but Dr. Loomis chose to use a legal phrase.

It's an interesting idea. Convincing, though? Not really.

But Navarre's theory about what happened to the murder weapon does make sense. The house was thoroughly searched for a murder weapon, but nothing was found. But in the basement, they discovered a number of sections of two-by-four that had been sharpened to be used as stakes for a wire enclosure when Frank was putting down sod for his lawn. The copes stretched out the wire and assembled the stakes – there was one missing.

He believed that Frank first struck his wife with his fist, then went to the basement and got the two-by-four, with which he struck her three times on the back of the head, killing her.

The wooden stake – like the bloodstained shirt – went into the furnace.

DID FRANK KILL HIS WIFE? PROBABLY, but we'll never know. The case will always be a mystery. A line from a piece written by a newspaper reporter after the doctor's suicide provides the perfect ending to our story. The reporter wrote: "So far as was known, and so far as has ever been learned, a lone canary in a cage in the sun-room was the only living witness to Mrs. Loomis' death."

And that canary, like Frank Loomis, never sang.

"FORBIDDEN LOVE"
Dr. James Howard Snook and Theora Hix

HER BODY WAS FOUND ON THE MORNING of Friday, June 14, 1929, by two young men – Paul Krumlauf and Marion Miller – who were on their way to a shooting range just outside of Columbus, Ohio.

The boys headed over to warn a local farmer, Ephraim Johnson, who was plowing his field, that they were going to do some shooting. On their way toward where he was working, however, they stumbled across something in the brush.

At first, they thought her crumpled body was just an abandoned pile of clothes, but the cloud of flies and the drying blood quickly told them a different story. They ran to tell the farmer, who promised to watch over things while they called the police.

He didn't, though. He actually left the scene to go and put his horses in the barn, but in the end, it wouldn't matter.

The boys drove to the Parsons Avenue Police Station, and nearly an hour passed before they returned with Corporal John May and Officer Emmett Cloud, who secured the site and waited for the arrival of the coroner and a crime scene photographer from the state's Bureau of Identification.

When Coroner William Murphy arrived, he was met by the gruesome scene of the body lying facedown in the grass. The woman was wearing a blood-soaked, belted, brown crepe dress with a white collar. She was lying on her left side, with her right arm extended in front, her hand clutching a bloody handkerchief. Her throat had been slashed, her hair was matted with blood, there were stab wounds on her back and abdomen, her nose had been broken, her face was battered almost beyond recognition, and her skull had been shattered.

Murphy, who had been the coroner since 1921 and had seen many murder victims, waited for Homer Richter, the police photographer, to snap some images and then help him turn her over.

A reporter and one of the two boys who discovered the body of a young woman on the rifle range on the morning of June 14, 1929.

The first thing he saw were four bruises on the inside of her left arm and a corresponding bruise on the outside. Someone had held her with a firm grip, he knew, and she'd probably tried to get away.

He noted that her throat had been cut from left to right with a sharp knife and three wounds to her forehead – two on the left side and once above her nose. One of the wounds was so deep Murphy could insert a finger into it.

Discovering the time of the woman's death was simple. When she was turned over, Murphy saw she was wearing a wristwatch. The crystal had fallen out, and the hands had stopped at 9:58. This seemed to correspond with the temperature and rigor of the body.

Her clothing was intact, and as far as the coroner could tell, this hadn't been a sex crime.

After his cursory review at the scene, Murphy ordered the unidentified young woman to be taken to the Glenn L. Meyers Mortuary for an autopsy.

She wouldn't stay unidentified for long.

About the same time the two marksmen discovered the body, two sisters, Alice and Beatrice Bustin, were wondering why their roommate had not returned the night before. The three women shared a small apartment above the State Drug and Supply Company, about a block away from Mack Hall on the Ohio State University campus. As a roommate, the missing young woman was an enigma to the Bustin sisters, but she had never stayed away from the apartment overnight without telling them. It wasn't until most of Friday had passed that the sisters became worried and called the police.

When the newspapers with a story about the dead woman hit the streets that afternoon, Alice and Beatrice were not the only ones who feared they knew the identity of the body found at the shooting range. Bertha Dillon, a switchboard operator at the Ohio State University hospital, had been irritated when the young woman she'd been training hadn't returned from a date the night before. She'd sat with Bertha for an hour or so on Thursday evening, learning the layout of the switchboard, until she announced she had a date and would be back soon.

She never returned.

The police brought Bertha and the Bustin sisters to the mortuary, where they viewed the body of the young woman found that morning.

All three of them identified her as Theora Kathleen Hix, an Ohio State University medical student who was just two months shy of her 25th birthday.

THEORA HIX WAS A 22-YEAR-OLD MEDICAL student at Ohio State University, and she had been born on Long Island, New York, to parents who had been married more than 20 years and had given up hope of ever having children. She was cherished as a "miracle child" and raised with every opportunity her family could give her.

Theora's early school years were within the New York Public Schools system, where her father, Melvin, was a principal. Her parents then sent her to the Northfield Seminary in Massachusetts, where she graduated as the only senior in 1922. Northfield was a storied East Coast preparatory school that boasted a long list of illustrious graduates. It was also a religious school, which was important to her parents, who sent her there so she would be exposed to significant moral and religious influence.

On the surface, she took the education to heart. Although described by some as shy and reserved, she announced plans to become a doctor – which was then still mostly a man's profession – and to please her parents, she spoke of becoming a missionary with medical training. Her desire to attend medical school took her to Ohio State University.

Theora Hix – a young woman raised in a conservative Christian home, but one who it was soon discovered lived a secret life at college.

After her death, the police began trying to find out all they could about Theora after she came to Ohio, and they soon found that the deeper they dug into her life, the more mysterious she became. No one they spoke with who was acquainted with Theora really knew her at all. Detectives found many who spoke of what a pleasant, polite, hardworking young woman she was, but none of them had any information about her that wasn't superficial. They described her as a quiet, very smart, sometimes standoffish co-worker, roommate, or lab partner – nothing more.

She played tennis and golf and liked to talk walks. She was a good worker, and she always showed up on time, said her boss at the veterinary school, where she worked as a stenographer. She was shy, some people said, while others called her moody. Men who knew he said she had little interest in them. One of her classmates, Flora Peddicord, noted that she always chatted freely with the other girls but knew it was useless to ask about a date she'd been on. "She wouldn't tell us," Flora said.

As far as anyone could tell, she seldom went on dates and almost never with the same man twice. There were rumors, though, that she'd been seeing an older man who was connected to the university. She didn't talk about it, and no one pressed her.

Detectives who searched Theora's room found her bank passbooks, which only deepened the mystery. They found one account at the Buckeye Building & Loan Association that contained $615 and another that showed she'd recently closed an account at the Columbian Building & Loan Association containing $1,863. That's the equivalent of more than $32,000 today, and to provide a little perspective, Theora could have bought a brand-new car and put down half the cost of a house in Columbus with that kind of money at the time.

It was unusual, to say the least, for a college student – even a working student – to have that much money in the bank. No one, including her parents, could say where it came from. Her father told investigators he gave his daughter $600 to live on each year. Even stranger, Theora had been known to take advantage of the university's short-term loans for students program. Why, if she had that kind of cash in the bank?

And then they found something else that raised even more questions – Theora kept a .41-caliber pistol in a drawer.

The police also found several letters that Theora had saved that were signed by someone named "Janet." They contained musings that the detectives thought hinted at a physical relationship between the two women, which might explain why Theora didn't seem that interested in men.

As salacious as they sounded to the cops in 1929, they were uncovering just the tip of the iceberg when it came to Theora Hix. She was living the kind of secret life that went far beyond their imaginations.

EARLY ON SATURDAY, JUNE 16, DETECTIVES got their first break in the case when a man came forward who said that he had been Theora's boyfriend. Marion T. Meyers was a 35-year-old horticulture expert from the agriculture department at OSU. He lived at the Gamma Alpha fraternity house near campus and was once so enamored of Theora that he'd proposed marriage. That proposal and her laughing rejection ended the relationship, but the pair remained friends.

As a "jilted suitor," Marion was a prime suspect and was questioned by the police. They knew that Theora was seeing an older man on campus, and they assumed it was Marion.

And Marion, acting on the naïve belief that his innocence would be proven, and he'd be set free, came across as having something to hide. The news of the murder clearly shook him, and his naturally nervous temperament made him seem like he had a guilty conscience. His answers to even basic questions were vague and lacking in detail, making him seem uncooperative. He wasn't – he was just an odd and nervous man.

He also didn't help himself by saying that the relationship between Theora and himself ended after the proposal. He had to backtrack and admit that while the two of them did meet up for casual sex, they were no longer dating.

Marion was intensely questioned before finally sharing with the police that there was another man from Ohio State University in the picture. He didn't know much about him, but he'd seen letters from him in Theora's room, and she'd confessed he was also her lover.

Marion Meyer was eventually cleared of the murder, but his admissions about his sex life didn't do him any favors. He was fired from the university soon after his release for "moral turpitude."

What the police wanted now was to track down the man that Marion and other witnesses called the "older man." Only Marion knew the man's name – Dr. James Howard Snook.

JAMES SNOOK WAS A 49-YEAR-OLD PROFESSOR of veterinary science who had worked at OSU since graduating from there in 1908. Tall and fit, he was smooth-shaven but with a thick, dark beard that gave him a perpetual five o'clock shadow. He was a serious-looking man with a bald head, and short cropped hair that ringed the back of his head from ear to ear. With his round, wire pince-nez glasses clipped to his nose, he was the stereotypical example of what you'd expect a quiet, well-established college professor to look like.

What he didn't look like was the kind of man that would attract a pretty 22-year-old coed, but those were different times, I suppose.

Dr. James Snook

Snook was acclaimed as a veterinarian by both the school and the community and had received grateful thanks from farmers in the region for stopping an outbreak of hog cholera in 1914. During World War I, he served as an instructor at the aviation school.

At the time of his arrest, he had several claims to fame – he'd been the American rapid-fire pistol shooting champion eight times in the past. He won a gold medal for shooting as a member of the 1920 United States Olympic team in Antwerp, Belgium. He was also the inventor of what was called the "Snook Hook," a surgical instrument for dog and cat spaying procedures that is still used today.

Snook had a well-rounded education and was a cultured and charming man. He was a member of the exclusive Scioto Country Club in Columbus and a pair of shooting clubs that frequently used the range where Theora's body was found.

In 1922, Snook married Helen Marple, and the couple had two children – a son who died in 1925 and a daughter who was almost two when he was arrested. Her name never appeared in the newspaper coverage of the case.

On Saturday, June 16, Detective Larry Van Skaik and reporter James Fusco knocked on the front door of the home Dr. Snook shared with his family. They were met by the professor, who was about to sit down for breakfast. The men noticed that his right hand was bandaged.

He was asked to step outside with them, where he admitted that he knew Theora. Van Skaik then told him that he needed to take him downtown for questioning.

Snook agreed to go but seemed more concerned about missing his breakfast than an interrogation. Van Skaik wasn't going to wait around for the man to eat, so when Snook asked to drive himself to the police station, the detective agreed. As the professor turned to go back into the house, the detective asked

how he'd injured his hand. Snook said he'd hurt it while repairing his car on Wednesday.

Soon, the cop and the reporter were on their way downtown, with Snook following in his own vehicle. Unbelievably, they stopped at a restaurant on the way so that all three men could have breakfast. Strange, but, in the end, it's really only notable because Dr. Snook never returned home after that – that breakfast was his last meal as a free man.

DR. SNOOK'S FIRST INTERROGATION WAS LOW-KEY, almost friendly, and certainly not threatening. Snook was assured he was not a suspect, just a person of interest. Detectives just wanted to see what he knew.

Snook acted like a man with nothing to hide. He admitted that he'd met Theora in 1926 when she was working as a typist and stenographer in his department. They'd chatted a few times, and once, he gave her a ride home during a rainstorm. Beyond that, he claimed, there was nothing more between them other than a casual office acquaintance.

When he was asked what he thought had happened to Theora, he suggested that she took a ride with someone she didn't know and was killed. Of course, he couldn't be sure because he hadn't seen her since the previous Wednesday night.

Where was he on Thursday evening? At his office, he said. He'd gotten there around 7:30 or 8:00 and finished some articles he was writing for a couple of magazines. He wasn't sure what time he'd left, and no, there was no one around that saw him leave. He did pick up a newspaper on the way home, though, and was sure it was 9:30 P.M. when he walked in the door.

Chief of Detectives Wilson Shellabarger was in the interrogation room with the professor – as was Police Chief Harry French, Detective Otto Phillips, and Franklin County Prosecutor John J. Chester, Jr. Detective Shellabarger turned up the heat a little. "Did you ever loan money to Miss Hix?" he asked.

After pausing to think, Snook admitted he had – two years earlier. He said she had written to him from New York, needing funds, and asked him to meet her in Pittsburgh. He sent someone else with the money for her, though.

"Why would she ask you for the money?"

"We did take some rides together," he said. "I was negotiating with her to type a manuscript for a book I'm writing."

"So, you would say that you knew her more than just... what did you say? You knew her more than just 'casually.'"

Snook shrugged his shoulders and said nothing. After a few more questions, the interview ended. Snook was taken to the county jail, where he was booked and photographed. The authorities were going to hang onto him a little longer and see what they could find.

Investigators looking at his car found some peculiar stains on the passenger side door and the upholstery – stains that looked like blood. The city chemist later confirmed that they were. Behind the seats, they found a glove that was also stained with blood and a hairpin.

Across town, Detective Howard Lavely executed a search warrant at the Snook home. He failed to find any weapons that could be linked to the murder, but he did discover the remains of a fire still smoldering in the basement incinerator. Mixed in with the normal household trash were several pairs of men's pajamas and a man's shirt that appeared to be bloodstained. He also reported that there were some articles of "a feminine nature," but they didn't belong to Theora.

Helen Snook could not explain the pajamas but said she had been burning trash on Friday. The shirt, she supposed, had animal blood on it. She said it was not unusual for her husband to destroy clothing that was soiled during his work. She also confirmed with the police that Dr. Snook had come home at 9:30 on Thursday evening.

Detective Van Skaik had tried to re-investigate the crime scene at the shooting range but arrived too late. It had already been trampled by hundreds of curious men, women, and children who wanted to see where the murder happened. It was said the high grass had been flattened in a 150-foot radius around the spot where the two young men first saw Theora's body.

Investigators were unsure what to do next. None of the evidence they'd found was a "smoking gun" that linked Snook to the murder. It could all be explained. The blood – on his clothing and in his car – could be animal blood. It took too long to check back then. His burned shirt meant nothing.

And then they got the break they needed.

It came as a telephone call from a woman named Margaret Smalley, who owned a boarding house on Hubbard Street. She had seen a photo of Dr. Snook in the newspaper, and she identified him as "Howard Snook," a salt salesman who traveled with his much younger wife. She didn't know the wife's first name, but she knew her face because she was in the newspaper, too – Theora Hix.

Detectives were soon at her door. The small flat – which newspapers would dub the "Love Nest" – was small and dominated by a large brass bed and a single high-backed wooden armchair. It overlooked the rear of the boarding house and allowed the occupants to come and go discreetly through the back entrance.

Margaret would likely never have seen them at all if Mr. Snook hadn't stopped by each Friday to pay the $4 weekly rent – until June 14 anyway. On that Friday, he came by to say that he was giving up the room and wouldn't need it anymore.

The landlady had only met "Mrs. Snook" one time when she showed up a little early to clean their room and saw her in the hall when she was leaving. Nevertheless, when she was taken to the mortuary, she positively identified Theora as the woman who stayed at her boarding house.

She also accompanied detectives to the jail, where Margaret came face-to-face again with the man who'd told her he was a traveling salesman – that man had been Dr. James Howard Snook.

The noose had drawn just a little bit tighter around Snook's neck.

MEANWHILE, BLOOD TESTS WERE BEING conducted that showed the blood on Dr. Snook's clothing as human, not animal.

The contents of Theora's stomach were shown to include an undigested roast beef sandwich, as well as powdered marijuana and *cantharides*, or Blister Beetle extract, which has the more notorious name of "Spanish Fly." This legendary aphrodisiac is used in animal husbandry to induce animals to mate. It doesn't make the male more amorous but merely helps it to perform sexually. Contrary to popular myth, it doesn't have an effect on females except to increase blood flow to the urinary tract.

It looked as though Theora might have been surreptitiously drugged by her killer since no one was aware of her using any kind of drugs.

To make matters worse, there was a bottle of the extract in Dr. Snook's office. It had a medicinal purpose in the veterinary lab as an external ointment for blisters.

Was that the only way the doctor used it?

By now, circumstantial evidence was piling up against the professor – enough that D.A. Chester was able to get him indicted for Theora's murder. As the investigation continued, the authorities learned more and more about Snook's movements before and after the murder and had many questions that needed answers.

Theora was last seen riding in a blue coupe, the kind of car Snook owned. There was human blood on the passenger door – and on the doorjamb – while Theora's right hand was broken and bloody. The break could have been caused by having her hand slammed in the door.

Investigators found human blood on the shirt in the Snook incinerator. The cops felt the injury to Snook's hand had not been caused by working on his car. Plus, he said it happened on Wednesday, but a doctor said he had treated it on Friday.

Snook gave up the apartment after Theora was murdered and removed her clothing from it. The female clothing in the incinerator might have been those clothes.

Detectives found a hammer and a pocketknife with blood on them in Snook's garage.

Snook had Spanish Fly in his office, as well as several books about sex. In 1929, these things indicated a deranged mind.

But, once again, this was all circumstantial evidence. It's the kind of evidence that requires a jury to infer other facts that may reasonably follow. While, by itself, it had sent many criminals to prison, juries really wanted direct evidence that proved a fact. D.A. Chester had no such evidence. More importantly, he couldn't tell a jury why Snook would have killed Theora. A motive wasn't required to get a conviction, but the jury wouldn't be happy unless they had a good reason to send a killer to the electric chair.

This meant one thing – they needed a confession.

WE WILL NEVER KNOW FOR SURE WHAT happened in that interrogation room. We do know that it was a scene right out of an old movie – a hot, cramped room filled with cops and prosecutors, a frosted glass door that let in just enough light, an oscillating fan that blew cigarette smoke over the heads of those seated at the table, and in one of the chairs was a sweating, shaking professor who was trying to maintain his cool.

Both sides had their own version of the events that occurred. The police and prosecutor left with a confession, while Dr. Snook would maintain the confession had been coerced. He was beaten, starved, and not given water for 19 hours, ordered over and over again to talk. He said that Jack Chester struck him several times in the face, saying, "Damn you, go ahead and tell the story; you have got to tell it; we know that you know more, and you must tell it."

But Police Chief Harry French, who agreed that Snook had been slapped, stated the professor's only reply to that was, "Now, Mr. Chester, don't resort to that; don't resort to that."

By 1:45 A.M., Snook was nearly broken. Detective Otto Phillips was demanding to know where Snook had gotten Theora's key to their secret apartment. If he hadn't seen her, how had he gotten her key to give back to the landlady?

"You know where I got it," Snook said and began to weep.

For Phillips, Snook's noncommittal answer – accompanied by tears – was good enough. He considered the professor broken and knew he was about to admit that he'd gotten the key from the girl after she was dead. Then, Jack Chester entered the room and said something Phillips couldn't hear, and at that moment, Snook found his backbone again.

"I want to speak to my lawyer," he said.

The detective clenched his fists and shot an angry look at Chester. Phillips stormed out of the room, and Chester followed, saying he would summon Snook's attorney and get him some breakfast. Snook was taken to a holding cell, where he wept quietly.

Chester found Wilson Shellabarger speaking to reporters, telling them that Snook had confessed. The district attorney was confused and immediately told the newsmen that no confession had been made. He pulled Shellabarger and Phillips into an empty office where a shouting match could be heard. Chester was adamant – the statement Snook made about the key wasn't enough. He wanted a "point-blank confession," and nothing else would do.

Chester was livid when he spoke to the press again, telling them that no confession had been made. No one other than himself, he told reporters, would release information about a confession. If any paper printed anything about such a confession, they'd regret it.

By this time, Snook's sleepy attorney, John Seidel, had arrived. Chester pulled him into the same office. "John, if you don't get that man to confess, damn you, I'll ruin you," Chester snapped. "I'll give the newspapers the whole story."

Seidel was taken aback by the threat. "I'll be damned if you will," he shot back. "But if there is any confession in that man, I'll wheedle it out of him and give it to you."

Chester told him he'd give him 10 minutes with his client.

Seidel spoke with Snook in his cell as the professor ate breakfast, and then he returned to Chester and told him that

Snook had no intention of confessing. Seidel said he wanted to be present from that point on when his client was questioned. Chester agreed but said that if Seidel "uttered one word he would throw him out."

At about 7:00 A.M., Snook was returned to the detective bureau, when questioning began again. He was exhausted and was slow to answer. When Seidel barked at Chester for asking questions too fast, Chester ordered him out of the room. Inexplicably, Seidel grabbed his coat and hat and left the room – and left his client to the wolves.

At one point, when Snook refused to answer any other questions, Chester lost his temper. That was when the disputed slaps took place. After that, Snook started to talk, and a stenographer was brought into the room to take his statement.

At noon on Thursday – one week to the day after Theora was killed – the district attorney met with the press and triumphantly announced that Dr. James Howard Snook had signed a written confession to the murder of Theora Hix.

The story he told was not only strange, but it was shocking and scandalous, especially to the people of 1929. In fact, much of it turned out to be so shocking that statements made in the courtroom couldn't be printed in the newspapers.

IT WAS IN THE SUMMER OF 1926 THAT THE affair began. It began with short conversations, which eventually led to Snook offering Theora a ride home in the rain. More rides followed, and they became longer and more frequent. They began taking rides into the country, and within a month after their first acquaintance, they became lovers.

Dr. Snook had been in a bad place when the two met and was not inclined to make wise choices. His son had died. His wife was in mourning. He felt he had nothing left to achieve professionally or as a marksman. The future looming ahead of him seemed to be one of department meetings, lonely dinners, long nights, and tedious weekends. He and Helen got along, but there was no spark between them. They spent more time apart than together, even sleeping in separate bedrooms. Snook had his work, and Helen had her church work. They'd eventually have another child, but that gave Helen something else to focus on other than her husband.

Helen had also noticed the distance between them, and even though she claimed ignorance of the affair, she consulted an attorney about getting a divorce in 1928. She never went through with it and steadfastly maintained that she loved her husband. She defended him to the bitter end.

Discussions between the professor and the coed quickly became intimate. Theora spoke about her other sexual partners and even told Snook that she was more knowledgeable about sex than he was and that he'd better "read up" about the subject. She offered titles of several books, such as *The Art of Love*, a book written by a physician, for Snook to study, and he did.

From early autumn 1926 until June 1927, the two slept together at least once a week, renting rooms or making love outdoors on a blanket that he kept in the car for them. The couple took a four-day trip to Camp Perry along the shore of Lake Erie before Theora decided to move to New York and continue her education there.

While she was in New York, Marion Meyers visited her for a week, and they rented a hotel room because Theora's rooming house prohibited male visitors. She didn't stay in New York for long. She returned to Columbus in the fall of 1927 and resumed her relationship with Snook.

In early 1928, though, Snook had surgery to correct a deviated septum and suffered some complications. While he was recovering, he didn't see Theora for several weeks, so she started dating Marion again. Then, in February, the pair were caught having sex and were fined by the justice of the peace. Not long after, their relationship ended for good with Marion's ill-advised marriage proposal, and she was back with Snook.

During this time, he taught Theora how to shoot pistols and rifles, and she eventually became a good shot. Snook presented her with a .41-caliber pistol for protection, and she started carrying it in her purse.

The affair continued, but by 1929, things had taken a much darker turn. Snook claimed he was chafing under Theora's constant criticism and demands, but I'm convinced he didn't want to admit to the male prosecutors and cops just how he'd allowed the young woman to dominate him.

Theora tormented him, acting moody and disagreeable to the point that Snook tried to avoid her until she reeled him back in again. She would tell Snook that her other lover, Marion Meyers, was better in bed than he was or had a larger penis and could satisfy her more than he could.

He insisted that their relationship was physical – neither he nor Theora cared deeply for one another. "We didn't love each other, we satisfied each other's needs," he later testified in court.

Theora, aside from being demanding of his time and somewhat petulant about Snook's need to take care of family obligations, often used drugs, he claimed. She introduced him to cannabis, cocaine, and Spanish Fly, which she took from his veterinary drug room. She urged Snook to ingest some of it, and he did.

Of course, he did. He did everything she told him to do. He undoubtedly didn't care to admit just how much he was under her power, but his actions demonstrated it. During their affair, Snook performed a vasectomy on himself to avoid getting her pregnant.

There was no question that Theora was the dominant partner in the relationship – especially in bed. She knew what she wanted and had no shame in taking it. She also was able to hold her own against the professor physically. She was a tall girl and weighed about 145 pounds. She was athletic, and more than once said she could defend herself against any man of similar stature.

Snook made sure to mention her physical aggressiveness and sadistic behavior. Her behavior would become so extreme that he literally had to fight her off – which, he claimed, was exactly what happened on the night of her death.

On Thursday evening, June 13, the pair made plans to meet up, but according to Snook's story, they missed each other. Theora found him anyway. He was mailing some letters when she walked up to this car and got inside. As they drove, she ate a sandwich and discussed giving up the room at the boarding house on Hubbard. Theora handed over her key.

They went for a drive and ended up near the rifle range, a secluded area after dark, where they often went to have sex. But things weren't romantic on this night, especially after Snook told Theora that he was taking his wife and daughter out of town to see his mother that weekend.

"I don't want you to go," Theora whined.

Dr. Snook's automobile, being checked for blood by detectives.

"I'm sorry. I promised Mother that I would come and bring Helen and the baby."

The mention of Helen sent Theora into a rage. Snook had expected this. More than once, Theora had demanded he not go on a trip, and outings that involved his family were especially upsetting to her. Snook said nothing as she sank back into the seat, her arms crossed and her mouth in a firm line. When she was in this kind of mood, there was nothing he could do.

Suddenly, she turned and glared at him. "Damn you!" she cursed him. "I'll kill your wife and baby!"

"Now, now," the professor tried to calm her.

"And I'll kill you, too!"

Snook said that the expression in her eyes that night made him think she might be serious. She had been acting strange and unpredictable lately. He saw her reach for her purse, and he immediately thought of the gun that he'd given her. He was convinced she was going for it.

But Theora reached for the door handle instead. But it was too late. Snook was already moving. He'd shoved his hand into the toolbox he kept in the back and grabbed a ball-peen hammer. He raised it and hit Theora on the back of the head with the hammer. She was staggered by the blow but tried to get out of the car.

"Damn you!" Theora cried out, and Snook hit her again, this time in the forehead. He was trying to stun her, he said, but the blows seemed to have no effect.

She managed to get the door open and stumbled out of the car. Snook slid across the seat and followed her. Theora tried to slam the door on her pursuer, but her own hand was in the way, and she injured herself. She stumbled back a few feet and reached into her purse, pulling out a handkerchief.

Snook was now out of the car. Freed from the confines of the small space, he extended his arm and brought the hammer down on Theora's head with a crushing blow. She fell to the ground.

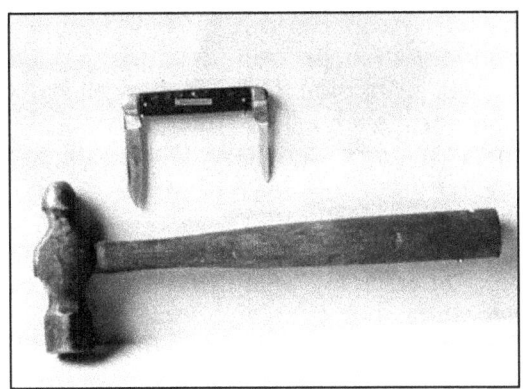

The hammer and pocket-knife that Dr. Snook used to kill Theora.

"Damn you..." she groaned and slipped into unconsciousness.

Snook slid down to a seating position on the running board of the car, looking over at the silent form of his lover. She was still alive, but he didn't want to see her suffer, so he used a pocket-knife to slice her jugular vein and carotid artery. He sat and watched as she bled out.

In shock but feeling lucky to be alive, Snook picked up Theora's purse and tossed it into the car. He looked inside for her gun but was stunned when he saw it wasn't there. She couldn't have killed him after all.

It was now almost 9:30, and he was afraid that someone might come along and see him, so he sped away. At some point, he realized he still had her purse, so he threw it off a bridge into the Scioto River as he drove home.

It was 11:00 P.M. when he arrived home.

Once inside the dark house, he quickly washed the blood from the knife and the hammer in the kitchen and then made a sandwich.

"Is that you?" Hellen called from upstairs.

He said nothing, and Helen came downstairs in her nightgown. The kitchen was dark, so she didn't see the blood on his shirt. He ate his sandwich in silence and then went to his room and began packing for the weekend trip. He tried to sleep but couldn't.

On Friday, he took his bloody suit and some other clothing to the dry cleaner and dropped off his car with the veterinary school custodian to have it washed. After that, he went to the Hubbard Avenue flat and cleaned it out, then turned over the keys to Mrs. Smalley. When he returned home, he lit the incinerator and burned a shirt and items from the boarding house.

He'd thought of everything, Snook confidently decided.

On Friday evening, the Snooks saw the mention of a young woman's body being discovered. However, the article didn't prompt any conversation between them until Saturday morning, when the victim's name was published. Dr. Snook mentioned that he knew Theora Hix because she worked in the steno pool in his department.

He was just going to say how tragic the murder was when someone knocked on the door. It was a detective and a reporter, and they wanted to have a word with him.

BY THE TIME DR. SNOOK WAS PREPARING FOR trial, he had two lawyers working for him – John Seidel and E.O. Ricketts. They'd later be joined by a third, Max Seyfert. Snook was loudly proclaiming his innocence, telling anyone who would listen that his "confession" had been beaten out of him. His claims ended up getting Seidel to make a statement to the press that would later haunt him. "If Dr. Snook killed that girl, I helped him do it."

His attorneys pushed for a postponement of the trial but could only manage to have the opening date pushed back two days. They had three different defenses to consider – a false confession, self-defense, or insanity. It was unlikely that the first would work and the other two were dangerous, but if they chose insanity, it would be up to the state to prove that Snook was sane. His attorneys just had to make him seem crazy.

District Attorney Chester was also carefully weighing his options. He had a confession that he was sure would hold up in court against the claims of coercion that were sure to be made. He also had facts that were not in the confession but would work in his favor anyway. Snook's allegations of Theora's drug use and the intimate nature of their relationship had been brought up in the papers, but the depth of depravity to which Snook – at least in Chester's mind – had dragged Theora down to was still a secret. He knew that using that information would also expose Theora, but he felt it was worth it because those secrets were sure to damn Snook in the eyes of the jury.

The trial began on the sweltering day of July 24, 1929. The courtroom was packed to capacity with 200 people, some of whom had waited in line for hours to get a seat. Three long tables had to be placed across one end of the courtroom for the 40 members of the press who were covering the trial.

Snook and his attorneys E. O. Ricketts, left, and John F. Seidel, did not have to wait long for a verdict. The jury deliberated less than 30 minutes before finding Snook guilty of murder in the first degree.

The case was no longer just getting regional attention – it was in newspapers across the country.

The first order of business before the trial actually started was to settle the question of Dr. Snook's insanity. Three panels of doctors had been named to examine his mental state. The psychiatrists for the prosecution, who included the director of the State Hospital for the Insane in Columbus, reported that Snook was not insane. The three doctors who examined the professor for the defense, headed by the chief at the State Hospital for the Insane in Athens, found Snook's reactions "very peculiar... and that he presents a very difficult problem for diagnosis." They asked for an additional 60 days to observe him in a clinical setting, but Judge Henry J. Scarlett denied the request.

At this point, the defense withdrew its motion for an official insanity hearing. Ricketts was not ready to abandon the idea that Snooks was insane but believed he could get the question worked into the trial another way.

He wouldn't be able to, and, in fact, the whole insanity hearing mess ended up causing more trouble for Dr. Snooks than it turned out to be worth. He was severely injured when one of the doctors attempted to draw spinal fluid to see if the professor had a venereal disease that might cause insanity. The spinal tap was botched, and for several weeks, Snook was unable to sit upright and suffered blinding headaches. When Judge Scarlett refused to delay the trial while he recovered, Snook was brought to the courtroom wearing dark glasses and was allowed to sit in a canvas beach chair.

The trial lasted less than a month, but during that time, hundreds of individuals waited outside the courtroom, which was packed every day, in the hope of hearing some of the sordid testimony first-hand. People began arriving as early as 3:00 A.M., hoping to get a good seat when the doors were opened.

Jack Chester called a total of 21 witnesses, including Dr. Joseph A. Murphy, the Franklin County Coroner, who testified that he found several hammer blows to the victim's head, one of which had driven particles of bone into her brain. The cause of death, though, was the severing of the jugular vein and carotid artery, which appeared to have been done by someone knowledgeable and experienced in anatomy.

Forensic examination of Snook's clothing found human blood -- later determined to be Theora's – and the same blood was found in Snook's car and also on his pocket knife and a hammer.

The defense called a total of 42 witnesses, two of whom were Dr. Snook's wife and mother, whose weepy, pathetic testimonies moved many -- including Snook -- to tears. Helen claimed her husband was a peaceful and quiet man and that she had never seen him angry. Snook's mother recalled with pride her young son's desire to stay to himself, reading and studying animals rather than running around with the rest of the neighborhood boys. When she left the stand, mother and son embraced and sobbed for what one reporter noted: "seemed like an eternity."

On August 7, 1929, Dr. Snook himself took the stand before a packed, standing-room-only courtroom that was the temperature of a sauna. Judge Scarlett Had ordered that no one under the age of 18 was allowed inside, and the press reported that a majority of the spectators were young flappers anxious to hear the salacious details that had been previously only hinted at.

The defense, though, wasn't going to be rushed and spent an entire day discussing Snook's background, teaching history, and the early days of his relationship with Theora. When minutes stretched on discussing her shooting skills, even the judge got impatient and prodded Max Seyfert to move on.

Finally, they began to talk about the triangle that included Theora, Snook, and Marion Meyers, and the prosecution objected. When the judge asked what this had to do with the murder, Seidel spoke up and explained that the defense intended to show that details of the three-way relationship would bolster their claims of insanity. When Scarlett asked what he meant, Rickets replied, "No sane man could have entered into such an arrangement as existed between these three persons. They were all insane."

Snook allowed them to continue but instructed the jury to use the testimony only as it pertained to the sanity of the defendant and not to determine Theora's character.

The professor spent the rest of the afternoon testifying that Theora had shown him more about sex than he had known before and also recounted the incident when she and Marion Meyers had been caught having sex along the Scioto River by the police and were fined $20 each. She had lied about her identity and address to the arresting officer and the justice of the peace.

When the trial continued the next day, it began with chaos. The crowd outside the courtroom had swelled to the point that the noise made it difficult for the participants to hear. Extra deputies and bailiffs were called in to control the mob once they realized they were missing what was sure to be the most exciting point in the trial. Those who waited overnight only to be denied entrance to the already packed courtroom hurled abuse at the bailiffs and tried any means possible to get inside. They forged press credentials, invented newspapers they worked for, claimed friendships with the judge and the lawyers, begged and bribed. Finally, Judge Scarlett reached his limit and demanded that deputies arrest anyone who caused a fuss outside the courtroom.

Once things calmed down, Snook was brought in to continue his testimony. It turned out to be unlike anything that had ever been heard in a courtroom before.

His testimony began with the financial arrangements that he had with Theora. She was by no means a "kept" woman, but she did receive a great deal of money from him. This occupied an hour or so of the morning, but then things turned to what everyone wanted to hear about – sex.

The three-year affair was tumultuous, Snook testified, with Theora becoming more and more discontented with "conventional sex" and more demanding of Snook's time. She pressed him to engage in acts that in the 1920s were considered "not matrimonial" and "unnatural."

In addition to introducing the professor to various drugs, she also introduced him to fellatio.

Seyfert asked him, "I just want you to relate now, Dr. Snook, as near as you can, without going into too many details, in a generalized way, just what took place between you and Miss Hix?"

Snook replied, "Finally, she insisted that she be allowed to satisfy in the way she wanted to. She did so by taking my privates in her mouth."

This was an earth-shattering revelation. At a time when sex between unmarried people was a crime, oral sex was not only unlawful and grounds for divorce, but it was considered a terrible perversion.

Publicly, of course.

Let's not kid ourselves into thinking that no one in the 1920s was having oral sex. It's just that no one talked about it, and if you heard about it, you had to seem shocked. This was, by the way, the first time that fellatio was mentioned in court records in American history.

By now, there was nothing else to talk about but the events at the shooting range. For the most part, Snook's testimony was the same as what he said in his confession, but at the point they arrived there, his story took an unexpected turn. They didn't go there so Dr. Snook could distract Theora from her bad mood. They went there to have sex, he now claimed.

According to Snook, it was Theora's idea. "I like to go out some place farther where I can scream," she allegedly said, which must have titillated the spectators all over again.

He testified that he and Theora tried to have sex in the small car but decided that it was "unsatisfactory for both of us." Afterward, when he mentioned he wanted to leave because he needed to prepare for a trip out of town with his family, she became enraged.

After that, it was basically the same story he told the police – with a few pretty wild twists.

Snook testified that he told Theora he was taking his family to his mother's home for the weekend, and she replied, "Damn your mother. I don't care about your mother. Damn Mrs. Snook! I'm going to kill her and get her out of the way."

At this point in the testimony, Dr. Snook began to cry, saying that Theora continued to threaten his family, even going so far as to say she would kill his young daughter.

After Snook was allowed to collect himself, things really took a turn. He told the courtroom, "She said, 'You have got to help me out.' She grabbed open my trousers and went down on me then, and she didn't do it very nicely, and she bit me and got hold of my privates and pulled so hard I simply could not stand it. I got hold of something out of this toolkit and hit her with it. I finally got her loose, very nearly twisted her arm off, and she sat up there a little bit and said, 'Damn you, I will kill you, too.'

"She grabbed her purse and slid out of the car. I was in so much pain, and when I tried to straighten up, all at once it flashed through my mind that she was getting out and I knew if she got out, she would shoot me.

"I hit her once then, I hit her again and she slid right out on the ground, and I followed her out. I got up behind her and hit her once more with the hammer and she went down and her head hit against the running board, and that is all I can remember of hitting her."

Snook said he couldn't recall stabbing her or cutting her throat.

None of the local newspapers quoted any of the explicit testimony. However, a reporter for the *Columbus Citizen* wrote: "The Snook trial devotees have been rewarded for their long hours of standing in line and sitting in the stuffy courtroom. Thursday morning. They heard the dirt they had been looking for."

Almost immediately, some enterprising printer managed to get his hands on the court transcripts and started selling a booklet called *The Murder of Theora Hix: Dr. Snook's Uncensored Testimony*. As soon as the 70-page booklet hit the streets, it was declared obscene, and the police were ordered to confiscate every copy they could find. Only a handful of copies still exist today.

DURING THE CLOSING ARGUMENTS, Snook's wife and mother – who had wisely avoided the courtroom during his testimony – sat on either side of him and held his hands. They listened as the defense attacked Theora, blaming her for seducing a good, upstanding professor, and to the prosecution, who cursed Snook and demanded that the jury uphold the honor of the state of Ohio by finding Snook guilty. They remained beside him during Judge Scarlett's charge to the jury, which surprised the gallery by returning with a "guilty" verdict in just 28 minutes.

Afterward, a juror said that the first 15 minutes of the deliberations were taken up by selecting a foreman and praying for divine guidance.

There was only one sentence for first-degree murder at the time – death in the electric chair – and Judge Scarlett pronounced this on Snook one week after the verdict. Snook was taken to death row at the prison on the other side of the city to wait for his sentence to be carried out.

Justice moved quickly, and soon, his appeals were exhausted. The Ohio Supreme Court set his date of execution for February 28, 1930.

He spent most of that day with his wife and was allowed to have his last meal catered and shared with Helen, his minister, Reverend Isaac Miller, and the prison chaplain. Reverend Miller later stated, "It was as if we were on a picnic." The last meal included fried chicken, lamb chops, mashed potatoes, ice cream, and coffee.

At 7:00 P.M., Snook was taken to the death chamber. He said nothing as he sat in the chair, and only as the straps were being tightened across his chest did he show any kind of emotion. He blinked his eyes a few times, clenched his fists, and bit his lower lip.

Three blasts of nearly 2,000 volts were administered over three minutes. At the first shock, the professor strained against the restraints until the current stopped. Reporter H.T. Hopkins for the International News Service wrote, "The fists drew up into knots and the bald head blistered terribly from the heat of the thunderbolt. Thin wisps of smoke curled up from the electrodes on his head and leg. The smell of burned human flesh pervaded the chamber into which two score people had crowded to watch the man die."

Dr. James Howard Snook was pronounced dead at 7:09 P.M.

A few days after the execution, Snook's body was buried in Greenlawn Cemetery in Columbus. The grave is marked by a stone that reads only "James Howard." Local legend has it that his ghost is sometimes seen walking through the cemetery, perhaps still regretting the choices that he made that ended the life of a young woman and, in the end, his own.

"THE BLUEBEARD OF THE QUIET DELL"
The Murderous Harry Powers

Why be lonely? Register with us for a small fee and start corresponding with members of the opposite sex. Thousands of our members have met the ideal mate through the mail. Why not you?

"LONELY HEARTS" ADS WERE ALREADY BIG BUSINESS by the time Raymond Fernandez and Martha Beck started using them to look for victims in the 1940s. It's true that the publicity about their crimes came close to putting an end to ads looking for love in romance magazines and newspapers, but they survived.

It would take more than that to kill them off. Nearly a decade before, another killer had used the same kind of ads to claim his victims, creating a nationwide scandal and prompting the police and the churches to try and discourage people from looking for love in such a sorted manner.

But, of course, it didn't work.

Asta Eicher and her three children, Harry, Annabelle, and Greta.

Among the scores of desperate seekers of love in the 1930s was a 50-year-old Danish-born widow from Oak Park, Illinois, named Asta Eicher. She was the mother of three children -- Greta, 14, Harry, 12, and nine-year-old Annabelle. Asta was not a woman easily led astray. She was cultivated, socially prominent, artistically inclined, and wealthy, thanks to the estate of her late husband, a prosperous Chicago silversmith.

But she was lonely and hoped to find a man to fill the space that had been left in her life by the death of her husband. She wrote a letter in response to an ad that she saw in one of her romance magazines. In early 1931, she received a reply from a gentleman who identified himself as Cornelius O. Pierson of Clarksburg, West Virginia.

According to his letter, Pierson was a successful civil engineer with a net worth of $150,000 --- more than $2.5 million in today's money. He had what he described as a "beautiful, ten-room house, completely furnished." Because his hectic work schedule and his many responsibilities prevented him "from making many social contacts," he had turned to a match-making service to help him "make the acquaintance of the right type of woman."

From the information he could see about Asta, he felt that she might be a suitable partner for him. He wrote, "My wife would have her own car and plenty of spending money."

Over the next several weeks, the two embarked on a long-distance mail-order courtship. As their hand-written romance heated up, Cornelius plied the full-figured widow with his particular brand of sweet talk. In response to a photograph of herself that she'd sent, he exclaimed over how "well-preserved" she was and assured her that he "preferred plump women." He also let her know that he understood the deepest needs of the opposite sex. He wrote thrillingly, "The great trouble is that men are so ignorant that they do not know how women must be caressed."

That was pretty steamy stuff for the time.

At some point in the spring of 1931, at Asta's invitation, Cornelius made the first of several trips to her home outside of Chicago. There is no record of how she reacted to her first look at her long-distance suitor. From his letters, she expected a tall, handsome, distinguished-looking man with dark, wavy hair and "clear blue eyes."

What she got was a spectacle-wearing, beady-eyed, moon-faced man who stood barely five feet, seven inches tall and weighed nearly 200 pounds. But, as they say, personality goes a long way, and Cornelius must have won her over because she invited him back for several more visits and proudly introduced him to her neighbors as a man of substance with investments in oil and gas wells, farm property, and stocks and bonds. Anyone who still had a lot of money during the Depression – as Cornelius clearly did – was someone worth knowing.

On June 23, 1931, Cornelius returned for another visit to Oak Park. After staying for two days, he and Asta left on a trip together, leaving the three children in the care of the family nanny, Elizabeth Abernathy. Five days later, Miss Abernathy received a letter from Asta telling her that Mr. Pierson would be coming soon to pick up the children and asked that she please have them packed up and ready to join her in West Virginia.

Cornelius arrived on July 1. He spent the night at the Eicher home, and the next morning, he sent the oldest girl, Greta, to the bank with a check and a note, both signed by Asta. The note instructed the bank clerk to fill in the entire amount of Asta's bank balance on the check, cash it, and give the money to Greta.

After reading the note, however, the teller conferred with the bank manager and asked him to look at the letter and the check. As far as they could tell, by comparing the signature on the account, it didn't appear that Asta had signed the note or the check. Greta was sent home empty-handed with a stern warning not to play pranks with her mother's account.

When she returned without the money, Cornelius quickly packed up his car, loaded the three children into the back seat, and drove off. He refused to explain anything to Elizabeth Abernathy.

Elizabeth didn't know it then, but she'd never see any of the Eichers alive again.

Harm Drenth, who became infamous as "Harry Powers."

ON NOVEMBER 17, 1892, WILKO AND JANTIE Drenth welcomed a baby boy they named Harm into their family. They had no idea at this moment of happiness just how much trouble and pain Harm would cause them in the future.

In 1910, they left the Netherlands and immigrated to America. By now, Harm was 18 years old, and within a few months of their arrival, he was already in trouble with the law for stealing liquor and automobiles. More arrests followed. He committed robberies and skipped out on unpaid loans, and while he was a busy criminal, he wasn't a very good one. He always seemed to get caught. He spent a few years behind bars and, while locked up, vowed to become more skilled at lawbreaking.

Behind bars, Harm came up with a sure-fire way to get rich with very little work – he would court rich women and desperate widows through the listings in the back of magazines, using the lonely-hearts ads. He would romance them, propose to them, get them to give him their money for safekeeping, and then he'd promise to sweep them off their feet and take them away for a life of wedded bliss. He would, of course, never deliver on his promises and would disappear into the night.

What could go wrong?

Harm knew that the first thing he needed to do was to ditch his name. It would help him cover his tracks and erase his identity as an immigrant. Women wanted a good, strong American man, he told himself, and that's what he'd give them. He started using a string of aliases, including Harry Powers – and Cornelius Pierson. Harm Drenth was gone for good.

Harry – as he called himself most of the time – set up a post office box in Vandalia, Ohio, and a mailing address in the Ohio town of Mansfield. After receiving a list of eligible women's names, he went to work, striking up his first correspondence with a Hammond, Indiana, woman named Lena Fellows in the mid-1920s. Harry pursued her cautiously, but as the letters flew back and forth, he finally proposed through the mail and suggested they elope to a quiet location for a quick wedding and start their life together.

Since they wouldn't be returning to Indiana after the wedding, he instructed her to bring all her jewelry with her and close out her bank account, which had about $1,600 in it. She should bring the cash with her on their wedding trip.

When Harry arrived in Indiana, Lena was startled to find that he looked nothing like how he described himself in his letters. But she figured that she'd hedged a bit, too – subtracting both some pounds and some years – and decided that she'd love him for his personality. They quickly drove off, with Lena thrilled at how well things were working out for her.

They drove for hours, and it seemed like Harry had no real destination in mind. Lena was content, though, especially when Harry stopped at a service station for some fuel. She was hungry and thirsty and figured she'd find a drink and a snack at the station.

Before she got out of the car, Harry suggested that she lock her cash and jewelry in a suitcase in the backseat for safekeeping. He didn't want anyone to see it whenever they stopped for meals or gas. Lena thought this was a wonderful idea, locked things up, and then went inside while Harry had the attendant gas up the car.

She had a smile on her face when she walked out of the station, but her smile quickly disappeared. The car was gone, and so was Harry – and he'd taken the locked suitcase of money and jewelry with him.

Harry was eventually caught, though, and went to court over the incident. His attorney was able to convince the jury that he wasn't guilty. Lena had given him the cash and jewelry as gifts – he hadn't stolen them.

Harry learned nothing from his failure. He was still a lousy criminal and a man with no conscience. As soon as he was free, he went right back to working the lonely-hearts ads, searching for more victims.

Next time, he vowed, he'd do things differently.

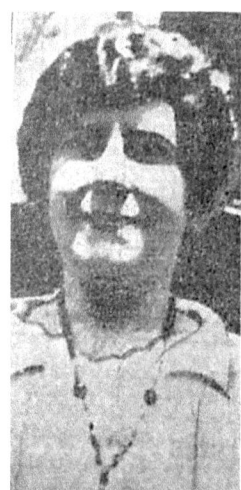

Luella Strothers, who Harry would swindle and marry, making her an unknowing accomplice to his crimes.

HARRY SOON HAD OTHER WOMEN ON THE HOOK. One of them was Luella Strother from Clarksburg, West Virginia. Luella, her mother, and her sister, Eva, owned a house, a store, and some land in a secluded spot called Quiet Dell – an unincorporated area about eight miles south of town.

They began exchanging letters. Harry's notes were filled with loneliness and hope, and Luella wrote chatty, flirty missives in return. Soon, he proposed marriage. I assume his original plan was to do the same thing he'd done with Lena Fellows, but for some reason, he didn't. Harry went through with the marriage, and they were wed on June 1, 1927.

But he hadn't fallen in love. He had simply decided to play the long game.

Good luck followed the wedding when Luella's mother died about three months later, leaving the house, store, and land in Quiet Dell to his wife and sister-in-law. His first order of business was to get the two of them to sign a power of attorney that would make him the legal authority over all of it. With a bit of gentle urging – and the built-in misogyny of the era – he soon had a document with both of their signatures on it.

In April 1931, Harry told Luella that he planned to evict a family that was living on their Quiet Dell property and build a garage on the land. He wanted to turn it into a workshop where he could tinker around in peace and quiet. Luella never questioned it.

He hired a local cement contractor to build the garage, using plans that Harry had created himself. Like Luella, the contractor never questioned any of Harry's additions. He was getting paid. That was good enough for him.

Around that same time, Harry went back to work with the lonely-hearts ads. Now posing as Cornelius Pierson, he described himself as a wealthy, 38-year-old civil engineer who was looking for the right kind of woman. He described his stately home, his memberships in the Elks and the Freemasons, and how well he planned to treat his future wife – giving her all the love and money she'd ever need.

His ad – no surprise – was a big success. Harry received more than 100 replies from lonely widows and spinsters. His post office box ended up with so many letters in it that it overflowed. To keep track of each woman, he invented a coded system that he could, at a glance, tell where in the correspondence he was with each of them individually and what benefits she could provide him with a proposed marriage.

One of the women at the top of his list was Asta Eicher, a widow from Oak Park, Illinois. She and her three children mysteriously vanished in the summer of 1931.

Just three weeks after Cornelius Pierson drove off with the three Eicher children, he turned up at the home of Mr. and Mrs. Charles Flemming in Northboro, Massachusetts. He was there to meet the object of another long and passionate correspondence -- Mrs. Flemming's sister, Dorothy Lemke. He had recently proposed to her, and Dorothy had accepted. Now, they planned to leave town and start a new life together.

St. Paul Victim of Bluebeard

Mrs. Dorothy Lemke, former St. Paul woman, who was one of the victims of Bluebeard Harry F. Powers at Clarksburg, W. Va. Mrs. Lemke was lured to Clarksburg by offers of marriage made by Powers through his matrimonial bureau. She and Mrs. Aste Eicher and the latter's three children were slain by the monster in his garage. The bodies were found where he had buried them nearby.

Before leaving town, Cornelius and Dorothy stopped by two local banks, where Dorothy withdrew $4,000 from her accounts. They were leaving for Iowa, where the two of them planned to get married. On the way out of Massachusetts, they stopped at a railway station to ship Dorothy's trunks. They looked forward to a leisurely sightseeing drive, and Cornelius wanted to have her trunks waiting for them at their Iowa hotel when they arrived.

But Dorothy didn't notice that the trunks were not sent to Iowa. Instead, they were sent to Fairmont, West Virginia, where a man named Harry Powers picked them up at the train station just a few days later.

As for Dorothy, well, she was never seen alive again.

DESPITE HOW IT MIGHT SEEM, HARRY'S criminal skills had never really improved since the time he was a terrible car thief named Harm Drenth.

It was the nanny, Elizabeth Abernathy, who first alerted the police that something strange was going on with the Eicher family. During a search of their home, detectives found 27 letters that had been written to Asta by Cornelius Pierson from a post office box in Clarksburg, West Virginia, and they immediately began trying to track him down. They searched through public records, telephone books, and city directories for Clarksburg, but there was no trace of anyone named Pierson.

They contacted the Clarksburg police and explained the situation, telling them that Pierson was wanted for questioning in the disappearance of Asta and her children. The police chief put a detective named Carl Southern on the case, and he also discovered that Pierson didn't seem to exist.

But he turned to the U.S. postal service for answers. He soon learned that a man named Cornelius Pierson had rented a post office box and had given his home address as 111 Quincy Street in Clarksburg. It turned out that the man's name was not Pierson at all – it was Harry F. Powers. Far from being a wealthy bachelor with money coming in from oil wells, dairy farms, and high-yield bonds, he was married to a local girl named Luella, who owned a little store near their home. Detective Southern was ordered to bring in Harry for questioning.

When the officers arrived at the house, Luella told them that her husband was out and would be back later. He had long before convinced her that he needed to travel often for his job as a vacuum cleaner salesman, and she had gotten used to him being gone for days and weeks at a time.

When Harry finally did return home, she told him that the police had been there and planned to return that afternoon. Harry shrugged off the news, pretending he wasn't interested, but then told Luella that he quickly needed to transfer $4,000 from his bank account into the store's account. He didn't tell her why – but obviously, he didn't want the police to find that kind of money in the account of a simple salesman. He'd never figure out a way to explain it.

When the police returned, Harry at first denied that he knew Asta Eicher. However, when he was confronted with photographs of the more than two dozen love letters that he had written to her, he grudgingly admitted that they had corresponded but nothing else. He insisted that he didn't know anything about her disappearance.

The cops didn't believe him.

Harry was arrested on a warrant from Illinois and taken into local custody. Before he was interrogated at the station, he was searched, and the police found four letters addressed to four different women in his jacket pocket. He said they had been written for fun, that was all – and he demanded a lawyer.

Under questioning, Harry admitted again that he knew the Eicher family, but if they were really missing, he was sure they'd turn up soon, safe and sound. Asta was only a friend. She had contacted Harry to help her sell some of her property, he claimed, and their friendship had turned flirtatious but remained innocent.

Harry's arrest was reported in the local newspaper, and the story was read with interest by a woman named Louise Watson. She telephoned Harrison County Sheriff Wilford B. Grimm to tell him that Harry had a garage on the property that adjoined land belonging to her mother at a place called Quiet Dell, a few miles outside of Clarksburg.

The sheriff badly wanted to get into the garage, so he went to a justice of the peace and obtained a warrant under bootlegging laws, even though there was no evidence that Harry had been making or selling illegal liquor.

But, you know, he could've been, and that was good enough for the justice of the peace. Sherriff Grimm got the search warrant on August 28, then joined by other local officials and Detective Southern, and he headed for Quiet Dell.

None of the men would ever forget what they found there.

There was a rundown cottage sitting in the middle of the secluded property. It had once been home to the family that Harry had evicted. It had clearly been empty for a while, and directly across a narrow dirt road stood a large, new structure – Harry's recently designed and built garage.

The door was secured by a pair of heavy padlocks that were pried open with a crowbar. The interior had been designed to hold at least three automobiles, but there were no cars inside – and no workshop, which was the excuse Harry had used to build the place.

In the middle of the dusty concrete floor was a pile of trunks and boxes that turned out to be packed with the personal belongings of Asta Eicher and her three children. Among the clothing and correspondence were letters that had been written to Cornelius Pierson.

As they poked around, one of the officers noticed a trap door on the floor – the garage had a basement level. Harry had designed it that way.

When the door was opened, a wave of horrible odor rushed up into the faces of the lawmen. It was coming from below. Shining their flashlights down into the darkness, several officers cautiously descended the creaking wooden steps. As they looked around, it became painfully clear that the cellar had been designed --and used -- as a prison.

The space was divided into four cramped cells, each of them fitted with a heavy wooden door. Small, iron-grated openings at the top of the exterior walls allowed some weak rays of sunshine to penetrate the gloomy interior. Otherwise, there was no light and no ventilation. And there were no furnishings – just a bare, filthy mattress on the floor of each cell.

Horrific discoveries were made in the cramped chambers. In one, they found a noose that could easily be used by a hangman. In another, they found a bloody footprint. They discovered a hammer with blood on it, clumps of hair that had been pulled out by the roots, and bloodstains on all the mattresses. A partially burned bank book and scorched, bloody clothing were later retrieved from some ashes near the building, but there was no sign of any victims.

Even so, any hope that the authorities had about the safe return of the Eicher family began to fade.

The search of the farm continued. The Clarksburg Fire Department assisted with pumping out an old well that was located on the property. It would have been the perfect place to dump a corpse. But they found it filled with rocks and water – no bodies.

While the search was going on at Quiet Dell, Harry was still being questioned in town. He suddenly remembered that Asta and her family had gone away with a man named Charles Rogers, who lived in Pittsburgh.

Enough was enough. Handcuffed and heavily guarded, Harry was brought to Quiet Dell and shown the boxes in the garage and the bloodstains in the cellar. He finally changed his story – Asta and her children had gone to Denver, not Pittsburgh. And while he recognized some of the bloody clothing as that of the Eicher family, he didn't know anything about the rest of the stuff in the garage. Someone must've been using the place without his knowledge.

Other than that, he said nothing.

THE NEWS OF THE GRUESOME DISCOVERIES in the garage spread rapidly across the area, and by late afternoon, more than 300 of the morbidly curious had gathered at the farm to watch what was taking place.

As news spread of the gruesome discoveries at Quiet Dell, hundreds of people flocked to the scene to watch the search.

Among these bystanders was a 15-year-old boy who lived nearby. He interrupted Sheriff Grimm to tell him that he had recently helped Harry dig a ditch for a sewer pipe that was supposed to stretch from the garage to nearby Elk Creek.

Officers from the sheriff's department and the state police grabbed shovels and went to work. As the excavation progressed, a road gang from the county jail was brought in to help. Soon, a terrible odor began to emanate from the trench.

Asta Eicher's body was discovered first. She had been strangled and wrapped in a burlap bag before being buried in the ditch. Her arms had been tied behind her. Clumps of hair had been ripped from her head. The bodies of her three children were also uncovered, wrapped in burlap, later that afternoon.

A few hours later, the diggers came upon the remains of a fifth person – who was later identified as Dorothy Lemke. By this time, she had also been reported missing.

According to the results of the autopsies that followed, Asta had been starved and tortured before being murdered. Evidence in the "death dungeon," as the newspapers began calling it, suggested that Asta had been hanged from the noose that was tied to a ceiling beam, likely in full view of her children. When her son, Harry, had tried to struggle free and save his mother, his skull had been beaten in by the hammer.

He had been castrated – while still alive – before his body was buried in the ditch. His sister had been strangled and dumped next to him. They had all been starved for days before they died.

The trench that was supposed to be for a sewer pipe from the garage was actually a trench to hide the bodies of Harry's victims.

Dorothy had been strangled, too, using a heavy leather belt. It was still twisted around her neck when her corpse was discovered.

Confronted with the corpses at the local mortuary, Harry viewed the remains with no emotion and claimed again that he had no idea how any of them had died. When he was taken back to jail, a mob had already formed around the building, screaming that Harry be turned over to them so that justice could be carried out.

But even then, Harry remained silent, maintaining his innocence. He insisted they had been buried there by someone else.

But at that point, on Friday night, August 28, the interrogation took a turn for the worse.

Police officials, sheriff's deputies, and even detectives from the Baltimore and Ohio Railroad took turns questioning Harry with their fists, boots, burning cigarettes, a rubber hose, and even a ball-peen hammer that was banged on his knees, elbows, and

Harry was in rough shape after his interrogation by police officers, sheriff's deputies, and railroad detectives. He eventually confessed to all the murders.

toes. He was jabbed with knife tips, his left arm was broken, and hot boiled eggs were pressed into his armpits.

Finally, around 4:00 AM the following day, he broke. He sobbed to the detectives, "I did it. My God, I want some rest."

Photographs taken of Harry over the next two days showed his badly swollen face, black eyes, bruises, burns, puncture wounds, and welts – all of which his captors insisted occurred when he "fell down the stairs" during questioning. In the jail's infirmary, he signed a confession to the murder of Asta and her children "by using a hammer and strangulation."

No matter how the confession was obtained – and keep in mind, there were no laws prohibiting that kind of interrogation back then – Harry did commit the murders.

And he may have committed others that we'll never know about.

The police found hundreds of letters that he'd received from lonely women around the country. Each of them had poured their hearts out to him, and he had professed his love in return. Detectives began reaching out to the women who had written him letters – trying to make sure they were still alive.

One of them was Edith Simpson of Detroit, who expected Pierson to marry her in September. She had already purchased her wedding dress and arranged to leave town with him after the ceremony. When shown a letter that Powers had written to Asta Eicher, Edith was amazed to see that it was an almost exact copy of one that he had sent to her – but still refused to believe he had done anything wrong until she was shown photographs of the bodies of his victims. She vomited on the spot – likely then realizing how close she had come to being next on his list.

But not all the letter writers were so lucky. A mother would later contact the police about her daughter, Maud Johnson, who had gone missing a few years before. One of the photos later found to be in Harry's possession was that of an unknown woman with the name "Maud Johnson" written on the back.

As news of the murders spread out of West Virginia and across the country, new letters began arriving from victims who were luckily still alive. One of them, June Dixon from South Carolina, claimed to be Harry's lawful wife, with a marriage license to prove it. It seems he would also be able to add bigamy to his list of crimes.

Speaking of wives, the authorities were running into trouble with their questioning of Luella. They were trying to figure out what she had known and if she could have been married to Harry for four years without ever suspecting that anything strange was going on. At one point, the cops were sure she was guilty and then, at other times, assumed she was merely stupid.

She claimed that she never asked Harry about his business or his frequent absences. She admitted that she did enjoy the stylish women's clothing that he often brought her, but it never crossed her mind to ask him where the used garments had come from.

So, maybe she was just stupid after all.

THE DISCOVERIES AT QUIET DELL WERE discussed in every home, church, general store, billiards parlor, and barber shop across the region. People were fascinated by news of the newly dubbed "Bluebeard of Quiet Dell," taking the name from the character in the French fairy tale who had a habit of murdering his wives.

Hundreds of people lined up to walk through the Romine Funeral Home in Clarksburg for a look at the five victims, who had been laid out in open caskets.

On Sunday, August 30, an estimated 30,000 curiosity-seekers overran the so-called "murder farm" at Quiet Dell turning the hot, end-of-the-summer afternoon into what newspapers called a "morbid holiday." A dozen county deputies were dispatched to the scene to direct traffic, but they were soon overwhelmed.

An estimated 30,000 people came to see Quiet Dell in late August.

A couple of enterprising local promoters quickly erected a six-foot wooden fence around the property and started charging people admission to get inside. Outraged at having the site of a tragedy transformed into what one observer called a "mass murder amusement park," someone soaked the fence with gasoline during the night and set fire to it. A second fence was also promptly torn down.

Rumors were still spreading about local citizens taking justice into their own hands. The rumors became real on the night of September 19, when a lynch mob of more than 4,000 men and women surrounded the jail, crying out for Harry to be turned over to them.

The fire department was called to the scene to try and help dispel the mob with water hoses, but the angry crowd tore lengths of hose from the trucks to keep them from operating, and several members of the mob tried unsuccessfully to overturn one of the fire trucks.

A contingent of heavily armed lawmen then confronted the crowd – the sheriff and his deputies, the entire city police force, and a detachment of state troopers – who warned them to stay back or be shot. Ignoring the threat, the mob surged forward. After firing a few warning shots over their heads, the police let loose a barrage of tear gas. But as the canisters were spewing their contents, members of the mob picked them up and hurled them back at the cops.

A cloud of tear gas hung over downtown for hours, burning the eyes of bystanders more than a block from the scene of the riot. Eight members of the mob were arrested before the crowd finally dispersed.

As it turns out, Harry wasn't in the jail anyway. He had been hustled out of a rear exit and into a waiting automobile. Escorted by two state police cars, he was driven to the state penitentiary at Moundsville, where he remained in solitary confinement until his trial.

The next problem that the authorities faced was finding a suitable place for that trial. The old courthouse was too small for the anticipated crowd, and the new courthouse was under construction. The temporary building, which would later serve as the City Hall and police station, was not nearly large enough for the number of spectators that were sure to come, so county officials arranged to hold the trial in the largest venue available -- Moore's Opera House. It had a seating capacity of 1,200 people, and every seat was filled during the five days of the trial.

Choosing a jury was even more difficult. Most of the locals had already traveled to Quiet Dell to gawk at the garage, and everyone in the area knew about the murder victims who had been found there. Harry's attorney demanded a change of venue. It was denied.

Eventually, a jury was seated, and the proceedings began on December 7, 1931, with the principal performers – the judge, jury, witnesses, defendant, lawyers, and prosecutors – all on the opera house stage. During the days that followed, the audience watched in rapt attention while Harry, in sharp contrast, just seemed bored by the whole thing.

Prosecutor Will Morris was seeking the death penalty and was confident he'd get it. Even though the defendant had been indicted for five murders, the prosecutors had elected to try the case based solely on Dorothy Lemke's murder because there was a more direct link to Powers.

Prosecutor Morris had a damning list of witnesses, including James E. Smith, the contractor who testified that he had constructed the garage at Quiet Dell for Powers.

Detective Carl Southern testified that Dorothy's body had been found in the ditch near the garage. He also stated that he had seized letters that Harry had that were addressed to Cornelius Powers.

City and county officers testified about bloodstains, clothing, and trunks found at the scene.

County Coroner Dr. Leroy C. Goff testified that Dorothy had been strangled with a man's leather belt.

Mr. and Mrs. Charles Flemming identified Harry as the man who had left their home with Dorothy while claiming to be Cornelius Pierson.

Employees from the express company in nearby Fairmont testified that Harry was the man who had picked up trunks and other baggage sent to Fairmont on Dorothy's behalf.

Three bank officials of the Second National Bank of Uniontown, Pennsylvania, identified Harry as the man who had cashed two checks totaling $4,287.21 that were drawn on Dorothy's account.

Three residents of Quiet Dell swore that they had seen Powers shoveling dirt into the ditch near the garage between July 30 and August 1.

And then there was the forensic psychiatrist who had interviewed Harry – just in case he tried to put on an insanity defense. Dr. Edwin H. Meyers, one of the best in the business, testified that Harry was legally sane. He knew right from wrong, even if he chose to ignore it. He was driven by greed, but he received his greatest satisfaction from planning and carrying out his murders and torturing his victims before he killed them. He was simply, Dr. Meyers said, "driven by the mere love of killing."

Harry took the stand in his own defense but offered a confusing mix of denials and accusations about two mystery men who he claimed had actually committed the murders. He said that he had only been an acquaintance of Dorothy's, and he had cashed the checks for the *real* murderers. His testimony was flat and disinterested, and none of the jury members believed what he had to say.

Harry also didn't seem all that interested when the jury returned a "guilty" verdict on December 11. They had only deliberated for two hours – just long enough to order one more lunch on the county's dime.

On December 12, the judge sentenced Harry to death on the gallows. Harry simply shrugged.

His attorneys tried to appeal the case several times but with no luck. Harry was already resigned to his fate.

On the day of his execution, Harry was nattily dressed in a black pinstripe suit, white shirt, and a gaudy blue necktie. He calmly walked up the steps to the gallows without assistance and looked out dispassionately at the 42 witnesses who had assembled to watch him die. Asked if he had any last words, he calmly replied, "No."

A moment later, at precisely 9:00 a.m. on Friday, March 18, 1932, three attendants stationed by three buttons pushed them simultaneously, and Powers dropped to his doom. None of the three men would ever know which button sprang the trap door. His neck broken, Harry dangled at the end of the rope for 11 minutes before the prison physician pronounced him dead.

Neither his father nor Luella claimed his body for burial, so he was buried in an unmarked grave in a Moundsville Cemetery. The location of the site remains a mystery.

THE STORY OF THE "BLUEBEARD OF QUIET DELL" ended, for most people, with the death of Harry Powers, but, in a way, the horror lived on.

His father, Wilko, couldn't live with the idea that his son had committed such atrocious crimes. He had already outlived his wife and all his other children. On October 6, 1933, at his farm in Ohio, Wilko put a shotgun to his chest and fired the blast that ended his life.

The crimes of Harry Powers divided Luella and her sister, Eva. They never spoke again after the murders were revealed. Eva took over the store, and Luella lived in the house. She withdrew from society and refused to leave home. The shame was just too much to bear, and she was never seen in public again. She died in isolation in 1957.

The infamous garage was later destroyed. A house trailer sits on the property as of the time of this writing.

As for Harry, he has managed to live on in infamy – or at least a fictionalized version of him has. In 1953, his life and crimes inspired a best-selling book by West Virginia author Davis Grubb, who had lived not far from Quiet Dell when the murders were revealed.

The book, called *Night of the Hunter*, was set during the Depression and told the story of a psychopathic ex-con named Harry Powell, who passed himself off as an itinerant preacher. In his relentless hunt for $10,000 in stolen cash, he courted, married, and then murdered a widowed young mother, then pursued her children, who ran off with the money.

Two years after the book was published to great success and critical acclaim, it was adapted into a film starring Robert Mitchum as the depraved killer with the words LOVE and HATE tattooed on his knuckles. It turned out to be one of the best – and most sinister – roles of Mitchum's long career.

If you're looking for a real chill some night, seek it out and give it a watch. If it scares you, though, remember that you chose to watch it. This is one of those rare times when you can't just tell yourself that it's "only a movie."

This is a case of fiction being inspired by fact, and, as most of us know already, truth is almost always stranger – and much more terrifying – than fiction.

"MY WIFE HAS BEEN GASSED!"
Richard and Delores Gladden

DAN POWER, THE SHERIFF OF CLINTON, COUNTY, INDIANA, made a sharp curve in his patrol car, the wheels of the vehicle screeching on the pavement. The engine roared. Sheriff Power was driving fast along State Road 39, heading north from Frankfort.

In the backseat of the car was a 22-year-old convicted killer named Richard Gladden, who was being closely watched by a deputized Frankfort merchant named Clyde Louck. Frankfort police officer Clifford Gray was riding shotgun – literally. He had a weapon gripped in his hands.

The Indiana State Penitentiary at Michigan City.

Their destination on that warm April morning in 1932 was the Indiana State Penitentiary in Michigan City.

For the first 93 miles of the journey, Richard seemed completely unconcerned about the prison cell that was waiting for him to spend a life sentence in. But after passing through the tiny LaPorte County town of Wanatah, where he spotted the "19 Miles to Michigan City" sign on the side of the road, he grew somber. A few minutes later, when the sheriff's car arrived within sight of the prison's high stone walls, Richard spoke, his voice uneasy. "So, this is where we're going," he said.

The sheriff scoffed. "This is it. This is where you'll spend the rest of your life."

Richard only laughed and shook his head. "Nah," he said. "I'll be eligible for parole in six months, and I'll bet I don't serve two years."

Three months earlier, Richard would have bet that he'd never even be accused of murder, let alone charged, convicted, and sentenced to life behind bars.

But that was before his 21-year-old bride, Dolores, had died in the front seat of his car.

RICHARD HAD MET HIS BRIDE-TO-BE, DOLORES RENFROW, HIS in January 1930 in Kansas City, Missouri, where he was then attending the Sweeney Automobile and Aviation School. It was, apparently, love at first sight. The couple was married three weeks later, and they briefly made their home with Dolores' mother and stepfather. Soon after, Richard's school went out of business – a casualty of the Great Depression – and he had to start looking for work while Dolores clerked at Woolworth's. In about a month, he landed a job at a local cafeteria, and the couple moved into a rooming house.

In January 1931, the pair relocated to Frankfort, Indiana, but over the next year, Dolores returned to Kansas City several times to see her mother, Dorothy Titsworth.

Her marriage, it seemed, was not going well.

And then, shortly before midnight on February 1, 1932, a man named John Young was awakened by the sound of someone banging on his door. He peered out the window. His house overlooked State Road 28 on Frankfort's east side, and by the lights on the roadway, he could see a car parked outside his front door. He opened it to find Richard Gladden on his porch. The young man was excited and upset. "Please, please, my wife has been gassed and I need an ambulance!" he cried. "Call eighty-eight!"

Young figured the man on his porch was drunk, but he made the call anyway – dialing eighty-eight, the number for Goodwin Funeral Home, which also operated the town ambulance. He turned to the young man and told him he'd made the call, and he watched as Richard stumbled across the state road toward its intersection with Maish Road.

Ambulance driver William Goodwin responded to the call. He sped to the scene, and when he arrived a few minutes later, he saw Richard standing in the road waving a flashlight. Goodwin stopped, threw open the passenger door, and told Richard, who seemed weak and confused, to climb in.

"What's the matter?" Goodwin demanded. "A wreck?"

"No," Richard replied, "gassed – carbon monoxide."

Richard directed Goodwin to turn north onto Maish Road and followed it until he found his car, a Whippet coupe, parked about a half mile away, just south of some railroad tracks.

"What time is it?" Richard asked.

"About midnight," Goodwin answered.

Richard gasped in shock. "My god! I've been out here since 8:30!"

He quickly explained to Goodwin that he and his wife had pulled over to talk, and because it was so cold, he'd left the car running to stay warm. He wasn't sure when they'd dozed off, but when he woke up around 10:30, he couldn't rouse his wife. His first thought was to take her to a hospital, but the motor had turned off while he was asleep and wouldn't restart. It was likely out of gas, so he had no choice but to leave and try and get help on foot.

Goodwin pulled the ambulance to a stop next to Richard's car. He could see Dolores in the passenger seat. She was slumped over, and her head was resting against the passenger-side window. Goodwin sprang out, and he quickly moved Dolores – who was still unresponsive – into the ambulance. In a few short minutes, he was roaring away toward the Clinton County Hospital.

When they arrived, a nurse checked Dolores' vitals and summoned Dr. W.L. Hammersley. He reached the hospital a few minutes later and immediately went to work on the unconscious woman. He tried to resuscitate her, but it was useless – Dolores was dead.

And soon after that, several events occurred that forever altered the course of Richard Gladden's life.

The first was when Dr. Hammersley included in his report on the incident that he'd found two bruises on each side of Dolores' neck. Although he said they were "hardly discernible," he was obligated to report them to Clinton County coroner Frank Strange and prosecutor Millard Morrison.

Both men began the second event – they recommended that Richard be taken into police custody on the spot.

Finally, Dr. Strange performed the autopsy on Dolores at Weidner and Kent Funeral Home, and the prosecutor announced that Dolores' death was "surrounded by mysterious circumstances" – even though he wouldn't actually see the autopsy report until the end of the week.

By then, though, a grand jury had already been assembled to decide if Richard Gladden would be indicted for murder.

ON WEDNESDAY, FEBRUARY 3, A GRIEF-STRICKEN Dorothy Titsworth had already arrived in Frankfort and was visiting her son-in-law in his jail cell. She stayed all afternoon, and the two met again the next morning at the funeral home so Richard could bid an emotional goodbye to his wife.

The co-owner of the funeral home, Oswell Weidner, would later testify that Dorothy asked Richard several times if he had killed Dolores, and each time, he swore, "I never touched her."

Two days later, Dorothy took her daughter home to be buried at Soldier Cemetery in Jackson County, Kansas.

While his wife's body was traveling home to Kansas, Richard retained local attorney Frank S. Pryor. Since no charges had been filed against him yet, Pryor immediately petitioned for his client's release. That paperwork was still sitting on someone's desk, though, when the grand jury indicted Richard for first-degree murder on February 6.

Richard appeared to be stunned by this turn of events. Protesting his innocence, his attorney appeared before Circuit Judge Brenton A. DeVol to request a bail hearing. A reporter from the *Frankfort Morning Times* was there and described Richard as looking much different than the handsome man who was a familiar figure in town. "He has not shaved in several days," he wrote, "and the strain of his incarceration is clearly evident."

The hearing was set for February 20, and Pryor appeared in court with his client to proclaim Richard's innocence and argue for his release on bond pending trial. Pryor pointed out that the "evidence is not evident nor the presumption strong" with the case against his client.

The prosecuting attorney challenged the bond, and the hearing dragged on for several days, with 19 witnesses appearing for the state. Pryor pointed out the ridiculousness of the witness list – for a hearing, no less – and even made a motion for a dismissal when two of the state's medical experts from Indianapolis refused to testify unless they were paid.

In the end, though, Pryor lost. Richard's bail was denied, but the hearing had provided the attorney with a preview of what the state planned to do at trial – overwhelm the jury with a dozen theories and see what sticks.

THE TRIAL BEGAN ON MONDAY, APRIL 11, and on that first day, everyone described Richard as looking gaunt and pale. Jury selection was grueling, lasting for more than two days, because nearly all the prospective jurors claimed to have already formed strange suspicions about Richard's guilt.

That was bad enough, but something worse soon happened – Dorothy Titsworth entered the courtroom and took a seat at the prosecution table with D.A. Morrison.

Richard was shocked by her unexpected presence. The last time that he had spoken with Dolores' mother was the day that he'd said goodbye to his wife at the funeral home. Had Dorothy returned as a witness? And if so, for whose side, his or the prosecution?

Richard had to know.

He got up from his seat at the defense table, and before a deputy could stop him, he walked in Dorothy's direction.

Dorothy recoiled in panic. "Get away! Get Away!" she shrieked at him, jolting backward in her chair and banging up against the table. And if that wasn't enough to shock the entire courtroom, she then screamed, "Dolores came to me from spirit land and told me you killed her!"

The case was already the talk of the town – in churches, the bowling alley, taverns, pool halls, barber shops, and beauty parlors – but an ear-shattering announcement about the ghost of the dead woman got everyone's attention. Interest in the case spread like wildfire, and the next day, available seats in the courtroom were so scarce that spectators were hiring stand-ins to save seats for them.

The going rate was 25 cents an hour.

When opening statements in the trial began, the prosecutor announced several very thin and completely unsubstantiated scenarios that, he claimed, would prove Richard's guilt beyond a reasonable doubt. Morrison insisted that any of his theories – strangulation, drugging, motor tampering, a rubber hose, arguments in the marriage, and life insurance – was more than enough to convict Richard of first-degree murder. Once that was accomplished, he told the jury, they'd have to decide if he would receive a sentence of life in prison or death.

Frank Pryor responded with promises – not wild claims. He promised that in the coming days, the defense would offer irrefutable, rock-solid evidence that would dismantle the circumstantial allegations made by the state.

Dream Brings Murder Conviction

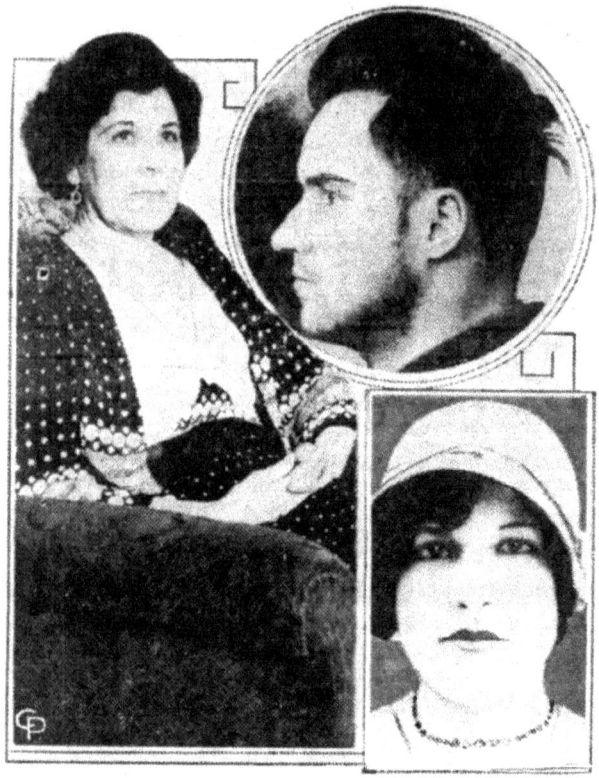

Richard Gladden, his wife Dolores, and his mother-in-law Dorothy Titsworth, who showed up unexpectedly during Gladden's trial to testify that her dead daughter came to her during a dream to tell her mother that her husband had murdered her.

The state only had theories about his client's guilt – none of which they could prove beyond a reasonable doubt for the simple fact that his client was not guilty.

In his opening, D.A. Morrison tried to shock the jury by offending their sense of morality. He knew it was easy to unsettle small-town folks about anything to do with sex. He called Richard a "feckless adulterer" and claimed he had been hatching a scheme for months to kill his wife and then cash in on her life insurance policy. It was money and sex, Morrison said.

Pryor laughed at these allegations and countered in his opening by reminding the jury that a grand jury indictment shouldn't be confused with evidence of guilt. He stressed, "Richard Gladden is an innocent man. He loved his wife dearly.

Finding her unconscious in the car, he did everything humanly possible to revive her. When his efforts failed, he rushed to obtain medical assistance."

Pryor also assured the jury that the couple had been very religious and had taken their wedding vows seriously. He said to them, "Why, just that Sunday night preceding the fatal Monday night, the young man and his wife attended church, as they frequently did. Such habits are not those of one with adultery – or murder – in his heart."

ONCE THE TRIAL OFFICIALLY BEGAN, THE STATE called an assembly line of witnesses to try and convince the jury that Richard was guilty. It didn't matter what motive they chose – there were so many – they could choose from any of them, and they'd clearly see that he'd killed his wife.

On Wednesday morning, April 13, Morrison called three witnesses affiliated with three different life insurance companies. They testified that Richard was the beneficiary of three different policies that covered the life of Dolores Gladden.

In the middle of a Depression.

Pryor used his cross-examination to show that these were the sensible precautions of a responsible married couple. The prosecutor had made the policies look suspicious, but he proved they had all been purchased with Dolores' knowledge and consent. Besides that, she was the beneficiary of a $15,000 policy that had been taken out on her husband.

When Morrison called Richard's younger brother, Robert, to the stand, he revealed he was the owner of the car that Richard and Dolores had been driving that night. He relentlessly quizzed Robert about repairs made on January 31 to the car's heater. Robert explained that the gas line, as well as the heater, frequently malfunctioned and that his passengers complained about headaches, which he'd also experienced. Morrison scoffed at his answers, suggesting the car had been tampered with.

Pryor brought a local mechanic to the stand later, who testified that the car's manifold heater was faulty. He said its grease- and soot-covered outlet tube could have caused carbon monoxide to leak into the car's interior.

But Morisson continued hammering on this theory – sort of. He tossed aside the heater that had been allegedly tampered with and came up with a new idea. A piece of rubber hose had been found in the trunk of the car, and he asserted that Richard had used the hose to direct poisonous gas fumes from the exhaust pipe to the car's interior.

But the mechanic that Pryor put on the stand had an answer to this, too. The hose was way too short. There's no way it could have stretched from the exhaust pipe to the window.

Then perhaps it was another type of poison?

Morrison used a medical witness to say that, based on the way she reacted, Dolores might have been drugged with luminal, a commonly used sedative. The fact that Richard bought some of the tablets on February 1 was apparently the basis for this story, even though Dolores regularly kept it in her medicine cabinet.

But Pryor put Dr. R.H. Karger, an associate professor of toxicology at the Indiana University School of Medicine, on the stand. He testified that tests showed conclusively that there were only two foreign substances present in Dolores' organs – carbon monoxide and a trace of acetylsalicylic acid – also known as aspirin.

Morrison must have felt that the bruises that had been spotted on Dolores' neck when she arrived at the hospital were sure to convince the jury of Richard's guilt because he waited for a dramatic moment to introduce them at trial. He was able to get a witness who stated that this showed possible strangulation.

However, Pryor's witness, a doctor in Frankfort, A.G. Chittick, testified that strangulation had not contributed to Dolores' death. The marks had not been deep, he said, and since air was found in her lungs, that deduction had been disproved."

Morrison also used several witnesses to try and show that Richard was a cold-hearted killer by focusing on how impassive he seemed about his wife's death. He questioned a Frankfort police officer who testified that Richard hadn't shed a single tear that night. William Goodwin, the ambulance driver, agreed, saying that Richard showed no outward signs of emotion.

But a witness of Pryor's told a different story about Richard's reaction when he saw his wife's body at the funeral home. "He knelt beside her body and cried bitterly," he said.

The prosecutor also tried to make the jury think that not only was Richard uncaring the night his wife died, but he was also probably drunk. He put John Young, the man whose door Richard knocked on that night, on the stand, and Young said he'd acted "queer and was probably drunk."

But Pryor asked Dr. Ivan Carlyle, former Clinton County coroner, to list the effects of carbon monoxide poisoning. He testified that, prior to death, victims experience extreme weakness, disorientation, headaches, and dizziness – any one of which could be mistaken for drunkenness.

Well, if he wasn't drunk, he was definitely a convicted felon. The prosecutor revealed that in 1929, Richard was convicted in federal court in Missouri of stealing U.S. mail. He was sentenced to spend one year and one day in a federal reformatory in Chillicothe, Ohio.

And not only that, but Richard was also a ne'er-do-well who rarely worked and sponged off his family. The prosecutor pointed out that both of his grandmothers had been "indulgent benefactors" for most of his life. But both women had recently grown tired of his laziness and cut him off.

These things had nothing to do with murdering his wife, but Pryor addressed them anyway. Yes, his client had been convicted, but his sentence was suspended, and he was placed on probation instead. Then, because of his client's good behavior, the probation was canceled, too.

Pryor also called witnesses to show that Richard's life had been a long series of setbacks, starting at the age of three, when his mother died. After that, his father abandoned him and left his son to be raised by his grandmothers. They hadn't gotten tired of helping Richard with his finances – their grandson had asked them to save the money. He was working, and the Depression had made things tight for everyone.

Finally, on April 21, Richard Gladden took the stand in his own defense. Pryor's line of questioning was surprisingly brief, and he started with a basic query: "I will ask that if, on February 1, 1923, you murdered Dolores Gladden."

"I did not," Richard quickly replied.

"I will ask if you loved your wife."

Richard took a handkerchief from his pocket and wiped his eyes with it – although at least one newspaper reporter noted that no tears were visible. "I did," he said.

Pryor spoke again. "I will ask if you bought any tablets at the drugstore on the night of February 1."

"Yes, luminal tablets," Richard replied.

"That's all," Pryor said and returned to the defense table.

The judge raised his gavel, ready to adjourn for the day, but Pryor turned to Richard and asked one more question. "Did you cry at the police station that night?" he asked.

"No, I didn't."

"Why not?"

"Death is something that has had much effect on me," Richard explained. "But with Dolores, I couldn't realize it. I... I knew she was gone, but I couldn't realize it."

ON TUESDAY, APRIL 26, MORRISON PRESENTED A dramatic closing argument to the jury. In his speech, he insisted that Richard had drugged, strangled, and gassed his wife for the insurance money. He walked over to within a few feet of Richard, pointed a finger at him, and shouted, "You've got blood on your hands, Mr. Gladden, and you know it!"

And with that, the prosecutor turned on his heel and stormed across the courtroom. He returned to his seat at the opposite table as though personally enraged by what he had accused Richard of doing. It was a moving performance and one that had kept the jury engaged.

Frank Pryor's closing argument followed. He walked the jury through the case, pointing out the fact that every theory the prosecutor had concocted turned out to be untrue and that not a single shred of hard evidence remained to show his client was guilty. Morrison's so-called evidence was all circumstantial – and should not be used to convict Richard Gladden.

The case went to the jury at 10:40 A.M. on Wednesday, and they deliberated for nine hours. Later that night, the courthouse bell rang, signaling that the jury had reached its verdict.

There was complete silence in the courtroom when the clerk read the verdict: "We the jury, find the defendant, Richard H. Gladden, guilty of murder in the first degree. And we the jury recommend life imprisonment."

All eyes turned to Richard, who was slumped over in his chair. He displayed no emotion – no sadness, no anger – but stunned disbelief.

The next morning, Richard stood before Judge DeVol for formal sentencing. The judge asked him if he had anything to say before judgment was pronounced.

He did. Richard looked directly into the judge's eyes and spoke loudly and clearly. "Though the jury has found me guilty, I am not guilty," he said.

But the judge was unmoved as the jury had been. Pryor filed a motion for a new trial, and Judge DeVol overruled it.

Richard was taken by Sheriff Power to the prison in Michigan City, holding the dubious record of being the defendant with the longest trial in Frankfort history. It was also the first time that Indiana had tried and convicted a defendant for murder by carbon monoxide.

WHAT HAPPENED ON THE COLD NIGHT OF FEBRUARY 1?
Does this really qualify as a murder that occurred because of love that turned bad?

Richard maintained his innocence for the rest of his life. At the start of his prison term, he was confident that his sentence would be reduced. He never changed his story about the night Dolores died – that her death was an accident, not murder. Initially, he was certain that regaining his freedom would be as simple as convincing the right person that he had been railroaded into a prison cell.

He tried to find a new attorney and tried to get a new trial, but each time he tried, his pleas were denied.

Richard might have earned parole if he'd changed his story – admitted that he killed his wife and expressed his remorse about it. But he refused to do it. As he wrote in a letter in 1954, "It might interest you to know that I am still doing life in prison because I will not ask for a parole. Parole is the tempering of justice with mercy, and I have always contended that there has been no justice in my case. A pardon or a discharge is all I'll take."

For the next several years, Richard disappeared from the press, but then, in January 1962, several Indiana papers reported that his latest request to have his sentence commuted had been denied. The brief story was mostly forgettable, except for a curious quote from prosecutor Millard Morrison: "Had Gladden not been convicted, a very great effort would have been made to have him hung on the courthouse lawn."

The next time that Richard made news was in February 1966. After spending 34 years behind bars, he'd had a change of heart about tempering justice with mercy. He finally played ball with the parole board and walked out of prison a free man in October.

But he was never able to repair his shattered life. Everyone he knew was dead or had abandoned him long ago. He quietly lived out his remaining years in Indiana's Tippecanoe County, and he died on December 30, 2007, at the age of 97.

He was buried at Rest Haven Memorial Park in Lafayette, but at his request, there is also a tombstone in a small cemetery in Jackson County, Kansas, that bears his name. It's engraved next to the name of the grave's occupant – Dolores Gladden.

RICHARD NEVER STOPPED LOVING THE wife the jury at his trial decided he had murdered on that night in 1932. But did that mean he didn't kill her? Not necessarily, because, as we've found within these pages, love doesn't stop someone from committing murder.

Sometimes, it's the reason for it.

But when we look back at Richard's trial, it seems almost impossible, based on what we read, that he could have been guilty. The evidence was all circumstantial, and his attorney managed to dismiss every theory that the prosecutor had suggested as a method or motive for the crime. It certainly seemed like an accident – but was it?

D.A. Morrison was convinced Richard had killed his wife – so convinced that he pulled out all the stops to try and make sure he was convicted and even suggested Richard might have been lynched "on the courthouse lawn" if he'd been found not guilty.

And the jury believed him. No matter what we think about the trial, as we read about it today, the jury found him guilty of murder in the first degree.

So, what did they know in 1932 that we don't know today? In hindsight, the trial seems like a farce, but no one thought that at the time. The people involved took it seriously. The judge denied the request for a new trial. Frank Pryor never represented Richard again. What don't we know that those involved in the trial knew back then?

There's no way I can answer that one, I'm afraid. The death of Dolores Gladden will always be a mystery. Murder? An accident? We'll never know.

"THE CLEAVER WIDOW"
Betty and Jerry Ferreri

THE CITY OF LOS ANGELES IS NO STRANGER to sensational crimes. Between murdered celebrities and serial killers, the city has seen more than its share of blood over the years, and much of it has been splashed across the front pages of the L.A. newspapers.

In 1948, residents were scandalized once more by a story that emerged from one of the city's wealthiest neighborhoods, Hancock Park. It involved sex, money, and a brutal murder that involved sex, philandering, and a meat cleaver.

Even in L.A., this was one for the books.

IN 1941, ELIZABETH "BETTY" LADAY WAS A GORGEOUS redhead and the daughter of Hungarian immigrants who owned a small diner in New Brunswick, New Jersey. Jerome "Jerry" Ferreri was a handsome ladies' man and one of their best customers. His father, Vincent, was an important man in New York politics, which in those days meant he was likely connected to the city's underworld.

Betty and Jerry met under uncomfortable circumstances. He was leaning on the counter one day, chatting up the cashier, who also happened to be Betty's little sister. He was pleading with her to go out with him.

Betty happened to be passing by and gave her sister some advice – "Don't go out with that man," she said. Her sister turned him down. Whether Betty had a gut feeling about Jerry or wanted to date him herself, she should have heeded her own advice.

Elizabeth "Betty" Ferreri and (below) her connected husband, Jerry.

Soon, the pair became hot and heavy. Ditching classes and meeting up with Jerry became Betty's favorite pastime. She was a whiz at math and hoped to be a chemist after college, but she threw all that away for Jerry. She knew he'd had a few brushes with the law – including arrests for auto theft, robbery, theft, and assault – but Betty believed she could change him. Her parents thought otherwise. When summer came, her parents sent her to stay with relatives in Asbury Park, hoping she'd be over him by the fall. But Jerry followed her there, and they eloped.

But Betty soon found out that Jerry was not exactly burning with ambition. He made very little money and couldn't hang onto a job. The couple lived on whatever Betty earned and whatever cash Jerry could get from his parents.

His father managed to get him a civilian job with the Army, but Jerry claimed to have heart trouble and ended up behind a desk. He clashed with his supervisors and was fired again.

In 1943, Jerry was arrested again, this time for assault and battery after he beat up Betty. But she refused to press charges – not out of love or weakness but because she didn't want him to be able to use his record as an excuse for not working.

It was around this time that Betty discovered she was pregnant, so the couple decided to move west to Los Angeles for a fresh start.

They were at the station, getting a

bite to eat while they waited for their train to leave when Betty got an inkling of what awaited her in days to come. The waitress who served them wrote her telephone number on the back of the check she handed to Jerry.

Later, Betty would admit she wasn't that surprised. "Women just fell for him and even gave him money," she said. "He was what you would call a great lover."

And maybe he was, but he was a lot of other things, too.

The move to Los Angeles really didn't change anything in their marriage. Jerry continued to be unemployed, and after Betty gave birth to their son, Vincent, whom they called "Butchie," Jerry convinced her to take a job as a carhop, which was essentially a waitress – often on roller skates – who served customers in their cars at restaurants.

Betty made good money – usually around $400 a month, which is equal to about $3,900 today – but that wasn't enough for the chronically unemployed Jerry. He pressured her, sometimes with his fists, into going along with his plan, which required him to do nothing and live on whatever Betty and his parents could provide. He told his wife that he wanted a Cadillac, so Betty bought him one. She was already learning an important lesson about her husband – when she gave him what he wanted, things went well.

But she had limits. Jerry was convinced that she could make even more money by turning tricks – if she really loved him, she'd prostitute herself for him. Betty didn't take this suggestion and kept working as a carhop.

Jerry was soon tired of living in their cramped rental house, so he convinced his parents to come up with $35,000 so they could purchase a large, sprawling home in Hancock Park, an area so wealthy and so white that residents there had recently circulated petitions to prevent singer Nat "King" Cole from buying a house there.

If only they had known how bad their newest neighbor was – the velvet-voiced singer wouldn't have seemed so bad.

The couple now had a mansion to live in, but Betty's carhop job and Jerry's lack of gainful employment weren't going to pay the bills. Strapped for cash, they rented out four rooms and hired Alan Adron, a 52-year-old handyman, to babysit and take care of the property.

The house that Jerry's parents financed for the couple in the Hancock Park neighborhood of Los Angeles.

The house was soon filled with Betty, Jerry, Vincent, now 5, and assorted guests and tenants like Jerry's cousin, Vincent "Charley" D'Angelo; Marion "Val" Graham, a professional singer; Maxine Gould; and live-in handyman, Allan Adron.

Fast women, big cars, and living large made Jerry happy, as did a little plastic surgery on his nose and ears, another gift from his parents. While his wife worked, Jerry cruised the streets of L.A., looking for attention from a string of disposable women. Occasionally, he even brought the girls home while Betty was out of the house.

About the only thing that Betty could count on from her husband was regular beatings. All the residents of the house had heard or seen Jerry verbally and physically abusing Betty, and cousin Charley once had to step in and keep him from harming little Vincent.

The beatings slowly grew worse. Betty later said she prayed to make it through the day without losing teeth, ending up with a black eye, or worse – turning up dead.

When Betty refused to have sex with an auto mechanic to whom Jerry owed $100 for repairs, he hit her so hard that he ruptured her eardrum. Angry over the doctor's bill that resulted, he hit her on the other side of the head while she was speaking to the doctor on the telephone. "Maybe he'll give you two for the price of one," he quipped.

This wasn't the last time that Jerry hit her or the last time that Betty swallowed her pain and shame and let him do it. But it wouldn't be long before she simply wasn't going to take it anymore.

ON THE EARLY MORNING HOURS OF OCTOBER 26, 1948, Val Graham and Charley D'Angelo saw Jerry pick up a fireplace poker and try to strike Betty with it. He was red-faced and screaming that he was going to kill her.

Jerry had driven past the house that night with another woman in his car, and Betty had spotted them. When he showed up a little later, Betty was angry, and Jerry went after her with the poker.

According to Val Graham, Jerry had the poker in his hand, and before he and Charley could get between them, he swung it hard enough to kill her if it had hit her squarely. But Betty ducked, and the bar only knocked her hat off and grazed the top of her head. "He swung once more – hard," she said, "and again he missed. He started a third swipe of the poker, but Charley reached out and held his arm."

The two men managed to calm Jerry down and talked him into leaving the house. They assured Betty that he wouldn't come back that night – but he did.

About 10 minutes after the scene in the living room, Alan Adron returned home from an errand, and a few minutes after that, Jerry was banging through the front door. Charley and Val intercepted him, telling him they were going out for a cup of coffee, and asked him to come along.

"No," he shook his head. "I've got something to take care of."

Graham and D'Angelo were still walking to the car at the curb when they heard two gunshots inside the house, followed by screams. They ran back inside and found Jerry lying mortally wounded on the floor of the pantry. Allan had shot him, and then Betty had taken a meat cleaver and had hacked her husband with it 23 times.

A few minutes later, the police arrived at the scene and took Betty and Allan to the station for questioning. Detectives then began to try and unravel Jerry's complicated love life, discovering the dead man didn't have one girlfriend – he had at least two. It seemed that the motives for his murder were multiplying by the minute.

Jerry's girlfriend, Loretta Salisbury Burge

An attractive 28-year-old blond named Loretta Salisbury Burge had been seeing Jerry for at least eight months prior to his death. The cops found her through a mysterious telegram found at the Ferreri home. It was addressed to Jerry, asked for a rendezvous, and was signed "Three Deuces." Loretta lived at 222 North St. Andrews Place, about a mile from Jerry's home.

Jerry had kept the "Three Deuces" telegram as a souvenir, and he'd also kept a red face powder compact that didn't belong to Loretta or Betty. It turned out to be the property of Floy Smock, a 20-year-old redhead and former model. She'd been out with Jerry on the night of his murder, so detectives wanted her to provide a detailed account of their evening together.

According to Floy, Jerry had picked her up around 9:00 P.M., and they drove around for a while, passing by his house at some point in the evening. That was when Betty had spotted them.

Floy then told the police, "At about 10:20, we stopped by Jerry's house. He ran inside. Then he came out again and drove me home. I guess it was about 10:35 then. He drove away, drove back... to that. I can't tell you anymore."

Even though it seemed clear to the cops what had happened in the pantry of the Ferreri house, they knew better than to assume it was as simple as it looked. The coroner still needed to tell them if it was the gunshots or the meat cleaver that had killed Jerry. In other words, who was going to get charged with murder – the wife or the handyman?

As it turned out, after the inquest, both were charged and Betty was soon dubbed by the press the "Cleaver Widow."

Over the next several months, the newspapers captivated the public with lurid accounts of the murder and the adulterous activities of the victim. Prosecutors admitted that Jerry was a terrible husband but claimed that Betty and her accomplice had planned his murder. Betty's attorney responded that his client had endured years of physical and emotional abuse at the hands of her philandering husband. The years of abuse, he said, had finally pushed her over the top.

But nothing about this case was going to be that simple.

AS THE NEWSPAPER TRIED THE CASE IN PUBLIC, investigators were gathering evidence behind the scenes. But then everything they knew about the murder was upended when a new twist took them by surprise. Vincent "Charley" D'Angelo, Jerry's cousin, revealed that his real name was actually Charles Fauci. He was using the alias because he was wanted in New York for grand larceny.

On the night of the murder, Betty told the police that she had given the gun to Allan, which he'd used to shoot Jerry. Charley said this wasn't true – the gun was his, and he'd loaded it and had it in his pocket up to a few seconds before Allan shot Jerry with it.

He said that he and Val Graham were leaving the house to go and get coffee when they heard Betty scream. Charley said he had the gun because Jerry had attacked Betty earlier that evening with a fireplace poker, and he was worried there might be more violence. Charley drew his gun and tried to enter the house, but the doors were locked. He ran to the window of Allan's room and shouted to him, "He's murdering Betty, Allan! Go open the door!"

Allan threw open the front door, and then, according to Charley, Allan snatched the gun from him and rushed back into the house, locking the door behind him. When Allan entered the butler's pantry and saw Jerry hitting Betty, he fired the gun at him two times.

While being interrogated, Charley confessed to having wiped his fingerprints off the weapon when he got into the house and later took a drive out to Long Beach, where he threw the gun, holster, and unused .38-caliber cartridges into the ocean.

He stressed to the police that if someone had not "taken care of" Jerry, the man would have murdered his wife that night.

After he stepped in and tried to help Betty and Allan, the district attorney decided that Charley would be joining the pair at the defendant's table.

But his tangled story wasn't quite over yet.

The cops were asking questions about Charley's alibi – who was Vince D'Angelo? Where was he? Did he even exist? Charley maintained that he was real and that Vincent D'Angelo had driven with him from New York to L.A. Once they arrived, Charley said that D'Angelo had turned the car over to him so he'd have some wheels.

But that story fell apart when the car was found in a local garage after the attendant recognized Charley's picture in the paper and identified him as the man he knew as D'Angelo. So, the police wired New York for Charley's criminal record, as well as all the information they had on Vincent D'Angelo and the car.

By the end of November, the cops had answers to some of their questions about Vincent D'Angelo. He was a real person, not just an alias of Charley's, and he was back home in Brooklyn. He reported that his car had been stolen, not loaned, and he was also Charley's cousin. He also had a lot to say to the police about his shady relative, stressing that Charley was in California because "no one in the family wants him around." Whether D'Angelo meant their mutual relatives, or another kind of "family" is unknown.

It turned out that some of the other information received from New York detectives temporarily sidetracked the investigation. They told their counterparts in L.A. that Jerry had once collected $100 for dropping a dime on a member of the infamous Murder Inc. assassination squad. It was interesting but not all that helpful, given that Jerry's wife and handyman were found in the pantry with the dead man, a smoking gun, and a bloody meat cleaver.

This was definitely not a Mafia hit.

But just because the mob didn't get to Jerry first didn't mean they didn't want him dead. In fact, someone may have recently planted a bomb in his car to send him a message about an unpaid gambling debt. About six weeks before he was murdered, Jerry reported that his car had been stolen from in front of his house. A few hours later, a muffled explosion was heard, and the gutted car was found smoldering a block away.

Jerry had lived a life complicated by uncontrollable rage, multiple girlfriends, a wife he didn't love and treated terribly, and a gambling problem. But according to the law, it was still about the three defendants in the case and the fact they'd committed murder.

BETTY WAS TEMPORARILY RELEASED FROM JAIL to attend Jerry's funeral. The gray sheriff's car that she rode in stood out among the black automobiles that made up the funeral procession. It traveled from the mortuary on the Sunset Strip to Holy Cross Cemetery. Betty sobbed as she stood by the grave.

Betty's father and brother traveled from the East Coast to support her during the trial. Jerry's family had also made the trip from back east, but not to stand by Betty's side. They wanted to try to take possession of the Hancock Park house and gain custody of her son, Vincent.

Betty was escorted to the preliminary hearing by Deputy Marjorie Kellogg, and as she entered the courtroom, two of Jerry's girlfriends – Loretta Burge and Floy Smock – angrily glared at her. Later in the day, Betty was even accosted by Loretta as she was escorted to the restroom. Loretta muttered something derogatory to her, and Betty took offense. She was led away before the encounter turned violent.

Then Val Graham learned that he was to be the prosecution's star witness, even though he was in full support of Betty and the other defendants. None of them held it against him, though, and Betty even kissed his cheek as she left the courtroom.

Betty entered a plea of not guilty by reason of insanity. Defense attorney Jack Hardy stated that she was a vulnerable woman, duped by her cheating husband, and a victim of years of verbal torture and physical abuse who finally snapped.

Charley Fauci also offered an insanity plea, but Allan Adron refused to let Jack Hardy portray him as crazy, so he hired his own attorney, Gladys Towles. She argued that he was temporarily insane at the time of the shooting, but with a twist – he had been under a hypnotic trance at the time but was now clear-headed. These allegations soon had the press mockingly calling him "Robot Man."

The trial began on February 1, 1949, and handyman Allan Adron shocked the courtroom on the first day by withdrawing his plea of not guilty and entering a plea of guilty. He would now be tried separately – and would testify against the other defendants, stating that the shooting was planned an hour before the shooting.

When Allan changed his plea, Jack Hardy immediately tried to minimize the damage to his clients. He tried to have the man declared insane and incompetent to testify, but the judge denied the motion.

Betty's fate hinged on whether her use of the cleaver was self-defense or was felonious assault after Jerry had fallen to the ground from the bullet wounds he'd sustained.

To make her case for self-defense – and temporary insanity – Betty had to testify about the abuse that she'd suffered for so many years at Jerry's hands. She frequently wept as she described the pain and torment she'd endured. Jerry beat her often and humiliated her in their home. She occasionally found undergarments that were not her own in the bed they shared, and Jerry merely laughed at her. She described her husband as a "sadist, an incorrigible brute, a bully, and a beast."

Once, during cross-examination, Betty became so upset that she fainted and had to be taken out to the hallway to be revived. Back on the stand, she testified not only about her own experiences with Jerry but shared some of the horrendous stories she'd heard from friends about him when he was a child.

She told the jury: "They said he used to string up dogs in the cellar and beat their brains out with a baseball bat. Then he would put them in a burlap bag and put them out at the front of his house."

Jerry's behavior as an adult – especially toward Betty – grew worse over time, and she described the nightmare of their life together: "He was out most of the night and slept all day. Sometimes, he would lock me in a closet and tell me to stay there. He would gag me. He would bring a girl up, and I would hear them. He would tell me not to make a sound, or he would beat my face. Then, he would come back and expect me to feed him. To cook for him."

Jerry even beat his wife on the morning she went to the hospital to give birth to their son, Vincent. In fact, it was likely the beating that caused her to go into labor.

Dramatic Gestures Mark Betty Ferreri's Testimony

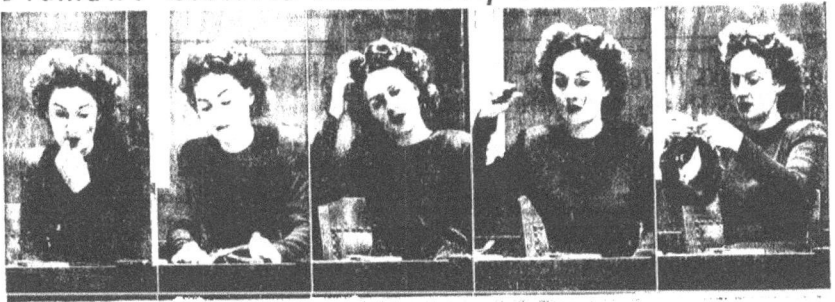

Eventually, the story of what happened on the night Jerry was killed finally came out.

When Allan came home after Jerry's initial attempt to hit Betty with the fireplace poker, she had asked the handyman for protection. When Jerry returned, he angrily confronted his wife, and a violent altercation ensued in which Betty was dragged by her hair into the butler's pantry, where he continued beating her. Hearing her screams, Charley had given the gun to Allan. In the middle of the chaos, Allan had rushed to Betty's aid and, without saying a word, shot Jerry twice. Jerry went down, but he wasn't dead. Fearing that he might attack her again, Betty said, she grabbed a meat cleaver from the counter in the pantry and began viciously hacking at Jerry until she was sure that he was dead.

Betty struck him 23 times, spraying blood all over the walls, the floor, the ceiling, the pantry shelves, and all over Betty herself. The frenzy continued until Jerry was no longer moving.

The years of abuse finally drove Betty Ferreri over the edge.

AFTER BETTY'S HARROWING TESTIMONY, DISTRICT attorney J. Miller Levy put Jerry's mother, Laura Ferreri, on the stand to try and repair her son's tarnished image. She did all she could to make him seem sympathetic, but it's unlikely that anyone was buying it. She also spoke of Betty in bitter terms, saying that her daughter-in-law had once said that if she couldn't have Jerry, then nobody could.

Does that sound unlikely? It did to everyone else, too.

On March 18, the prosecution and defense summed up their cases, and the jury of seven men and five women began their deliberations. The following day, they acquitted Betty and her co-defendant, Charles Fauci. Charley had other problems waiting for him back in New York, but at least he'd been cleared of murder.

On March 29, Allan Adron was found not guilty by reason of insanity. During the brief trial, psychiatrists testified that he suffered from bouts of dementia but was not a dangerous man. His actions during the murder were blamed on the tension and chaos of the Ferreri home and his need to protect Betty from harm. Declared mentally ill, Allan was hospitalized for a short time but was eventually released from custody.

As for Betty, she was free, and even though her in-laws had fought hard to take her son from her, she regained custody of Vincent following her acquittal. She did lose the house, however. Jerry's parents threw her out and sold it at auction.

Even so, she apparently remained an optimist because less than six months after her acquittal, she got married again in Las Vegas. Her new husband was 28-year-old hotel maître de Jean Paul Roussos.

Whether they lived happily ever after is unknown.

THE PRICE OF OBSESSION
The Vanishing of Dorothy Jane Scott

THE MORNING OF AUGUST 6, 1984, WAS A HOT one in Southern California. The Macco Construction Company work crew that was toiling away in a ditch for a Pac Bell telephone line just northeast of Anaheim didn't expect anything different. It was summer in L.A. – why wouldn't it be hot?

But what they didn't expect was to find a partially charred human skeleton about 30 feet from the edge of the Santa Ana Canyon Road. The bones had been scattered about – in a 25-foot radius, investigators later discovered – but there was no doubt about it: they were human.

When Orange County Deputy Coroner Richard Rodriguez arrived at the scene, he was unable to ascertain the cause of death. But he did feel the charring of the bones had happened when a brush fire had swept through the area in 1982. That meant they had been there, undiscovered, for at least two years.

Investigators collected a complete skull, two femurs, a pelvis, and an assortment of other bones. They had been bleached white from the sun, but the skull contained a complete set of teeth that contained many fillings. While Rodrigues ran the teeth through the missing persons database, Judy Suchey, an anthropologist that he contacted from Cal State Fullerton, narrowed down the age and sex of the remains.

It didn't take long to discover the identity of the person who went along with the bones. Her name had been Dorothy Jane Scott, and she had gone missing four years earlier, on May 28, 1980, under very mysterious circumstances.

It was not so unusual that she had gone missing – since thousands of people vanished every year – but Dorothy had been a 32-year-old single mother who left a four-year-old son behind. She was also quiet, religious, rarely dated, spent most of her time at home, and, her friends lovingly said, lived a life that was "as dull as a phone book."

But there were the telephone calls – calls so menacing and strange that they turned Dorothy's ordinary world completely upside down.

And soon after they began, she disappeared.

OBSESSION.

It can make you feel powerless, distracted, even dangerous. You will think of nothing else, day and night. You'll lose your sense of reality and make bad choices. Obsession eats away at you, little by little, piece by piece until you are compelled to act.

There is no such thing as a healthy obsession. An obsession is the opposite of anything positive. It is also frightening in that we can become a victim of our own obsessions, eventually destroying ourselves.

Even more terrifying is becoming the object of someone else's obsession. The person obsessed with you may be a relative, a lover, a friend, or a stranger you passed once on the street and smiled at, not knowing you'd done the wrong thing at the wrong time.

But you'll soon know if it happened because obsession moves swiftly and, when unchecked, grows worse. And that's what happened to Dorothy Jane Scott. She found herself the object of someone's dangerous obsession and was unable to escape from it alive.

IN 1980, DOROTHY SCOTT WAS A SINGLE MOTHER, living with her son, Shawn, and her aunt, Shonti Scott, in Stanton, California, about a 20-minute drive from Anaheim, where her parents lived and where Dorothy worked.

Dorothy Jane Scott

Friends and family described Dorothy as a loving, giving person who almost never dated, preferring to stay home with Shawn. She loved her family, her friends, and God, which makes her job as a secretary for two stores in Anaheim seem a little odd. The two stores were Swingers Psych Shop and Custom John's Head Shop. One sold psychedelic accessories – like black-light posters, tapestries, and lava lamps – and the other was a "head shop," a retail outlet for tobacco and cannabis paraphernalia.

It seemed an odd choice because she was a religious homebody who didn't drink or do drugs, but her father, Jacob, had originally owned the shops, and she started working for him years before. After he sold them, Dorothy stayed on, and so did her father, sort of. He took care of repairs and general upkeep for his friend, John Kocyla, who now owned the business.

Dorothy was friendly and fun, and everyone loved her, including John, her other co-workers, and the eclectic mix of customers for the two stores. And Dorothy loved them back.

She only occasionally dated and had no steady boyfriend, but she wasn't lonely. She had her friends, and her relationship with her parents was always great. They watched Shawn while Dorothy worked and, of course, spoiled him, as grandparents are bound to do. Shawn's father was entirely absent from the boy's life. He'd relocated to Missouri when the two split up and had started a new family.

All in all, Dorothy had a happy life – a good job, good friends, a loving family, and a simple, consistent everyday life.

And then, as mentioned, the calls started.

In early 1980, Dorothy began receiving telephone calls at work. Soon, she started getting them at home, too. The calls were anonymous, but, as she told her mother, Vera, it was always the same man on the other end of the line. She couldn't identify the voice, but it always sounded vaguely familiar to her – as if she knew the man but couldn't come up with his name. Sometimes, he was kind and happy, professing his love for her and declaring his devotion. At other times, he seemed angry and suspicious, becoming hostile and threatening. The caller told Dorothy that he followed her and provided intimate and accurate details from her daily life to prove it. He told her what she'd been wearing, what she did, where she went, and once, he went so far as to tell Dorothy to go outside because he had left her a gift.

She later found a single dead rose on the windshield of her car.

In the weeks that followed, the calls became more aggressive. In the most haunting call, the man told Dorothy that he was going to get her alone and "cut her up into bits" so that no one would find her. The kind-hearted, compassionate young woman became so unnerved that she considered buying a handgun for protection. Her mother discouraged her since she had a young son in the house, and so Dorothy enrolled in self-defense courses instead.

Friends and family knew about the harassment and the fear that it was causing Dorothy, but no one knew what to do about it. It was a different time, and no one felt they could "bother" the police with what was just prank phone calls.

But they would soon discover the calls weren't just pranks.

ON THE EVENING OF MAY 28, DOROTHY dropped off Shawn at her parents' house so she could attend an after-work staff meeting. The meeting was still going on around 9:00 P.M. when

Dorothy noticed that her friend and co-worker, Conrad Bostron, looked sick and that he had a terrible red mark on his arm that seemed to be spreading. Dorothy insisted on taking him to the emergency room, and another co-worker, Pam Head, volunteered to go with them. The two women got Conrad into the car, and they headed toward the hospital.

Dorothy and her son, Shawn. Friends and family knew that the single mother wouldn't have left her son behind.

Instead of taking the sick man directly there, though, Dorothy said she had to stop first at her parents' house and let them know she would be later than she'd planned. Pam thought she should wait and call them from the hospital, but Dorothy assured her the stop would be quick. She stopped and hurried inside, and when she came back out, Pam noticed that Dorothy had switched the black scarf that she had been wearing for a red one. In hindsight, this seems a strange thing given the circumstances, but regardless, they were now on their way to get help for Conrad.

At the UC Irvine Medical Center, doctors discovered that a black widow spider had bitten Conrad. Dorothy and Pam waited in the lobby while he was being treated, and Pam later said that Dorothy never left her side.

Around 11:00 P.M., Conrad was released, and while he was picking up a prescription, Dorothy went to the restroom and then out to the parking lot to bring her car around to pick up the others at the front door. She didn't want Conrad to have to walk that far.

But it was the last time her friends ever saw her alive.

Pam and Conrad, with his medicine in hand, waited outside for Dorothy to arrive. When she didn't come in 10 minutes or so, they assumed there had been some sort of miscommunication or even a problem with her car. They decided to walk over to where Dorothy had parked and were relieved when they finally saw Dorothy's white Toyota station wagon coming toward them. Suddenly, though, it accelerated, made a sharp turn out of the parking lot,

A white Toyota station wagon like the one that Dorothy was driving when she disappeared.

and sped away. The headlights were so bright that they couldn't see Dorothy, or whoever it was, behind the wheel.

Pam ran after the car, waving her arms, wondering what her friend was doing – but it was gone. Worried about an emergency with Dorothy's son, Pam, and Conrad waited for two hours for Dorothy to return. They called Dorothy's parents, but Jacob told them they hadn't seen her since she'd dropped by on the way to the hospital.

Concerned now, Pam and Conrad contacted hospital security, but they told them there didn't seem to be a reason to worry. When they called the police to report Dorothy missing, the authorities also dismissed their concerns. They were advised to get a cab home. Dorothy was an adult – they were sure she was fine.

And then things took another turn.

Around 5:00 A.M., police officers on routine patrol discovered a white Toyota station wagon parked in an alley about 10 miles from the hospital – and it was on fire. The car turned out to be Dorothy's, but she was not inside. Any clues that might have been left behind had been destroyed by the flames.

A week later, the telephone calls started again.

Her mother, Vera, received the first one. A man's voice asked, "Are you related to Dorothy Scott?" Vera said that she was, and the man replied, "I've got her," and hung up.

It was the first call they received, but not the last.

The same voice called every Wednesday afternoon, usually asking if Dorothy was home. Sometimes he said that he had Dorothy, and other times he claimed he'd killed her. The calls were always brief and always when Vera was home alone – as if the caller was watching and waiting for that moment to call.

The police tried to trace the calls, but the man never stayed on the line long enough for them to find out where he was calling from. The police asked the Scotts not to get the press involved in the investigation, telling them this would only slow things down. Jacob begged them to at least release the audio to see if anyone could recognize the man's voice, but investigators refused.

As another week passed with Vera being taunted and harassed by the caller, Jacob impatiently decided that he'd waited long enough. He went to the local newspaper, the *Santa Ana Register,* with the story of his missing daughter. The story ran the next day, with Jacob offering a $2,500 reward for anyone with information regarding Dorothy's whereabouts.

On the day the story ran, June 12, the newspaper's editor, Pat Riley, received an anonymous call of his own. He heard a man's voice on the line that told him, "I killed her. I killed Dorothy Scott. She was my love. I caught her cheating with another man. She denied having someone else, so I killed her."

The mysterious caller offered details about what Dorothy was wearing on May 28, her changing to a red scarf, and why she was at the hospital to prove his story was genuine. He claimed that Dorothy had called him from the hospital, but Pam Head insisted this was not true. Dorothy had never been out of her sight until she went to get the car.

Except when she went to the bathroom, of course.

But why would Dorothy have called the man who had been stalking her and making her life hell for the past six months?

No one had an answer for that or where Dorothy had been taken. The information the man gave to Pat Riley made the police believe he was likely her kidnapper, but they knew nothing else. They hadn't thought to try and trace any of the callers to the newspaper's reward line.

The police investigation led nowhere. However, over the next four years, Dorothy's parents continued to receive a call from the stalker every Wednesday afternoon. The calls finally stopped in April 1984 after the telephone rang a little later than usual, and Jacob picked up. When he spoke, the line immediately went

Killer calls, mom says
Man terrorizes parents of murdered daughter

ASSOCIATED PRESS

SANTA ANA, Calif. — For four years, the parents of Dorothy Scott were "tortured" by phone calls from a man who claimed to have killed their daughter. Now, after her remains were finally found, the calls have begun again.

Vera and Jacob Scott say they believe the anonymous caller is the same one who repeatedly harassed their daughter, Dorothy, 32, before she vanished in May 1980.

"Dorothy got one call just before she disappeared that upset her horribly," Mrs. Scott said in an interview published Sunday in the *Los Angeles Herald Examiner*.

"The voice said, 'OK, now, you are going to come my way and when I get you alone, I will cut you up into bits so no one will ever find you.'"

Last week, a set of bones unearthed Aug. 6 at a remote construction site were identified as those of Dorothy Scott.

Two weeks after her daughter disappeared, Mrs. Scott received the first of the chilling calls from a man who said, "Are you related to Dorothy Scott? Well, I've got her."

The caller's knowledge "of things no one else could have known, like what color her scarf was and where she was and what she was doing," convinced Mrs. Scott that she was speaking to Dorothy's kidnapper.

"She was my love," a man said shortly afterward in a telephone call to *The Register*, an Orange County, Calif., newspaper. "I caught her cheating with another man. She denied having someone else. I killed her."

Police who investigated that message agreed that the caller was Miss Scott's killer.

"For four years, (the caller) has tortured us," her mother said. The couple didn't change their telephone number because they hoped that if the man had Dorothy, he would allow her to speak to them.

The calls stopped about three months ago, when Jacob Scott answered the phone for the

Please see CALLER, A-5

---

dead. It was as if the caller knew, unlike Vera, Jacob would recognize his voice.

After that, the stalker only called two more times – after the case took another heartbreaking turn.

In August 1984, a construction worker found human remains in a rugged area north of Anaheim. They were believed to be Dorothy's, and this was confirmed after Vera identified a turquoise ring and a watch among the bones.

The watch had stopped at 12:30 A.M. on May 29, 1980, about an hour after Pam and Conrad last saw Dorothy's car race out of the parking lot at the hospital.

Dorothy's cause of death could not be determined from her bones, but their discovery did manage to bring a little peace to her family and friends. A memorial service was held for her eight days later, on August 22.

The story of the discovery of Dorothy's remains was widely reported across Southern California, and her stalker and killer apparently saw it.

Four months after the calls had stopped, they began again. Jacob and Vera were at the funeral home making arrangements for Dorothy when a man called their home two times. Their son, Allen, answered, and each time, the voice on the line asked, "Is Dorothy home?"

That was the last straw for the Scotts. Dorothy was gone. They didn't have to hold out hope that the caller might let them speak

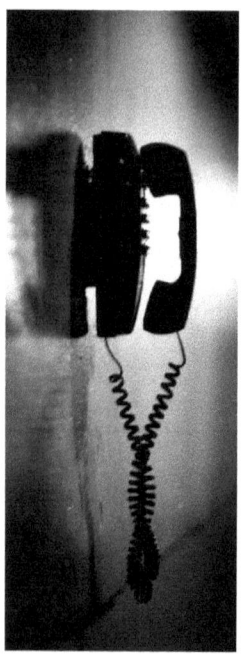

to her or let her come home – not anymore. The Scotts changed their number, and they never heard from the man again.

Dorothy's son, Shawn, was raised by his grandparents, who passed away in 1994 and 2002 without ever knowing who had taken their daughter. Shawn remains dedicated to figuring out what happened to his mother, though, and has come to believe that it was someone she knew – a man Dorothy had worked with.

His name was Mike Butler, and he was the only suspect the police had ever looked closely at. After Jacob Scott sold John's Head Shop, Butler briefly owned it, and Dorothy worked there as a secretary. According to co-workers, Butler pursued Dorothy during his time at the shop, repeatedly asking her out on dates and harassing her at work. Butler was known for being reclusive – he lived alone in the Santiago Mountains – and was often considered unstable.

Although Butler turned over the shop to John Kocyla, he was able to keep tabs on Dorothy because his sister still worked there and was close to Dorothy. Shawn believes she inadvertently gave her brother details about Dorothy's schedule and activities.

Also, Butler knew Dorothy's father, Jacob, and this may have been why the caller seemed to panic and hang up when Jacob picked up the phone that one Wednesday evening. He knew Jacob could recognize his voice.

Unfortunately, Mike Butler passed away in 2014, so there's no way anyone will ever know for sure if he was the one who stalked, kidnapped, and murdered her. I have no doubt that will haunt Shawn Scott for the rest of his life.

"Is Dorothy home?" the voice on the line asked one final time in August 1984.

Of course, the answer was "no." Dorothy was never coming home, and her killer—whoever he was – knew it. What happened to Dorothy Scott on that early morning in May 1980 remains unsolved to this day.

"MEET THE CREEPER"
The Madness of Dennis Depue

IT WAS EASTER SUNDAY, APRIL 15, 1990, and Ray and Marie Thornton were driving along Snow Prairie Road, a rural highway about 12 miles outside of Coldwater, Michigan. Ray was at the wheel, Marie was next to him, and the couple were playing a game they'd made up – trying to make words and phrases out of the license plates they saw.

But things were quiet along the secluded road that morning, and they hadn't seen another car in a little while. Suddenly, though, a green Chevrolet van appeared in the rearview mirror. It aggressively roared up behind them and then passed them at high speed.

Marie won that round of the game. Spotting the GZ on the van's license plate, she remarked, "Geez, he's in a hurry."

They laughed and would've thought no more about it if they hadn't seen the green van again a short time later. As they passed an abandoned schoolhouse, Ray and Marie saw it parked on the side of the building – but that wasn't all they saw.

The driver was outside the vehicle and was carrying a large bundle wrapped in what appeared to be a bloody sheet. He was walking toward the back of the ramshackle building.

Although shocked, they really weren't sure about what they'd seen or what to do about it. Finally, Ray suggested they call the police and let them figure out what to do about it. Marie agreed and wrote down what she could remember of the van's license plate number. They kept driving, now intent on finding a telephone.

And that's when Ray saw the van coming up behind them again in his rearview mirror. Gaining speed quickly, the van menacingly rode their rear bumper for the next two miles. As Ray and Marie worried about what the driver pursuing them might do, they turned off the highway just as the van suddenly pulled off the road.

Determined to see the rest of the van's license plate number for the police, Ray turned around, and they approached the van from the opposite direction. As they slowly passed, they saw a tall man in a hat standing at the back of the van with the doors open, changing the rear license plate. He'd also left the side door open, and the couple saw that the interior of the van was soaked with blood.

If any of this sounds familiar to you, it's because this incident inspired the opening of a film that came out a decade later – a film called *Jeepers Creepers*.

It became one of the most terrifying horror films of the early 2000s, but what happened in real life turned out to be even scarier.

Dennis Depue's high school senior picture

DENNIS HENRY DEPUE WAS BORN IN 1943 AND grew up in Michigan, where, as an adult, he began working as a property assessor. In 1971, he married Marilynn McLenahen, who became a well-liked high school guidance counselor in Coldwater. The couple had three children – two girls and a boy – but after 17 years of marriage, Dennis' controlling ways had worn Marilynn down. She had confided in friends that Dennis was a bully. He had become paranoid, sullen, and withdrawn. He isolated himself from the family and frequently accused his wife of "turning the children against him."

In 1989, Marilynn filed for divorce, telling her attorney that she could no longer allow Dennis to control every decision in her life. During the settlement that followed, though, he offered Marilynn whatever she wanted and made no claim on the house, although he still used the guest house as an office.

But things didn't go smoothly. One day, Marilynn came home to find Dennis sitting on the couch in her living room despite her having changed all the locks. When their divorce was finalized in December, Marilynn likely breathed a sigh of relief.

Tragically, though, less than five months later, she'd be dead.

On Easter Sunday, 1990, Dennis arrived at the family home to pick up two of the children. Joint custody had been part of the divorce settlement, but their daughter, Jennifer, refused to go anywhere with her father. He had expected to pick up Julie and Scott, but Julie decided she didn't want to go either. When he went into the house to find Scott, he began yelling at the boy, claiming that he was stalling. When Marilynn intervened, his anger increased, and soon, Dennis became unhinged.

Marilyn and Dennis Depue

Dennis grabbed Marilynn, shouting accusations, and in his rage, he pushed her down the stairs while their horrified children looked on. Dennis charged to the bottom of the stairway and began pummeling Marilynn with his fists. With the children pleading with him to stop, Jennifer ran to a neighbor's house to call the police.

When she came back, she found Dennis outside. Marilynn was seriously injured, and he said he was taking her to the hospital. He put her into his green Chevrolet van and sped away – but they never arrived at any of the nearby emergency rooms, and Marilynn was never seen alive again.

The Michigan State Police and the Sheriff's office began a widespread search for the couple, but Ray and Marie Thornton had spotted Dennis first. When they saw him by the school, he was trying to dispose of the bloody sheet that had been wrapped around his ex-wife's body. After their last attempt to copy down his license plate number – when they saw the bloody interior of the van – they returned to the school and found the sheet before alerting the police.

A forensics team closed off the area around the abandoned school. A pool of blood was found, as well as tire tracks that would turn out to be a match for those on Dennis' van.

The abandoned school building where Dennis had left the bloody sheet that he'd wrapped Marilyn's body in.

The police knew that Marilynn had been badly injured in the fight with her ex-husband, but after hearing the account of the Thorntons and finding the blood at the school, investigators feared the worst.

The fears proved valid the next morning when a highway worker discovered Marilynn's body in some brush next to a quiet road that was halfway between her home and the schoolhouse. She'd been badly beaten and then shot in the back of the head.

Dennis DePue, though, had vanished.

IN THE DAYS AND WEEKS TO COME, DENNIS remained in the wind, but while hiding out, he sent a series of bizarre, rambling letters to friends and family, trying to justify Marilynn's death. He sent 17 in all -- postmarked in Virginia, Iowa, and Oklahoma – and in them, he ranted about the wrongs that he felt she had done to him. One letter read:

Marilynn had many, many opportunities to treat me fairly during this divorce, and she chose to string it out, trick me, lie to me, and when you lose your wife, children, and home, there's not too much left. I was too old to start over.

Three months after Marilynn's murder, he sent another letter. This one was 13 pages long and quoted verses from the Bible and contained long strings of incoherent ramblings about the unfairness of his life and about how Marilynn deserved to die for turning his children against him.

And then he went silent.

The police were no closer to finding him than they had been in the days after the murder.

THE TELEVISION WAS ON IN THE LIVING ROOM when the Dallas, Texas, woman came home from work on March 20, 1991. She wasn't paying much attention to it, however. She had been surprised when she parked in the driveway and saw that her boyfriend's van was sitting in her way. It was unusual because he usually insisted on keeping it in the garage.

She could hear her boyfriend, Hank Queen, in the bedroom, and she called out to him. There was no answer, so she turned down the volume on the television, which had been turned to the latest episode of the show *Unsolved Mysteries*. When the sound lowered, Hank popped his head out of the bedroom, a look of surprise on his face.

"Everything okay?" she asked him.

"Yes, of course," he replied. "I just didn't hear you come in."

She saw that Hank had a large duffle bag sitting on the bed. He was gathering clothing and personal items and stuffing them into the bag. When she asked what he was doing, he explained that he had to make an emergency trip home – his mother was very sick.

Hank carried the bag into the living room – keeping one eye on the television – and picked up a few other items and placed them in the bag, too.

"Do you want me to come with you?" she asked. "I can see if I can get the time off work."

"No, no," he told her. "I'm not sure how long I'll need to be gone. But you could do me a favor – would you mind making me some sandwiches for the trip?"

She agreed, not realizing that he was trying to keep her distracted in the kitchen so that she wouldn't see the next segment of *Unsolved Mysteries* – which featured a story about a man named Dennis DePue, who was wanted for the murder of his ex-wife.

When Hank said goodbye to her that night, driving away in his green Chevrolet van, she had a strange feeling that she would never see him again.

Her suspicions proved to be correct.

Hank – who was, of course, Dennis DePue – left so quickly because he was sure one of his girlfriend's friends would recognize him on the popular show and call the police.

And he was right. Within the hour, state and county law enforcement officials knew who he was and where he'd been living and had the number of the false Texas license plate on his van.

It took Dennis four frantic hours to drive across the state. He was heading for Mississippi, but he had to cross both Texas and Louisiana to get there. Louisiana state troopers were the first to spot the van. They tried to pull him over, but the traffic stop turned into a high-speed chase for the next 15 miles. Across the state line, Mississippi authorities waited for him, alerted by their counterparts in Louisiana and the FBI.

Dennis DePue was wanted for murder and should be considered armed and dangerous.

Warren County Sheriff Paul Barrett set up a roadblock, and deputies were told to shoot out the van's tires if he didn't stop. Dennis blasted through the roadblock, as the sheriff predicted, and they opened fire, hitting both back wheels.

But Dennis kept going. He managed to drive on rims for another half mile as cop cars tried to force him off the road. Dennis leaned out the window and shot at them, shattering windows. Finally, the van came to a halt around 4:00 A.M.

Deputies surrounded the car, ordering Dennis to throw out his weapon and surrender. Instead, he turned the gun on himself. A booming sound was heard from the van, and when an officer approached, he found Dennis still clutching the pistol with his thumb on the trigger.

The chase had ended, and the long nightmare that began one year before with the murder of Marilynn DePue was finally over.

"THIS IS NOT ACCIDENTAL"
The Story of Zack and Addie

IT WAS OCTOBER 17, 2006, AND THE NEW ORLEANS POLICE department received an unexpected call from the Omni Royal Orleans Hotel in the French Quarter. It wasn't a complaint about drunken tourists or some petty crime. The hotel was reporting that a guest witnessed a man jump off a ledge in the rooftop bar and fall seven stories to the top of a parking garage below.

Needless to say, the man had died on impact.

When the police arrived at the hotel on St. Louis Street, they went to the top of the garage next door and found the body of the reported suicide. Investigators searched the body for identification and discovered that he was 28-year-old Zack Bowen, a local bartender. In a plastic bag in the dead man's right front pocket, they found Zack's army dog tags, the key to his apartment on Rampart Street, and a note that had been written to the police. It contained his address, the name of his landlord, and permission to search the apartment.

There was also a short message that read, in part:

This is not accidental. I had to take my own life to pay for the one I took. If you send a patrol car to 826 N Rampart, you will find the dismembered corpse of my girlfriend Addie in the oven, on the stove, and in the fridge and a full signed confession from myself.

The New Orleans detectives – who'd probably seen and heard just about everything in their years of service – were shocked by the note. What had started as a suicide had just turned into something much worse.

They would soon discover one of the most gruesome murder scenes in the city's recent history – a murder committed for love.

ZACKARY BOWEN WAS BORN ON MAY 15, 1978, IN Bakersfield, California. He grew up in the Golden State, a reasonably average all-American boy. It wouldn't be until he reached high school that Zack began to show signs of depression and mental illness. He had always been one of those children who worried about letting down the people around him and was concerned about what others thought of his successes and failures, but it wasn't until he was older that it began to seriously trouble him.

Zack decided the best way to deal with his mental state was to start over fresh somewhere else, so he moved from Sacramento – where he'd been living with his mother – to New Orleans, where his father lived. Zack finished high school there, and when he turned 18, he got a job as a bartender on Bourbon Street.

It was while working in the French Quarter that Zack met 28-year-old Florida native Lana Shupack. She had come to New Orleans a few years earlier, and when the pair met, she was working as a stripper at one of the Bourbon Street clubs. Despite the 10-year age difference, the two of them immediately hit it off and started dating. Then, just months after they met, Lana discovered that she was pregnant.

Although Zack felt too young to be a father, he embraced the situation, and the couple eventually got married. After their son Jackson was born, Zack decided to quit bartending and find a better way to support his family. He joined the U.S. Army.

Zack served as a military police officer in Kosovo and Iraq – including spending time at the infamous Abu Ghraib prison. In time, he'd earn the rank of sergeant, but his promotions came at a cost, leaving him with severe Post Traumatic Stress Disorder. One experience in particular that friends said "messed him up" the most was when a young girl he'd befriended in Iraq was killed – along with her whole family – when her family's shop was bombed. Zack was weighed down by tremendous guilt, causing further decline of his mental health.

Despite earning a NATO medal and the Presidential Unit Citation for his service – plus his commanding officer's recommendation that he receive an honorable discharge – Zack left the service with only a general discharge. That meant that while he qualified for VA benefits, he couldn't get the GI Bill education benefits. This left Zack bitter, feeling like all the trauma and guilt that he'd been left with had been for nothing.

He returned home to New Orleans, but Lana hardly recognized him as the same man who had left for the military. His PTSD had turned him into a different person, and arguments, stress, and marital issues soon led to their separation. Zack was ordered to pay child support – they'd had a second child while he was in the service – so he went back to work as a bartender in the French Quarter.

It was then that he met co-worker and future girlfriend, Addie Hall.

ADDIE HALL WAS KNOWN TO HER FRIENDS AS A creative free spirit. She had grown up in North Carolina but came from a toxic and abusive home. She had been molested as a young girl and, like many abuse victims, went on to have a string of abusive relationships as an adult. But once she moved to New Orleans, she seemed to leave her past behind her and become her own creative individual. She considered herself a poet, a dancer, an artist, and a seamstress. Bartending wasn't her life – it was just a way to support her art – and she was a familiar figure in the French Quarter, riding her bicycle back and forth to work each day.

But under the surface of her independent, bohemian lifestyle was a young woman with demons. According to many of Addie's friends, she struggled with undiagnosed bipolar disorder, and it's likely she also had PTSD from her early abuse. She was also known to get very aggressive and nasty towards her friends after having too many drinks.

When Addie first became interested in Zack, she tried flirting with him and teasing him to see if he could really handle her. But he could, and, in fact, he was interested in her from the start. They began loosely dating, spending time together outside of work, and testing the waters. Addie had her history of bad relationships and didn't want to get involved in another.

Zack – the tall, good-looking charmer – and Addie – the free-spirited artist – shared the same love of music, fun, and nightlife. They loved going out at night, partying with friends, snorting cocaine, and drinking – a lot. Zack finally seemed to shake off the deep depression he'd brought home from the service and started to open up and let loose with Addie. They were both adrenaline junkies, who wanted to live life to the

Zack and Addie outside their apartment on Rampart Street

fullest, but their friends were skeptical about whether the relationship could last. Fueled by drugs and alcohol, it seemed destined to crash quickly, but it didn't.

And then came Hurricane Katrina at the end of August 2005.

In the days leading up to the storm, city residents were advised to evacuate and warned that it wouldn't be safe to stay behind. Lana asked Zack to leave with her and the children, but he refused. He wanted to stay behind and ride out the storm with Addie. It seemed dangerous, reckless, and – in Lana's opinion – very stupid, but there was no way to change his mind.

As it turned out, Katrina seemed to be the best thing that could have happened to the relationship between Zack and Addie. They holed up in her small upstairs apartment on Rampart Street and waited out the worst of the storm. For the most part, the French Quarter was spared, while flood waters badly damaged other parts of the city after the levees broke.

Once the storm passed, the couple found themselves stranded with a small community of people who had stayed behind in the French Quarter. They had no electricity, no running water, no air conditioning, and limited resources, and yet, they loved everything about this post-apocalyptic-like situation.

Zack and Addie went into abandoned bars and gathered alcohol to make cocktails in the street in front of their apartment to exchange with others for food and water. They burned debris to cook with and to stay warm after dusk. With no job or bills to worry about, it seemed more like an extended camping trip than a natural disaster.

To make sure that the police kept circulating through the neighborhood in case of emergencies, Addie flashed her breasts whenever police cars drove past the apartment. No one complained.

Zack and Addie's colorful version of survival, the favors they did for others, and their antics around the French Quarter after Katrina caught the attention of the media. The couple was featured in several newspapers, including the *New York Times*, and were dubbed the "King and Queen" of Katrina survivors.

At this point, Zack and Addie were head over heels in love.

But the party had to end sometime. After weeks of adventure, the city around the couple started to open back up again, and people started coming home. Eventually, New Orleans came back to life, and, as it did, the relationship between Zack and Addie began to take a downward spiral.

Neither of them was prepared to go back to their real-world responsibilities. They didn't want to work, pay bills, or follow a routine. Zack had no interest in paying child support, co-parenting, or dealing with Lana. And Addie didn't want the baggage that came with Zack. She wanted Zack – not Zack's life. Life in post-Katrina New Orleans began putting a lot of pressure on two people who had plenty of other issues to deal with.

According to friends, the pair began arguing constantly, and the more they argued, the more drugs and alcohol they consumed. They bickered and complained about the other person to friends. Their fights became more explosive and more physical, and they began a constant cycle of breaking up and getting back together again. None of their friends had any idea what the state of their relationship was at any given time.

After several months of this, Zack told Addie that he wanted to end the relationship for good, but Addie convinced him to give things one more chance. She asked Zack to "start fresh" with her and move back into her apartment at 826 North Rampart Street. Zack hesitated, then agreed. He paid for the first two months of rent in advance, and the lease was put in both Addie's and Zack's names.

But the "fresh start" didn't last long.

On October 4, Addie went to their landlord and asked that Zack be taken off the lease. He had cheated on her, she said, and she was kicking him out. The landlord didn't comply but instead told her to go home and work it out with her boyfriend.

That was the last time anyone other than Zack saw her alive.

It's unknown exactly how things spiraled out of control that night, but they did. In an eight-page confession letter that Zack wrote in Addie's journal, he described what happened after they had a heated argument:

I killed her at 1:00 A.M. Thursday, 5 October. I very calmly strangled her. It was very quick.

Zack simply snapped. He was likely drunk or high, or both, but had reached a breaking point with his mental health.

After he killed her, He sexually violated Addie's corpse several times before he passed out next to it. The next morning, he got up, dressed, and went to work like it was any ordinary day. While he was at work that day, serving cocktails to tourists and revelers on Bourbon Street with a smile on his face, he had the corpse of his girlfriend lying on the floor of the apartment they'd shared.

When he returned home from work, he moved Addie's body into the bathtub, where he dismembered it using a knife and a hacksaw. As he cut her apart, he placed the pieces in pots and pans and then stored them in the refrigerator and oven. He eventually decided to cook the remains to make them easier to dispose of. Despite how the crime scene looked when the police found it – and the rumors that started because of it – there were no human remains found in his system during an autopsy.

It took four days for Zack to decide that he was going to cook Addie's remains, though. During those days, he went on about his life as usual. Friends who saw him between the murder and his suicide said he seemed to be in good spirits and even talked about taking a vacation.

But many of those friends began to wonder where Addie was. When asked, Zach said she'd gone home to North Carolina. While some were surprised by this answer, others shrugged it off. Addie's bipolar disorder often made her unpredictable, so it seemed fitting that during a tumultuous time in her relationship, she'd run off to someplace she really didn't want to be.

As days passed, Zack began to realize what he'd done and started to fall apart. It was later discovered that his body was covered with cigarette burns – 28 of them, in fact. He had burned himself one time for every year that he had been a failure.

In his confession, he expressed a great deal of regret: "I scared myself not only by the action of calmly strangling the woman I've loved for one and a half years but by my lack of remorse. I've known forever how horrible a person I am – ask anyone."

It was at this point that Zack began trying to kill himself – although not by throwing himself off a building. Not yet. Instead, he spent all the money he had going to strip clubs, drinking, doing drugs, and sleeping with prostitutes. In the confession letter he left behind, he stated that he wanted to enjoy his last days on earth to the fullest, indulging in "good food, good drugs, and good strippers."

Once Zack was out of money, he went to the rooftop bar of the Omni Royal Orleans, where he opened a tab and started drinking. The security cameras captured Zack going to the railing of the terrace and looking at it several times. Finally, he downed his last drink and threw himself over the edge to his death.

WHEN THE POLICE REACHED THE APARTMENT ON RAMPART Street, they discovered a scene that was like something out of a horror movie.

Despite the warm October weather, the apartment was frigid because Zack had turned the air conditioning down all the way to slow the decomposition of Addie's remains. Zack had meticulously cleaned the bathroom after he had dismembered Addie's body in the tub, but the rest of the apartment was in chaos.

The walls were spray-painted with haunting messages of regret and pain. "I love her," one of them read and included instructions to call Zack's wife and deliver that message. A second scrawled message said, "I'm a total failure."

The shop on Rampart Street with the apartment upstairs where Zack and Addie lived.

Another message directed the police to the stove. In a pot on one of the burners was a human head, burned beyond recognition. In another pot were hands and feet. Inside the oven, in a large roasting pan, were arms and legs, also scorched.

Inside the refrigerator, in a large plastic bag, they found Addie's torso.

But it would be in the bedroom where investigators would discover Addie's journal and the confession letter that Zack had written that explained the details of this sad, grisly tale.

AND YET, THIS IS NOT THE END OF THE STORY.

Not surprisingly, in a city filled with ghost stories, the apartment at 826 North Rampart Street gained a reputation for being haunted. Stories were told of uneasy feelings in the space – not a shock considering what happened there – feelings of being watched, whispers that were heard, and even the ghostly figure of a young woman peering out the window.

A recording that was made inside the apartment was said to have picked up a disembodied voice that said, "Please don't hurt her." Some believe it was referring to Addie.

It was inevitable that the apartment would earn this kind of reputation, especially in New Orleans, which is home to hundreds of eerie tales and, it often seems, just as many people telling them. Usually, locals would think nothing of another such story – it's a town that's notoriously open about its history of gruesome crimes.

But something about what happened next managed to trigger even the most accepting residents of the city. The exploitation of the murder and suicide of Addie and Zack made many people very angry.

Less than a decade after the murder, the building on Rampart Street was leased by a local ghost tour company, and, for a fee, visitors began to be allowed upstairs into Zack and Addie's apartment to see the stove and refrigerator where Addie's remains were found. Worse, the apartment was cheaply decorated with fake  blood and horror film props to give the tourists a thrill.

It was a horrible event – but it was history – and it appealed to people fascinated by true crime. But history wasn't how it was presented. Decorating the place like a scene from a cheap slasher flick turned it into gratuitous entertainment, erasing the reality of the two people who lived and died in that apartment.

The owners defended their decision, saying it educated people about the crime, but eventually, they bowed to pressure, and the trashy decorations were removed. The public applauded the decision, locals, true crime buffs, and even others interested in haunted history.

We can love true crime and ghosts – but I guess we need them to be in good taste.

There's no question that the murder of Addie Hall - and the ghost story attached to it – appeals to the public's fascination with death. Addie's story has become, over time, just another tale of murder, horror, and ghosts. Those are three things of which we never seem to be able to get enough.

For centuries, executions were public affairs. Eventually, they were moved out of sight, but we found that if we couldn't witness death, we still wanted to learn about it. Most of the first mass-produced newspapers were dedicated to the lurid retelling of murders, accompanied by detailed illustrations.

And this industry has only grown larger over the years – from local tour operators to writers to television and movie production companies – all dependent on murder. Hotels with murders and other tragic events are quick to capitalize on it because they know people are willing to pay to stay in a room that might be haunted. Crime tours and ghost tours roam the streets of small towns and big cities, delighting in the most sensational stories of crime and horror each place has to offer.

Are we terrible people profiting off the absolute worst human behavior imaginable? No, I don't think so.

While some may turn up their nose at our morbid curiosity, there are ten times that number of people who eagerly embrace it. We just always must remember that there is a fine line to walk when it comes to the way that we present the history of true crime -- a middle path between exploitative and pretending it never happened.

Respect the victims, but don't hide the reality of the crime.

We can't change human nature, but we can change the way we talk about death.

"COME PREPARED TO STAY FOREVER"
The Murder Farm of Belle Gunness

IT WAS A COLD, CRISP DAY IN EARLY JANUARY 1908 when the train pulled into the station at LaPorte, Indiana. A handful of passengers left the cars and stepped down onto the wooden platform outside the small station house. One of them, a thick, blond man wearing a heavy fur jacket, had the handle of his leather satchel gripped tightly in his fist. He looked around for a moment and then walked over to a wagon that was standing near the station.

He spoke to the dirty, slightly ruffled man that was standing next to the wagon and the equally ruffled mule that was hitched to it and struck up a bargain with him – the man, not the mule. The mule didn't care where he went so long as he was fed, watered, and warm at night. You could probably say the same thing about the man.

The blond man placed his bag into the back of the wagon and climbed up onto the seat next to the driver. He pulled his hat down low to cover his ears from the cold and then pulled on a pair of woolen gloves. His pale cheeks were bright red from the chill, but it didn't bother him much. He'd come to Indiana from the open plains of Aberdeen, South Dakota. The weather here didn't seem very cold to him.

Andrew Helgelien as a young man

The driver snapped the leather reins on the back of the mule, and the wagon jerked forward, the wheels crunching over the frozen ground. He steered through town, and his passenger looked at the stores and businesses of LaPorte as they made their way toward the road that would take them out of town to the farm where his beloved lived.

The man, Andrew Helgelien, glanced at a feed store, a restaurant, a grocery, the post office, and the bank where he'd find himself in just a few days, waiting patiently to make a cash withdrawal from his bank back home. He watched the people who walked past, many of them offering a friendly wave to the broad-shouldered man in the long fur coat while others simply stared at him with curiosity.

They'd later remember seeing Andrew on that cold morning, and they'd later tell their children and grandchildren that they had been on the street that day when he'd passed by.

Soon, the wagon left the city limits and rolled out into the barren countryside. A layer of white covered everything as far as he could see – the fields, the trees, the houses, and barns, but again, it was nothing like the snow on the ground back in South Dakota – or back in Norway when he'd been a boy.

Even so, there was a feeling of gloom in the gray sky overhead. Andrew heard the call of a crow in a stand of trees that had lost their leaves months before and would see no more until spring. He heard the crow, and he shivered a little.

He knew what would cheer him up, though. He reached into the pocket of his coat and felt the bundle of letters that he kept there, wrapped with a scarlet ribbon. They were the beautiful letters that had been sent to him by the woman who would become his wife. To Andrew, they were like poetry, conjuring images of green grass and sunshine.

Others, who would later read them, would call them clumsy and stupid, but they weren't to Andrew. "We shall be so happy once you get here," she had written to him, "then I will make a cream pudding and many other good things. You have been there long enough and worked hard for many a day, and now you must take it easier for the rest of your days."

Just thinking about the letters made Andrew's heart melt. There were 80 of them in all, each begging him to come to Indiana and bring all his money with him, promising him a part of her wonderful farm and the pleasures of love and marriage.

Andrew wondered if he deserved a woman as fine as this. The thick-necked Norwegian hadn't lived a perfect life. He had spent time in prison for robbing the post office in Red Wing, Minnesota, and then burning down the building to hide the evidence. But since his release a decade earlier, he had stayed on the straight and narrow. He was now a prosperous farmer, living not far from his brother, Asle, and his sister, Anna.

But his past haunted him, and it kept him from pursuing the few chances at domestic bliss that had come along – until now.

He'd first received letters from her nearly two years before, and, at first, he dared not dream that love could be his. He began writing back to her, planning to visit, but some trouble or another on the farm had kept him away. Finally, he could wait no longer, and he finally kept the promise that he had made to his beloved many months before.

He was finally here in LaPorte, and in a very short time, he would meet the woman he loved face-to-face for the very first time and arrive at the farm that she had described as paradise on earth.

Andrew thought back to one of the letters she had sent him, and there was one line that he could never forget. He thought of it often.

"Come prepared to stay forever," Belle Gunness had written to him, and Andrew was filled with hope that his dreams were finally about to come true.

And they were – but as nightmares rather than dreams. But one thing was certain: Andrew would come to stay on Belle's farm forever.

AFTER THE GREAT FIRE REDUCED THE CITY OF Chicago to ashes in 1871, the city roared back to life in the decade that followed and, by the early 1880s, had resurrected itself as the "gem of the prairie."

The growing metropolis drew not only hordes of eager young men and women from the small towns, villages, and farms of the Midwest, but it also attracted tides of immigrants from across the sea – Germans and Poles, Scottish and Irish, Italians and Jews – from every corner of the globe.

Many of the newcomers to the Windy City hailed from Norway. In fact, Norwegians had been some of the earliest settlers of the area, establishing homes there when Chicago was just a collection of wooden buildings on the swampy shores of Lake Michigan. Their numbers grew in the years after the Great Fire, doubling then tripling and becoming an essential part of the new and shiny version of the city.

Like their fellow Scandinavian immigrants, the Norwegians of Chicago were regarded as frugal, industrious, hard-working people who made the city better by their presence in it.

By the late nineteenth century, Chicago's Norwegian population – now the third largest in the world outside of the two largest cities in Norway – numbered more than 20,000. The wealthiest among them – the doctors, lawyers, businessmen, and bankers -- had turned the neighborhood of Wicker Park into a tightly knit ethnic community, with more Norwegians seemingly arriving every day.

Among the arrivals in 1881 was a 22-year-old woman from Norway's west coast. She was a notably unattractive woman with

Brynchild Poulsdatter Størset, who would eventually become more infamous as Belle Gunness.

a large head, small eyes, a short nose, and a wide, fat-lipped mouth that, when she frowned, made her look like a frog.

The woman's origins, like most of her life story, are shrouded in legend and deliberate inventions, but she was born Brynchild Poulsdatter Størset on November 11, 1859, in Selbu, in northern Norway. Her father, Paul – her second name, "Poulsdatter," literally means "daughter of Paul" – was a poor farmer who kept his entire family in poverty.

He didn't even own the farm he worked on. It belonged to distant relatives, and Paul leased the land to grow barley, oats, and potatoes and raise a few sheep. During the winter months, he supplemented the family's meager income by working as a stonemason. Hunger and poverty loomed over Brynchild's early life, and she was sent to work as a dairy maid and cattle girl, hired to shepherd the livestock to the mountain pastures for fresh grazing. Any money that she earned was turned over to her father to help with the family expenses.

Years later, some of the locals in Selbu would remember Brynchild – truthfully or not – as a malicious young girl with bad habits and a taste for lies. People mocked her and called her a "twig girl" because the family's poverty forced her to gather sticks to be sold as kindling, which was a lowly job. The cruel nickname subjected the young girl to mockery and ridicule from children and adults alike. There was no question that Brynchild and her family occupied the lowest rung of the town's social ladder. The resentments she undoubtedly felt toward the more fortunate in the village built up in the young woman until a defining tragedy in her early life created a powerful anger that would return repeatedly as a violent retribution towards men – and a strange feeling about children.

In 1877, when she was 17, the church-going Lutheran girl discovered she was pregnant, scandalizing her family and bringing even more shame upon herself. She was already an outsider in the community, and this gave the gossips something else to whisper about. After this scandalous news spread through the community, Brynchild attended a dance one evening and was physically attacked by the son of a wealthy local family – a man far above her own station in life.

She fought back against his sexual advances and, rebuffed by a woman he felt should have welcomed his attentions, the angry young man kicked her viciously in the abdomen. Brynchild miscarried, but officials in Selbu did nothing to prosecute her attacker. Strangely, though, the young man died a short time later, allegedly from stomach cancer. Considering her later crimes, there has been speculation that she poisoned her attacker and thus claimed her first victim.

Truth or fiction? Who can say?

Her part in his death will always remain a mystery, but what is known is that Brynchild was never the same after her miscarriage. Her personality changed, and she became increasingly morose and resentful. All the dreams that she once had of settling down with a loving husband in a happy marriage disappeared. All she carried about now was making the money needed to escape the terrible place she called home. As her sister, Nellie, would later say: "Money became her god."

Brynchild would leave Norway for America, where popular myth claimed that even a person from the humblest beginnings could make their fortune.

Over the next three years, she saved her money and worked hard to make her dream come true. She labored in pigpens, milked cows, and tended horses, putting every penny aside. Several years before, her older sister, Olina, had moved to the United States, settled in Chicago, and met and married a man named John Larsen. Nellie, as she now called herself, invited Brynchild to come and live with her and her husband and helped her come up with the rest of the money that was needed for the ship's passage. Brynchild boarded a steamship on September 8, 1881, and made the Atlantic crossing, choosing a new name to give to immigration authorities when she arrived.

She was now Belle Peterson.

She made her way to Chicago and moved in with Nellie and John in Wicker Park – an arrangement that became quickly unsuitable. Life with the Larsens offered security but proved difficult. John was not fond of his sister-in-law, and the relationship between Belle and Nellie became strained.

Belle stayed away from home as much as possible, working – as most unmarried Scandinavian women of the time did – as a domestic servant. She did laundry, did piecemeal sewing, and cleaned homes for meager wages that she handed over to the Larsens for her room and board.

This kind of work was nothing new for a former farm girl, but Belle hadn't come to America to keep performing the menial tasks she'd done back home. She was ambitious, and she longed for the finer things in life. The deprivation of her childhood had left her with a lust for money.

As for marriage, Belle made no secret about what she looked for in a man. Nellie later said, "She never seemed to care for a man for himself, only for the money and luxury he was able to give her."

Years later, Belle would admit that she only stayed with her first husband – the father of her children and, by all accounts, a kind, loving man – because he provided her with a nice house.

That first husband was Mads Anton Sorensen, and they married in 1884. The only photographs that exist of him show a large, powerfully built, bull-necked man with strong Nordic features and a fashionable handlebar mustache. Five years older than Belle, he was one of 800 employees at the Mandel Brothers department store at State and Madison. He worked there as a night watchman.

They were married at the Evangelical Lutheran Bethania Church on Grand Avenue, and in their wedding photograph, Belle poses proudly in a black taffeta dress. The color was more common for wedding dresses in those days, but in hindsight, black would be a premonition of things to come.

LITTLE IS KNOWN ABOUT THE NEXT 10 YEARS in the lives of Belle and Mads, although most of what is known about Belle's life in Chicago came from Anton Olsen, a close friend of her husband.

Olsen was an engineer at the Munger Laundry Company in Chicago, and he had become friends with Sorensen through the Wicker Park Chapter No. 121 of the Independent Order of Mutual Aid, a fraternal lodge associated with the trade union he belonged to that sold life insurance policies to its members.

In 1890, Olsen lost his wife to typhoid fever, leaving him to care for an eight-month-old infant girl named Jennie. He couldn't care for an infant in diapers without a woman in the house to help him, so he allowed his neighbor and friend, Mads, and his wife, Belle, to adopt the little girl.

This was not as unusual as it sounded at the time. Belle seemed to have a desperate need to take in boys and girls that no one seemed to want or those whose parents could not afford to clothe and feed them. Thanks to Belle's attack and subsequent miscarriage as a young woman in Norway, she was apparently unable to have children of her own. This seems to have fed her desire to adopt children off the streets. It was said that almost every Norwegian Sunday School child in Chicago knew her for her kindness.

But Nellie's son and Belle's nephew, John Larsen, would see this differently, later saying that Belle was a "queer woman with a weakness for adopting children."

His mother, Nellie, became aware of Belle's fixation with children after she allowed her daughter, Olga, to stay with Belle for about six weeks. When it came time for Olga to go back home to her parents, Belle tried to adopt the girl. Nellie refused, and angry words were exchanged. The argument led to a serious falling out, and the two sisters did not speak for years.

So, when it came to little Jennie Olsen, Mads assured his friend that Belle was the "right kind of mother" to raise Jennie in their loving home.

About three weeks before Olsen's wife died, a Lutheran minister drew up the adoption papers outlining the agreement between the Sorensens and Anton Olsen. Anton, wracked by guilt over the situation but knowing it was for the best, wanted it understood that Jennie would legally remain his daughter and that she would eventually come back to live with him when he remarried.

Everyone agreed to these terms, although it would never quite work out that way.

Though Mads only brought home about $15 a week in wages – which is about $450 today – he and Belle somehow managed to come up with enough money to purchase a small candy store – or confectionary as it was called at the time – at 318 Grand Avenue in Chicago. The wood frame building sold tobacco, cigars, newspapers, magazines, stationery, a few grocery items, and the popular candies of the time. Despite its prime location in a busy commercial district, the shop failed to prosper, and Belle watched as the money she loved so much slowly drained away.

The store had previously been owned by a man named Charles Christiansen. Mads took over running the business while Belle looked after children that other people didn't want or couldn't care for. In addition to Jennie Olsen, Belle would eventually have three children with her in Indiana – all loosely "adopted" – Myrtle, Lucy, and Phillip.

Living in a small apartment above the confectionary, the Sorensens had a rather drab existence. Their life revolved around the shop, Norwegian fraternal societies, the Lutheran Church, and their daily routines.

Angry quarrels over money punctuated it. Belle was unhappy with the store's income and warned Mads that they would have to give up the business if things didn't improve. Then she suggested to him that he might want to increase his life insurance coverage in case anything ever happened to him. She was sure that he wouldn't want his family to starve in the event of some calamity.

And then a calamity occurred, although it wasn't a fatal one – not this time, anyway. Less than a year after Mads and Belle bought the confectionary, it burned in a mysterious fire.

Belle was home alone with the children at the time. She hurried them to safety in front of the building, where she began screaming at the top of her lungs. Belle claimed that a kerosene lamp had exploded and started the fire. No lamp was ever found in the ruins, but the insurance money was paid. The interior of the building was destroyed.

Soon after, Sorensens pocketed the insurance check and sold the building to the brother of the original owner.

The confectionery had been heavily insured – just like Mads – and the tidy sum allowed Belle and Mads to move their family into a large home at 620 Alma Street, between Chicago Avenue and Ohio Street, an area usually reserved for the well-to-do.

They settled into the three-story, wood-frame home with a large backyard and began bringing in extra income by renting office space on the upper floor of the house to a physician.

The house at 620 Alma Street (now Latrobe) in Chicago's Austin neighborhood

Mystery followed the family to Alma Street. The origin of the Sorensen children continued to raise questions. Belle took great delight in parading her daughters about in the finest clothes they could afford. Many people knew that Jennie Olsen came to live with the family after her mother had died, but where had the other children come from?

The sudden appearance of a baby boy named Axel in the Sorensen home soon raised many eyebrows. Belle passed off the infant as her own, but Dr. J.B. Miller, the North Avenue physician who rented space on the upper floor of the Alma Street home, later told a curious tale to the *Chicago Daily News*. He told a reporter, "A few days before the appearance of little Axel, I was asked by Mrs. Sorensen to hold myself in readiness to attend her in childbirth. To me as a physician this announcement came as a surprise."

He had no idea that Belle was even pregnant, let alone just about to give birth. A few days later, someone put a note under Miller's door advising the doctor that he was wanted immediately and to come at once to Belle's bedroom – she had been in labor all night, and the baby was on its way. Again, the doctor was astonished. He had worked late the night before and slept in a room adjoining his office but had heard no sounds in the house. He assumed he was the only one home at the time.

When he arrived in Belle's room, she demanded to know where he'd been. She looked for him everywhere, but when he couldn't be found, she called another doctor to deliver her baby.

Dr. Miller never found another physician who would admit to attending the birth of the baby – a baby that Belle was holding that morning and appeared to be older than a newborn.

Belle would eventually claim to her neighbors that she had given birth to four children. However, it struck them as very peculiar that a woman who had failed to give birth in the first 11 years of her marriage had allegedly delivered four children within the span of the next three years.

One neighbor, Mrs. William Diesling, stated that she'd gone to the Sorensen house one day and had found an infant crying on the couch. She asked Belle why she didn't feed it, and Belle replied that she didn't have time to take care of it. Mrs. Diesling asked who the baby belonged to, and Belle said that a relative had sent it to her to look after. The next day, the baby was gone. Belle claimed the relative had returned for it.

But was this really the case? Or did the baby meet with a more tragic end? According to burial records, Caroline Sorensen, a three-month-old girl, died on August 24, 1896, and an infant boy named Axel passed away in April 1898. Both children exhibited symptoms of acute colitis – inflammation of the large intestine – and both were buried in Forest Home Cemetery.

It's very possible that the "colitis" could have been caused by the ingestion of poison. However, that's just a rumor. At a time when the infant mortality rate in America was shockingly high, no suspicions were aroused by the deaths of the two babies. My suspicions are aroused in hindsight, though, especially when we consider that Belle collected significant insurance claims on the lives of both children.

After moving to the Alma Street house, Mads went to work for the Chicago and Northwestern Railroad. He was only bringing home $12 a week when what seemed like a golden opportunity came his way.

On October 1, 1897, a man named Angus Ralston called at the Sorensen home. He presented himself as the agent and chief engineer of the Yukon Mining and Trading Company. The company – which owned mines throughout the west and in Alaska and the Klondike – was hiring men to go to Alaska for one year for the chance to strike it rich in the gold fields.

To Mads, after 13 years of a troubled marriage, this must have seemed like not only a great adventure but an escape from Belle. She encouraged him to sign up, and Mads was hired to depart for the Alaskan gold friends on April 1, 1898. He would receive wages that matched those of other miners in the area, as well as one-fourth interest in all the mines he located, plus stock shares in the company. Since Mads would be away, Belle would receive $35 per month to make ends meet at home.

Belle, blinded by the idea of dazzling wealth, agreed to invest a considerable chunk of their savings to cover his supplies for a year. She signed a promissory note over to the company, using the deed to the Alma Street house as collateral.

The idea of going off into the wild and returning with a fat bank account seemed almost too good to be true – because it was. The Sorensens never suspected that they had fallen for a scam. It wouldn't be until they heard no further word from the company – and found out their promissory note and deed had been sold to a real estate broker for $500 – that they discovered they'd been fooled.

Even though the Sorensens filed a lawsuit that returned their deed, their get-rich-quick scheme had come to an embarrassing end. Mads returned to his earlier job as a night watchman at the department store, while Belle seemed to accept the idea that she was destined to spend the rest of her life as the wife of a blue-collar worker who was only getting by.

But she didn't accept it. Belle had other plans.

On the evening of Tuesday, April 10, 1900, a fire – allegedly caused by a broken heating apparatus – broke out in the Alma Street house.

Though firefighters arrived in time to save the building, the Sorensens suffered a loss of roughly $650 in household goods – or that's what they told the insurance company. Another check was collected and cashed, but Belle wasn't finished yet.

At the time of the fire, Mads belonged to a mutual benefits association that provided him with a $2,000 life insurance policy that was set to expire on Monday, July 30. He decided to let that policy lapse and took out a new one for $3000 that started that same day.

As bad luck would have it – on that very day – Dr. Miller, who had once rented offices in the Sorensen house – received an urgent call from Belle. He hurried to the Alma Street house, and when he arrived, he found Mads, fully clothed, lying in bed.

He was dead.

By then, another doctor, Charles Jones, had also arrived. They questioned Belle, and she said that Mads, who had been suffering from a cold, had come home from work that morning complaining of a terrible headache. She had given him a dose of quinine powder and then had gone downstairs to make dinner for the children. When she came back upstairs a little while later, she found him dead.

Thinking that perhaps a druggist had accidentally given Belle morphine instead of quinine, Dr. Miller asked to see the paper in which the medicine had been wrapped. Belle told him that she had thrown it away.

Dr. Jones couldn't help but notice how strange Mads looked. He almost didn't appear dead. He also wondered about the medicine that Belle had given to her husband, but there was little he could do. With no other evidence to go on other than what Belle told them, the doctors decided that Mads had died from a cerebral hemorrhage.

Mads' death turned out – by coincidence, I'm sure – to be a gold mine for Belle. Since he'd died on the same day one insurance policy lapsed and another began, she ended up with a payout of $5,000, or what would roughly be $150,000 today.

Three days later, on August 2, Mads Sorensen was laid to rest next to his two infant children at the Forest Home Cemetery. Among those attending the funeral was Nellie, Belle's estranged sister. No one knows if they spoke that day, but according to Nellie, at some point in the service, she was gripped by a terrible and dark premonition.

She later recalled, "While I was there, a terrible feeling came over me. I felt like something bad was going to happen."

The sensation struck her with such force that she became dizzy and couldn't stand up. But it would be another eight years before she understood the meaning of the dread that seized her that day.

By then, it would be too late to warn anyone.

AFTER MADS DIED, BELLE REMAINED LIVING in the Austin neighborhood – much to the dismay of most of her neighbors – for another year. Repairs were made to the house using the insurance windfall that arrived after Mads' death and Belle and her children endured both the fear and curiosity of those who lived nearby.

Most of them believed Belle to be an arsonist and a poisoner, but they kept silent, either too courteous or too frightened to cause a fuss. But they talked quietly among themselves, gossip

Belle Gunness's most famous family photo. Belle with Phillip (on lap), Myrtle and Lucy

that their children overheard. The children whispered in the schoolyard, where they taunted the children whose "mama had killed their daddy." They were tormented mercilessly, and almost everyone shunned Belle.

Eventually, Belle would be as disgusted with the people of the neighborhood as she had become with the villagers back home in Norway. Eventually, Belle would leave Chicago for Indiana – where she would go from merely being a subject of local gossip to something far, far worse.

How exactly Belle came into the possession of the farm on McClung Road, outside of LaPorte, Indiana, is a bit of a mystery. Some say that she made a property swap with Arthur F. Williams, president of the Trade Circular Advertising Company, giving him the Austin house in exchange for the 60-acre farm, but others are not so sure. Regardless, the property already had a checkered past before Belle showed up.

LaPorte, Indiana, around the time when Belle arrived there.

LaPorte had been founded in 1833, luring white settlers to the area with promises of cheap government land. As the little community began to grow, it became the county seat and the largest place of local employment. The arrival of the railroads brought farmers, carpenters, mechanics, and businessmen to town, which was now just a train ride away from the booming city of Chicago.

New residents built homes and started farms, and commerce, industry, and rich soil helped the town grow after the Civil War, although it was eclipsed by Michigan City, its larger neighbor to the north. Despite this, local publications called LaPorte "unquestionably the handsomest city in Northern Indiana, if not the state."

When the news of Belle's "Murder Farm" broke in the spring of 1908, it shattered the optimistic notion that this tranquil farm community was somehow removed from the clamor, noise, and urban horrors of Chicago. When people from across the country read about the case, it dawned on them that rural America's small towns, farms, and fields were not immune to the evils they believed only lurked in the big city.

But the people of LaPorte already knew that.

Even before a horrific crop of corpses was unearthed on the farm, they thought there was something strange about the place out on McClung Road.

A picture postcard of the Gunness farm.

Even today, a dispute lingers among the townspeople about the real history of Brookside Farm, the property that Belle purchased near Fish Trap Lake. There is even an argument about who built the place. The one thing that they can agree on, though, is that the land was soured even before Belle arrived and began her brutal killing spree.

The history of the property appears to go back to 1831, when it was purchased by Adam Polke, one of the first white men in the region. He bought the land from the government in November of that year, selling his interests to S. Treat, a cattle buyer, in 1842. Treat then transferred ownership of the land to his brother, George, who then sold it to Dr. B.R. Car, a homeopathic physician who constructed a log house on the property in 1857. He lived at the site and conducted his medical practice there, putting aside a portion of the property for a private cemetery that became filled with unmarked graves. Frontier medicine was primitive in those days, and many patients didn't survive.

Dr. Car likely would have lived out his days in peace, caring for the sick and injured, if not for the actions of his son, Hill, the leader of a gang of Midwestern holdup men and outlaws.

They began using the property as a rendezvous point. Based on the stories, the peaceful farm turned into the "terror spot" of Northwest Indiana. Illegal gambling, liquor distilling, horse racing, and general lawlessness were everyday occurrences along McClung Road during this time. Eventually, the younger Car moved west to Denver, where he was killed in a shootout. Dr. Car, after attempting to make a living in the coal and lumber business, moved away from LaPorte in disgrace in 1875, leaving behind a stack of unpaid bills.

In 1877, the August Drebing family replaced the log cabin with a sturdy brick home, although some versions of local history have it that John Walker, one of the original settlers of the area, actually built the brick home for his daughter, Harriet Holcomb, and her husband, John. No one really knows for sure.

But whoever built the house, it was obvious that they intended to make it the finest residence in the area – a task at which they failed miserably. Locals called the house "sinister" in appearance long before Belle moved to town. It was lavishly built but heavy and gloomy and brought nothing but misfortune to its owners.

Legends state that the Holcombs had been Confederate sympathizers during the Civil War, which put them at odds with the people of Northwest Indiana, who had sent more than 2,500 men to fight for the Union cause. Eventually, they were pushed out of the LaPorte area for good.

In 1888, the property was sold again to a farmer named Grovesnor Goss, who died, leaving it to his wife, Sarah. Two years later, a Chicago streetcar conductor turned real estate speculator named C.M. Eddy bought the land from Mrs. Goss. She was eager to get rid of the cursed place after her son committed suicide by hanging himself earlier that same year.

Eddy's hope for a quiet life in the country was crushed after his wife died in the house a short time after they moved in.

In 1892, Eddy sold the house to a woman who briefly had the title of "the most notorious woman in Northern Indiana." Her name was Mattie Altic, and she had been the owner of a high-class brothel in the vice districts of Chicago. She had decided to move her sporting house out of the city and relocate it to LaPorte. Not surprisingly, her presence in the community became a terrible scandal.

The flamboyant Mattie – who was a tall, striking woman in the image of the Gibson Girl of the era -- was unconcerned about gossiping old ladies, offended ministers, and the opinions of the wives of her best clients.

She transformed the place into the region's classiest whorehouse, complete with a marble-topped bar in the front parlor, a fancy carriage house, a boathouse, new furniture, a dance floor, and spacious bedchambers to accommodate her patrons when the evening's revelry came to an end. A flashy, fringe-topped surrey was used to pick up her clients when they arrived by train from Chicago.

Each night, the sound of dance music and the merry laughter of the patrons and prostitutes echoed into the quiet woods and across the nearby lake. This was no mere sporting house. It was, as Mattie said, "Chicago Southeast."

The quiet, religious town of LaPorte was horrified by the wild behavior of Mattie, her girls, and the men who came to see them.

But Mattie wasn't around to offend the town for long. She died suddenly one night after hours of drinking and dancing. The official cause of death was heart disease, but stories persisted that she had either taken her own life after being jilted by a lover or had been poisoned by her sister, a rival brothel owner with a sporting house in South Bend.

The "sordid reputation" of the house kept it empty for the next two years, and then it went through a series of owners who either never lived in the house at all or stayed there for only a very short time.

In time, it came into the hands of Belle Sorensen, whose infamy would make Maggie Altic seem as respectable as a Midwestern school teacher.

Whether Belle traded land for the farm or saw it advertised in a newspaper, as some claim, we know she eventually ended up there. The idea of leaving the city and settling on a farm may have first started to appeal to her after the death of her husband when she paid a visit to a relative on a farm in Fergus Falls, Minnesota. Whatever the reason for the move, a deal was struck in November 1901, and Belle and her three children – Jennie, Myrtle, and Lucy – began making plans to move to LaPorte.

But Belle had a stop to make along the way. She was searching for a new husband, a man to do the hard work and heavy lifting on her new farm. With her children in tow, she went to Janesville, Wisconsin, to look for wedded bliss. Her intended target was a man named Peter Frederickson. She hoped to convince him to sell his home, increase his life insurance -- not a good sign -- and move with her to LaPorte. She had placed a matrimonial advertisement in the local newspaper, and, at first, Frederickson responded enthusiastically.

Belle had discovered that his home was completely paid off, and he was worth at least $1,500. "You must come with me to Indiana where it is much nicer and there is so much to do," she urged him, but Frederickson stalled. A wedding supper was planned, but no one on his side of the family agreed to attend. Peter's family believed that marrying a woman that he met through a lonely-hearts ad in the newspaper was a terrible idea.

I'd have to agree – and eventually, so did Peter. He took their advice and called off the wedding. Belle left Janesville disappointed, but she wasn't ready to give up just yet.

When Belle and Mads were first married, they briefly rented a room to a man named Peter Gunness. He was a big, burly, Viking-looking man with a heavy blond beard and mustache. He had immigrated to America in 1885 from Oslo and joined his brother, Gust, in Minneapolis. In 1893, the two men moved to Chicago and rented a room from the Sorensens while working in the stockyards.

When he returned to Minneapolis in June 1895, he married a woman named Jennie Simpson and moved into a home on Hennepin Street. Peter went to work for a grocer, and they lived happily for a time. Their first child, a girl named Swanhild, was born in 1897. Four years later, though, Jennie died while giving birth to a second daughter.

During Belle's earlier trip to visit her relative in Fergus Falls, Belle had made a point of going to Minneapolis to become reacquainted with her handsome – and suddenly available -- former tenant.

The years had not been kind to Belle. Hardly a beauty at any age, she had turned into a rough, mannish-looking figure as she got older. Even so, she had no trouble attracting men, even one as handsome as Peter Gunness. Some say it was her money, others her farmland, or her cooking, but whatever it was – she soon had Peter on the hook.

The couple and the children departed for LaPorte with plans to marry there, and on April 1, 1902, wedding bells rang at the First Baptist Church.

But sadness followed wedded bliss. Just five days after the wedding, Peter's second daughter died. Her official cause of death was "edema of the lungs." Her body was shipped to Chicago, and she was buried at Forest Home Cemetery next to the remains of the other two infants who had died under Belle's care.

Belle, Peter, and the remaining children settled into the former brothel at Brookside Farm, and the newlyweds began their married life.

Peter Gunness, Belle's last husband.

But it was a marriage that wouldn't last long.

MEANWHILE, POOR ANTON OLSEN – THE father of Jennie, the little girl Belle and Mads had adopted when his wife died -- was back in the picture and looking for his daughter. He'd gotten remarried and now wanted his daughter back. He lived on the South Side of Chicago with his new wife, who wanted to care for Jennie as his own.

It was a great idea – but Belle wasn't going along with it.

When Anton first came to her, asking for Jennie, Belle was still living in the Austin house. She told him she was too busy to make the trip to his new home to drop Jennie off. Anton offered to come to her, but Belle said she'd be out of town with the children. When Anton tried again, Belle ignored him. He came to her home, and she refused to answer the door. He threatened to take her to court, and Belle informed him that she'd hire her own lawyer. Finally, he returned to the Austin house again – this time with a friend who was a police officer – and discovered she no longer lived there. Belle was gone and had taken Jennie with her.

Anton refused to give up. He kept looking for Belle and Jennie, but they were nowhere to be found. And then, thanks to a neighbor in Chicago, he learned about Belle's marriage to

Peter Gunness. Anton finally tracked down Belle in Indiana and demanded once again that Jennie be allowed to return home.

This time, Belle grudgingly agreed – but only to allow Jennie to come and live with him for one month. She would allow this with the understanding that Jennie could choose to live wherever she wanted, either with her father or with Belle.

Anton agreed, and Jennie traveled to her father's home. He enrolled her at the Cornell School at 75th Street and Drexel Boulevard, and she seemed to adapt to her new life and family very well.

And then Belle came to Chicago to visit her.

Belle's foster daughter, Jennie Olsen

She went directly to Jennie's school and took her out of class. She then sent a letter to Anton stating that since Jennie didn't have enough food or clothing at her father's house – which wasn't true- she was taking Jennie back home with her to Indiana. Anton immediately responded to the message, hurrying home before Belle could take his daughter away. He tried to reason with Jennie, but the girl was determined to leave and go away with Belle. Whether she had threatened the girl in some way or simply convinced her that life would be better in LaPorte, Belle had managed to turn Jennie against her father.

Anton reluctantly went along with his daughter's wishes and took her to the train station. As the train left the station, Anton sadly watched it go. Belle had been very kind to him before they left Chicago, trying to ease his pain about the loss of his daughter.

But that moment on the station platform, with the train pulling away and Belle and Jennie waving from the window at him, became the last moment when Anton would ever see his daughter alive.

Later, after shovels wielded by grim-faced men began cutting through the mud and muck of the hog pens and backyard of the Gunness farm in LaPorte searching for human remains, Anton vividly recalled the last words that Belle spoke to him before she took his daughter away.

"Don't worry. I am a Christian woman," she told him, "with a passion for God. Jennie will be safe with me."

IN THE SPRING OF 1903, ANOTHER CHILD ARRIVED AT the farm on McClung Road. The little boy's name was Phillip, and he was said to be the son of Belle's husband, Peter Gunness.

But like the births of Belle's earlier children, people were asking a lot of questions about the circumstances of Phillip's birth. A neighbor had come over to help Belle deliver the baby but arrived to find the front door locked. Belle refused to let anyone into the house to witness the birth. Another neighbor noticed how odd it was that Belle had been out in the yard, chasing pigs and washing clothing in the well just two days before Phillip was born.

If Belle actually gave birth to Phillip, she would have been 44 years old at the time. It was not a physical impossibility, but it was still unlikely. A midwife named Mary Swenson later told investigators that she had been called to the Gunness farm but arrived too late to deliver the baby. When she saw the infant for the first time, she was amazed to find the child washed, clothed, and appearing too old to be a newborn.

If that sounds familiar – it's the same thing that Dr. Williams – who had rented space for his office in the Sorensen home – had said when he'd seen Belle's last baby.

Some of the women around LaPorte had the same suspicions that Belle's neighbors in Chicago had. They believed Belle was faking pregnancies and claiming other people's children as her own. No birth certificate for Phillip was ever found, and many surmised that the boy had been "dropped off" at the Gunness farm in the middle of the night – just like someone would a stray dog or cat.

You might wonder why no one asked Peter Gunness for his opinion on the matter. Well, unfortunately, Phillip's father – if he was his father, which is, again, unlikely – hadn't lived long enough to see Phillip be born. On December 16, 1902, Peter had met with a fatal accident.

It's a good thing he had all that life insurance.

It had been around 3:00 on that cold December morning when Swan Nicholson and his family were startled awake by someone banging on their front door. Hurrying downstairs, they found Jennie Olson standing on the porch. "Mama wants you to come up," Jennie said. "Papa's burned himself."

When they arrived at the Gunness farmhouse a few minutes later, Swan and his son, Albert, found Belle seated in the kitchen, so upset she could hardly speak.

Her husband, dressed in a long white nightshirt, was face down on the parlor floor in a pool of blood. Swan felt for a pulse but couldn't find one. He tried to rouse Peter, but there was no response.

He sent Albert into town to fetch a doctor, and a short time later, he returned with Dr. Bo Bowell, a physician who also served as the country coroner. He hurried into the parlor and got to his knees to examine Peter while the others – Swan, Albert, Jennie, and a sobbing Belle – stood in a circle around him.

The doctor could tell that Peter had been dead for some time. His body was already growing stiff. The back of his head had an ugly wound on it, thickly caked with blood. His nose was broken and bent to one side. It was clear, as far as Dr. Bowell was concerned, that Peter Gunness had been murdered.

Belle – who the doctor described as nearly hysterical – was led into the kitchen and seated in a chair. He tried to find out what had happened, though the story he got out of the inconsolable woman raised more questions than answers.

From what he could gather, Peter had gone into the kitchen to get his shoes, which he kept near the stove to keep warm. As he bent down to pick them up, a meat grinder accidentally fell from a shelf above him, striking the back of his head and overturning a bowl of hot broth that scalded his neck. Although hurt, he assured Belle that he was all right and had laid down to rest. A few hours later, she discovered him dead on the parlor floor.

Though Dr. Bowell found this convoluted story highly suspicious, he decided to reserve judgment until the postmortem the next day. Albert Nicholson, though, had no doubts. As he and his father walked back home, he made it clear that he believed Peter had been murdered. His father cautioned him not to repeat that – it might cause trouble for Mrs. Gunness, he said.

Reports of Peter's death in the newspaper that next day showed the same caution that Swan Nicholson had taken with his son. It was only noted that Peter's death had been "mysterious," and there had been some "indications" of foul play.

Later in the afternoon, Dr. Bowell, assisted by another local physician, Dr. H.H. Martin, examined Peter's body. In his report, he stated that he found no burns or scalding on the body. His nose was broken – consistent with being struck by a heavy, flat object like a board -- and the wound on the back of his head was so severe that portions of his skull were visible. That wound had been the cause of his death.

Dr. Bowell felt that he was no closer to solving Peter's mysterious death. The autopsy had only made Belle's story harder to believe. Determined to find the truth, he announced his intention to impanel a coroner's jury and conduct an inquest.

It was held two days later in the room where Peter had died at the Gunness house. Belle, who was the main witness, underwent a lengthy and often pointed interrogation by Dr. Bowell.

When describing the events of the night when Peter died, she said that she had been stuffing sausage casings with freshly butchered pork that Peter had ground for her that afternoon. After finishing, she washed the meat grinder and then went into the parlor where Peter was reading the newspaper.

It was nearly 11:00 PM when Peter decided to go to bed. Moments later, she heard a terrible noise from the kitchen.

Belle hurried to the other room and saw Peter getting up from the floor with his hands on his head. She said that the pot of broth boiling on the stove had spilled on him. She had planned to put it away before she went to bed. She also saw that the meat grinder that she had put on the shelf above the stove to dry had fallen and hit him.

She had no explanation for why he decided to put on the shoes that were warming by the kitchen stove when he was going to bed.

Belle seemed more concerned with possible burns from the broth than with the wound on his head. She put Vaseline on his skin to help his burned skin.

Dr. Bowell asked if she had noticed the wound on the back of his head, and Belle said that she had. "Was it bleeding?" he asked her.

"Not very much. The bleeding seemed to be all stopped."

Belle continued to minister to Peter's burned skin, she said, even though Dr. Bowell knew that there had been no burns on Peter's neck or head. She said that Peter kept complaining about it. Finally, he took off his wet clothes and put on his nightshirt. He had decided to rest in the parlor rather than go upstairs to bed. He said he was too uncomfortable to sleep. Belle fixed up the couch for him and told the inquest jury that she had gone upstairs, instructing Peter to call for her if he needed anything.

In dramatic turns and in her thick Norwegian accent, she told the jury what happened next. She explained that Peter began calling loudly to her, waking up both Belle and the children. Peter was walking around the parlor, complaining about his head. Belle looked at the wound, but it didn't look that bad, she said. Even so, she decided to send Jennie over to the Nicholsons, and then she'd ask one of them to fetch the doctor from town.

When she returned from getting Jennie dressed, Peter was holding his head and saying that he felt that he was going to die. He stretched out on the floor, and soon, he was unconscious.

"When Nicholson came to the door," she told the jury, "I was rubbing his head, and I opened the door, I think, and they come in, and he then thought he was gone, but I did not think he was gone before you came. I think he was only unconscious.

It was quite a story, but it did not fit the timeline, or the statements of the others involved, including Dr. Bowell, who knew that Peter had been dead long before he arrived.

When Belle was asked how she thought Peter's head had been hurt, she said she didn't know. "I picked up the meat grinder from the floor," she told the jury. "I think it must have tumbled on him in one way or another. That's what I think, but I didn't see it."

"Did he say anything about it?" the doctor asked.

"He didn't say anything about the hurt on his head."

"When you found the cut, did you tell him his head was cut?"

"I asked him where he'd been with his head because it was sore in the back, but he didn't tell me."

Belle added that Peter never told her how the hot broth had tipped over on him either, other than to say that he must have bumped against the pot in some way. He also didn't tell her how he'd broken his nose. Belle claimed she didn't know it was broken until the doctor told her. She hadn't seen it bleed.

Dr. Bowell asked her one final question regarding Belle's relationship with Peter, whose death just two days before had caused her a terrible bout of sobbing, weeping, and grief.

"You always lived happily together, you and him?" the doctor asked her.

"As far as I know," a dry-eyed Belle replied with a shrug.

Jennie Olson testified next, and her account of what happened on the night of Peter's death matched precisely with the one given by Belle – which is really no surprise.

She gave the same sequence of events and then said she had gotten up when Peter had called from downstairs and saw him lying on the parlor floor. She had gone straight to the Nicholsons to get help and had returned with Swan and Albert. Belle, she said, had been beside herself.

Dr. Bowell asked her how she thought Peter might have gotten the cut on his head.

"I couldn't tell you or Mama either," Jennie said. "But when she came out there that thing was on the floor."

"Didn't he tell her?"

"Not that I know of."

"Don't you suppose he knew his head was cut?"

"Well, I suppose he did, but I don't know."

Suspecting that Jennie was just repeating what Belle had told her to say, Dr. Bowell asked if the two of them had talked about how Peter was hurt. Jennie shook her head, though, insisting they hadn't talked about it at all.

It's unlikely that Dr. Bowell believed her denials. He was convinced she had been coached because there were some deeply troubling aspects to the story given by Belle and echoed by her foster daughter.

Even as heavy as it might have been, could the meat grinder suddenly fall from a shelf and strike a man hard enough to fracture his skull? How could Belle and Peter spend two hours together after the accident and never discuss what caused it? Why didn't he mention his head wound? How could she not notice his broken and bloody nose? Why was there no evidence of the burns that Belle kept mentioning?

Many of the doctor's questions to Jennie make it clear that he had some serious doubts about Belle's version of events. He asked if Peter had any life insurance. Did he leave a will? Had he brought money with him when he moved to LaPorte?

To each of these questions, the soon-to-be 13-year-old girl gave the same answer – "I don't know."

The inquest concluded with testimony from Swan Nicholson, who said that he "didn't see no burns" on Peter's body. Nor had he seen any blood on the couch where the seriously wounded man had been lying down. Asked if he thought that the meat grinder falling from where it did and hitting Peter on the head could have fractured his skull, he replied: "I think it could have possibly, but I never thought there was anything else but the way she told me."

Dr. Bowell ended his questions by asking directly if Swan thought Belle might have killed her husband. This time, his answer was more direct: "No, I never thought that. No sir. They be like a couple of children and the same as the day they were married."

It was a strange answer, especially since just a few minutes earlier, at the start of his testimony, Swan had said that he knew virtually nothing about his new neighbors. So, how had he come to know so much about their allegedly happy marriage?

We don't know. No one asked him.

By the time the inquest was finished, rumors were swirling around town about the circumstances of Peter's death. Residents scoffed at Belle's explanation of a meat grinder dropping on his head.

Her behavior at her husband's funeral also raised eyebrows. The service took place in the parlor of the Gunness home on Friday, December 19. It was conducted by Reverend George Moor, the same minister who had performed Peter and Belle's marriage ceremony just eight months earlier.

During the service, Belle sat moaning loudly with her hands covering her eyes. However, some witnesses would say that she frequently peered between her fingers to see who was watching her as she put on her performance.

They weren't fooled, and neither was Albert Nicholson. After the funeral service, he wouldn't stop sharing his opinion that Belle had killed her husband until his father told him to shut up.

But Albert was hardly alone in this belief, which is why it came as such a shock to many in town a few days later when Dr. Bowell issued his autopsy findings and stated that Peter had died by accident.

The report read: "After having examined the body and heard the evidence, we do find that the deceased came to his death by the accidental falling of the auger part of the sausage mill falling from the heating shelf of the cook stove in his kitchen and striking him on the back of the head. The impact of said auger part of sausage mill causing a fracture of the skull and inter-cranial hemorrhaging resulting in death." The report may have officially put an end to the case, but it didn't stop the speculation and rumors.

And then there's what little Myrtle Sorensen – only five years old at the time of her stepfather's death – told her classmates at school soon after Peter was buried.

"My mama killed my papa. She hit him with a meat cleaver, and he died. But don't tell a soul."

AFTER THE CORONER'S REPORT OFFICIALLY CLEARED her name, Belle expected things to go back to normal, not only with the townspeople and her neighbors but with her family, as well.

But among the most skeptical about the official verdict on Peter's death was Belle's brother-in-law, Gust. He not only suspected foul play in his brother's death but in the sudden death of Peter's seven-month-old baby with his first wife, who had died less than a week after the wedding. He was also now very concerned about the welfare of his niece, Swanhild, who remained in the care of her stepmother. He knew that, prior to the marriage, Peter had taken out a $2,500 life insurance policy naming Swanhild as the beneficiary. He wanted to make sure the money went where it was supposed to – and that Swanhild stayed alive long enough to spend it.

At some point in early 1903, Gust traveled to LaPorte from his home in Minneapolis. He was reassured to find that Swanhild was well, although she was lonely and wanted to go home to Minnesota. But he was less happy when he asked about the $2,500 that Swanhild was supposed to get. When he asked Belle about it, she said that Peter had cashed out the policy shortly before his death and had turned the money into mining company stocks. If the stocks ever amounted to anything, Belle said, Swanhild would be a very rich girl. When Gust asked to see the stocks, Belle couldn't find them.

Gust decided enough was enough and made plans to take Swanhild home with him, but Belle refused. She assured Gust that she would be better cared for in Indiana on the farm. She proposed that Gust stay, too, and manage the farm for her.

"We can get along nicely together," Belle told him. "And we will make good money here, for I know you are a good farmer."

But Gust dismissed the idea. He later told a reporter, "I didn't like her eyes, and I didn't like the place, so I refused. I tell you – I'm glad I didn't take that offer."

Gust stayed at the farm for a few days with a growing sense of unease. One morning, less than a week after he arrived, Belle awoke to find that Gust had disappeared in the middle of the night – and that he had taken Swanhild with him.

The young woman would spend the rest of her days convinced that her uncle had saved her life.

AFTER PETER'S DEATH, THE FRIENDLY RELATIONS Belle had enjoyed with her neighbors came to an end. Belle's troubles with the Diesslin family began over some stray cows. Belle's cattle kept wandering over onto their property to graze, and William Diesslin angrily warned her that he was going to start charging for the use of his pasture. The next time the cows came onto his land, he made good on this threat. He locked the cows in his barn and refused to return them unless Belle paid him $1.

Soon after, Belle retaliated. She drove some of Diesslin's cows onto her land, and when Diesslin came to get them, she demanded $1 for their return, even threatening him with a pistol.

She had also had a falling out with the Nicholson family. Her pigs kept getting into their corn, and finally, Swan Nicholson penned them up and demanded Belle pay $11 to get them back and to repay him for the damage they had done. After that, the Nicholsons and Belle Gunness never spoke or set foot on each other's land again.

With Peter gone, Belle did all the work around the farm that generally would have been performed by a man. She did her own planting and harvesting, pitched her own hay, and milked her own cows. Wearing a man's coat and hat and an old pair of her husband's shoes, she would join the men at farm auctions. At livestock sales, she would buy a 200-pound hog and then lift it up and toss it into her wagon as easily as if it were a sack of laundry. When it came time to butcher the animal, she "handled the business herself," one local farmer later said. "She shot it, she bled it, scalded it, gutted it, and cut it apart."

The south side of Belle's farm – where the hog lots were located. They'd see a lot of use over the next few years.

Even for a woman of Belle's exceptional strength and abilities, such a substantial farming operation like the one she had was more than she could manage on her own. By the winter of 1904, she was greatly in need of a man.

And not just one to help with the farm work.

In February of that year, Olaf Lindhoe, a 30-year-old Norwegian immigrant who had arrived in Chicago three years earlier, discovered a HELP WANTED ad in a Norwegian-language newspaper. It was an ad looking for a hard worker on a farm in LaPorte, Indiana. Olaf packed up his belongings – including his life savings of $600 – and went to Indiana, where Belle hired him to do farm work – and other things.

Soon after his arrival, neighbors noticed that he and Belle seemed to enjoy an unusually close relationship – so close that many mistook him for her new fiancée. From a letter he wrote to his father and conversations that he had with other Norwegians in the community, it soon became apparent that Olaf believed they were going to be married.

He definitely had the wrong idea.

A short time later, Belle put out the word that she needed a new hired hand. Olaf had left her right in the middle of a big job. She told one neighbor that he had gone to St. Louis to see the World's Fair and maybe buy some land in Missouri. Swan Nicholson heard that Olaf had returned to Norway to see the new king crowned. And when Olaf's father – after not hearing from his son for months – wrote to ask Belle about his whereabouts, she sent back a letter that said that, from what she understood, Olaf had gone west and started a homestead there.

The truth was, though, Olaf was still on her farm. But it would be four years before he – or what was left of him – was seen again.

DURING THE SECOND WEEK OF APRIL 1905, A neighbor named Chris Christofferson was at the Gunness farm when a stranger arrived from town. He introduced himself as Henry Gurholt and explained that he had come there to work for Mrs. Gunness. He had a heavy trunk with him, and Christofferson helped him carry it up to the room that Olaf Lindhoe had recently vacated.

Henry was happy with his room, with the farm, and with Belle. In a letter written to his mother a week after his arrival, he described the farm as the nicest in the community and said that he was being treated like one of the family.

Christofferson continued to see Henry over the following weeks, sometimes with Belle and sometimes by himself. But then, one day in August 1905, during the oats harvest, Belle came to the Christofferson home and asked him if he would help her stack oats. Henry, she told him, had suddenly quit.

He became sick and left the farm, leaving with only a satchel full of clothes. His trunk and most of his belongings, including a heavy fur coat, had been left behind. Belle was seen wearing that coat all over town during the following winter.

Henry's mother later wrote and asked what had become of her son. Belle pled ignorance. All she knew was that Henry left in August with plans to go to Chicago and work as a horse trader in the Union Stockyards.

Christofferson asked Belle why a man would want to go live in Chicago without a heavy coat and Belle just shrugged – she never heard from Henry again.

One of the things that everyone always remembered about Henry Gurholt was the fancy, thick black mustache he always wore – a mustache like the one still attached to a corpse that was later unearthed on the Gunness farm.

IN THE LATE SUMMER OF 1905 – SOON AFTER Henry Gurholt had disappeared – Belle found a new place to advertise for men. She began putting "lonely hearts" ads into the matrimonial notices of the largest Scandinavian newspaper in the country. It had a huge circulation, especially in the Midwest and Plains states like Minnesota, Wisconsin, and the Dakotas. Chicago was the hub of Scandinavian immigration, where Norwegians, Swedes, and others lived in their own neighborhoods and spoke the languages from back home.

Thanks to this, the newspapers thrived, connecting rural and urban immigrants who were separated not only from home but from each other across great distances. These newspapers made it possible for men and women to interact with one another socially and even broker marriages through the placement of personal notices. The newspapers became an opportunity for Belle Gunness to look for potential husbands – and for victims.

Belle inserted her first ad, which read:

Personal - comely widow who owns a large farm in one of the finest districts in La Porte County, Indiana, desires to make the acquaintance of a gentleman equally well provided, with view of joining fortunes. No replies by letter considered unless sender is willing to follow answer with personal visit. Triflers need not apply.

Interested parties were invited to write to "BG" in care of the newspaper.

Precisely how many replies this ad got is unknown, although D.J. Hunter, who delivered mail to Belle's farm, later reported that she sometimes received as many as eight or ten letters in a day.

One of the first to reply was a middle-aged Norwegian immigrant named George Berry, who traveled from his home in

Tuscola, Illinois, to LaPorte in January 1906 with plans to work on the farm and later marry Belle. He had $1,500 with him when he left home, but both he and his money disappeared.

A few weeks later, Christian Hillkven of Dover, Wisconsin, sold his farm for $2,000 and bid farewell to his friends after having his mail forwarded to his new address in LaPorte, Indiana. That was the last time he was ever seen.

After telling his boss that he was going away to marry a rich widow, Emil Tell, a Swedish bachelor from Osage, Kansas, quit his job in a furniture factory and left for LaPorte with at least $2,000 in his pocket. He vanished without a trace.

And there were more. A lot more – a string of men with money in their pockets who traveled to the farm, intent on proving they were men of substance who were worthy of the attention of a beautiful widow. But what they got when they arrived was something far different than what they had expected.

BUT NOT EVERY MAN WHO SPENT TIME AT THE Gunness farm died there. Emil Greening was a 17-year-old carpenter who worked on Belle's farm as a handyman and farm worker. Emil became infatuated with the pretty, blond-haired, blue-eyed Jennie Olsen, so he likely spent more time hanging around the farm than anyone else.

Emil later spoke about some of the things he saw. "Mrs. Gunness received men visitors all the time," he said. "A different man came nearly every week to stay at the house. She introduced them as 'cousins' from Kansas, South Dakota, Wisconsin, and from Chicago. Most of the men who came brought trunks with them, but they rarely took trunks away. Mrs. Gunness kept the 'cousins' with her all the time in the parlors and her bedroom. She was always careful to make the children stay away from her 'cousins' who rarely tried to show them any affection."

None of the men stayed very long, though, and neither Emil nor anyone else ever witnessed their departure. Strangely, every one of them left his trunks behind. Eventually, Emil recalled, "There were about 15 trunks, and one room was packed full of all kinds of men's clothing. Mrs. Gunness said that the cousins had left their clothes, and she wasn't certain they'd be back for them."

In the summer of 1906 – between visits from Belle's "cousins" – Belle hired a local man, a Polish immigrant named William Brogiski, to dig several large holes in the muck of her fenced-off hog pens. She was clear of the size they needed to be – six feet long, three feet wide, and four feet deep.

"They are to be rubbish pits," Belle told him.

William later testified that he never saw what went into those pits, and he did not know when they were filled. However, several years later, William, along with the rest of the world, discovered the true purpose of the pits he'd dug that summer.

BY THE FALL OF 1906, JENNIE OLSEN had turned into a very pretty young woman of 16, and she was starting to attract many male admirers.

One of these was, of course, Emil Greening, the young farmhand. During the time that he was working for Belle, he and Jennie became close. "She told me a great deal about herself when we were alone," he later said.

Sometime during the winter that followed, she told Emil that her mother had decided to send her to college in California and had arranged for one of her professors to come to LaPorte and escort her to school.

Shortly before Christmas, Emil was told – by Belle, not Jennie – that the professor had arrived. Early the next morning, Emil was sent on an errand. When he returned, he asked to see Jennie to tell her goodbye, but Belle said he was too late – Jennie was gone.

Emil would later realize that no one had seen her leave, and no one else met the mysterious professor. He wrote two letters to Jennie and gave them to Belle to send, but he never received a reply.

John Weidner, a young carriage shop worker who had also courted Jennie, had a similar experience. During a visit to the farm about ten days before Christmas, Jennie told him that she was going to Los Angeles to attend college. Her mother had made all the arrangements. John was heartbroken, and Jennie didn't seem all that excited about the situation either. She made him promise that he would return the following Sunday to say goodbye.

When Sunday came, John went out to the farm in a blustery snowstorm. The weather was terrible, but he desperately wanted to see Jennie one last time. When he arrived, he knocked on the door and was told by Belle that Jennie had already left.

"Is that so?" John asked. "How funny. She asked me to come see her before she went."

"Yes, she left on Wednesday," Belle shrugged.

Over the course of the following year, he sent several letters to Jennie in California but never received a reply. One day in October 1907, he ran into Belle in town and told her of his failed attempts to reach Jennie.

"Oh, that's all right," Belle said with a laugh, "I heard you had gotten married and wrote to tell Jennie."

John explained that it had been his brother who had gotten married and asked Belle to write to Jennie and tell her he was still single.

"She said she would," John later said, "but Jennie never wrote to me."

Of course, the only way that Jennie Olsen could have communicated with anyone at that point was during a séance.

ODDLY, THOUGH, THERE WAS ONE PERSON who seemed to be aware of Jennie's fate before Belle Gunness' many secrets were revealed to the world. That person was Anton Olsen, Jennie's long-suffering father.

According to his account, he was awakened from a disturbing dream one night around the time that Jennie supposedly left for California. He was not a superstitious man and did not believe in premonitions or psychic visions, but he was so shaken by the dream that it gave him a terrible feeling of dread. In the dream, he had seen Jennie lying in a shallow, unmarked grave. Rain was falling, and the wet landscape around the grave appeared to be a farm.

Anton had a sinking feeling that the farm might be the place in Indiana where his daughter was living with Belle Gunness.

Anton had not seen Jennie for nearly five years since she had returned to the farm with Belle. He had been looking forward to his reunion with Jennie when she turned 18, but the dream had filled him with terror.

He lay in his bed, awake for nearly an hour, but then finally went back to sleep. He dismissed the nightmare as nothing more than anxiety or something he'd eaten that upset his digestion. He was nervous about seeing Jennie again. She was almost a grown woman, and he had no idea what she even looked like now. His nerves had gotten the better of him, he thought, as he closed his eyes and let sleep take him again.

Anton wouldn't think about that dream again until he heard about the horrific things that were discovered on Belle's farm. He knew right then that he would never see his daughter again.

WITH JENNIE GONE, WORKING AT THE GUNNESS farm lost whatever charm it once had for Emil Greening. In June 1907, six months after Jennie's departure, he quit his job and headed west.

A short time later, Belle hired his replacement, Ray Lamphere, a 37-year-old local man whose father had once been one of the most prominent men in the community. However, the former schoolteacher, politician, and justice of the peace had become a raging alcoholic who ruined his career and his family. Ray, like his father, was overly fond of the whiskey bottle.

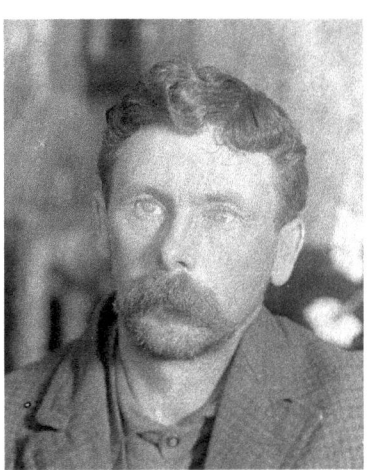

Ray Lamphere

When sober, he was a skilled carpenter and jack-of-all-trades and had spent 20 years in the Carpenter's Union. When drinking, though, he spent his money on liquor, prostitutes, and gambling and was reputed to have lost $50 in a single night on a backroom saloon slot machine – which was a huge sum of money in rural Indiana at the time.

Accounts of how he ended up working for Belle vary quite a bit. Some claim she'd had her eye on him for a while, and one day, she stopped him on the street and proposed that he move to the farm and work for her. Others say that Ray simply heard about carpentry work that needed to be done on the farm from a fellow carpenter, met Belle for an interview, and she hired him on the spot.

Whatever the case, it is certain that by July 1907, Ray was living on the Gunness farm, occupying the room on the second floor where other farmhands had once stayed.

As their relationship unfolded, it seemed there was nothing Ray wouldn't do to please Belle. He had – as he regularly boasted to his drinking companions – become her lover. Although the idea of the short, scrawny man becoming involved with the coarse 280-pound woman who was 11 years older than he was might not have been appealing to everyone, Belle's motherly presence in Ray's life seemed to ease his loneliness so much so that he missed many of the warning signs that would have sent others running for their lives.

Belle proposed marriage to Ray on several occasions, always encouraging him to take out a life insurance policy on himself with her as the benefactor.

The fact that Ray was dragging his feet about the idea shows that he was either lazy or perhaps not as dim-witted as he seemed. His refusal to act would eventually lead to a bitter falling out between the two of them, but while he was still in her good graces, Ray kept her secrets.

He really had no choice.

Ray continued his heavy drinking while living with Belle. Almost every night, he could be found drinking alone or with one of his cronies in town. When he was drunk – which, according to locals, was most of the time – he became gloomy about his life on the farm and his role as a keeper of Belle's secrets.

He likely feared that his days might be numbered if Belle ever thought he might spill those secrets. He wavered back and forth between loving and fearing Belle, concerned that one day he might pay dearly for his role in her crimes. Belle would either kill him, or he'd spend the rest of his life in prison.

But when Ray wasn't drinking, he relished his place on the Gunness farm. Throughout the fall of 1907, Ray and Belle were often seen together, riding into town in her wagon or strolling side by side on the streets of LaPorte. To his pals, he bragged about how Belle begged him to marry her, and he flaunted the gifts she gave him, including a fine silver watch.

He had been the town drunk, just like his father had been, and now he was in charge of the largest farm in the community. It didn't matter that the townsfolk disliked and feared Belle in equal measure. Ray believed that by managing her property and keeping her happy in the sack, he'd finally earned a little status in town.

He was as happy as he had ever been in his sad, miserable life, but in January 1908, it all fell apart when Andrew Helgelein showed up in LaPorte and ruined everything.

There had been other men who had shown up at the farm during Ray's time as the hired hand, but... well, none of them stuck around for long.

But Helgelien was different – in many ways. And as it would turn out, the unraveling of the mystery left in Andrew's wake by his brother would eventually mark the end of Belle's life of crime.

STARTING IN THE SUMMER OF 1906 – EVEN while others were responding to her ad and visiting the farm – Belle had been corresponding with Andrew Helgelein, the bachelor farmer from Aberdeen, South Dakota. He had seen her advertisement in a Norwegian-language newspaper and had started writing her. Over the next 18 months, Belle sent him dozens of letters – all written in Norwegian, sloppy in their diction and spelling, but working a sinister spell on the recipient, who couldn't believe his good fortune at winning the heart of a beautiful young woman from Indiana.

That Belle spent a year and a half setting a trap for Andrew says a great deal about not only her malevolent cunning but about Andrew himself. As flattered as he might have been with her attention, he wasn't the easy prey of most of her victims – perhaps because he was no gentlemen farmer or rich widower. Andrew had done time. He'd been on the wrong side of the law, and perhaps he needed to make sure that what Belle was offering was on the up and up.

When Belle wrote back to Andrew the first time, she boasted of her "beautiful home" and all her land, which she claimed was worth at least $14,000 – which would be about $400,000 today. To see if he was a candidate worthy of her attention, she asked to know more about him and, most importantly, how much cash he had to invest in the farm.

Although Andrew's side of the correspondence no longer exists, it's clear from Belle's letter to him, dated August 20, that he wrote back right away and that his response was satisfactory to her. She wrote:

You impress me with being a good man with a strong and honest character. A real genuine Norwegian in every respect, and it is difficult to find such a man and not every woman appreciates. There are plenty of American dudes around here, but I would not even look at them, no matter how often they asked me.

She bragged that LaPorte was truly a place of golden opportunity with the railroad, farms, markets, and proximity to Chicago. She added that she had chosen him to be her partner out of 100 applicants and urged him not to delay his trip to see her. She told him, "Take all your money out of the bank and come as soon as possible."

More letters traveled back and forth between them, and it was clear that Belle was already treating Andrew not as a business partner but as a potential husband. One letter said:

I long so to know you better but I will try to wait with patience until you get here. I have now thrown away all other answers I got and keep all yours in a secret place by themselves. You truly do not know how highly I prize them.

She told Andrew that he towered above common men and that she could not wait to devote herself entirely to his needs. She gushed:

I do not think a queen would be good enough for you and in my thoughts, you stand highest above all high and I will not let anything stand in the way of my doing anything for you.

We shall be so happy once you get here and then I will make cream pudding and many other good things. How lonesome it must seem for you to be up there all alone, but you must hurry and come to me as soon as you can. You have been there long enough and worked hard for many a day and now you must take it easier for the rest of your days.

Before she ended her letter, she made sure to emphasize the things that she would repeat many times in the months to come:

Now sell all that you can get cash for, and if you have much left, you can easily take it with you, as we will soon sell it here and get a good price on everything. Leave neither money or stock up there but make yourself free from Dakota so you will have nothing to bother with up there.
Now, my dearest friend, come soon.

But Andrew didn't come at once – he didn't come at all. In a letter that Belle received in late October 1906, he mentioned to her that he had been sick. Belle, of course, offered advice for him to stay healthy and hinted that if he had been with her already, she could have been his nurse. She again urged him to come and see her – and to come alone when he did. She asked:

Do not take anyone from up there with you before we become a little acquainted. Do you not think that would be best if we were alone, especially at the beginning?

To reinforce what she had in mind, she added:

Now I must close because I am getting sleepy. I will now go to bed and think of you.

When Andrew still failed to come, the tone of Belle's letters became more urgent. She implored him to come to Indiana before the harsh winter weather arrived. She told him that he should bundle up for his journey so that he would not become sick again. But his health was not her sole concern. She wrote:

You talk of leaving some of your money up there. This I would not do if I were you, especially when you are going so far away, rather, sell your things. If you read only just a little every day, you find the newspapers are full of bank robberies and bank failures; it is either one or the other. I am sure you will find just as good a place for them here, as you will find up there.

She stressed that he should keep all his financial business a secret, as well as his love life. She added:

This is a secret between us and no one else. Probably we will have many other secrets between us, not so, dear friend? We will have many things between us which no one else will know which we will enjoy, won't we? I will surely see to it that you enjoy yourself.

But Andrew still hesitated. Belle kept writing. She sent him pressed roses and wrote longingly of a Norwegian Christmas. She drew pen and ink portraits of the two of them snuggling on the couch in front of a fire, warm and cozy as snow fell gently outside. When he did not make it down for the holidays, Belle's correspondence began to reflect a growing impatience. Disappointed as she was, though, she assured him that she would continue to wait patiently for him. She wrote:

I place you higher in my affections than anyone on this earth and will remain true until you come.

With her usual calculation, she ended one letter with a picture of domestic bliss that must have been tempting to a lonely bachelor fending for himself on a cold Dakota farmstead:

If only you were here with me and were sitting in a rocking chair talking to me. Then I would go and get you a glass of fruit wine which I made myself, but you will get it when you do come, my dear friend.

Shortly after the New Year, Andrew received news from Norway that his mother had died, further delaying his visit to Indiana. Belle wrote a consoling letter that urged him to live for the people who are still among the living and do the best he could for them. In his case, this meant hurrying to the side of the person who eagerly awaited his arrival.

When spring arrived – and still no Andrew – Belle started to apply more pressure. Addressing him not merely as her "dearest best friend" but as her "very best and faithfullest friend in the whole wide world," she relentlessly filled her letters with rosy pictures of their future life together. She wrote glowingly of the farm in spring – the new leaves, the green grass, the calves, little pigs, and chickens...

Several weeks later, she wrote about how she was fixing up the inside of the house for his arrival. She wrote:

It will be real comfortable and pleasant when it is all ready and then I hope you will be here and everything is all right. Then we will be so cozy and have some good homemade cake and some good coffee and cream pudding and many other good things. Then we can also sit and talk and talk until we get so tired we cannot talk anymore. Yes, my dear friend, we will make up for this long waiting, that you can be sure of. Oh, if you only knew how I would love to talk with you about everything, my good friend. It will be so pleasant.

And yet, still no Andrew.

Apparently, he had told her that he hoped to join her in the summer of 1907, but he postponed his departure again. That fall, for the first time, Belle finally gave in to her frustration in a letter, writing:

Now it is already the 25th of September and last year at this time I waited for you and yet you haven't come to me. I know you are a man I can trust and therefore I have waited so faithful but it is tiresome and lonely to wait much longer and the fall is here again and I have the whole year managed the best I could without steady help because I have waited for you from one time to another as you have promised and promised and it seems as if you will never get your belongings in order up there.

She ended the letter with a thinly veiled ultimatum, insisting that he make up his mind as soon as possible, or she would no longer be waiting for him.

What Andrew wrote in return is unknown, but he seems to have taken her message to heart and assured her that her long wait was almost over. In late 1907, she wrote back:

No woman in the world is happier than I am. I know that you are now to come to me and be my own. Think how we will enjoy each other's company. You, the sweetest man in the whole world. We will be all alone with each other. Can you conceive of anything nicer? I think of you constantly. When I hear your name mentioned, and this is when one of the dear children speaks of you, or I hear myself humming it with the words of an old love song, it is beautiful music to my ears. My heart beats in wild rapture for you, My Andrew, I love you. Come prepared to stay forever.

Andrew might not have planned it that way, but he did indeed stay on the farm forever.

AFTER HAPPILY SETTLING INTO HIS ROLES as Belle's carpenter, farmhand, and lover, Ray Lamphere was hit with a hard dose of reality on the morning of Friday, January 6, 1908, when a burly stranger in a shaggy fur coat arrived at the farm.

Later that day, Belle informed Ray that she was turning his bedroom over to the new guest and that Ray could sleep in the barn.

At daybreak the next morning, Ray returned to the house and, following his usual morning routine, started building a fire in the parlor stove to warm up the room before breakfast. He was just finishing when the stranger came downstairs. The two of them struck up a conversation that was interrupted when Belle appeared and angrily motioned Ray aside. She insisted that Ray leave the man alone.

The arrival of the big Norwegian farmer from South Dakota literally changed Ray's relationship with Belle overnight. She had no more use for the scrawny little carpenter, but she had plenty of use for Andrew – and, of course, for his money.

On January 6, Frank J. Pitner, a cashier at the First National Bank of LaPorte, was at his usual place in the teller's cage when Belle came in with a broad-shouldered man wearing a long fur coat. Introducing himself as Andrew Helgelein, he presented three certificates of deposit from the First National Bank of Aberdeen, South Dakota. He announced that he wanted to redeem them for their full value. When Frank explained that he would have to send them to the issuing bank for collection, Belle asked him how long that would take.

Frank guessed that it would be four or five days.

Though Andrew accepted the delay without complaint, Frank would later recall that Belle couldn't conceal her annoyance. She argued with him, but there was nothing he could do. The couple eventually left the bank without the cash.

On January 11, a draft for the full amount arrived at the LaPorte bank, but three more days passed before Belle and Andrew returned. When Frank remarked with a smile that they seemed less in a hurry for the money now, he was told that Mr. Helgelien had been sick for the past few days.

The amount of the draft was a large one -- $2,839, which is about $75,000 today – so Frank suggested he write Andrew a cashier's check. Andrew seemed willing, but Belle insisted they be given the entire sum in cash. As Frank counted out the money – half in gold coins and half in currency – he asked Andrew what he planned to do with all of it.

"Mind your own business!" Belle snapped at him, then took Andrew by the arm and led him out of the bank.

Later that same day, Tuesday, January 14, Belle sent Ray off on an errand. She had arranged a horse trade with a cousin of hers named John Moe. Ray was to meet him in Michigan City, where the transaction would take place. If, for some reason, John didn't show up that night, Ray was supposed to spend the night there and meet her cousin in the morning.

Belle would be staying at home alone with her handsome new suitor, Andrew Helgelein.

Ray left for Michigan City around 5:00 that evening. It was a 20-mile trip, so he brought along a friend, a brewery wagon driver named John Rye. There was no sign of Belle's cousin at the livery barn where the swap was supposed to take place, so Ray and his pal killed a few hours, first at an oyster house and then at a five-cent vaudeville show.

Around 8:00 P.M., after checking in at the livery barn again, Ray decided to ignore what Belle told him and go back to LaPorte. They caught the 8:15 interurban train, which arrived in LaPorte about an hour later.

Saying that he "wanted to see what the old lady was up to," he told Rye that he'd meet him later at Smith's saloon and walked off into the darkness toward the Gunness farm. John waited at the bar for an hour, but Ray never showed up.

As for Andrew Helgelein, the big-shouldered Norwegian farmer, he was never seen alive again.

WHEN ANDREW HELGELEIN FINALLY MADE THE TRIP to LaPorte in early 1908, he'd been instructed by Belle to tell no one where he was going, but Andrew had – he'd told his brother, Asle. He said he expected to be gone for about a week and would come and see him when he returned. Asle had no idea why his brother was going to Indiana – only that he planned to return soon.

Asle Helgelein, the brother of Belle's missing beau, Andrew.

But he didn't.

Nine days passed, and Asle heard nothing – no letter, no telegram, no word at all from Indiana or Andrew's home in Aberdeen. Thinking that perhaps his brother might have gone to see a family friend named Minnie Kohn in Minneapolis, Asle sent her a letter. She said that Andrew had paid her a visit but had only stayed for an hour. She was surprised to hear that he was not back home. But he wasn't. As far as Asle could tell, he'd never left Indiana.

John Huluth, a farmhand who was taking care of Andrew's livestock, had also started to wonder about his employer's whereabouts. Looking around Andrew's house for some clue, he came upon a dozen or so letters, which he promptly turned over to Asle.

All of them were signed "Belle Gunness."

WHILE ASLE HELGELIEN WAS STARTING THE search for his brother, Belle was having problems of her own with Ray Lamphere. What exactly happened between the two of them in early February 1908 is unclear. Some say she fired him, and others say that he quit after an argument about unpaid wages, but whatever happened, it was something bitter. Ray left the farm in such a rush that he left all his clothing and carpenter tools behind.

Less than a week later, Belle hired a replacement, Joe Maxson, to take over management of the farm, take care of chores, feed the animals, and whatever else was needed – although it appears that Joe was never involved in any of Belle's more sinister work on the farm.

In the meantime, Ray had consulted a local attorney, who suggested that he return to the farm, demand his money and belongings, and, if refused, inform Belle that he planned to sue her. He did, and Belle laughed in his face.

Joe Maxson

Not only did she then chase him off the property, but she wrote several letters to the County Sheriff Albert Smutzer, claiming that Ray was harassing her.

Undeterred by threats of arrest and unwilling to leave Belle alone, Ray continued to hang around the farm and was often seen following Belle when she was in town. Alcohol and jealousy turned out to be a bad mix for the squirrely little man. Acting on Belle's complaint that Ray had repeatedly trespassed on her property and had cut down a wire fence, the sheriff arrested him on March 12 for committing an act of harassment.

He was fined $1, a paltry sum that was allegedly given to him by Elizabeth Smith, an African American woman that some of the people in LaPorte accused of practicing voodoo and witchcraft.

Meanwhile, back in the Dakotas, Asle Helgelein was growing increasingly worried about his brother. After confirming with the LaPorte postmaster that Belle Gunness was a resident of the city, he sent a letter to Belle and to the First National Bank, where he'd learned Andrew had deposited his savings in January. He got a letter back from cashier Frank Pitner, who said he had conferred with Mrs. Gunness about Andrew and that she would be in touch with him concerning his brother.

Soon after, Asle received a letter from Belle. She wrote:

You wish to know where your brother keeps himself. Well, this is just what I would like to know but it almost seems impossible for me to give a definite answer.

In a feeble attempt to calm Asle's suspicions, she informed him on March 27, 1908, that Andrew had left LaPorte to search for another of his brothers, a professional gambler who had disappeared in January. After failing to find him in Minneapolis, he stopped briefly in LaPorte before continuing the search. According to Belle, he planned to look for the missing brother in Chicago and New York but feared he'd returned to Norway. If that was the case, Andrew was going to follow him there.

The last time she'd heard from him, she said, was in a letter from Chicago saying that he wouldn't write again until he'd found his brother.

Since then, I have neither heard nor seen anything of him. Now this is all I can say about this matter. I have waited everyday to hear something of him.

While writing letters to Asle Helgelein, Belle was also still dealing with Ray Lamphere. On March 28, she filed a second complaint against him for trespassing. He was fined again – this time $19.

The fine was paid by John Wheatbrook, who owned a farm in Springville, six miles north of LaPorte. He hired Ray to work off the debt on his farm, hopefully keeping him away from Belle and out of trouble.

However, having Ray out of town was not enough to satisfy Belle. With tears in her eyes, she begged the court to issue a peace bond against him, claiming that he followed her around town and showed up at the farm, both day and night, threatening her life. She claimed that Ray was not in his right mind and was a menace to the public. She asked the authorities to hold a sanity hearing for him, stating that she had noticed the "first signs of insanity" in December 1907 when he told her things that were not true and unreasonable. She wrote, "He comes to my house every night, at all times of night. He looks in the windows and commits misdemeanors."

I'm not sure what she meant by "commits misdemeanors" – and I'm not sure I want to – but it's evident in hindsight that Belle was trying to make Ray look insane in case he ever decided to talk about the crimes he'd helped her to commit.

But her attempts to send Ray to an asylum didn't work. Ray's doctor testified that he had never treated him for any kind of mental imbalance and didn't consider him insane. The three-member insanity commission felt the same way. Other than being "slightly nervous," he seemed intelligent, coherent, and not insane.

He was, however, still trespassing on the farm and Belle had him arrested again in early April. His new trial was set for the 15th.

While Belle had her hands full with Ray Lamphere, she was also still fending off prying inquiries from Asle Helgelein. He wanted to see the letter that his brother had supposedly sent Belle from Chicago. Belle replied that she couldn't because it had been stolen by a man named Lamphere, who had worked for her awhile. She added:

This Lamphere began to find so many wrong things to talk about until at least they arrested him, and they had three doctors examine him to see if he was sane. They found him not crazy enough to put in a hospital. But perfectly sane he is not. He is now under bonds and is going to have a trial this week. But one thing I am sure of is that in one way or another he has taken the letter from Andrew, he had sent me. Others have told me that Lamphere was jealous of Andrew and for that reason, troubled me this way.

Not only was Belle trying to make Ray look insane, but she was also laying the groundwork to set him up for murder if necessary.

At Ray's new trial, he retained the service of local attorney Wirth Worden, and during his cross-examination of Belle, Worden, trying to undercut her credibility, launched into a series of increasingly hostile questions about her past.

He asked Belle: "Peter Gunness, your husband, died very suddenly, didn't he?

The state's attorney, Ralph Smith, was immediately on his feet. "Objection!"

"He carried a considerable life insurance policy, didn't he?" Worden went on.

"Objection!" Smith shouted again.

"You collected that life insurance, didn't you?"

Smith, angrier by the minute, told Belle that she didn't have to answer that.

But Worden went on: "Mrs. Gunness, how did that sausage grinder come to drop on Mr. Gunness' head anyway?"

Smith was now enraged. He demanded that Judge Robert Kincaid stop the defense attorney from browbeating and insulting a defenseless woman.

If there was one thing that Belle was not – it was defenseless. But legally, he had a point. But Wirt Worden didn't care. He kept after her, asking about Mads Sorenson, how he'd died, and if he'd also had a life insurance policy.

The judge had sustained all of Smith's objections, but Worden kept asking questions about Mads' death and whether there was talk of exhuming his body to see if he'd been poisoned.

Smith continued to be outraged. "I object to these questions! They have nothing to do with this case. I demand they be stopped!" Then he turned to the witness stand and said to Belle, "Mrs. Gunness, you would be justified in waylaying this man on his way home!"

But Judge Kincaid finally stepped in and noted that the questions had gone too far.

Wirt Worden seemed to regret what he'd done and started to dismiss the witness – but then he turned around and asked one more startling question. "Oh, just a moment. When will your daughter, Jennie Olson, return, Mrs. Gunness?"

Belle was told not to answer, and the judge brought the cross-examination to an end.

It was obvious when she left the stand that she was visibly agitated. Ray Lamphere had been talking to his attorney. He knew too much. Between Ray and the fear that had been aroused by Asle Helgelein's inquiries into his brother's whereabouts – Belle's crimes finally seemed to be catching up with her.

DURING THE TRIAL, ANOTHER LETTER arrived from Asle Helgelein. She replied to him on April 24, saying that Andrew's whereabouts were as great of a mystery to her as they were to Asle. It was very strange to her that a man would go away without all his belongings. She told Asle that Andrew was no longer in LaPorte and boldly suggested that if he wanted to come to Indiana and look for this brother, she would help conduct a search.

However, she cautioned him that hunting for a missing person was often an expensive proposition. If she were to be involved in such an endeavor, Asle would have to pay her for her efforts.

Eventually, Asle would come to Indiana, but when he did, it would not be to search for this brother – it would be to identify his corpse.

Despite her daring words to Asle Helgelein, Belle was worried. Ray Lamphere still represented a danger to her, and Asle was making inquiries that could potentially send her to the gallows. There wasn't much she could do to control Asle, but she could fix Ray Lamphere.

Miss Bertha Schultz – a clerk at the Chicago Leader dry goods store in LaPorte who frequently waited on Belle – later reported that Belle had come into the store during the last week in April looking very distressed. When Bertha asked what was troubling her, she recounted her troubles with Ray Lamphere.

She returned the next day, once again talking about how Ray was harassing her and prowling around her farm. Bertha would say afterward, "She told me she feared he would someday set fire to her home and building and that he would murder her and her children."

And it wasn't just the dry goods store. Clerks at the hardware store also told similar stories about Belle and her problems with Ray Lamphere. So did a teller at the bank, a waitress in a restaurant, a man at the feed store. The stories were going around.

On April 27, Belle showed up in the office of her attorney, Melvin E. Leliter, and tearfully informed him that she wanted to draw up a will. She feared for her life and the lives of her children because Ray Lamphere had threatened to kill her and burn her house down.

The attorney advised her that the simplest way to deal with Ray was to "fill him full of buckshot" the next time he showed up at the farm uninvited, but Belle dismissed this suggestion. She wanted to make sure her last will and testament was in place in case Ray made good on his threats.

Leliter wrote out the document according to Belle's instructions. She appointed Wesley Fogle, a local farm implement dealer from whom she had purchased tools and equipment the previous year, to serve as the executor of her estate. Belle left all her property to her children – Myrtle, Lucy, and Phillip. Jennie Olsen – who was allegedly in California attending school – was never mentioned.

Once the will was finished and signed, Belle took it to the State Bank, where she placed it in a safe deposit box and made a cash deposit of $730.

Her next errand was at a store where she purchased candy, cake, and a toy train. She told the clerk that she was going to give her children a little treat.

"Is it a birthday?" the clerk asked.

"No," Belle said. "I am just going to give them a little surprise."

Belle's last stop that afternoon was at John Minich's general store, where she purchased groceries for that evening's dinner. She also bought something else – two gallons of kerosene in a five-gallon can that she borrowed from the store's owner. She said she had searched for her own can before she left home but hadn't been able to find it.

Belle was carefully setting the stage for the final act to follow.

AFTER HER STOPS IN TOWN, BELLE WENT HOME. She got there around 5:30. It was already dark. Joe Maxson helped her carry her purchases inside. He placed the can of kerosene oil in the entry, under the back stairs.

An hour later, the family sat down to supper – bread and butter, salmon, beefsteak, and potatoes. Cookies and jam followed it.

When the meal was done and the table was cleared, the whole family – including Joe – went into the parlor to play games. By 8:30, Joe was having trouble staying awake. He was usually up every morning before dawn to take care of chores. He said good night to everyone and headed for the stairway.

Joe later recalled, "The last I saw of Mrs. Gunness, she was sitting on the floor with her daughters and son, playing with a toy engine and passenger coaches that she had bought earlier that day for the children."

Officially, that's the last time that Belle Gunness was ever seen alive. Unofficially, though, that may be a different story.

MRS. GUNNESS WAS ALREADY UP AND COOKING breakfast.

That was Joe's first thought as he woke up later that night. From the smell, though, it seemed the hotcakes were burning.

He wearily swung his legs out of bed and reached for his pants, which were hanging on the post at the end of the bed. As he did so, he saw tendrils of smoke sifting up between the floorboards from the kitchen below. More smoke was drifting under the bedroom door.

Joe was suddenly wide awake. There wasn't anything burning on the stove – the house was on fire! He stumbled to the window, trying to put his pants on, and threw it open. He was right – the house was burning. He yanked on his boots and tried to yell, "Fire!" but the smoke was so thick he could hardly breathe.

He stumbled blindly to the door and pulled it open. Smoke filled the hallway, and the ominous flicker of flames could be seen farther down the hall. He called out as loudly as he could for Belle and the children, but there was no answer. Belle's room was just steps away. The room was always kept locked, and while he had been forbidden to enter, Joe kicked at the door with all his strength. It shuddered on its frame, but it refused to open.

Choking on the smoke, he raced down the rear stairs, clutching a satchel that held most of his belongings. He ran to the carriage shed that was about 50 feet from the house, tossed his belongings inside, and ran back to the burning house. He tried to get back upstairs, but the flames drove him outside.

He called loudly for Belle and the children, shouting their names and pounding on windows. There was still no response. In the thick smoke, and from what he could see through the windows, no one was moving inside.

Joe continued to run around the house, calling for help. He explained later, "I was yelling to attract the attention of Mrs. Gunness and the children, but I didn't hear any sound except the roaring of the fire. I picked up bricks and threw them in the windows, but no one showed up."

Not far away, Mrs. Ella Clifford rose as usual at 4:00 A.M. to make breakfast for her husband, Michael, who left for work before daybreak. Looking out the window, she saw their neighbor's house on fire. She called to her teenage son, William, rousing him from his sleep. Within minutes, he was on his bicycle, pedaling furiously toward the Gunness house to wake up everyone there if he could.

His father, Michael, and uncle, William Humphrey, also ran toward the Gunness farm. When they arrived, they found Joe Maxson standing helplessly by the front door with an ax in his hands. He managed to chop a hole in the front door – just before the ceiling in the parlor collapsed.

"Where do they sleep?" Humphrey asked, yelling to be heard over the roar of the fire.

Joe pointed to two upstairs windows on the west side of the house. Humphrey found some loose bricks and hurled them up at the windows. The glass shattered, and flames spurted out, but no one responded from inside.

"Is there a ladder around here?" Humphrey called to Joe, who immediately ran for the woodshed.

He returned a moment later, dragging a ladder. With Michael and William on one side, Humphrey scaled the rungs and peered into the broken window. There was an empty bed in the corner – just a mattress, no sheets, and no bodies. The fire was coming through the floor.

Hurrying down, they moved the ladder to the second window, and Humphrey climbed up again. He saw nothing but another empty bed. He thought of climbing inside, but seeing the flames between the floorboards, he decided against it.

Humphrey then sent his nephew to alert Daniel Hutson, who lived with his family a short distance away. Roused from bed by

Michael pounding on his door, Daniel went to the door, still in his nightshirt.

"Are you going to let your neighbors burn while you sleep?" the young man demanded – which seemed unusually harsh at 4:00 A.M.

Daniel looked in the direction the boy was pointing and saw the Gunness house was ablaze. He threw on some clothes and rushed toward it, not even stopping to tie his shoes. When he reached the house, he saw there was nothing he and the others could do. The house was completely engulfed in flames. He turned to Joe Maxson and told him that he had better notify Sheriff Smutzer. They got four horses hooked up to a wagon, and Joe raced off into the early morning darkness.

Joe later said he wasn't sure what time he arrived at the jail but thought it was just before 5:00. Deputy Sheriff William Antiss was handling the desk, and when Joe told his story, he accompanied him to the sheriff's house a few blocks away.

After rousing the sheriff, Joe and Deputy Antiss hurried back to the Gunness farm. Sheriff Smutzer followed in his red Ford automobile, arriving just ahead of the volunteer fire brigade.

There was nothing they could do either.

By the time they arrived, only parts of three walls were still standing. They could do nothing but watch until the flames died down. After that, the fire brigade threw buckets of water on the embers until they started to cool down.

By then, at least 50 of the morbid curious had gathered at the scene. That number would soon grow into the hundreds.

Though the blaze had burned itself down by daybreak, heat from the smoldering ruins kept the sheriff and everyone else at a distance. Finally, a bucket brigade tossed enough cold water on it that it was cool enough to approach. By the cellar door, the men saw signs of a fire that was so concentrated that it had to be man-made – it was the work of an "incendiary," they said, what an "arsonist" was called at the time.

Rumors spread through the crowd that perhaps the eccentric Belle had lost her mind and started the fire herself. But Sheriff Smutzer and others, who knew the details of her ugly feud with Ray Lamphere, thought otherwise.

They were firmly convinced that Ray had burned down the house in revenge.

Sheriff Albert Smutzer

Sheriff Smutzer assigned two of his men to find the former farmhand while the sheriff and about a dozen volunteers began making plans to search the blackened ruins for the bodies of Belle Gunness and her children.

As preparations were made, the corps, under the direction of Chief Thomas Whorwell, used ladders, ropes, and hooks to tear down the still-smoking walls of the house so that searchers could work in the ruins without fear of a brick falling on their heads.

With Sheriff Smutzer leading the way, the men began digging through the cellars while firemen did their best to cool off the smoldering ruins of the once-fine house with buckets of water.

The ruins remained a hotbed of coals, from which smoke and steam continued to rise. After hours of labor, the men found little more than pieces of blankets, bed frames, blackened tools, and even an old pistol, but nothing else. They began to wonder if the remains of the family were even in the ruins.

Only one area – the southeast corner -- remained unexplored. The men were shoveling through the wreckage there around 3:45 in the afternoon when they made a gruesome discovery.

"Here they are," one of the men said to Sheriff Smutzer.

Newspaper stories that appeared the following day presented a heroic death scene of a mother who tried valiantly to save her children from the flames. A blanket had been wrapped around the little boy, Phillip, which made his corpse the least gruesome of the four. Even so, his face was blackened, and his legs had been burned away below the knees.

The bodies of the two sisters were lying perfectly on each side of their mother. They had also been burned to death. Their bodies were two nearly unrecognizable masses of scorched flesh and bone.

But it was Belle whom newspapers described as presenting the "most ghastly appearance." Her body was so badly burned that bones protruded through her flesh. Most appalling was what wasn't with her body – her head. It was surmised that it had been burned away by the fire, which sent the diggers on a search for whatever remained of her skull.

Ruins of the Gunness house after the fire.

The four corpses were removed from the debris and placed on boards until the town's undertaker, Austin Cutler, could arrive with his wagon. After that, they'd be taken to the morgue.

A local reporter wrote that the only glimmer of good news about the fire was that one member of the family had escaped the blaze – Belle's adopted daughter, Jennie. As he wrote, "Even now, she is on her way from California to this city. She is expected to arrive here in a day or two, and it is thought she might be able to throw some light on this mystery.

But Jennie was a lot closer than anyone thought.

Volunteers and law enforcement officers searching the ruins of the house for clues.

And the mystery of Belle Gunness was a lot bigger than anyone could have imagined.

THOUGH REPORTS CLAIMED THAT RAY LAMPHERE had "disappeared" on the morning of the fire, he hadn't. The previous night, Ray had shown up at the cabin of Elizabeth Smith, the alleged "voodoo woman," where he sometimes stayed. She let him in to sleep off the booze, and then early the next morning, he headed out to John Wheatbrook's farm, where he'd been working.

He was still there when Deputies Leroy Marr and William Antiss showed up that afternoon. When they reached the front gate, he went out to talk to them, and Deputy Marr told him to get his coat and come to town with them.

If Deputy Marr had any doubts that the little farmhand had some involvement in the fire, they were dispelled by the first words out of Ray's mouth. "Did those three children and the woman get out of the fire?" he asked.

Asked how he knew about the fire, he said that he just happened to be passing the Gunness farm that morning and noticed fire and smoke billowing from the roof. Ray didn't stop to help, nor did he notify any neighbors. He just kept walking. He said that if anyone knew he was there, he'd likely get blamed for it.

And he was right.

Sheriff Smutzer knew all about Ray's alleged threats against Belle and her children – almost everyone in town did. Her attorney, M.E. Leliter, came forward and told the sheriff about

Belle's will and how she feared that Lamphere would kill her family and burn down her house.

Ray was taken to the county jail, where he was subjected to the first of what would be a string of "sweatings," as interrogations were often called at the time. They were conducted by Deputies Antiss and Marr, Sheriff Smutzer, and State's Attorney Ralph Smith, who had hurried to the jail when he heard about Ray's arrest.

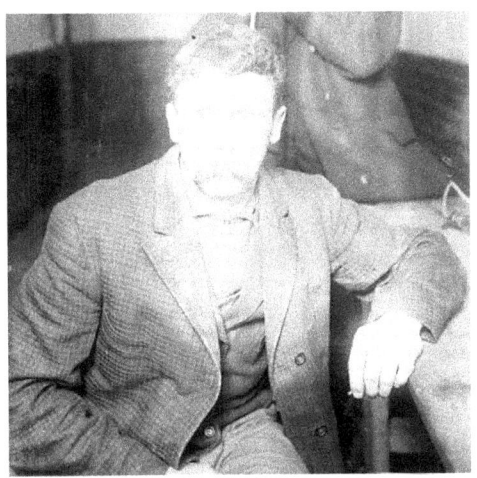

Ray Lamphere – in trouble again. He was now accused of killing Belle and her children.

Ray stuck to his story. He swore that he didn't start the fire. He offered Liz Smith as his alibi. Liz – who was once known as one of the loveliest women in town and one who had won the hearts of many men, not all of whom were black – was now in her 70s, and any beauty she'd once had was long gone. She was frail, hunched over, and scarecrow-like. Many in town, primarily children, believed she was a witch and a so-called "voodoo woman." But Liz's advanced age and physical infirmities seemed to make no difference to Ray Lamphere, a man who was apparently blessed with very flexible standards for feminine beauty.

Liz did confirm Ray's whereabouts at the time of the fire, but this did little to dispel the almost universal belief in his guilt. Newspapers all over the Midwest branded him a "maniac," a "homicidal firebug," and a man whose mad infatuation with Belle Gunness drove him to set her house ablaze because she didn't reciprocate his passions. It was hinted that some people in town were making plans that would end with Ray's lynching.

Repeated questioning of Ray failed to produce a confession, so Sheriff Smutzer resorted to another time-honored technique for breaking a suspect – he put cuffs on Ray and took him to the Cutler funeral home to see the bodies of the Gunness family.

Confronted with the hideously charred remains of Belle and her children, Ray turned pale and began to tremble. "My god," he gasped.

"There is some of your work," the sheriff said to him. "What do you think of it?"

"Awful..." Ray managed to say. He seemed about to collapse.

Deeply shaken, Ray was hustled back out to the car and taken directly to court for his arraignment. He was charged with arson and four counts of murder. After pleading not guilty, he was ordered held without bond and returned to his cell to await the actions of the circuit court grand jury, which was scheduled to meet in May.

IN THE MEANTIME, MEN WERE STILL DIGGING through the rubble of the house, searching for Belle's missing skull. Rumors swirled that Ray had decapitated Belle to steal the gold in her teeth, but Sheriff Smutzer scoffed at this idea, saying it wouldn't be worth the money or the trouble.

The postmortem exam confirmed his opinion. A team of doctors, led by Dr. J. Lucius Gray, concluded that Belle's head had not been cut off before death. It was believed that the ferocity of the fire had burned her head from her neck, but he admitted it could have been cut off after the woman had died.

Regardless, the head – or at least the skull – should be in the ruins of the basement. It was just a matter of time before they found it, everyone thought.

Volunteers and local officials continued to search through the rubble of the house.

While they were searching, Asle Helgelien came back into the picture. He was still looking for his brother, Andrew, and knew he'd been in LaPorte. He had written again to Frank Pitner, the cashier at the First National Bank who'd handled Andrew's affairs, and he sent him a photograph of his brother. Frank had quickly written him back and assured him that Andrew was, without a doubt, the man who had come into the bank with Belle Gunness to cash some certificates of deposit.

On Friday, May 1, Asle received another envelope from Frank Pitner. Inside was the front page of the LaPorte newspapers for April 28, reporting on the fiery destruction of the Gunness house and the deaths of its occupants. Asle packed his bags and, the next day was on his way back to Indiana.

He arrived on May 3 and checked into a hotel in town. His next stop was the local newspaper office, where he purchased all the back issues from the date of the fire until that day, poring over them for the next hour. He then went to the office of Sheriff Al Smutzer, who listened to his story and then drove him out to the Gunness farm.

At that point, only two men were digging in the rubble – Belle's hired hand, Joe Maxson, and her neighbor, Daniel Hutson. Asle, who wondered if the farm could offer any clue as to his brother's fate, decided to lend a hand. They didn't know what they were looking for – aside from Belle's missing head, that is.

They didn't have much luck, only uncovering charred debris. However, that night, Asle accepted the hospitality of other neighbors, the Swan Nicholson family, who were happy to feed and shelter a fellow Norwegian. When Asle returned to work at the Gunness farm early the next day, he found Joe and Daniel already shoveling through the ruins of the cellar.

Asle decided to look around the rest of the property, hoping to see something suspicious. He didn't find anything. There was a small lake on the property, and he wondered whether a body could be sunk in it. But Joe told him the lake had been a solid sheet of ice all winter, before and after Andrew Helgelein had been there.

Discouraged, Asle decided there wasn't much point in continuing to wander around the farm. If he were to find clues to his brother's whereabouts, they wouldn't be in LaPorte. He said goodbye to the other men and started to walk back to town. He didn't get far, though. He had an idea and ran back to ask Joe

In search of the men who'd come to the farm and never left, volunteers began in areas of the farm where Belle told Joe Maxson she wanted to bury some garbage.

about it. Did Joe remember any holes being dug on the property that spring?

As a matter of fact, he did. Sometime back in March – he didn't recall the exact date – he had helped Belle load up a wheelbarrow with old cans, shoes, and other garbage, and they hauled it to a pit that had been dug in a fenced-off section of the yard that was used as a hog pen, about 50 feet from the house. At Belle's direction, he'd dumped in the rubbish and filled the hole. Asle asked Joe to show him the spot, and the three men, shovels in hand, headed for the yard and started to dig.

It wasn't long before they were slapped in the face by a terrible smell. Joe said that Belle had thrown out a lot of tomato and fish cans with that garbage, and maybe that explained the stink. But Asle didn't think so. The rank odor that rose from the pit smelled nothing like rotting tomatoes and old fish.

Their shovels found the source of the smell about four feet down. It was hard and wrapped in a gunny sack. There was a rip in the fabric, and they peered inside. It was the side of a man's head, and next to the bag in the dirt was a man's severed arm.

Joe Maxson was, once more, racing to town to fetch the sheriff. Meanwhile, Asle found some clean gunny sacks in the barn and laid them over their grisly find. Then, he and Daniel picked up their shovels and cleared away more of the dirt in the makeshift grave.

They had just widened the hole when Sheriff Smutzer arrived with Coroner Charles Mack. Under his watchful eye, the men carefully raised the decomposing body out of the earth. The head had been separated from the torso, and each arm had been cut away. The legs had been cut off below the knee. The face – or what remained of it – was, in the words of one of the men, "a thing of horror." It had sunken holes for eyes, a hash for a mouth, and a jagged crack from the top of the skull to the forehead.

Whoever the man had been, he had fought hard for his life. The body was cut with deep blows, and defensive wounds marked his hands and arms. In one mutilated hand was clenched a clump of brown hair that had been ripped from the head of his murderer.

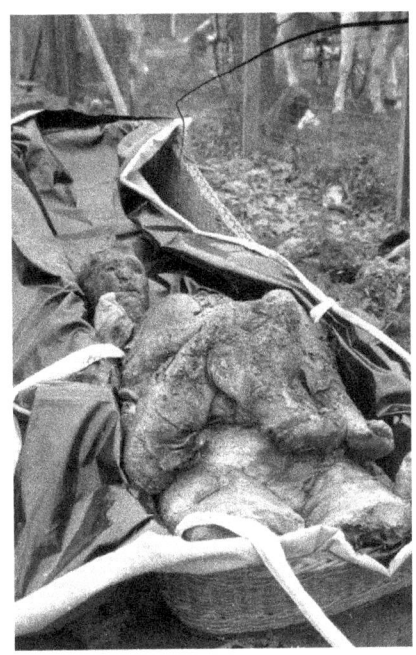

Andrew Helgelein's body was the first one found buried on the farm.

The ghastly face – looking more like a bizarre mask than anything human – still had enough of its features to make identification possible.

When Asle Helgelein looked down into the face of the dead man, he saw the familiar features of his own brother. His search for Andrew had finally come to an end in a trash pit in Belle Gunness' farmyard.

AFTER THE HORRIFIC DISCOVERY OF Andrew's remains, Sheriff Smutzer reluctantly asked Joe Maxson if he knew of any other places on the property where holes had been dug and covered with dirt. Joe's hand shook as he pointed to another spot a short distance away.

As more remains were discovered, the digging continued. Word began to spread and soon, small groups of curiosity-seekers started arriving at the farm – there would be many more to come.

A drizzling rain had started to fall on the farm. While they had been digging, a small crowd of curiosity seekers had gathered, peering over the fence and trying to catch a glimpse of the macabre scene as Joe, Daniel, and the sheriff started to dig.

Three feet down, beneath another pile of rubbish, they found a jumble of decomposing body parts – naked torsos wrapped in burlap, heads, arms, legs, hands, and feet scattered around.

The buggy shed was turned into a makeshift morgue, and before sundown, the putrefied remains of four more victims were found. The bodies, deteriorated by quicklime, were unwrapped to reveal they were two men, an adult woman and an adolescent female. The coroner was unable to determine a cause of death, and all were in terrible condition.

Only one body had a distinguishing feature -- the body of the young woman. A long, matted bundle of blond hair was still clinging to a fleshless skull.

Jennie Olsen had not been sent away to school in California. She had not gotten married and gone on a honeymoon, as some claimed. She was not on her way back to LaPorte by train. She had never left. She had been chopped up into a half-dozen pieces and then dumped in a trash pit in her foster mother's hog pen.

Her body had been discovered on May 5, 1908 – the date that would have been Jennie's 18th birthday.

While the people of LaPorte were stunned into shocked silence by the murders in their own backyard, the newspapers went ballistic. The Gunness case became front-page news all over America and even overseas. Newspapermen flocked to the small community, setting up headquarters in the town's only hotel and cranking out stories that were being printed everywhere.

Overnight, Belle – at first praised for trying to save her children from the flames – was transformed into a monster. The *Chicago American* newspaper branded her as both "the most fiendish murderer of the age" and "the most fiendish murderess in history."

That same newspaper would go on to help create a mystery that has plagued the story of Belle Gunness ever since. It suggested that, with as diabolically cunning as Belle was, wasn't it possible that the headless body found in the ruined cellar wasn't Belle at all? Was it another of her victims left behind in her place?

What if – maybe, just maybe – Belle Gunness was still alive?

ONE PERSON WHO THOUGHT THIS IDEA WAS worth considering was Ray Lamphere, who had just been informed of Sheriff Smutzer's discoveries on the farm.

"My god," Ray gasped. "I knew the woman was bad, but nothing like this."

When Ray was taken from his cell to speak to reporters, he insisted he knew nothing of Belle's crimes. Whether this was true or not is open to debate, but that's what he told the press. He did hint that he suspected some things about Belle's activities, though.

When he was asked to elaborate, he told of a time after Andrew Helgelein's arrival when Belle sent him into town to buy some rat poison. Another time, he said, she sent him to buy chloroform. He also mentioned that he knew some of the men who came to visit the farm suddenly left without taking their trunks and suitcases with them.

But he didn't kill anyone, Ray insisted, not Belle, not her children, and not anyone found buried on her farm. He didn't know what happened to Andrew Helgelein either. He just knew that Belle had once gotten mad at him for talking to Andrew. He told the reporters that she had come into the house and found the two of them chatting in the sitting room. Belle got angry at

Ray and told him to never speak to Andrew again. "I told her I'd speak to him if I felt like it," Ray recalled.

A few days later, Ray was at the farm, and Andrew was gone. When he asked Belle about him, she said that she'd told him that he'd never talk to Andrew again.

"I didn't know what she meant," he told the reporters, "but now I understand."

AFTER THE STORY OF WHAT THE PRESS WAS SOON calling the "Murder Farm," hit the papers, more and more people started showing up in LaPorte. The road leading out to the farm was so choked with buggies, wagons, bicycles, and people on foot that Sheriff Smutzer had trouble getting through the traffic when he returned to the scene.

A massive crowd of men, women, and children – a number that would eventually grow into the thousands – surrounded the hog lot fence, eager for a glimpse of the next horror to come out of the ground.

They didn't have to wait long.

The sheriff, along with Joe Maxson, Daniel Hutson, and a few other men with strong stomachs who had been recruited for the search, started digging at a spot about five feet from the scene of the previous day's discovery. Almost immediately, their spades pierced the earth, and a noxious smell flooded their noses. A few people a dozen feet away groaned in shock. About three feet down, they found the butchered remains of another victim. More rotting burlap was clinging to a rib cage, pelvis, and spine. A skull – with a large gash in it – as well as some sawed-off leg bones were a few feet away.

After this discovery, the men somehow managed to stop and eat lunch before returning to their task.

Within 30 minutes, they found an abandoned spot where an outhouse had once stood. In the muck, they found more than a dozen pairs of men's shoes. Under the shoes were a tangle of human bones.

There were three bodies in the hole. They had been wrapped in burlap and so poorly covered in quicklime that pieces of decaying flesh were still on the bones. The bones had been hacked apart by an ax. Such force had been used to cut them that the bones were crushed where they had been

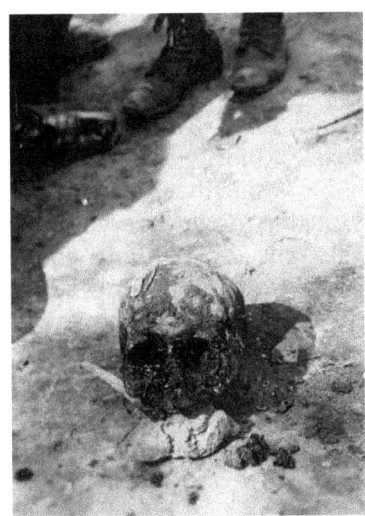

Skulls, bones, piece of bodies – all began turning up around the farm. With no way to identify all of them, the carriage house on the farm was turned into storage for the various remains.

separated. Two of the skulls were near each other. They had been buried face up. Quicklime had been spread on their faces and stuffed in their ears. It was impossible to tell if they were men or women, let alone who they might have been.

The relics were placed in buckets and carried to the buggy shed morgue from which, one reporter noted, "there was such a stench that even more most resolute curiosity seeker is daunted."

Added to the five bodies from the previous day, the latest discoveries brought the death toll from Belle's hog lot to nine.

The newspapers were still having a field day, especially those in Chicago, which was so close to LaPorte. They printed sensational stories, lurid tales, half-truths, and outright lies, suggesting that members of Chicago organized crime had been dumping bodies on Belle's farm. There was no real evidence of this, but it was a good story, and when a reporter convinced Assistant Police Chief Herman Schuettler to consider the idea, the papers decided that he had endorsed it.

The suggestion that Belle had accomplices in Chicago also helped push the idea that she might still be alive, especially after an unnamed witness was interviewed stating that he had spotted a "cloaked figure" boarding the Chicago train from LaPorte on the morning of April 28, the day of the fire. The press speculated that Belle might have met up with one of her accomplices and was now hiding out in Chicago, waiting for a chance to escape to Norway.

A massive hunt was launched for the murderess in the Windy City. Every depot, post office, express office, hotel, and train station was soon under watch by the police.

While the police searched for the fugitive, reporters began tracking down everyone who knew Belle while she was living in the city, looking into the death of Mads Sorensen and anyone else who died suspiciously during that time. Assistant Chief Schuettler, going along with the idea that she might be hiding in Chicago, ordered an immediate investigation into the records of all missing persons who vanished from the Austin neighborhood while she'd lived there. Meeting with reporters, he announced that his men were going to dig up the backyard of the home that Belle and Mads had shared on Alma Street. "We confidently expect to find bodies in this yard," he told the newspapermen.

They didn't.

But, they did manage to link Belle to a business that might explain all the random babies and young children who were in and out of her house while she was in Chicago. In the late nineteenth and early twentieth centuries, unwed women, prostitutes, or women with too many children to care for often consigned newborns to caregivers who, for a monthly fee, would provide a home for the babies or find them suitable families for adoption.

They called them "baby farmers," and while some of them treated the children in their care well, most were utterly callous and sought to maximize their profits by supplying the babies with the bare minimum of care.

Some did even worse things.

There were many cases of women who murdered the children in their care after accepting the money to find them a good home. Chicago authorities became convinced this was what Belle had been involved in – taking in babies for cash until they could be conveniently put out of the way.

There were many bodies discovered on Belle's farm – none of which had been dropped off there by gangsters -- but if we add in the children who may have died by her hand, the actual number of her victims may be so high that it will never be known.

A DRENCHING RAIN FELL ON THE FARM on May 7, putting the digging on hold. With the grim work suspended, Sheriff Smutzer traveled to Chicago to confer with more experienced lawmen.

He was still away when a messenger arrived at the jail and told Deputy Antiss that a pair of men had broken into the locked buggy shed on the Gunness farm, where the exhumed bodies and bones were stored. He hurried to the farm and was met by Joe Maxson, who told him that he'd seen two men fleeing out the shed's back window. He couldn't see much of them in the heavy rain, but he'd called out to them. They replied that they were doctors and had a right to go inside. Joe knew they were lying and sent one of the neighbor boys into town to alert the sheriff. By the time Antiss arrived, they were long gone.

Rumors, of course, spread through town that the two men had been Belle's accomplices, who'd been sent to destroy evidence against her, stealing several bottles of poison and mixing up the bones to prevent identification of the bodies.

The truth turned out to be much less exciting – they were just a couple of curiosity-seekers who wanted to sneak a look at the gruesome relics found on the farm.

Around 1:30 that afternoon, just before Sheriff Smutzer returned to town, two young men arrived in LaPorte from Iola, Wisconsin. They were accompanied by an older man, a hardware dealer named Edwin Chapin.

The two younger men were Mathias and Oscar Budsberg, Wisconsin farmers. They had read about the terrible discoveries at the "Murder Farm" and were now in town on a somber mission --- they needed to view a human skull thought to be that of their father, Ole Budsberg.

Fourteen months earlier, Ole – a 51-year-old widower and subscriber to a few Scandinavian newspapers – told his sons that he was taking a trip to LaPorte to see about managing a farm there. To his brother, though, he told a different story – he was going there to marry a wealthy widow.

He left Iola on the third week of March 1907, returning a week later to settle his affairs before moving to Indiana. He sold his farm to his son, Mathias, for $1,000, and on April 7, with cash from the sale and an additional $1,000 mortgage note on some

Wisconsin farmer Ole Budsberg turned out to be another victim of Belle Gunness.

other land he owned, he left town by train, assuring his sons he'd write as soon as he got settled.

The following day, Ole showed up at the First National Bank in LaPorte and requested that the money from his mortgage note be sent there from Wisconsin. He was back on April 16 to pick up the money – with Belle Gunness. The cashier who assisted him, J.W. Crumpacker, said it was the last time that he had ever seen Ole Budsberg.

By late April, having never received any word from his father, Mathias sent a letter to the only address he had for the Gunness farm. It was returned to him as undeliverable. In the meantime, a payment had come due on Ole's mortgage note. A cashier at the Farmers State Bank in Iola sent an inquiry letter to cashier J.W. Crumpacker in LaPorte, who had to admit that he had not seen Mr. Budsberg lately.

He passed the letter on to the bank president, who took it upon himself to drive out to the Gunness farm to see if Ole was there. Belle answered his knock at the door but didn't invite him inside. She had no idea where Budsberg was. During a visit to Chicago, she explained he'd been robbed of all his money, which caused him to decide to go out west and try to earn back what he'd lost. She couldn't remember the date but said she had taken him to the train depot, where he bought a ticket for Oregon. That was the last she'd seen of him.

A letter was sent to the bank officers in Iola, informing them of what they knew. That seemed to be the end of the story – until the fire at the Gunness farm and the discovery of the bodies. Assistant cashier Crumpacker quickly sent an envelope stuffed with newspaper clippings to the bank in Iola, and they had notified the Budsberg brothers. Fearing the worst, Mathias and Oscar had set out at once for LaPorte.

Deputy Antiss drove the Wisconsin men out to the Gunness farm around 2:00 that afternoon. Despite the bad weather, 20 or so local men – drawn by the quickly spreading story about the break-in – were gathered to stand guard around the buggy shed. When Antiss led the men into the foul-smelling building, several of the volunteers followed them inside.

By the dim glow of an oil lamp, Mathias and Oscar looked over the wooden planks that held the remains dug out of the barnyard. Atop one mass of bones was the skull they had come to see. They bent close to look it over.

Though the head retained few recognizable features, there was no mistaking its distinctive facial hair – a long, red mustache that dropped down over its fleshless mouth.

When they saw it, the two brothers straightened up, exchanged a grim look, and then pushed their way out of the shed and into the fresh air. They stood aside, engaged in a short, whispered conversation, and they walked over to Deputy Antiss, who was waiting for them.

"It's him," Mathias said. "I sure of it. It's what we feared."

The Budsberg sons had found their father.

SHERIFF SMUTZER'S TRIP TO CHICAGO HAD been a fruitful one, even if it didn't lead to any more clues about the case. The newspapers were still spreading sensational theories about Belle, but Assistant Chief Herman Schuettler had changed his mind about Belle's connections to organized crime. After speaking with the sheriff, he realized that Belle had been personally acquainted with everyone discovered dead on the farm.

But Chief Schuettler was still convinced that Belle was alive. "I cannot believe she is dead," he told the press. "She was too expert of a criminal to be caught that way. She may well be in Chicago."

Schuettler wasn't alone in this belief. An acquaintance of Belle's had reported to the police that she had seen her on board a North Clark streetcar at Summerdale Avenue. Just a day before that, several witnesses claimed they had encountered her around Wabash Avenue in Chicago's South Loop. One of them was a druggist named Al Levi, who had a store in the Commercial Hotel Building at Wabash and Harrison Street. After seeing her photograph in the *Chicago Tribune*, he contacted the paper and told them that she had come into his store and bought morphine within four or five days *after* the Gunness house had burned. He had been certain it was her.

Convinced now that Belle's murders had been confined to her Indiana farm, Chief Schuettler called off plans to search for missing persons in the Austin neighborhood and called off the digging at the Alma Street house. But his decision failed to reach a gang of reporters with shovels who showed up there. Before they could dig, though, they were confronted by the current owners – two burly plumbers from Wisconsin. They firmly convinced the reporters to leave.

Schuettler's belief that Belle cheated death was also shared by LaPorte's mayor, Lemuel Darrow – a cousin of soon-to-be-famous lawyer Clarence Darrow – and his police chief, Clinton Cochrane.

Sheriff Smutzer and Prosecutor Smith, of course, were adamant that she was dead. They had to be. To admit otherwise would destroy the case they'd built against Ray Lamphere for arson and murder.

BY FRIDAY MORNING, MAY 8, THE FLOODING that had been falling for the past 36 hours finally slowed to a drizzle. At daylight, a great caravan of buggies, wagons, and assorted conveyances began making their way toward the "Murder Farm." By 8:00 A.M., more than 1,000 men, women, and children had arrived to watch the grave hunting resume.

Locating a spot where the earth seemed soft not far from the pit they'd uncovered on Wednesday, Sheriff Smutzer, Joe Maxson, Daniel Hutson, and a few others started their task. The wet soil turned easily under their spades. It only took a half hour to strike something solid – a rotting wooden box.

Inside were rotting pieces of burlap that had once been wrapped around the tangled pieces of bone and flesh in the box. One skull was on top. It still had strands of dark hair clinging to it.

The bones were brought to the surface and examined by Coroner Mack. Like all the other victims, they had been carved up before they were buried. Arms and legs had been severed to make concealment easier. From the size of the bones, Mack concluded the remains were an adult male – even though two pairs of women's shoes had been tossed into the box with the body.

The mystery of the women's shoes was solved a few minutes later. Digging in the same hole, Daniel Hutson soon turned up another tangle of bones. Smutzer suggested they were the bones of the same person, but Coroner Mack said it was impossible – "if those bones belonged to the same person, you'd have a monstrosity, someone 10 or 12 feet high," he said. Mack's expert eye told him the second skeleton was that of a woman.

Placed in separate buckets, the two skeletons – the tenth and eleventh to be found – were taken to the buggy shed to join the rotted remains of Belle's other victims.

THE GRUESOME FINDS AT THE "MURDER FARM" continued to make front-page headlines across America. Relatives and friends from all over the Midwest hurried to LaPorte, further adding to the chaos at the farm. Local police officials began to be flooded with letters from people who also feared their missing loved ones had ended up in the mud of Belle's hog lot.

The letters often spoke of lonesome fathers, brothers, uncles, and cousins who had vanished after going away to meet with possible fiancées. Some of them even spoke of Belle Gunness by name. Others simply hoped for answers, unsure of whether the missing had gone to Indiana or not.

William Stern, a Philadelphia saloonkeeper, wrote to ask about his employee Charles Neiberg, a recent immigrant from Sweden who had dreamed of marrying a wealthy widow. He spent all his time answering matrimonial ads, Stern said. He had vanished in June 1906, telling his employer that he was going to Indiana to marry a widow with a large farm. He had left his bicycle and a trunk of clothing behind, saying that he would send for them when he was married. Stern never heard from him again.

Another letter came from G.R. Burk of Tuscola, Illinois, asking about a former farmhand named George Bradley. The previous October, Bradley had announced that he planned to marry a widow who owned a nice farm near LaPorte. He sold about $1,500 worth of property and left for Indiana. He left some books and clothing behind with Mr. Burk, saying he would come back for it, but he never did.

The wife of Benjamin Carling, an agent for the Prudential Life Insurance Company in Chicago, sent a pleading letter about her husband, who had gone to LaPorte the year before after telling her that he had secured a splendid investment through a rich widow. He was excited about the plan and even borrowed several thousand dollars from friends who were interested in the scheme. He took another $1,000 that belonged to the insurance company when he left Chicago. That was the last time anyone had seen him.

Mrs. Kullers of McKeesport, Pennsylvania, contacted the sheriff's office about her missing father, John Hunter. He had left home in November 1907 for Northern Indiana to marry a rich widow. He had taken a large sum of money with him and told his daughter he wasn't sure when he'd be back.

Gustav Thomas of Washington, Pennsylvania, also told his family and friends that he'd been in contact with a wealthy widow in LaPorte. He'd left town with $1,000 in his pocket and hadn't been seen since.

And there were dozens more – letters and telegrams, all asking for help. They sent along photographs and descriptions of the missing, but those were, for the most part, utterly useless. Given the condition of the exhumed bodies – which were piles of hacked bones, rotting flesh, and skulls that sometimes still had hair and skin attached – it was impossible to put names to most of them.

There was circumstantial evidence that helped to identify some of them, however. The authorities concluded that Belle's hired hands – Olaf Lindhoe and Henry Gurholt – were two of her earliest Indiana victims. Another man, Olaf Jensen, had written to relatives in Norway to say he was leaving his home in Carroll, Indiana, to marry a rich widow who owned a farm in LaPorte. He disappeared soon after cashing a large check at the First National Bank in town. When neighbors asked where he'd gone, Belle used her regular answer – he'd gone west.

Arthur Peglow, an assistant cashier at the First National Bank, was able to identify another of her victims – John Moe of Elbow Lake, Minnesota. He'd arrived in town after informing relatives that he was moving to a place in Indiana, not far from Chicago. In December 1906, John Moe had come into the bank to cash two checks totaling about $1,000. He was never seen again. Peglow remembered Moe from a photograph.

In early 1906, Christian Hilviken of Dover, Wisconsin, had left home abruptly after selling his farm for $2,000 in cash. He had forwarded the delivery for the Norwegian-language newspaper he subscribed to Belle's address in LaPorte.

Some came forward with what amounted to "near misses" in connection with Belle Gunness. Besides Carl Peterson – a Wisconsin man that Belle rejected because he didn't have $1,000 – there was Alonzo Townsend of Topeka, Kansas, who had arranged to visit Belle's farm in early May but was delayed by late spring rains that prevented him from putting in his crops on time. By the time he was ready to leave on the trip, the Gunness house was in ashes.

Townsend had been saved by bad weather, while a family emergency saved Olaf Catchousen of Illinois. After an ardent exchange of letters with Belle not long before the fire, Olaf had withdrawn $2,000 from his bank with plans to move to LaPorte. Just before he left, though, he received an urgent message to hurry to his parents' home. Had the message not arrived, he would likely have been one of the bodies unearthed in the hog pen.

George Anderson – a Missouri man who had responded to Belle's ad in 1906 – also had a close call. Satisfied with his finances, Belle had told him to convert his property into cash and join her in LaPorte, where they would be married. George did what she asked and was soon at the farm.

On the night of his arrival, he went to the bedroom on the second floor of the house and quickly fell asleep. Sometime around midnight, he was awakened by a disturbing dream and opened his eyes to find Belle standing over his bed. She ran out of the room. Frightened, he didn't close his eyes for the rest of the night. At daybreak, he fled the farm. After reading the horrific revelations about Belle, he was certain he had barely escaped death.

He was confident about something else, too. "I am convinced that woman is still alive," he told some reporters, "and that she set fire to the farmhouse herself."

Sightings of Belle were still coming in from Chicago. She was spotted on streetcars, on the street, and eating in restaurants. A waitress named May Wagner, who worked at a café on Van Buren Street, told police that a man and a woman -- matching Belle's exact description -- left a train and entered the restaurant to eat. The man ordered two steaks from May, who gave them a newspaper to read. The front page detailed the ongoing investigation in LaPorte.

The man, May said, took one look at the paper and threw it on the floor, and then he and the woman left hurriedly without eating the food that had just arrived at their table. May asked the man if there was anything wrong with it, and he told her there was nothing wrong; he just wasn't feeling well.

About an hour later, the same couple was seen eating a hurried breakfast at a restaurant on West Jackson and Halstead, and their secretive manner had attracted the attention of the owner.

As far as the newspapers were concerned, the eyewitness accounts left little doubt that Belle was at large in the city. One reporter for the *Tribune* dramatically wrote, "Fleeing from place to place, haunted by her conscience and in constant dread that she will be seized by the hand of the law, Belle Gunness is being sought by scores of detectives."

It was a newspaper competitor, though, the *Chicago Inter-Ocean*, that made the most dramatic claim about Belle. Its correspondent in LaPorte had somehow gotten into the embalming room at the Cutler funeral home, where the charred remains from the cellar had been brought.

Before the torso had been placed in a burial shroud, Cutler had weighed and measured it in the reporter's presence. Allowing for the missing head and feet, the undertaker calculated that, in life, the dead woman was five feet, two inches tall, and weighed 130 pounds. By contrast, Belle had been at least five feet, seven inches tall – some neighbors claimed taller – and weighed close to 300 pounds.

There was only one conclusion to be drawn from what the paper called an "astounding revelation" -- that Belle Gunness, "the siren who had lured a score of men to their deaths," was, beyond a reasonable doubt, still alive!

NO MATTER WHAT THE SENSATIONAL newspapers were saying, the authorities in LaPorte were firmly convinced that Belle was dead – slain by her accomplice, Ray Lamphere. Assisted by a trio of Pinkerton detectives, the sheriff's department believed they had gathered enough evidence to charge Ray with murder.

The newspapers thought so too – or at least that was the version of the story they printed when they weren't claiming Belle was alive and being spotted all over the country. She was dead on one page and on the run from the police on another page of the same newspaper. It was kind of a schizophrenic way of offering the news, but the public ate it up.

Every restless night that Ray spent behind bars was reported in the press as proof of his guilty conscience. With its usual shameless disregard for facts, the *Chicago American* portrayed him as a raving maniac, driven to madness by Belle's vengeful ghost, who haunted him in his cell. A quote that never came from Ray but was attributed to him anyway said, "She's pointing her finger at me! She is saying, I'll get you! I'll get you yet! I can't get away from her!"

Ray's lawyer, Wirt Worden, disputed the claims of the sheriff's department, insisting that his client was innocent. He told the papers that Ray was without criminal proclivities and, describing him in a way that he likely thought was doing Ray a favor, he called him "a man of mediocre mentality."

Wirt Worden, along with others in the community, believed that the headless woman found in the cellar was a corpse planted by Belle – because it was undoubtedly not Belle. This belief was bolstered by the continued sightings of her that flooded in from all over Indiana, East St. Louis, and Colorado, where Sheriff R.S. Williams telegraphed the LaPorte authorities about the reward because he was convinced Belle was now living in his town. Another telegram arrived from Willmar, Minnesota, where a resident claimed that Belle was now working as a housekeeper for a local farmer. The police were told to "come and get her."

Andre W. Thompson of Paulina Street in Chicago furnished the police with a photograph of Belle and swore that she was hiding in plain sight in his neighborhood. It was hard to dismiss Thompson's claims as he had been a boyhood friend of the late Mads Sorensen and had been best man at Mads and Belle's wedding. Thousands of copies of the Gunness photo were made and sent to police agencies in the United States and Europe, but a search of Thompson's neighborhood failed to produce Belle.

She was also spotted in Grand Rapids, Michigan; Hot Springs, Arkansas; Cincinnati, Ohio; Joliet, Illinois; Alberta, Canada; and traveling in Mexico, dressed in men's clothing.

Back in LaPorte, a self-described psychic named Jesse Dickensen came into Sheriff Smutzer's office on May 9 and announced that Belle was still nearby and that he had the power to locate her. All that he required, he claimed, was something that had been in the possession of Ray Lamphere, and he'd use that to tell the exact location of where she was hiding and solve the mystery. He failed.

Another person claiming to have powers from the spirit world, Mrs. A. James Smith of Milwaukee, announced that by studying the signs of the zodiac, she had deduced that Belle was either in Michigan City or Fort Wayne or maybe Terre Haute or possibly Indianapolis... Wherever she was, she was dressed as a man and working in a livery stable.

Sightings of Belle became such a common occurrence that many newspapers started treating them as a joke. One Indiana paper urged all "large-sized women to stay at home so they are not mistaken for Mrs. Gunness and held by the authorities."

Another observed that Belle had "been seen in so many different places at almost the same time that she seemed to have solved the problem of time travel."

But Sheriff Smutzer didn't treat any of this as a joke. He had a terrible crime on his hands – not only the murder of small children but a string of men who had been slain at the hands of a woman who was either dead or alive, depending on what version of the story you chose to believe.

The sheriff believed Belle was dead, so he went looking for a way to prove it. On May 9, he announced that he had retained the services of Louis "Klondike" Schultz, a local man who had worked in the California, Colorado, and Alaska gold fields as a prospector and miner. On Monday, he would set up his sluice on the Gunness property and begin sifting the ashes in the cellar in search of Belle's gold-capped teeth.

Klondike told the newspapers, "I will take my time and go over every particle of the wreckage. If the teeth are there, I will find them. And if it was Mrs. Gunness who perished in the flames, the teeth are there."

Belle's dentist, Dr. Ira Norton, agreed. Belle had visited him two times over the past year and noted that four incisors in her lower jaw were missing, and she had two gold crowns and a porcelain bridge of four teeth backed with gold. According to Dr. Norton, "If it was Mrs. Gunness whose body was found in the ruins, her teeth are intact among the debris. The fire was not hot enough to melt the gold or incinerate the porcelain."

Sheriff Smutzer's announcement about Klondike Schultz came at the end of a long and fruitless day of digging. For the first time since he and the other men had started their grim excavations, Belle's "Murder Farm" had yielded no bodies. When the search was called off at nightfall, the crowds that had been gathered at the farm since early morning were shocked and surprised. By then, Belle had grown into such a monstrous figure in the public imagination that it was generally assumed there were bodies buried pretty much everywhere on her property.

No digging was planned for the next day – partially because it was the Sabbath but primarily because of the enormous crowds that were expected to descend on the farm. Guards were posted at the ruins of the farmhouse and outside the building that had been turned into the morgue, but otherwise, spectators were allowed to roam wherever they wanted.

To cash in on the Belle Gunness frenzy, the Lake Erie and Western Railroad had arranged special excursion trains to bring visitors to LaPorte from Indianapolis and Chicago. Every hotel room in town – and in nearby Michigan City – had been booked, and extra cots had been set up in the hallways. Restaurants were doing a booming business and reporters commented that it looked as though the circus had come to town.

Livery companies were hiring additional drivers to take sightseers back and forth from the Gunness farm. They made countless round trips. According to at least one estimate, at least 10,000 people were expected to flock to the farm on Sunday – a day when no one would be digging.

But the prediction of 10,000 sightseers turned out to be wrong – it's estimated that there were at least 15,000 people who showed up on Sunday, May 10, maybe as many as 20,000.

Thousands of people converged on the "Murder Farm" to watch as human remains were uncovered. News that a new search of the house ruins for Belle's head brought even bigger crowds.

The first excursion train reached LaPorte at just after 5:00 A.M. Others, packed to overflowing, arrived regularly throughout the day, increasing the crowds by the hundreds. Locals used every carriage, buggy, and wagon to take new arrivals out to the farm. They waited at the train station and charged 10 cents for the one-mile ride. Once there, passengers were informed that the return trip would cost a quarter.

By midmorning, McClung Road was jammed with every kind of vehicle imaginable, as well as an army of pedestrians. At least 50 automobiles brought smartly dressed visitors from Chicago, South Bend, Elkhart, Niles, and other midwestern towns. Young men on bicycles, mothers pushing baby carriages, and even old folks on crutches hurried along the roadway while motorcycles shot through the crowds at frequent intervals. Given the congestion, it seems a miracle that only one accident occurred when an automobile spooked a horse that was pulling a buggy with a young couple inside. The lady was thrown from the rig and broke her arm.

The mood at the farm was weirdly festive. Vendors sold peanuts, sandwiches, and drinks from roadside stands. A crew of young men, hired for the occasion by a local printer, roamed the grounds selling picture postcards of the studio portrait of Belle and her children for 10 cents. Gruesome images of the remains of Andrew Helgelein sold out in minutes. Other postcards included panoramic views of the "Murder Farm" and images of the diggers standing knee-deep in graves. Many visitors brought new Kodak Brownie cameras and took their own photos, posing their children in front of the ruins of the farmhouse or at the edges of the pits in the excavated hog lot.

Several enterprising youngsters peddled authentic human skeleton fragments, allegedly dug up on the farm, but those who snapped up these relics later learned they'd purchased hog bones. Other eager souvenir hunters took whatever they could find – like chunks of brick from the burned house, charred pieces of wood, bent nails, burned shoe buttons, and even twigs from the trees on the property. Scavengers ignored the guards, rooted through the cellar, and groveled in the dirt for ghoulish keepsakes.

Many of the early arrivals went straight to the buggy shed, where the stinking remains of the exhumed corpses were still laid out on wooden planks. Sheriff Smutzer himself, standing guard at the door, lined up the visitors in single file and allowed them into the makeshift morgue a few at a time. By 9:00 A.M., though, the crowd trying to get in had become so large and out of control that the sheriff had to padlock the door. After that, people pressed their fingers into cracks in the walls, trying to pry them apart to see inside, while men lifted women up high to peer into the dusty windows.

Picnickers packed lunch baskets and spread blankets in the grass. Baseball games were played within a few hundred feet of the crime scene while laughing children ran through the crowds or followed around a local character dubbed "Uncle Ben," who roamed the property with a forked willow dowsing rod, claiming he could detect the graves of undiscovered witnesses. "There are 37 in all," he told reporters at the end of his search.

Young men pocketed money by assisting visitors with parking and then making more money by offering "insurance" to make sure nothing happened to their carriage or automobile. Pickpockets conducted a brisk trade by roaming through the spectators at the farm and on the train platform as visitors made their way home.

Sheriff Smutzer sighed and offered a sad comment on the happenings: "Awful, isn't it? There does not seem to be any horror in these people. I never saw folks having a better time."

Water trucks were bought in for Klondike Schutlz's sluice box.

(Below) Sluicing for clues, bones and Belle's teeth and gold bridge in the ruins of the house.

ON MONDAY, MAY 11, KLONDIKE SCHULTZ spent the day constructing his sluice box – a narrow, wooden trough that was about 12 feet long and arranged at a downward angle on the ground.

While he worked, Joe Maxson and a few other men began hauling shovelfuls of ashes from the cellar of the farmhouse and dumping them in a big pile next to Klondike's apparatus.

The next day, with a water wagon providing the necessary stream, he began washing through debris in search of Belle's gold teeth.

In the two weeks since the fire, diggers in the cellar had already turned up watches belonging to three men. One of them was traced to Iola, Kansas, where a ledger showed Ole Budsberg had purchased it. The other two timepieces were also presumed to have belonged to Belle's victims. Now, as Klondike worked his sluice, other watches were found – five more, making a total of eight.

Except for one rainy day when work was suspended, Klondike Schultz continued his macabre prospecting for the next week. Besides the watches, he turned up several corroded knives, part of a gilded picture frame, a plain gold ring, some keys, a belt buckle, a few bone fragments, and the remnants of a book about anatomy.

But so far, no teeth.

Large crowds of spectators gathered at the farm each day to watch Klondike do his work. Among them were the three Pinkerton agents that Sheriff Smutzer had hired to gather evidence against Ray Lamphere. Their presence was not welcomed by Ray's lawyer, Wirt Worden, who issued a statement to the press that alluded to the often-questionable tactics used by the Pinkertons. He suggested they were at the farm for the sole purpose of manufacturing evidence to fit their theories.

Thanks to the presence of the Pinkertons, he sarcastically told reporters, "There is no doubt in my mind that the gold teeth of Mrs. Gunness, with special identification marks of the dentist, will be found." The eye-roll that accompanied his statement implied that he believed the discovery of the teeth might not be credible.

And he was right. Just before noon on May 19, moments after shoveling a load of ashes into the sluice box, Klondike came up with a pair of dental bridges, an upper and a lower.

"They're found!" Sheriff Smutzer called out, throwing his hat into the air. Taking the bridges from the old prospector, he hopped into his car, sped into town, and headed straight for the office of Belle's dentist, Dr. Ira Norton.

Dr. Norton had no trouble identifying them. The upper bridge, which Belle had been wearing when Norton first examined her, was the work of a dentist in Chicago. The lower bridge was his own handiwork – four porcelain teeth backed with 18-carat gold and attached to molars on either side of her jaw. He told reporters there was no mistaking the bridge. It was positively the one he had made for Belle.

But one of the reporters asked the dentist what would have stopped Belle from removing the false teeth and throwing them in the fire before she left.

Norton stammered a bit and pointed to a small bit of molar that was still attached to the lower bridge. To do that, he explained, Mrs. Gunness would have had to extract one of her own teeth.

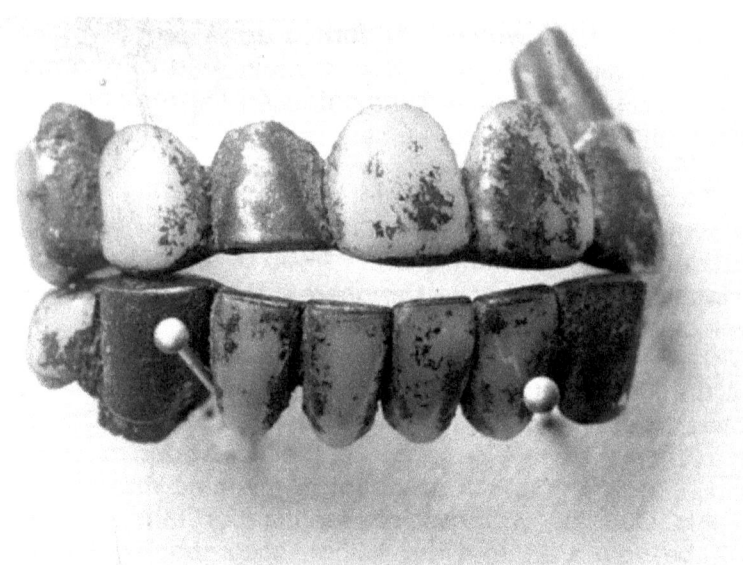

The bridge and false teeth found in the ruins of the house, alleged to belong to Belle. This would become a controversial discovery during Ray Lamphere's trial.

But, pretty clearly, she had. Or someone had. The bridge hadn't burned out of her mouth. It had been pulled out, which was why there was a natural tooth still clinging to the metal.

Thanks to this, many of the reporters were unconvinced --- along with a lot of other people. Wasn't Belle cunning enough to have left the bridgework behind? Because, if it was Belle, how was the fire hot enough to completely incinerate her skull and leave her false teeth mostly undamaged?

They were good questions, but officials didn't feel like answering them. Norton's identification of the teeth – and his belief they had been in Belle's mouth when she died – was all the convincing they needed to firmly say that Belle Gunness was dead.

Up until this point, Coroner Charles Mack had left the verdict in the case open. However, after the teeth were found, he was confident in saying that the headless body of the adult woman found in the cellar was Belle Gunness, and the other remains were those of her children. Death, it was ruled, was caused by suffocation, followed by burning.

Two days later, on Friday, May 22, a grand jury returned indictments against Ray Lamphere, charging him with arson and the first-degree murders of Belle Gunness, her three children, and Andrew Helgelein.

MANY OF THOSE WHO ACCEPTED THE official version of events and became resigned to the fact that Belle was actually dead still believed that her presence remained in LaPorte – now as a vengeful spirit.

In early July, Daniel Hutson was driving a wagon load of hay past the old Gunness farm and claimed to see Belle walking in the orchard.

His daughter, Eldora, reported a similar sighting a short time later. She was walking down McClung Road when she saw a buggy coming toward her, drawn by a gray horse that she had once seen in Belle's barn. When the buggy came closer, she swore she saw Belle in the driver's seat.

That same day, two boys walking near the Pine Lake Cemetery spotted a heavily veiled woman they swore was Belle Gunness.

Another witness was driving past the farm one summer evening and saw a woman in black looking around the southeast corner of the ruined house as if searching for something. The woman gave up and walked away, and at that moment, lightning flashed in the sky, and he recognized the face of Belle Gunness.

As these accounts made the rounds, one observer suggested the best way to rid the community of Belle's presence would be to pile all her goods into a great heap and purge them in a bonfire.

But the town decided to hold an auction instead.

Arranged by her executor, Wesley Fogle, the sale drew an enormous crowd, perhaps as many as 5,000 people. By the time the auction ended, every item had been sold, with bidders paying as much as ten times the original cost for the privilege of owning one of Belle's kitchen utensils or gardening tools. Belle's dog and her children's pony – each selling for more than $200 each – along with two chickens, an old house cat, and her kittens were purchased by a carnival showman named W.W. Hans, who put them on display in Chicago.

To the editor of one Indiana newspaper, the purchasers of Belle's personal effects were making themselves vulnerable to malevolent forces. Citing the paranormal theory of psychometry – the belief that objects retain the residual energy of their former owners – the writer warned that Belle's belongings possessed an aura of evil that might infect anyone who came into contact with them. Those who were foolish enough to have purchased what he called "these blood-spattered goods" were behaving as recklessly as a mother who bought rattlesnakes for her children to use as toys.

ON THE AFTERNOON OF WEDNESDAY, JUNE 17, undertaker Austin Cutler transported the remains of the woman officially identified as Belle Gunness, along with the corpses of the three Gunness children, by Lake Shore train to Chicago.

When they arrived at Union Depot, the caskets were transferred to the mortuary wagon of a local undertaker. At 10:00 A.M. the following morning, the bodies were interred without ceremony at the Forest Lake Cemetery. There was no service, and no mourners were present. Belle's sister, Nellie Larson, refused to attend.

Readers in LaPorte learned of the funeral in a local newspaper article that was published on June 25. The headline read – "Mrs. Gunness Dead At Last."

But was she?

Not everyone thought so. Despite the coroner's verdict and the burial at Forest Lake Cemetery, it was believed that at least three-quarters of the people who lived in LaPorte were convinced that she was still alive.

It didn't help matters that sightings of Belle were still coming in from around the country. Less than two weeks after the funeral, she was spotted in Detroit. Later that summer, Belle was reported in Birmingham, Alabama; Minneapolis; Portland, Maine; Passaic, New Jersey; and Galveston, Texas, where she was seen boarding a steamer that was bound for Hamburg, Germany.

In late summer, a traveling salesman named George Robinson told police that, while riding the Katy Flyer through Texas, he was standing at the water cooler when a woman in a black mourning dress approached him and asked for a drink. In his statement, he said:

When she lifted her veil to drink from the cup, I at once recognized her as Mrs. Gunness. When I spoke to her and called her by name, she suddenly turned and went back to her seat in a hurry, and after packing a few things that she carried, left the train at the next station.

A few months later, Henrik Fritz, a former resident of LaPorte, had a similar experience aboard a train between Fort Worth and Denver. Passing through the Pullman car, he saw Belle walk out of the restroom. Recognizing Henrik, she quickly dropped a heavy veil over her face, hurried back into the bathroom, and locked herself inside.

Were any of these sightings possible? Or was Belle dead, and people were mistaking other women for the murderess?

As it turned out, it wasn't just random people across the country or what State's Attorney Smith called "uneducated people in LaPorte" who believed that Belle had escaped her fate.

Dr. Harry Long, the prominent LaPorte physician who had assisted Coroner Mack at the postmortem, also believed the body found in the ruins of the house was not Belle Gunness.

Dr. Long had measured the remains and, making allowances for the missing head, stated that the dead woman had been about five feet, three inches tall, and had weighed no more than 150 pounds – much shorter and lighter than Belle.

Neighbors and people who knew Belle and saw the body taken out of the cellar had argued about the size of it. They were assured that it was Belle's corpse. It just looked smaller because of the fire damage and the missing head. But they weren't so sure and went on record saying they didn't believe it was Belle.

Detailed measurements of the body were compared with those on file with several LaPorte stores that had made dresses for Belle. Dr. Long became convinced that the body was not Belle Gunness.

Again, he wasn't alone. Questions were being asked about some of the other evidence that had been found in the sluice box of Klondike Schultz – the evidence that wasn't as highly publicized as the false teeth.

In the ashes of the basement – near where the body of the woman had been found – Klondike discovered three engraved gold rings. The inscriptions on two of them read: "PG to JS Aug-23, 94" and "PS to JS, 5-3-96."

Sheriff Smutzer and State's attorney Ralph Smith stated that the rings had belonged to Belle, even though there was nothing that proved that. They were found near where the woman's corpse had been discovered after the fire, so they must be Belle's.

Case closed.

But not so fast. The initials in the rings were certainly not Belle's, even if the "S" stood for "Sorensen." There were no clues as to the identity of the people who might have matched the inscriptions inside the rings.

Did Belle leave them behind in her hasty escape? Or did they belong to the mysterious woman that Ray Lamphere would soon claim had been lured to the farm from Chicago soon before the fire occurred? Was she the body found in the burned-out cellar? Or was it really the body of Belle Gunness?

Rumors continued to spread as other events in the case also began stealing the spotlight.

AS SUMMER TURNED TO FALL, RAY LAMPHERE waited in jail for his trial to begin. It was said that at some point, Ray confessed to some of the crimes that he committed while in Belle's employ to Reverend E.A. Schnell, but on the advice of his attorney, he shut up and said nothing else. He continued to maintain that he had not killed Belle – or Andrew Helgelein – and he had not burned down the Gunness home. As for the other things he'd done... well, let's just say that the accounts of him being near nervous collapse by the time the trial began were probably accurate.

The trial began on the afternoon of November 9, 1908. Jury selection in Judge Carl Richter's oak-paneled courtroom took four days. Hundreds were called, but 12 men – and some alternates – were finally seated on Friday the 13th, which was also Ray's birthday.

Not exactly the gift he wanted.

The trial was contentious – a bitter battle of wills between political rivals, each determined to destroy the reputation of the other. The hapless Ray Lamphere found himself caught in the middle.

The Republicans had prevailed in the 1908 fall election. William Antiss had replaced his former boss, Albert Smutzer, as sheriff. Charles Mack was defeated for re-nomination as coroner in the LaPorte County Democratic Convention because he believed that the body of the woman in the cellar was Belle Gunness, which ran counter to the case that Mayor Darrow and attorney Wirt Worden were building for Ray's defense. That led to Mack being unceremoniously dumped by the Democrats for going against the interests of the party.

Prosecutor Ralph Smith defeated his challenger, Philo Q. Doran, following a blistering campaign in which the handling of the Gunness case was called to account by the Democrats and defenders of Ray Lamphere.

Wirt Worden continued to push the theory that most people had come to accept as the truth: that Belle had escaped from the fire.

With local politics in disarray, various factions within the local government warring against one another, and the possibility that Northwest Indiana's most famous murderer was still on the loose, the trial of an alcoholic lay-about farmhand with criminal tendencies – who was in truth just a stand-in for the greater evil of his former employer – was finally underway.

WHILE WIRT WORDEN WAS SURE HE COULD PROVE that Ray hadn't killed Belle Gunness, Prosecutor Ralph Smith was equally confident about his strategy for pinning the murders of Belle and her children on Ray. He had also planned to try him for the murder of Andrew Helgelein, but he scrapped that just before the trial in hopes of streamlining his case.

Even so, he still had to deal with the rumors – and widespread local belief – that Belle had faked her death. He gave an irritable interview to the *Chicago American* just before the trial began. He told a reporter:

I am tired of this silly rot that she is alive! I am going to put a stop to all this talk about her being seen in 40 different places in the country by every Tom, Dick, and Harry who thinks he is a detective!

When it came to Ray's trial, he was sure about the outcome, and he added:

There is no possibility in my mind that the verdict will be anything other than guilty. I anticipate a good deal of trouble securing a jury owing to the wide publicity that has been given the case, but a special group of men has been drawn. That the dead woman found in the house was Mrs. Gunness we have conclusive proof. I have the evidence to hang the man in my office! The effort to make political capital of the case has failed.

One of the reporters reminded Smith about the recent findings of Dr. Walter Haines, an eminent Chicago toxicologist. Dr. Haines was called to LaPorte to analyze the three bodies of the children removed from the basement. He discovered large quantities of two poisons – arsenic and strychnine – in the children's stomachs. In his opinion, the poison had caused their deaths. He stated publicly that the state would have a hard time proving that Ray had poisoned the victims and then set fire to the house, especially with Joe Maxson on the property.

When the reporter asked Smith how he expected to prove that occurred, Smith shook his head and walked away.

With both excitement and strong feelings about the case throughout the entire Midwest, nearly 1,000 people jammed into the courthouse, hoping to gain admission into a courtroom that only seated 300. Numbered tickets were given out to spectators on a first-come-first-served basis to try and prevent overcrowding.

It was apparent to everyone in the courtroom that there were political benefits to someone if Ray was acquitted. The handyman and drunk – who didn't have a dollar to his name – had a legal team that consisted of Wirt Worden, Mayor Darrow, and Darrow's co-counsel, Ellsworth E. Weir, one of the most distinguished lawyers in the state. Asked by a reporter where he was going to get the money to pay his legal fees, Ray just shrugged his shoulders.

The usually scruffy Ray had been cleaned and scrubbed for his courtroom appearance. He was washed, shaved, and dressed in a suit, looking more like a respectable bank clerk than a man who spent most of his time and money in neighborhood dive bars. His elderly mother would make a tearful plea on her son's behalf during the trial. She evoked sympathy from nearly everyone in the room when she told of her son's early circumstances and the terrible poverty they had endured because of her husband's drinking and abuse.

The daily courtroom proceedings were unpredictable and lively, especially when the grandstanding Ellsworth Weir asked the circuit clerk to issue a summons for Belle Gunness to appear on November 14. This action provoked anger from the prosecution and laughter from the audience.

But Weir was serious. He was quoted the next day in the LaPorte newspaper, saying, "In my opinion the woman is not so far away that she could not answer the subpoena and her coming into court or otherwise will depend largely on the advice of her counsel. It might not be so easy of a matter to convict Mrs. Gunness of a crime as many people seem to suppose."

AS THE TRIAL GOT UNDERWAY, EYEWITNESSES recounted startling stories of the strange events that went on at the Gunness farm.

On the fifth day of testimony, jurors were told about a late-night visit to the farmhouse by Addie Landis, a young woman who was to meet with Belle about a possible job. A buggy driver, Leo Wade, said that he had driven Miss Landis to the house and watched as she left the carriage, went to the back door, and looked into the window.

Suddenly, the girl let out a scream and ran back toward the buggy, falling down several times on the way. Obviously upset, she demanded that Wade take her to the home of Pearl Corey, another prospective employer. Weeping, she cried out, "I've seen the most awful thing I ever expect to see!"

According to the testimony of the driver, Mrs. Corey refused to let Miss Landis into her home, so he let her off downtown. He found out the next day that she had taken the train to Valparaiso, Indiana. Within a week, Addie went mad and had to be institutionalized at the Logansport Hospital for the Insane.

Pearl Corey verified the driver's story and said that Addie was supposed to come to her house that evening about a job. She would have let her in, she said, but she was raving like a maniac about what she had seen at the Gunness house. She told the court, "I could not make much sense out of what she said except that it was about cutting up a body, and I believed the girl was a lunatic. In light of other developments, I am inclined to think that what she saw that night drove her crazy."

Joe Maxson took the witness stand and offered some confusing testimony about events at the Gunness house on the night of the fire. Had Belle tried to kill him? Or had Ray Lamphere? He didn't seem to know.

First, he claimed that he had spotted Ray lurking in the trees near the house and then running across a nearby field. But then he recalled Belle's apparent nervousness that night and said he believed that she had injected dope into an orange that she gave him so that he'd fall asleep. A strange feeling of drowsiness came over him soon after eating the fruit, he said. After going to bed, he never heard any sounds downstairs, and he was lucky to have awakened when he did. Maxson wholeheartedly believed that Belle had intended for him to die during the fire.

He didn't seem to know what direction he was going with his testimony, and no one asked him to clear it up.

A grocer's clerk named George Wrase took the stand. He recalled selling Belle some supplies in town on the day before the fire. Her purchases included two gallons of kerosene. As she was paying for the items, Ray came into the store to purchase a five-cent plug of chewing tobacco, and for a long moment, the two of them stared at one another.

George couldn't say if they looked at each other with hatred or – as Prosecutor Smith prompted him to say, which prompted many objections from the defense – if some secret, silent communication passed between them.

It was very disturbing, the grocer's clerk recalled. The oil can that he gave Belle that day was later found in the ruins of the cellar, under a pile of bricks, a few yards away from the four bodies.

On the witness stand, Peter Colson, who had worked on the farm for two years, told of Ray's obsession with Belle – and his fear of her. Colson admitted to also sleeping with his employer.

"She made such love to me!" he rapturously exclaimed as loud murmurs from the mostly female audience in the courtroom interrupted the proceedings.

The judge had to order the courtroom back into silence so that Colson could continue. He said that he was both attracted to Belle and repelled by her. Eventually, he left the farm and said that he spent the next six months sleeping in a haymow on a farm a half-mile away – because he simply couldn't stand to be too far away from Belle.

At this point, the prosecutor asked that Coroner Mack's findings that Belle had perished in the fire be admitted as evidence, and the judge agreed – at first. But then Judge Richter reconsidered the matter and reversed his ruling. It was a setback for the state, but the jury and the audience still had the vivid and gruesome reminder of the horror right in front of them.

Across the front of the courtroom was a row of jars that contained human bones, fragments of flesh, bits of cloth, and other evidence that had been pulled out of the burned farmhouse and dug from the grounds that surrounded it. It was almost impossible to keep from staring at the grisly display.

The prosecution called 40 witnesses to the stand. Only one – Klondike Schultz, who was in Arkansas – failed to show up. Former Sheriff Smutzer, the most important part of the prosecution's case, identified the three rings that were found in the ruins of the house as those that he had seen Belle wearing when she came to his office shortly before the fire to complain about Ray Lamphere. Smutzer hotly denied an allegation by Wirt Worden that he had any "special interest" in the case other than a duty to the community. He denied that his testimony had anything to do with politics.

The prosecution also called Dr. Joseph Meyer to the stand. He was a prosecution witness, but his testimony turned out to be better for the defense. Meyer had assisted with the autopsies and had conducted the postmortem of four-year-old Phillip Gunness. Asked about the condition of the boy's body, he provided a description that – though delivered in a dry, clinical tone – was horrifying enough to produce shudders from the audience.

Dr. Meyer testified:

The body was severely burned. The legs were burned off at the knees entirely. The forehead was burned away, exposing the brain. The back was badly burned, the spinal cord was exposed. One of the arms was missing. The lungs were partially preserved by cooking. The heart was contracted, containing no blood. All the organs were well-cooked.

The prosecutors asked him if he could determine a cause of death, but Dr. Meyer said that he couldn't – but he did have a professional opinion. He believed that, like his colleague Dr. Walter Haines, the boy had been killed by poison. He was already dead when his body was burned in the fire.

Any suggestion, of course, that the family had not died because of the arson committed by Ray Lamphere undermined the state's argument. As one writer put it, this was a prosecution witness testifying for the defense.

Caught off-guard by the response, the prosecutor quickly ended his questioning. Wirt Worden, though, drove his statement home for the jury, scoring points for Ray's defense.

Worden had a tougher time with Belle's dentist, Dr. Ira Norton when he took the stand. He said the teeth found in the burned house were, without a doubt, those of Belle Gunness. He had attended to her dental needs and knew the woman well.

Prosecutor Smith underscored the testimony with a long pause. The teeth seemed to provide the physical evidence needed to convict Ray. The hired hand's jealousy, Belle's rejection of him for Andrew Helgelein, and his alleged thirst for revenge already provided ample motive – or so it seemed.

But the defense had another theory about the mysterious teeth and bridgework. Worden found evidence that contradicted Dr. Norton's identification. A local jeweler testified that the gold in the bridgework had emerged from the fire almost unscathed, even though the heat from the blaze had damaged several watches and other pieces of jewelry that were recovered from the ruins of the house.

Doctors hired by the defense replicated the conditions of the fire by attaching a similar piece of bridgework to a human jawbone and placing it into a blacksmith's forge. The real teeth crumbled and fell apart; the porcelain teeth came out pitted and marked, and the gold parts melted out of shape. It was

much more damaged than the bridgework being used to confirm Belle's identification – even though the conditions were identical.

In addition, Joe Maxson and another man claimed that they had seen "Klondike" Schultz take the bridgework out of his pocket and plant it just before it was "discovered." As mentioned, old Klondike was conveniently out of town when Ray's trial took place.

WHEN IT WAS THE DEFENSE'S TURN, WIRT WORDEN was happy to take the stage, offering an eloquent speech on the inadequacies of the state's case and telling the jury and courtroom audience what he planned to prove in the testimony that followed.

As he spoke, several of the jurors edged to the front of their seats to listen. When he finished, there was a profound silence. Worden made his assertions in such a masterly manner that if he proved able to back them up with his witnesses, he might save Ray's neck from the noose after all.

In his speech, Worden stated that all the circumstantial evidence pointed away from his client and toward Belle faking her own death and substituting someone else's body in the place of her own. Worden's next words must have electrified the jury. He told them:

We will prove by testimony that on the afternoon of April 27, Mrs. Gunness had a conversation in front of the First National

Bank building with a certain man in which she said, 'It must be done tonight, and you must do it!' Something was done that night. A torch was applied to the Gunness house and the bodies of the three Gunness children were found in the ruins. We will produce a witness who saw Mrs. Gunness drive out to her house on the Saturday preceding the fire in the company of a woman who has never been seen since unless it was her body that was found in the ruins of the fire.

Worden began building a case, calling the doctors and jewelers who could testify about the mysterious bridgework. He called witnesses to the fire, who said they saw it begin at least a half hour before Ray Lamphere had left Liz Smith's house. Joe Maxson and undertaker William Weird testified to seeing the oil can inside the house after the fire. It seemed a scattershot defense that amounted to almost nothing. In fact, Worden even made a blunder at the end of the day by calling his opponent, State's Attorney Smith, to the stand.

He questioned him about a mysterious trunk that he had secretly hauled away from the Gunness carriage shed the previous spring. When the trunk was brought into the courtroom and opened, however, it was found to contain neckties, books, and letters that had nothing to do with the case.

Reporting on the day's developments, more newspapermen agreed that the defense had gotten off to a sloppy start. He struggled more over the next two days as Worden brought in witnesses to bolster his argument that Belle Gunness was alive and Ray hadn't killed her or her children.

They included Daniel Hutson, who spoke about the women that he and his daughters saw around the Gunness home during the summer after the fire. "I could plainly see her face," Daniel told the courtroom, and even when questioned by the prosecution, he said that he knew Mrs. Gunness enough that he could not be mistaken.

Another neighbor, John Anderson, offered evidence to advance the theory that the headless body in the ruins was a different heavyset woman, lured to the farm, slain, and switched for Belle. On the Saturday before the fire, he was working in his garden when Belle drove past in her buggy and stopped to talk to him. Seated beside her was a strange woman – "a large woman, although not quite as large as Mrs. Gunness," he said. Wirt Worden asked him if he had ever seen the woman again, and Anderson shook his head. "Never," he said emphatically.

More witnesses followed, including more neighbors, Joe Maxson revealing the shocking testimony of seeing Klondike Schultz fishing the mystery teeth from his pocket, another dentist, volunteers who excavated the basement, and, finally, Dr. Walter Haines from Rush Medical College, whom the reporters had asked Prosecutor Smith about before the trial began.

He was, the defense believed, their ace in the hole. Dr. Haines was not only a respected scientist but had been a chemistry professor at the medical school for nearly 50 years. During his long and distinguished career, he had been involved in several sensational murder cases. He was also a leading figure in the field of forensic science, even though it was in its infancy in those days.

His testimony in court was no surprise – he explained how he had found enough strychnine and arsenic in each body to kill three people. It was exactly what Wirt Worden wanted to hear.

But then came the cross-examination.

When asked if he could state with certainty that the persons whose stomachs he'd analyzed had died from poisoning. He said he could not.

Prosecutor Smith stated that the bodies had been in the morgue for ten days and had been viewed by hundreds of people. Could the poison have been injected into the bodies at that time? Dr. Haines agreed that it was possible.

The doctor was followed to the stand by LaPorte undertaker Austin Cutler. The state had called him as a rebuttal witness. As soon as he was sworn in, Smith asked him if he had treated the remains with any kind of poison. Cutler nodded his head, "Why yes, I did put poison on those bodies. I thought it strange that you never asked me before. I scattered about two gallons of formaldehyde embalming fluid and 15 pounds of arsenic preserving powder over them when they were at my place."

Smith allowed himself a smile. "Was this before the autopsy, when the stomachs were put in the jar for testing?"

"Of course it was," Cutler replied as if astonished at being asked such a silly question.

When Smith asked him why he had never come forward with this information before, Cutler said that no one ever asked him about it.

Though Cutler's testimony helped the state by offering an alternate explanation for the presence of arsenic, it didn't explain the lethal dose of strychnine.

Worden put Dr. Haines back on the stand and asked if strychnine was used for any kind of embalming fluids. He stated it was not – it has no antiseptic or preservative qualities.

This reply undid some of the damage done by Cutler but not all of it. The defense believed this was merely a setback, but the press believed it was much, much worse than that.

ON WEDNESDAY, NOVEMBER 25, THE DAY before Thanksgiving, closing arguments in the case began. Martin Sutherland, Smith's co-counsel, was the first to address the jury, appealing to their common sense and mocking the defense's claims that the body found in the ashes was not Belle Gunness. He spoke about the body, the teeth, the bridgework, and sarcastically spoke of any other explanation than the fact that Belle was dead was ridiculous.

He then took the jury through Ray's motives – his jealousy and greed, his anger, and his questionable reputation in town. He claimed that Ray had contradicted himself with the various stories he told the police and had even confessed to the fire to Deputy Antiss.

He took another shot at the lack of credibility of the defense and asked the jury to use actual facts, to sum up the matter and to use common sense to decide it in favor of the prosecution.

He was followed by Worden's co-counsel, Ellsworth Weir. He attacked Sutherland for using sarcasm and flights of fancy to make his case. He also criticized him for ignoring the evidence of the bridgework, saying how easily it could have been for a fake set to have been made and substituted.

Weir also asked why the prosecution ignored the poison that was found in the victim's stomachs. The undertaker had used arsenic powder, but where had the strychnine come from? For Ray to have committed murder, it would have been necessary for him to get into a tightly locked house, administer the poison, and then carry Belle and the three children to the cellar before setting the place on fire – all in a few minutes. Weir told the jury that it couldn't be done. He told the jury:

As far as Ray Lamphere is concerned, there is no evidence that he did anything except occasionally drink, and many men drink. Ray Lamphere may be bad, but he did not commit this crime, and as he did not, he should be freed by you gentlemen.

Tomorrow is Thanksgiving. You of the jury go home tomorrow, your task completed, to the hearts of your families. This man, if you condemn him, will have nothing before him! Think! Think long and hard before you seal the doom of a human life!

Wirt Worden was next, laying out a passionate case for his client's innocence and reminding the jurors of the concept of reasonable doubt. Every point the prosecution had made, Worden said, was open to doubt, beginning with the claim that Belle had died in the fire.

Worden even used his time to suggest that Joe Maxson might have even played a part in Belle's scheme to fake her death. He said to the jury, "I am of the opinion that Joe Maxson knows more than he has been willing to tell. I believe he had his clothes on that night. There was no yelling, no cry of fire, no calling of the neighbors."

He also insisted that Dr. Norton's testimony was flawed – that there was no evidence that the teeth that had been recovered had gone through a fire. They were, he claimed, part of a diabolical plot to convince the world that Belle had perished in the flames.

His final words were delivered with what the newspapers called "a ringing intensity of feeling." He nearly shouted them:

They say that Lamphere made damaging admissions. Suppose you agree that Lamphere lied to Antiss. Would you hang him for lying? Then we must all prepare for death. But I believe that if you act as your conscience dictates and according to the law and evidence, there will be no question about your verdict!

States Attorney Smith was the last to speak. He began quietly and calmly, dismissing the defense arguments as hopelessly confused. One moment, Mrs. Gunness was alive, and the next, she was dead. He shook his head.

Where was Klondike Schultz to answer the claims made against him? Where was Liz Smith, who could vouch for where Ray Lamphere was when he was supposed to be burning down a house? Where was the evidence that anything Dr. Norton said was not the absolute truth about the teeth?

The list of questions went on, each trying to poke holes in the claims of the defense attorneys. Then he turned his attention to Ray, who was sitting silently at the defense table. He jabbed a finger at him and made a dramatic change in his tone, and he addressed the jury. Smith cried out: "The badness of Mrs. Gunness is no defense for Lamphere. She was as rottener than hell. Lamphere was associated with her. Lamphere was going to marry her."

Ray struggled – with limited success – to appear unshaken by the attention.

Smith continued his remarks. His face was red, and he was shaking his fist in anger. He made it clear that he cared nothing about Belle Gunness but said to the jury:

My feelings are for those innocent children, slain by a man who hides and sneaks about and sets a fire with such consequences.

I say to you that if you don't believe Lamphere is guilty beyond a reasonable doubt, then don't bring in a verdict of guilty. I do not ask you to vindicate that bad woman, but I have a right to plead in the name of god on behalf of those three innocent children!

In his instructions to the jury, Judge Richter defined "reasonable doubt" and stressed that just because Ray didn't take the witness stand, that should raise any kind of presumption about him.

If the reader wondered about this, too, Ray's attorneys had wisely chosen to let other witnesses speak on his behalf.

The judge told the jurors that, under the law, they could return with one of several different verdicts. There was murder in the first degree, which carried a sentence of death; murder in the first degree that meant life in prison; Second degree, which was also a life sentence; Manslaughter, which meant two to 20 years in prison; arson, which also meant a sentence of up to 20 years; or, of course, not guilty.

It took the judge 15 minutes to read his instructions. After days of bitter and contentious arguments between the prosecution and the defense, the jury finally retired to try and reach a verdict at 5:30 P.M.

However, it soon became clear that after five hours of heated debate and four ballots, the decision wouldn't be quickly reached. At nearly 11:00, they ended the argument for the night and resumed it the following day after breakfast. Twice on Thanksgiving Day, they requested additional information from the judge and were told both times that the court could only re-read the judge's instructions to them. The 12 jurors filed in, took their seats in the box and listened to Judge Richter read through them again.

Rumors began to spread that the jury was deadlocked. As they continued their deliberations into the afternoon, the rest of the participants went home for holiday meals, and the lights in the courtroom were turned off.

As evening neared, a group of newspapermen who were hanging out on the street saw the courtroom windows suddenly light up. Word spread rapidly that the verdict was coming, and people rushed to the courthouse. The room was nearly filled when it became clear that it was a false alarm. Sherriff Antiss had friends visiting from out of town for the holiday and took them to the courtroom to show them around.

Another hour passed, and then 15 minutes after returning from supper, the jurors sent word to the bailiff that they had come to a decision after their 19th ballot.

After notifying the judge and the attorneys by telephone, the bailiff turned the courtroom lights on. By the time everyone arrived, the room was packed – every seat was occupied, with people lining the walls and standing in the aisles.

A few minutes later, Ray Lamphere was brought over from the jail and took his seat at the defense table. A deputy sheriff stood directly behind him in case Ray made what he called "any undue movements" after hearing the verdict.

On the surface, things didn't seem to look good for Ray, but his attorneys remained confident – they had raised considerable doubt about the prosecution's case. Besides that, Ray couldn't have killed Belle if she wasn't actually dead.

The judge asked: "Gentlemen of the jury, have you reached a verdict?"

The foreman, Henry Mills, confirmed they had and passed a paper to the bailiff, who handed it to Judge Richter. A few tense moments passed, and then the judge read the verdict aloud: "We, the jury, found the defendant, Ray Lamphere, guilty of arson."

The crowd, who had been warned about any kind of demonstration, listened in silence. Ray grew pale, and those watching closely said that his hands trembled. Otherwise, he showed no reaction. His attorneys, though, seemed to take the verdict harder than their client. Wirt Worden took an angry step forward as though he was going to offer a protest but stopped himself.

Ray was ordered to stand, and the judge asked him if he had any reason to state why sentence should not be pronounced on him. Ray, his face slack and his eyes downcast, slowly replied, "I have nothing to say right now."

With that, Judge Richter sentenced Ray to spend the next two to 20 years in the Michigan City Penitentiary.

Tears squeezed from Ray's eyes as the deputy sheriff standing behind him led him back to the county jail.

Interviewed in his cell that night, Ray seemed reconciled to his fate. He was a man who had just given up. He told a reporter, "It could have been worse. I don't have a particular complaint. The evidence was pretty strong against me, so I'm willing to take my medicine. Sure, I was hoping for an acquittal, but my conscience is clear, and that helps some."

Hoping to settle some of the questions left hanging after the trial, the reporter asked him why – if he didn't set it – didn't he wake people up that morning when he saw the fire?

Ray shrugged and shifted uncomfortably on his bunk before he spoke, "Well, I suppose if I'd realized what was going to happen and knew what I know now, I guess I would have done so. I got scared and did things I shouldn't have done, and that made me look bad."

The reporter then asked if he believed Belle was dead or alive. Ray replied, "Oh, she's dead, all right. That was her body and the children they found in the fire."

Finally, the reporter pressed him on what he had seen at the Gunness farm the night he'd come home early from Michigan City – the night that Andrew Helgelein disappeared.

"I didn't see anything," Ray said to him, and that was the last question that he'd answer.

That night, with the suspense finally over, Ray slept better than he had at any time in the previous five months.

LAMPHERE TAKEN TO PRISON TODAY

Defendant In Gunness Case Found Guilty of Arson.

MURDER CHARGE WAS IGNORED

RAY MAY HAVE ACCEPTED HIS FATE, BUT others were not so quick to do so. Wirt Worden, for instance, was venting his outrage to anyone who would listen, promising to make a motion for a new trial and, if that wasn't granted, appeal the case all the way to the Supreme Court.

Both a new trial and an appeal were unlikely, though. First, no one could afford the costs of either, and even if the jury's decision was overturned and the state declined to try Ray again on that charge, the prosecution made it clear they'd try Ray for Andrew Helgelein's murder next. Once things cooled down, gossip around the courthouse said, everyone would realize that Ray was lucky to get off as easily as he did. The best thing for the defense to do was to accept the verdict as gracefully as possible.

Newspaper editors had their own thoughts about how things turned out. Most seemed to feel that Ray had gotten off lightly. One wisecracking writer from the *Chicago Daily News* remarked that if Belle had been on trial instead of Ray, the jury would have probably found her guilty of operating an unlicensed graveyard.

Another editor agreed that Ray should have been found guilty of murder, but when it came to Belle, there was no reason for the jury to impose a harsh sentence. "If Lamphere took the life of Belle Gunness," he wrote, "he should have been presented with a gold medal."

Later that week, Ray was taken to the prison in Michigan City by interurban railroad. Sheriff Smutzer and several newspapermen accompanied him. He chatted easily with them and repeatedly said he was going to prison with a clear conscience. When asked what he meant by that, Ray replied, "I'm lucky to be here! Why? I might have been chopped up and put in a hole in old woman Gunness' chicken yard. I didn't do any more than hundreds of others in my place would have done."

With Sheriff Smutzer at his side, he was escorted to the chief clerk's window when he arrived at the penitentiary. His name was entered into the register, and he was assigned a number. He was then taken to the receiving room for a bath, was photographed and measured, and then issued a gray prison suit.

Before being taken to his cell, Ray shook hands with Sheriff Smutzer and thanked him for the good treatment he'd received while he'd been locked up at the county jail. He added, "I hope you'll put in a good word for me when I come up before the parole board in a few years."

Before Ray was led away, a reporter asked him one more question – was he ever going to tell anyone what he saw that night between Belle and Andrew Helgelein?

"No, I don't think I ever will," Ray told him and was taken away to spend his first night in his cell – a place that he would never leave.

RAY LAMPHERE NEVER SPOKE ABOUT THE NIGHT he returned home early from Michigan City – officially, he never spoke about the case at all.

He also never finished the two years of his minimum sentence.

Ray was diagnosed with tuberculosis, and by October 1909 – less than a year after his conviction – it became clear that he was dying. Hoping to win Ray's release, his brother-in-law, H.L.

Finley, traveled to Indianapolis to meet with Governor Thomas R. Marshall but was told by the governor's secretary that the state parole board would not be meeting until December.

Finley offered the man a grim reply, "Ray will come home in a box by then."

The governor agreed to consider a pardon and contacted James Reid, the warden at Michigan City, and William Antiss, who was now the sheriff in LaPorte. Reid believed there was no point in releasing him, stating that Ray would receive better medical care in prison than he would at home. Antiss simply said he didn't believe Ray deserved a pardon unless he "unsealed his lips."

According to newspaper reports, the authorities, and even Prosecutor Ralph Smith, Ray was going to make a confession that would clear up every detail of the Gunness death farm mystery.

But that was just wishful thinking.

On December 30, Ray began to fail so rapidly that his sister was contacted by telephone and told to come at once. He was dead by the time she arrived a short time later.

Whatever knowledge Ray had about the night when the Gunness house was burned to the ground went with him to the grave, for he made no statement before his death that would throw any light on the Gunness case. Those who expected that he would confess before he died were disappointed, as were those who hoped that in his dying moments, he would prove his innocence.

Ray's wake was held at his sister's home on Sunday, January 2, 1901. He was buried at a cemetery in Rossville. He was only 38 years old.

But Ray wouldn't be able to rest in peace.

Soon after Ray's death, a fellow convict named Harry Myers came to see Warden Reid. He claimed that Ray had confessed to him when he realized that he was going to die. The warden dismissed the stories as lies from a convict hoping to shorten his sentence, but there were, of course, those who took Myers seriously.

According to Myers, Ray told him that Belle wasn't dead and that he'd helped her escape from LaPorte. He had driven her in a buggy to a point nine miles from town, where she met a man who was to take her to Chicago. According to Ray, she had carried two large suitcases with her and a small tin box containing stacks of $100 bills and expensive items of jewelry with which she intended to finance a new start in life.

So, who was the woman in the fire? She was from Chicago, Ray allegedly told Myers. Belle had met her on State Street during a shopping trip to the city. Belle struck up a conversation with her, promising to give her a good-paying job as a housekeeper in Indiana. The woman happily agreed and traveled with Belle back to the farm – that's when Ray had met her.

Myers said that Belle had then told Ray to build a wooden box measuring two or three feet square, which would be large enough to hold the severed head of the woman. Belle killed her and brought Ray the head, wrapped in a rug, and placed it in the box. She nailed the lid shut and ordered Ray to bury the box in the orchard. Myers said that Ray couldn't remember the exact spot where he had buried it.

There was a lot about the story that raised doubts for the warden, and he chose to ignore the far-fetched tale. Wirt Worden, though, decided to investigate it further.

He employed some men to dig on the farm, but the box was never found. Wirt insisted it might be there, though. He told a reporter that he thought the story had "an air of truth."

Wirt Worden may have thought so, but no one else did. Besides that, it wasn't long before word leaked of *another* confession by Ray Lamphere, and this one came from a much more reputable source than a convicted burglar and thief.

It came from a minister named Reverend E.A. Schell.

Reverend Schell had, until recently, been the pastor of LaPorte's First Methodist Church, and he had been a frequent visitor for Ray at the county jail. The minister was well-respected, and after a long career as a pastor, church administrator, and writer for popular magazines, he was appointed president of Iowa's Wesleyan University.

Reverend Schell spoke about Ray after he was first arrested:

He is not a vicious man. He was just a farmer's son who had picked up a little knowledge of the carpenter's trade and, of course, cannot be expected to rate high mentally. But there is little in his past life to believe he would be guilty of firing a house containing four people. He is a drunk, and his relations to women are open to criticism, but he is not a bad man.

In the weeks that followed, Schell became Ray's closest friend, engaging him in conversations that lasted for hours. Badgered by reporters after his visits, he refused to repeat what Ray had told him, but he often couldn't resist dropping little hints, saying things like "the Gunness children were chloroformed" or that the woman's body found in the ruins of the house was not Belle Gunness. He also startled reporters by saying that he believed Ray was innocent of all but the Helgelein murder. Of that man, the minister said, Ray was jealous.

When a reporter first asked him if Ray had confessed to that murder, Reverend Schell clammed up, saying that it wouldn't be right to reveal what Ray said to his minister.

After hinting for so long that he possessed Ray's darkest secrets, Schell began to be pressured to reveal them after Ray died. At first, he refused. He told one reporter, "I would give $500 if I had not heard the story told to me by Ray Lamphere."

But then the minister spilled everything. On January 13, 1910, a shocking banner headline appeared on the front page of the *St. Louis Post-Dispatch* promising an exclusive confession given by Ray Lamphere to Reverend Schell.

Unlike the confession offered by convict Harry Myers, the story told by Reverend Schell offered dramatic revelations that had not been heard before.

In his confession, the minister said Ray spoke often about Belle, whom he called a "human monster. Ray told him that he had not murdered anyone, but he had helped Belle bury many of her victims. When one of the men would arrive at the farm, Belle charmed him with promises of wealth, good meals, and her warm bed. Once she had his money, she drugged the man's coffee and then murdered him – sometimes with a weapon and other times using poison or chloroform. The victim would then be taken to the basement and butchered like an animal.

Some of the bodies were buried in the hog lot, while others were rendered down in the vat used for animal fat. The remains were then covered with quicklime. If Belle was tired, though, she just chopped the bodies up and fed the remains to the hogs.

Reverend Schell said that Ray assured him Belle was dead. It had been her body in the fire, just as he'd told reporters on his way to prison.

Ray had been kicked off Belle's farm after they had quarreled over his share of the profits. He started drinking heavier after that, and during the early morning hours of April 28, an inebriated Ray and his companion, Liz Smith, had entered the Gunness house with plans to steal Belle's money. Sober, Ray would have never done it, but drunk, he was brave enough to go through with the plan.

Sneaking into the bedrooms, Ray had chloroformed Belle and the children – a skill he'd learned from Belle herself – and then he and Liz had ransacked the house by candlelight. Much to their disappointment, they found less than $70.

They fled the house near dawn, and Ray denied starting the fire. He had no idea how it could have happened unless he or Liz had accidentally knocked over a candle. A short time later, when he was on his way to work, he saw smoke and flames coming from the house.

He hadn't wanted anyone to die, especially the children. He hadn't even wanted to kill Belle. He was wracked with guilt over the fact that he might have accidentally started the fire.

Was this story true? Many doubted it. Ray had told a lot of whoppers when he was still alive, and the minister – no matter how respected he was – seemed to love the attention that he got from reporters. Had the reverend been the one who made the whole thing up?

Even Wirt Worden was skeptical of the story – and that's saying something. But Wirt didn't believe that Ray and Liz would have been able to subdue a woman of Belle's size and strength so easily. She would have almost certainly awakened during any attempt to drug her and would have called out for the children or Joe Maxson, who was also in the house.

The reverend seemed to have forgotten that Joe was around when he cooked up his story.

A local doctor was just as dismissive as Wirt Worden, saying that the statement was the most ridiculous thing he ever saw in print. No matter how deeply Belle and the children had been sleeping, they would have awakened when attacked.

Ray's supposed confession made headlines in papers across the country, but no one believed it in LaPorte. Prosecutor Smith even said the entire account was a "story of the cock and bull variety."

Even though the police didn't think it was plausible, they hauled in Liz Smith for questioning anyway. She strongly denied every word of it and was released a few hours later.

THE MAIN REASON WHY MOST PEOPLE IN LAPORTE so easily dismissed the confession offered by the minister because of one simple fact – they still believed Belle was alive.

In early March, Wirt Worden called a press conference and told reporters that some sensational developments had taken place that confirmed his long-held belief that Belle Gunness was alive.

Locals were delighted – but not surprised. They were still convinced by the story passed on by Gunness's neighbor Daniel Hutson, who claimed to have encountered Belle in July 1908 – more than two months after the fire. His daughters had seen Belle, too, as had a farmhand named Frederick Lambright. All of them stuck to their stories and swore their sightings were genuine.

However, when Daniel tried to report the incident to the police, Sheriff Smutzer refused to take his statement. He didn't understand why the police were so close-minded about the matter and suspected it was some kind of cover-up, or worse, that some local officials were in business with Belle Gunness. They weren't. It's just that Daniel didn't know about all the politics and in-fighting that was going on with the case.

He did recall being angry, though, when Sheriff Smutzer laughed at his story and told him, "Belle Gunness is dead, and she ain't coming back. You sure you didn't see a ghost?"

But Wirt Worden believed that Sheriff Smutzer wouldn't be laughing for long. Belle Gunness had been located in Grand Rapids, Michigan. She had been identified by a local policeman, who immediately wrote to Sheriff Antiss in LaPorte and urged him to send a deputy to arrest her.

The announcement was greeted with surprise and, of course, skepticism. Just two months earlier, newspapers had announced that Belle had been found in Willmar, Minnesota, where she was working as a housekeeper under a false name. In February, word came from Washington state that she was living on a ranch about 16 miles from Bellingham.

As with both of those instances, the Michigan story turned out to be untrue. The woman identified as Belle was merely a Norwegian woman who had inserted ads in Norwegian newspapers looking for a husband.

Wirt Worden was disappointed again.

But Belle sightings continued. Before the year was out, she was reported living in Moscow, Idaho; Greenville, Illinois; and Galcon, Oklahoma. Most of the tips were so unbelievable that LaPorte authorities paid no attention to them.

One, however – a telegram from police in Lethbridge, a small mining town in Alberta, Canada – was taken seriously enough that LaPorte's police chief, William Meinke, was sent to investigate.

Prosecuting Attorney Smith was adamant that every lead had to be investigated. Although he was sure Belle was dead, he insisted on running down each lead, intent on proving that any belief that Belle was still alive was without foundation.

This one, though, was a little unnerving.

The woman described in the telegram was said to be about the same weight and height as Belle and kept three trunks securely locked in her basement. It was also said that a witness had seen a letter that had been written to her that started with the words, DEAR BELLE.

But the trip to Canada turned out to be a waste of time. The chief returned to LaPorte in January 1913 and announced that the woman in question was not Belle Gunness.

If she was really still out there – no one had found her yet.

TIME PASSED. STORIES CHANGED, EITHER forgotten or lost when people died or moved away.

On March 17, 1916, Elizabeth Smith, the daughter of Virginia enslaved people, Ray Lamphere's lover, and the woman everyone in LaPorte thought was a Voodoo woman or a witch, died in the ramshackle house near the railroad tracks where she'd lived for years. No one knew how old she was when she died, but a doctor who tended to her in her last days guessed that she was around 80. Her body was frail, her teeth were gone, and she simply faded away.

Knowing that her end was near, she had asked to see Wirt Worden because she had promised him many times over the years that she would tell him all she knew about Belle Gunness and the Murder Farm, but Wirt was out of state on business at the time. By the time he returned to Indiana, Liz was already in the ground.

Whatever secrets she may have had went with her to the grave.

And it wasn't just Liz who carried the story of Belle Gunness from one world to the next.

Wirt Worden left criminal defense after Ray's trial and briefly became a county prosecutor. He later became a circuit court judge and had a long, distinguished career. Wirt died of a heart attack in January 1934 at the age of 69. His obituary recalled his many accomplishments, but the most space was given to his successful defense of Ray Lamphere in the Belle Gunness case.

Wirt never abandoned the belief that Belle had escaped.

Albert Smutzer left law enforcement behind after his term in office ended. He moved away from LaPorte to work in the building trade in Chicago for many years but later returned to live out the rest of his days with his daughter in 1933. He died in October 1940, never able to escape the notoriety that came with the Gunness case.

As the dust continued to settle in the story of Belle Gunness, more and more of those once connected to it passed away or vanished into history. Occasionally, though, someone with a connection would find his name in the newspapers.

In January 1915, Joe Maxson – the last of Belle's farmhands and the lone survivor of the fire – was arrested in LaPorte and charged with beating his wife and threatening to kill her and their children. He died eight years later, on Halloween 1923, when he was killed at work, struck fatally on the head by a piece of falling lumber.

A year later, a nephew of Belle's, Adolph Gunness, was in the news. A former soldier who had been gassed and suffered shellshock during the Great War, he was a patient at the Speedway Hospital for disabled veterans in Chicago. While there, he met and began a romance with a young nurse named Anna

Furness. They were married on July 20, 1923. A few months later, he stole $1,400 of her money and ran off to Madison, Wisconsin, where, it turned out, he had another wife named Ella, whom he'd married in 1920. Arrested and returned to Chicago, he was convicted of bigamy and sent to Joliet prison for a five-year stint.

There's an apple that didn't fall far from Belle's tree.

More years passed, and more of the characters in the story of Belle Gunness vanished with time. The sightings of Belle continued to sometimes occur, but eventually, the sheriffs and prosecutors who came after William Antiss and Ralph Smith started to ignore them, dismissing them all as mistaken identity and wild imagination. Eventually, the authorities in LaPorte grew weary of the many false reports. They informed the public that no taxpayer dollars would be used to dispatch detectives on wild goose chases across the country.

The only person who wasn't let down by the false leads seemed to be Wirt Worden, who died believing that Belle was still alive. He never abandoned hope that she might be found – and it finally seemed like he would have his wish in the spring of 1931.

That's when another possible Belle Gunness encounter occurred – and it's one that still has people wondering today if one of Indiana's most prolific killers managed to escape from that burning house in April 1908.

ON THE NIGHT OF FEBRUARY 9, 1931, THE telephone rang at the home of Peter Lindstrom, a Chicago meat packer. When Peter answered, he was given the bad news that his father, August, had died suddenly that afternoon in his home in Lomita, California, a suburb of Los Angeles.

On the surface, there was nothing suspicious about his death. The wealthy, retired lumber dealer was 82 years old. He lived a long and happy life. But the news was still a shock to his son. Just one day earlier, Peter had received a letter from his father saying that he was "feeling fine" and expected to live to be 100 years old.

August's body was taken to the Stone and Myers Funeral Home, where the deputy chief coroner signed the death certificate, citing the cause of death as heart failure. The remains were then sent to Williams, Arizona, where August had lived for many years, and were buried on February 11.

This should have been the end of the story, but it wasn't – not even close.

A few days after the funeral, Peter traveled to Los Angeles. Something was bothering him about his father's death. How could a man, even one who was 82 years old, be fine one day and dead the next? His father had always been in good health. Peter couldn't remember a time when his father had been sick or missed a day of work.

Peter needed to know more, and he also needed to handle his father's estate. His first stop was the home of Mrs. Esther Carlson, a widow who had been August's housekeeper for the past 15 years.

Esther Carlson

Esther's late husband, Charles, had been close friends with August. They had formed a friendship years earlier when August was the superintendent of a logging camp in Arizona, and Charles ran a nearby saloon. One day, after firing a group of Mexican men and replacing them with a group of Swedes, August was attacked by the Mexican men on the main street in Williams. He managed to get loose and ran into Charles' saloon with his attackers close behind him. He burst through the door and found Charles standing in front of the bar with a pistol in his hands.

Charles shot three of the pursuers, and the others fled. From that point on, the two men had been – as one newspaper who printed this story as a humorous anecdote put it – "almost inseparable companions."

Charles and August later became neighbors in Hemet, California, where Charles died after a long illness in 1925. Soon after, August moved to Los Angeles and took Esther with him as his housekeeper.

When Peter arrived at the Carlson home, Esther told him that on the afternoon of February 9, she had telephoned a local physician, Dr. Jesse Lancaster, and informed him that August had become violently ill. The doctor told her to come to his office, where he gave her medicinal powder for the patient. A half-hour later, August was worse, and Esther called again, saying that August had taken a turn for the worse. By the time Dr. Lancaster arrived at the home, August was dead.

Peter listened carefully to her story, but he was now more suspicious than ever. She had no idea what Peter had learned before he'd even left Chicago.

A week before his father's death, Esther had arranged with the Lomita branch of the California bank to make August Lindstrom's bank account a joint account for herself and her employer. Almost as soon as August died, a close friend of Esther's, 42-year-old Anna Erickson, appeared at the bank with a letter of authority from Esther and withdrew all the cash from the account.

Peter immediately shared his suspicions with his brother, Charles, a state highway official in Arizona. On Wednesday, February 18, August's body was exhumed and taken by train back to Los Angeles. The next morning, Esther Carlson and Anna Erickson were brought in for questioning by Captain William Bright of the LA County Sheriff's Department. He questioned them for almost an hour, speaking loosely about the circumstances around August's death. With their version of events now officially on the record, he let them leave. They said they were going to Esther's house for coffee.

A new autopsy was performed on August's remains by the county chemist R.A. Abernathy. He reported to Deputy DA George Stahlman that he had found two and a half grains of arsenic in August's stomach – enough to kill 40 men – and a quantity of split pea soup.

Murder warrants were issued for the arrests of Esther Carlson and Anna Erickson.

Within minutes, though, the district attorney got word that Anna Erickson had been rushed to the hospital with violent stomach pains and convulsions. When her stomach was pumped and analyzed, it was discovered that she had ingested a strong dose of arsenic. The doctors said there was little hope she'd survive.

That must have been some really bad coffee.

Just before midnight, Esther Carlson was arrested. When the D.A. and Captain Bright questioned her, she wouldn't say anything about August Lindstrom. All she'd say about her poisoned friend Anna was, "She got me into this."

Defying the prediction of her doctors, Anna Erickson not only pulled through, but she was soon strong enough to point the finger at Esther Carlson as the mastermind behind August's murder. She told the D.A. from her hospital bed that about three weeks before August's death, Esther had come to her and said that she couldn't stand him anymore and wanted him out of the way. However, Anna found out that August was actually making plans to move back to Arizona and live with his son, Charles. If it did that, he'd no longer need Esther as a housekeeper.

Two days later, DA Stahlman took another statement from Anna when she leveled more charges against her friend. As Stahlman told reporters after this second bedside interview, Anna stated that Esther often said to her that she was tired of "taking care of old men" – and you know what that means.

And she didn't mean just August Lindstrom. She hinted that she had also killed her husband, Charles, and another man who had also died around the same time in 1925.

Reporters soon dug up that dirt, too. The other man was an 80-year-old Swedish immigrant named Gustav Ahlzen. He'd only recently arrived in America and was staying with the Carlsons in Hemet. Soon after he moved in, though, he became ill. A doctor was called and diagnosed the problem as heart disease and prescribed a then-common drug for the condition – strychnine tablets, to be taken one at a time, as needed.

A short time later, Gustav was dead. He had taken the entire box, either by accident, to commit suicide or, more likely, because he had a little help.

A few months later, Charles Carlson also died. He'd suffered from severe stomach pains, and doctors believed he had stomach cancer when he passed away, but no one checked.

Not then. They were certainly going to check now, though.

On February 24, an inquest was held into August Lindstrom's death at the county morgue. Along with the dead man's two sons, witnesses included the county chemist, R.A. Abernathy, undertaker Charles Myers, B.A. Peckham, the bank manager who had turned over the contents of August's account to Anna Erickson, and a deputy sheriff named Harry Brewster, who testified that he found an empty strychnine bottle in the handbag of Mrs. Carlson.

Esther herself refused to testify. Anna, just out of the hospital, was there, too. After initially declining, she agreed to testify. Aided to the witness stand by Deputy Sheriff Hazel Brown, she moved slowly to the witness stand, where she admitted that she had given August a piece of apple pie on the morning of his death but declared she had also given a neighbor a slice from that same pie. If it had been poisoned, she insisted she didn't know about it.

The coroner's jury was not impressed with her claims of innocence. Though officially ruling that August had died from poison administered with homicidal intent by a person or persons unknown, they recommended that Esther and Anna be held pending further action in the case.

That same evening, D.A. Stahlman issued murder charges against the pair.

The investigation was in full swing now. Detectives were sent to Hemet, where they discovered that Esther had purchased poison from a local pharmacist in 1922. Inspecting the medical records of Gustav Ahlzen, they learned that even though his death had been listed as natural causes, he'd had symptoms of arsenic poisoning before he died. They were also told of unverified reports that strychnine poisoning may have caused Charles Carlson's death, too. After learning this news, D.A.

Stahlman told reporters that the bodies of both of those men might be exhumed, as well.

A few days later, a pharmacist in Long Beach named L.L. Willis – who'd been following the case in the papers – came forward to report that a month earlier, Esther and Anna had tried to purchase arsenic from him. Suspicious of why they wanted it, he turned them down.

This report prompted the police to make another search of Esther's home, where they found a piece of paper with writing on it that claimed it was a recipe for ant poison. The recipe read:

3 cups of sugar in a jar
2 cups of boiling water poured over the sugar
Add 2 teaspoonfuls of arsenic
Put it in little cans

The cops were then sent on a mission to check with druggists in Los Angeles, Long Beach, Redondo, and other nearby communities to see if any women brought in the recipe as a pretext to buy arsenic.

On Friday, a preliminary hearing was held in the case. By then, Anna had fully recovered from her brush with death, but it was Esther who appeared terribly weak and unsteady. The court – as well as readers of all the city's newspapers – learned that she had an advanced case of tuberculosis.

County chemist Abernathy was the first to take the stand, testifying that August's body was saturated with arsenic.

Charles Lindstrom described the suspicions that led to him having his father's body exhumed and returned to California for a coroner's examination. He testified:

Mrs. Carlson told me that my father came home ill one day, refused to eat lunch, and was violently sick in the afternoon. She said that he refused to allow her to call a doctor. She finally did so around 7:00 PM, when his condition grew worse. But he was dead when the physician arrived.

That physician, Dr. Lancaster, testified about giving medicine to Esther for August to take on the day of his death. He confirmed that, when he arrived at Lindstrom's home that evening, August was dead. Dr. Lancaster then added:

Several days afterwards, I was called to attend Mrs. Erickson, who was ill. I found her sick and vomiting and administered treatment, removing her to the hospital. A chemical test of the contents of her stomach showed arsenic. She told me that she became ill after drinking a cup of coffee which Mrs. Carlson gave her.

At the close of the hearing, Judge H. Parker Wood ordered that both women be held for trial on charges of murder. Their attorneys requested they be released on bail, but the judge denied the request.

Three weeks later, both women pleaded not guilty when they were brought before Judge William C. Doran in Superior Court. He ordered them to go to trial on April 30.

But before that date arrived, something happened that put Esther Carlson – who had only achieved local notoriety at that point – onto the front pages of newspapers across the country, especially in LaPorte, Indiana.

IN ADDITION TO HER ANT POISON RECIPE, the police had found something else of interest in their second search of Esther's home – a battered trunk that contained a lot of old photographs. Among them was a photograph of two young girls and a little boy.

Exactly how this photograph was seen by Mrs. Mary Kruger of Huntington Park, California, is unclear, but what we do know is that Mary was a former resident of LaPorte, Indiana, and had once known Belle Gunness and her children. When she saw the photograph, she positively identified the children as Belle's son, Phillip, and her daughters, Lucy and Myrtle.

How did the photograph end up in the possession of Esther Carlson?

Informed of this startling turn of events, D.A. Stahlman and his boss, Buron Fitts, immediately announced an investigation into whether or not Esther Carlson was, in reality, the mysterious Belle Gunness.

Across the country, the newspapers plastered their front pages with headlines about this sensational development. They ran side-by-side photographs of the two women – the famous formal portrait of the menacing and moon-faced "Female Bluebeard" and various shots of Esther Carlson, who, allowing for the passage of many years and a severe case of tuberculosis, might well be an old, thin Belle Gunness. As one newspaper put it: "In the 23 years since the Gunness horrors came to light, sightings of the murderess had averaged one a month. Of all those Gunness suspects, Mrs. Carlson seems to be the hottest."

ARE THESE TWO THE SAME WOMAN?

At left is Belle Gunness as she appeared 20 years ago when she was the operator of a "murder farm" at La Porte, Ind. At the right is "Mrs. Esther Carlson," accused Los Angeles poison slayer, who has been identified, since her recent death, as being the longsought Mrs. Gunness. California authorities are skeptical, for Mrs. Carlson was supposed to have lived in New England when Mrs. Gunness assertedly killed 14 men on her "love farm."

Confined to her bed in the prison ward of the County Hospital, Esther – whose condition had taken a turn for the worse – denied that she was Belle Gunness.

But, of course, everyone back in LaPorte said that's precisely what Belle would say!

Esther, though, claimed her maiden name was Johnson and that she had immigrated to America from Sweden in 1892 when she was 25 years old. She'd worked as a housemaid in Hartford, Connecticut, until 1907, when she married Charles Hanson. Just nine months later, her husband had drowned, so she'd moved west and ended up in Williams, Arizona, where she met and married Charles Colson. After he died in 1925, she moved to Los

Angeles and worked for August Lindstrom. She told reporters, "I have never lived in Indiana, or indeed, ever set foot in that state."

Like the folks in Northwest Indiana, the authorities were unconvinced and vowed to investigate the years that she claimed to be working in Connecticut.

In LaPorte – where the newspapers reported that the townspeople had been whipped into a state of high excitement – current sheriff Tom MacDonald expressed doubts about Esther's denials. He told reporters:

If Mrs. Carlson is not Mrs. Gunness, the case is about the strangest one I can imagine because so many details dovetail. The ages, the nationalities, and many of the racial features...

The sheriff was unaware or forgot that Belle was Norwegian and Esther claimed to be Swedish, but hey, it's the same part of the map. He went on:

... that fact that each woman had three children, two girls and a boy, with ages corresponding, and, from pictures, with similar features, these things are responsible for my strong feeling that Mrs. Carlson may be Mrs. Gunness.

D.A. Stahlman had sent photographs and a detailed description of Esther to Sheriff MacDonald. MacDonald also contacted two men – both former residents of LaPorte – who were now living in Los Angeles.

One of them was Dennis Daly, a 70-year-old boilermaker and a neighbor of Belle's between 1902 and 1908. He had spoken to her hundreds of times, he claimed.

The other man was John Yorkey, a one-time LaPorte saloon owner who had seen Belle many times around town.

On May 7, 1931, with introductory telegrams from Sheriff MacDonald, Daly and Yorkey went to Stahlman's office and were immediately taken to see Esther Carlson so that the question of her identity could be settled.

Only one small problem, though. Esther died on May 6.

When he had learned that Esther only had a few hours to live, D.A. Stahlman had rushed to her bedside in hopes that she might clear up the mystery of August Lindstrom's death. Stahlman bent down close to the barely conscious woman's ear and asked if she had poisoned Lindstrom. A barely audible sound – which would be described variously as a mumble, a sigh, and a croak in various reports -- escaped her lips.

Stahlman thought it sounded like "yes."

"You admit that you have him arsenic?" he then asked, and she answered with the same sound.

Stahlman accepted that as her deathbed confession.

A few hours later, one reporter wrote, "Death sealed her lips forever."

Driven to the morgue by Stahlman the next day, Dennis Daly and John Yorkey spent about 40 minutes with the corpse. Afterward, they spoke with reporters. Daly said that he was positive the dead woman had been Belle Gunness. He said:

I haven't the slightest doubt about it. She had a particular twist to her mouth that was very noticeable. Her eyes are the same color. Her hair, although faded with age, is the same general color and texture. The cheekbones are high, too. The last time I saw Mrs. Gunness she was rather heavy, but the tuberculosis could have worn the body down through the years.

John Yorkey was equally sure that the body on the slab was that of Belle Gunness. On Monday, May 11 – the same day that Esther Carlson was laid to rest next to her second husband, Charles, who she likely murdered – Yorkey sent a letter back to Indiana. It was addressed to Wirt Worden, and one line read:

I did not go and see her while alive, but you can bet all you got that was Belle Gunness of the old murder farm.

We'll never know what Wirt Worden thought about John Yorkey's claim that the dead woman in LA was Belle Gunness, but it's likely he believed it. Wirt believed more than anyone else that Belle had somehow escaped the hangman. He went to his grave, probably feeling that his long-held convictions had been correct.

But as years passed, there became better ways to determine the identity of a person than simply sending a couple of guys who once knew the person down to the morgue to look over the body.

In November 2007, a team of forensic anthropologists and researchers led by LaPorte native Andrea Simmons, a historian and Indianapolis attorney, and Dr. Stephen Nawrocki, a board-certified forensic anthropologist and a professor from the University of Indianapolis, opened the grave of the woman who had been buried next to Mads Sorensen and Belle's children in Chicago's Forest Home Cemetery.

Their purpose was to conduct scientific testing on the skeletal remains and to hopefully solve the mystery that had been baffling LaPorte residents – and crime buffs – for years. The fragile remains were removed and taken to the University of Indianapolis Archaeology and Forensics Laboratory, where DNA was extracted. Those samples, along with the original envelopes from Belle's letters to Andrew Helgelein, were sent to the State Police Forensics Laboratory in Indianapolis for analysis. Later, additional samples were sent for DNA testing to a university laboratory in Texas.

Results were hoped for by April 28, 2008, the 100th anniversary of the fire at the Gunness farm, but they were, unfortunately, inconclusive.

There's no way to know if the body in the grave really does belong to Belle and if she really died on the night of the fire. The team had also hoped to discover whether the children who died that night were actually Belle's children or if they had been adopted or stolen by Belle. But that mystery wouldn't be solved either.

Not yet, anyway. More tests might occur in the future that tell a different story, but until then, the mystery of whether Belle is buried in that grave will remain unsolved.

But there is one thing that we do know – if Belle did escape, she didn't become Esther Carlson, no matter what Dennis Daly and John Yorkey believed.

In 2014, Knut Eric Jensen, a native of Selbu in Norway, where Belle was born, went on a research mission to settle the question of Esther Carlson's true identity. After consulting census books, cemetery records, city directories, and hundreds of documents, he managed to establish what authorities at the time didn't bother to do – he found that every detail that the dying Esther Carlson had offered about her background was true.

She was *not* Belle Gunness.

SO, WHAT HAPPENED TO BELLE GUNNESS?

The answer hasn't changed – no one knows. She either died in the fire or she escaped. We only have those two options. If we believe the legal authorities in LaPorte in 1908, she died, but if we believe all the various accounts of her escaping from the fire and being seen afterward, then we must at least consider the idea that she got away.

There is no question, though, that Belle Gunness left an indelible bit of her presence behind everywhere she went. Not much remains that is physical today, though.

Belle's home on Alma Street – which is now Latrobe Avenue – in Chicago's Austin neighborhood was torn down many years ago. For a long time, it was simply an empty lot. Like many other locations that have been connected to crimes or notorious people, the land was considered cursed for years – or so the stories in the neighborhood claimed.

But available land in Chicago is worth too much to waste. Eventually, the empty lot on North Latrobe Avenue was redeveloped, and a new home was built there in 2003.

Outside of LaPorte, the fire debris was eventually cleared away from the farm on McClung Road, leaving only the brick cellar of Belle's farmhouse behind. The land became overgrown and neglected, and prospective buyers steered clear of the property after they learned the history behind it.

Then, in 1930, a Russian immigrant named John Nepsha, who had arrived in LaPorte two years after the Gunness affair, purchased the former "murder farm" and began building a house atop the old foundation where Belle's home once stood. The newspaper soon reported:

The new owner has laughed at the superstitions which have kept the property vacant for the last two decades. He thinks so little of such ghost stories that he plans to make a garden of the graveyard which yielded body after body of the woman's victims.

But Nepsha wasn't laughing for long.

Bad luck followed, just confirming for LaPorte residents that the property was as cursed as they believed it was. He became involved in a bitter divorce battle after his wife left him, announcing that she couldn't live in such a terrible place.

In 1936, during a fight over property lines, a surveyor dropped dead in the yard as he was measuring the private cemetery on the property. Visitors came from all over the country to see the place where the infamous murders occurred, showing up at all hours of the day and night and asking to take home souvenirs.

Finally, Nepsha had had enough, and he moved out, selling the farm at a loss.

As time passed, and the legend of Belle Gunness began to fade, the land was sold again – and again. Owners have frequently come and gone over the years, none of them staying too long.

In 2006, an interview with the owners at the time revealed that their son "saw dead people" on the property. They moved away soon after.

Such a revelation shouldn't come as a surprise to anyone aware of the history of the farm – and the story of Belle Gunness. It shouldn't be a surprise, just like the fact that any kind of digging on the farm takes the nasty chance of turning up a human bone or two.

For now, the story of Belle Gunness has come to an end, but you never know what the future might bring. Or what may be discovered on the "Murder Farm" in the decades to come.

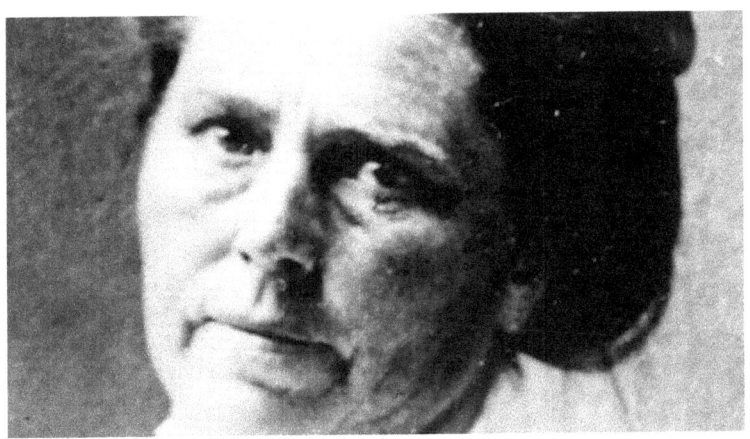

BIBLIOGRAPHY

Battz, Simon – *The Girl On the Velvet Swing*, New York, NY, Little, Brown & Co., 2018

Barry, Michael Thomas – *California's Deadly Women: Murder and Mayhem in the Golden State*, Atglen, PA, Schiffer Publishing, 2018
-------------------------------- - *Murder and Mayhem: 52 Crimes that Shocked Early California*, Atglen, PA, Schiffer Publishing, 2012

Bartlett, Evan Allen – *Love Murders of Harry F. Powers*, Sheftel Press, 1930

Bartlette, Delani R. – *Senior Citizen Serial Killers*, 2029

Battisi, Linda and John Stevens Berry, Sr. – *Twelfth Victim*, Omaha, NE, Addicus Books, Inc., 2022

Baumann, Edward and John O'Brien – *Murder Next Door*, New York, Diamond Books, 1993

Beaver, Nannette, B.K. Ripley and Patrick Trese – *Caril*, New York, NY, Lippincott, 1974

Blumenthal, Karen – *Bonnie and Clyde: The Making of a Legend*, New York, NY, Viking, 2018

Brown, Ethan - *Shake the Devil Off: A True Story of the Murder that Rocked New Orleans*, New York, NY, St. Martin's Press, 2010

Buhk, Tobin T. – *Cold Case Michigan*, Charleston, SC, History Press, 2021
------------------ - *The Lonely Hearts Killers*, Jefferson, NC, Exposit Books, 2020

Burt, Olive Wooley – *American Murder Ballads and Their Stories*, New York, NY, Oxford University Press, 1958

De la Torre, Lillian – *The Truth About Belle Gunness*, New York, NY, Fawcett / Gold Medal, 1955

DeFord, Miriam Allen – *The Real Bonnie and Clyde*, New York, NY, Ace, 1968

Engel, Howard – *Crimes of Passion*, Toronto, CA, Key Porter Books Limited, 2001

Farr, Louise – *Sunset Murders*, New York, NY, Atria Books, 1992

Gribben, Mark – *The Professor and the Coed*, Charleston, SC, History Press, 2010

Guinn, Jeff – *Go Down Together: The True Untold Story of Bonnie and Clyde*, New York, Simon & Schuster, 2009

Helmer, William J. and Rick Mattis – *The Complete Public Enemy Almanac*, Nashville, YN, Cumberland House Publishing, 2007

Holbrook, Stewart – *Murder Out Yonder*, New York, NY, Macmillan, 1941

Hynd, Alan – *Murder, Mayhem & Mystery: An Album of American Crime*, New York, NY, Stratford Press, 1958

Jones, Ann – *Women Who Kill*, New York, NY, Fawcett Crest, 1980

Langlois, Janet – *Belle Gunness: The Lady Bluebeard*, Bloomington, IN, Indiana University Press, 1985

Lesy, Michael – *Murder City*, New York, NY, W.W. Norton and Company, 2007

Lindberg, Richard C. – *Heartland Serial Killers*, Dekalb, IL, Northern Illinois University Press, 2011

Marlowe, John – *Chambers of Horror*, London, UK, Acturus Publishing Limited, 2018

MacClean, Harry N. – *Starkweather: The Untold Story of the Killing Spree that Changed America*, New York, NY, Penguin Books, 2023

MacGowan, Douglas - *The Bluebeard of West Virginia: The Infamous Quiet Dell Murders*, Quarrier Press, 2017

MacKellar, Landis – *The "Double Indemnity" Murder*, Syracuse, NY, Syracuse University Press, 2006

Mappen, Marc – *Prohibition Gangsters*, New Brunswick, NJ, Rutgers University Press, 2013

Meares, Hadley – "Forty Years Ago, the Sunset Strip Killers Terrorized L.A., *Los Angeles Magazine*, 2020

Milner, E.R. – *The Lives and Times of Bonnie and Clyde*, Carbondale, IL, Southern Illinois University Press, 1996

Rasmussen, Cecilia – "Sex, Money, Death in Hancock Park," *Los Angeles Times*, March 1999

Renner, Joan – *Deranged L.A. Crimes*, 2012-2023

Ritchie, Jean – *Kiss of Death*, London, UK, Michael O'Mara Books, 2020

Rule, Ann – *Fever in the Heart*, New York, NY, Sphere Books, 1996

Schechter, Harold – *Butcher's Work*, Iowa City, IA, University of Iowa Press, 2022
----------------------- - *Hell's Princess: The Mystery of Belle Gunness, Butcher of Men*, New York, NY, Little A, 2018
----------------------- - *Psycho USA: Famous American Killers You Never Heard Of*, New York, NY, Ballantine Books, 2012

Schneider, Paul – *Bonnie and Clyde: The Lives Behind the Legend*, New York, NY, Henry Holt and Company, 2009

Shelton, Gene – *Manhunter: The Life and Times of Frank Hamer*, New York, NY, Berkley, 1997

Taylor, Troy – *Hell Hath No Fury 2: 13 More Spirits of Depravity & Despair*, Jacksonville, IL, American Hauntings Ink, 2022

Thornton, Janis – *No Place Like Murder*, Bloomington, IN, Quarry Books, 2020

Treherne, John – *Strange History of Bonnie and Clyde*, New York, NY, Briarcliff Manor, 1985

Uruburu, Paula – *American Eve*, New York, NY, Penguin Books, 2008

Wolf, Marvin J. and Katherine Nader – *Fallen Angels*, New York, NY, Facts on File, 1986

Chicago, IL American
Chicago, IL Daily News
Chicago, IL Inter-Ocean
Chicago, IL Tribune
Columbus, OH Dispatch
Decatur, IL Herald
Edwardsville, IL Intelligencer
LaPorte, IN Argus-Bulletin
Los Angeles, CA Times
Mount Carmel, IL Daily Republican-Register
Murphysboro, IL Daily Independent
New York, NY Sun
New York, NY Times
New York, NY Tribune
Taylorville, IL Daily Breeze

SPECIAL THANKS TO
April Slaughter: Cover Design
Becky Ray: Editing
Samantha Smith
Athena & the "Aunts" - Sue, Carmen & Rocky
Brianna Snow
Orrin and Rachel Taylor
Rene Kruse
Rachael Horath
Bethany Horath

Elyse and Thomas Reihner
John Winterbauer
Cody Beck
Tom and Michelle Bonadurer
Lydia Rhoades
Cheryl Stamp and Sheryel Williams-Staab
Joelle Leitschuh and Tonya Leitschuh
Scott and Hannah Robl
Jake and Emily Fink
Dave and Donna Nunnally
And the entire crew of American Hauntings

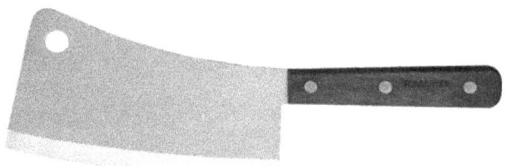

ABOUT THE AUTHOR

Troy Taylor is the author of books on ghosts, hauntings, true crime, the unexplained, and the supernatural in America. He is also the founder of American Hauntings Ink, which offers books, ghost tours, events, and weekend excursions. He was born and raised in the Midwest and divides his time between Illinois and wherever the wind decides to take him. See Troy's other titles at:
www.americanhauntingsink.com

www.ingramcontent.com/pod-product-compliance
Lightning Source LLC
Chambersburg PA
CBHW071655170426
43195CB00039B/2197